Python for Algorithmic Trading Cookbook

Second Edition

Recipes for designing, building, and deploying algorithmic trading strategies with Python

Jason Strimpel

<packt>

Python for Algorithmic Trading Cookbook

Second Edition

Portfolio Director: Sunith Shetty
Relationship Lead: Apeksha Shetty
Project Manager: Shashank Desai
Content Engineer: Tiksha Abhimanyu Lad
Technical Editor: Seemanjay Ameriya
Indexer: Manju Arasan
Production Designer: Deepak Chavan
Growth Lead: Merlyn M Shelley

First published: August 2024
Second edition: July 2026

Production reference: 1190626

Published by Packt Publishing Ltd.
Grosvenor House
11 St Paul's Square
Birmingham
B3 1RB, UK.

ISBN 978-1-80666-203-6
`www.packtpub.com`

Contributors

About the author

Jason Strimpel is the founder of PyQuant News, co-founder of Quant Science, and Managing Director of Global AI and Advanced Analytics at a top-tier consulting firm. His 20+ year career spans trading, quant risk, ML, and enterprise data across Chicago, London, and Singapore. At BP, he managed $20B in counterparty credit exposure, then led quant engineering globally for BP's derivatives book. In Singapore, he led engineering, data science, and analytics at Rio Tinto Commercial, scaling the team behind its $60B commodities trading business. At AWS, he joined the firm's GenAI operations organization, building internally facing GenAI tools. He holds a Master's in Quantitative Finance from Illinois Institute of Technology.

About the reviewer

Sudarshan Sawal specializes in quantitative finance with a background in economics and engineering. Currently working at a high-frequency trading (HFT) firm, he leads the quantitative research efforts by managing and guiding a team of researchers focused on developing systematic trading strategies and machine learning-driven research pipelines. Formerly, as Head of Products (Quant) at PredictNow.ai, he enhanced trading models and improved client portfolios, contributing notable research in portfolio optimization using Conditional Portfolio Optimization (CPO). Earlier at QTS Capital Management, he researched trading algorithms and supported clients with machine learning models. He has also represented PredictNow.ai at financial conferences.

Table of Contents

Chapter 4: Visualize Financial Market Data with Matplotlib, Seaborn, and Plotly Dash

Chapter 5: Build a Quantamental Research Database with Hedge Fund Tools 157

Chapter 6: Conduct Market Research with Advanced AI and Agentic Workflows 185

Chapter 7: Build Alpha Factors for Stock Portfolios 221

Preface

Algorithmic trading combines statistical models, programming, and quantitative methods to systematically trade financial assets. Markets now generate orders of magnitude more data than a discretionary trader can process, and the firms producing the best risk-adjusted returns are the ones with the most disciplined research, backtesting, and execution infrastructure. *Python for Algorithmic Trading Cookbook, Second Edition* gives you 68 hands-on recipes across 15 chapters to design, backtest, and deploy your own algorithmic trading strategies in Python. The code spans 51 annotated Jupyter notebooks and 17 modular Python trading applications, plus four GPU-accelerated research scripts.

Most trading books still focus on technical analysis indicators applied to small datasets. Those approaches rarely survive contact with live markets. This book brings professional techniques and tools to non-professionals in small, digestible recipes. You will learn how to source institutional-quality data, accelerate analysis with columnar engines, store research datasets free from lookahead bias, build alpha factors, evaluate them rigorously, and execute strategies through a production-grade Interactive Brokers trading application.

This second edition reflects how the algorithmic trading toolchain has evolved in the past two years. Three chapters are new. *Chapter 3* covers Parquet, Polars, and DuckDB for fast, scalable analytics over financial datasets. *Chapter 5* introduces ArcticDB, the high-performance DataFrame database used by Man Group to manage petabyte-scale market data. *Chapter 6* covers AI and agentic workflows built on LangChain and LlamaIndex, including an AI equity research analyst, multi-agent comparative analysis, and converting research papers into executable Python. *Chapter 15* has been rewritten end-to-end to GPU-accelerate the research stack with NVIDIA RAPIDS, demonstrating how to wrangle 267 million rows with `cudf.pandas`, train factor models with `cuml.accel`, compute correlation networks across 10,000 stocks with `nx-cugraph`, and solve Mean-CVaR portfolio optimization with NVIDIA cuOpt.

I have spent 20+ years inside real trading environments building, trading, and managing risk across the U.S., Europe, and Asia. I started on a Chicago hedge fund desk, became a risk manager at JPMorgan, traded derivatives, led production risk technology for an energy derivatives firm in London, served as APAC CIO of a financial software company in Singapore, and built the data science function for a global metals trading firm. The techniques in this book reflect the workflows used in those environments. I have taught the same material to 1,700+ students through my course, *Getting Started With Python for Quant Finance*.

Python gives you direct access to financial data, fast numerical computation, the broadest ecosystem of quantitative libraries in any language, and a path to production. This book takes you from raw market data to live algorithmic trading without skipping the parts in between.

By the end of this book you will have a working toolkit to design, validate, and deploy systematic strategies. Markets change. The advantage goes to traders who can iterate on research and ship code faster than the competition.

Who this book is for

This book is for traders, investors, and Python developers who want practical recipes for designing, backtesting, and deploying algorithmic trading strategies. The three target personas are:

- **Active traders and investors**: Individuals already investing in the markets who want to use algorithmic methods to enhance performance. You will learn how to acquire and process market data with OpenBB, build a research database with ArcticDB, and run AI-driven equity research with LangChain and LlamaIndex.
- **Python developers with market interest**: Developers comfortable with pandas and NumPy who want to apply their programming skills to financial markets. You will learn how to accelerate analysis with Polars and DuckDB, engineer alpha factors with PCA and Fama-French models, and run walk-forward optimization with VectorBT.
- **Aspiring algorithmic traders**: Readers with basic Python experience who want to enter the field. You will build production-ready backtests with Zipline Reloaded, evaluate factor quality with Alphalens Reloaded and Pyfolio Reloaded, build a modular trading application on the Interactive Brokers API, and deploy live factor, options combo, and intraday mean reversion strategies.

You should have basic familiarity with Python syntax and core libraries like pandas and NumPy. No prior trading experience is assumed, though comfort with financial markets terminology will accelerate your progress.

What this book covers

Chapter 1, Acquire Free Financial Market Data with Cutting-Edge Python Libraries, covers practical methods for sourcing financial market data. You will work with stock, futures, and options data through the OpenBB Platform, fetch Fama-French factor data with pandas-datareader, and bulk-download historical fundamentals with Financial Modeling Prep.

Chapter 2, Analyze and Transform Financial Market Data with pandas, covers the core pandas operations used throughout the rest of the book. You will work with index types, build Series and DataFrames, manipulate and transform tabular data, compute simple and log returns, measure volatility, generate cumulative return series, resample time series, handle missing data, and apply custom functions to financial datasets.

Chapter 3, Accelerate Financial Market Data Analysis with Polars and DuckDB, covers fast, scalable analytics over financial datasets. You will convert CSV files into compressed Parquet, manipulate time series with Polars, query Parquet directly with Polars expressions, integrate Polars with DuckDB for hybrid SQL and DataFrame analytics, and build a high-performance datalake with DuckLake.

Chapter 4, Visualize Financial Market Data with Matplotlib, Seaborn, and Plotly Dash, covers visualization techniques for financial data. You will quickly visualize data with pandas, animate yield curve evolution with Matplotlib, plot options implied volatility surfaces, visualize statistical relationships with Seaborn, and build an interactive PCA analytics dashboard with Plotly Dash.

Chapter 5, Build a Quantamental Research Database with Hedge Fund Tools, covers ArcticDB, the high-performance DataFrame database from Man Group. You will create bias-free historical datasets with versioning and time travel, build an options analytics tool over millions of rows, construct a Warren Buffett style value stock screener from historical fundamentals, and compute rolling metrics across massive datasets.

Chapter 6, Conduct Market Research with Advanced AI and Agentic Workflows, covers applying large language models and agentic workflows to automate market research. You will build an AI equity research analyst that queries annual reports, write Python code with AI to analyze stock performance, run agentic comparative analysis across companies, automate multi-agent equity research reports, and convert trading strategy research papers into executable code with LlamaIndex.

Chapter 7, Build Alpha Factors for Stock Portfolios, covers alpha factor construction. You will identify latent return drivers with principal component analysis, hedge portfolio beta with linear regression, analyze portfolio sensitivities to Fama-French factors, assess market inefficiency through volatility, and prepare a factor ranking model with Zipline Pipelines.

Chapter 8, Vector-Based Backtesting with VectorBT, covers high-performance vectorized backtesting. You will build technical strategies with VectorBT, conduct walk-forward optimization to test robustness out of sample, and optimize the SuperTrend strategy with VectorBT Pro at scale.

Chapter 9, Event-Based Backtesting Factor Portfolios with Zipline Reloaded, covers event-driven backtesting. You will backtest a momentum factor strategy and a mean reversion strategy with Zipline Reloaded, learning how to structure pipelines, schedule rebalances, and track portfolio performance under realistic execution assumptions.

Chapter 10, Evaluate Factor Risk and Performance with Alphalens Reloaded, covers factor evaluation. You will prepare Zipline backtest results for Alphalens, evaluate the information coefficient, examine factor return performance and decay, and measure factor turnover to assess the durability of an alpha signal.

Chapter 11, Assess Backtest Risk and Performance Metrics with Pyfolio, covers portfolio analytics. You will prepare Zipline results for Pyfolio Reloaded, generate strategy performance and return analytics, build drawdown and rolling risk analyses, examine holdings, leverage, exposure, and sector allocations, and break performance down to the trade level.

Chapter 12, Set Up the Interactive Brokers Python API, covers the infrastructure for live trading. You will build a modular algorithmic trading app, create Contract and Order objects with the IB API, fetch historical market data, request market data snapshots, stream live tick data, and persist tick data in a local SQL database.

Chapter 13, Manage Orders, Positions, and Portfolios with the IB API, covers trade and portfolio management. You will execute market, limit, stop, and trailing stop orders, manage placed orders, query portfolio details, inspect positions, and compute portfolio profit and loss in real time.

Chapter 14, Deploy Strategies to a Live Environment, covers live deployment. You will compute real-time performance and risk indicators, send orders driven by portfolio targets, and deploy a monthly factor portfolio, an options combo strategy, and an intraday multi-asset mean reversion strategy.

Chapter 15, Advanced Recipes for GPU-Accelerated Trading Research, covers NVIDIA RAPIDS for GPU acceleration. You will wrangle 267 million rows of global equity data with `cudf.pandas`, train Random Forest factor models and run KMeans regime detection on 2 million observations with `cuml.accel`, build and analyze a 10,000-node asset correlation network with `nx-cugraph`, and solve a Mean-CVaR portfolio optimization problem with NVIDIA cuOpt as the solver backend through CVXPY.

To get the most out of this book

You will need Python 3.11 to work through the examples. All notebooks specify Python 3 as the kernel, and the code in Chapters 1 through 11 follows a consistent procedural style with imports at the top, minimal abstractions, and one concept per cell. Chapters 12 through 14 build a modular Python trading application across 17 incremental recipe directories, each composed of `app.py`, `wrapper.py`, `client.py`, `contract.py`, `order.py`, and `utils.py` modules. Chapter 15 requires an NVIDIA GPU and the RAPIDS ecosystem.

The full list of libraries and versions used across the book:

<table>
<tr><th>Software/hardware covered</th><th>Operating system requirements</th></tr>
<tr><td>Python 3.11</td><td rowspan="11">Windows, macOS, or Linux</td></tr>
<tr><td>pandas 2+, NumPy</td></tr>
<tr><td>OpenBB Platform 4+, yfinance, pandas-datareader, ThetaData</td></tr>
<tr><td>Polars 1.35.2, DuckDB 1.4.2, PyArrow</td></tr>
<tr><td>Matplotlib, Seaborn, Plotly 6.5.0, Streamlit 1.51.0</td></tr>
<tr><td>ArcticDB 5.1.1 (conda install required)</td></tr>
<tr><td>LangChain 0.3.x, LlamaIndex 0.12.x</td></tr>
<tr><td>scikit-learn, statsmodels, TA-Lib</td></tr>
<tr><td>VectorBT 0.28.1, Zipline Reloaded 3.1.1</td></tr>
<tr><td>Alphalens Reloaded 0.4.6, Pyfolio Reloaded 0.9.9</td></tr>
<tr><td>Interactive Brokers API (ibapi), empyrical, exchange_calendars</td></tr>
<tr><td>NVIDIA RAPIDS (cudf.pandas, cuml.accel, nx-cugraph, cuOpt)</td><td>NVIDIA GPU required for Chapter 15</td></tr>
</table>

Specific installation instructions are included in each chapter where a library is first introduced.

If you are using the digital version of this book, type the code yourself or clone it from the GitHub repository linked in the next section. Doing so avoids errors from copy and paste and reinforces the patterns used throughout the book.

Download the example code files

You can download the example code files for this book from GitHub at `https://github.com/PacktPublishing/Python-for-Algorithmic-Trading-Cookbook-Second-Edition`. If there is an update to the code, it will be updated in the GitHub repository.

We also have other code bundles from our rich catalog of books and videos available at `https://github.com/PacktPublishing/`. Check them out.

Download the color images

We also provide a PDF file that has color images of the screenshots and diagrams used in this book. You can download it from the Packt product page for this title.

Conventions used

There are a number of text conventions used throughout this book.

Code in text: Indicates code words in text, database table names, folder names, filenames, file extensions, pathnames, dummy URLs, user input, and library names. Here is an example: "Import pandas as `pd` and call `pd.read_parquet()` to load a Parquet file into a DataFrame."

A block of code is set as follows:

```
returns = df.close.pct_change()
returns.name = "return"
returns.plot.bar(
    title="AAPL returns",
    grid=False,
    legend=True,
    xticks=[]
)
```

Any command-line input or output is written as follows:

```
$ conda install -c conda-forge arcticdb$ pip install vectorbt zipline-reloaded
```

Bold: Indicates a new term, an important word, or words that you see onscreen. For instance, words in menus or dialog boxes appear in **bold**. Here is an example: "Select **Paper Trading** from the **Account** menu in Trader Workstation."

> **Note**
>
> Warnings or important notes appear like this.

> **Tip**
>
> Tips and tricks appear like this.

Get in touch

Feedback from our readers is always welcome.

General feedback: If you have questions about any aspect of this book, email us at `customercare@packtpub.com` and mention the book title in the subject of your message.

Errata: Although we have taken every care to ensure the accuracy of our content, mistakes do happen. If you have found a mistake in this book, we would be grateful if you would report it. Please visit `www.packtpub.com/support/errata` and fill in the form.

Piracy: If you come across any illegal copies of our works in any form on the internet, we would be grateful if you would provide us with the location address or website name. Please contact us at `copyright@packt.com` with a link to the material.

If you are interested in becoming an author: If there is a topic that you have expertise in and you are interested in either writing or contributing to a book, please visit `authors.packtpub.com`.

Free benefits with your book

This book comes with free benefits to support your learning. Activate them now for instant access (see the "*How to Unlock*" section for instructions).

Here's a quick overview of what you can instantly unlock with your purchase:

Complete Code Bundle

Download the full source code for this book's examples and projects.

DRM-Free PDF Version

Download DRM-free PDF and ePub copies of this book.

7-Day Packt Library Access

Get 7-day unlimited access to 8,000+ books and videos. No credit card required.

Available for first-time Packt+ trial users only.

Next-Gen Reader Access

Read this book on Packt Reader with progress sync, dark mode and note-taking.

How to Unlock

Scan the QR code (or go to `packtpub.com/unlock`). Search for this book by name, confirm the edition, and then follow the steps on the page.

UNLOCK NOW

Note: Keep your invoice handy. Purchases made directly from Packt don't require one

Share your thoughts

Once you've read *Python for Algorithmic Trading Cookbook, Second Edition*, we'd love to hear your thoughts! Scan the QR code below to go straight to the Amazon review page for this book and share your feedback.

`https://packt.link/r/1806662035`

Your review is important to us and the tech community and will help us make sure we're delivering excellent quality content.

1

Acquire Free Financial Market Data with Cutting-Edge Python Libraries

A May 2017 Economist cover declared data to be the world's most valuable resource. It's no truer than in algorithmic trading. As algorithmic traders, it's our job to acquire and make sense of billions of rows of market data for use in trading algorithms. In this context, it's crucial to gather high-quality, reliable data that can adequately support trading algorithms and market research. Luckily for us, it's possible to acquire high-quality data for free (or nearly free).

This chapter offers recipes for a series of different Python libraries—including the cutting-edge **OpenBB Open Data Platform** (**OpenBB Platform** for short)—to acquire free financial market data using Python. One of the primary challenges most non-professional traders face is getting all the data required for analysis together in one place. The OpenBB Platform addresses this issue. We'll dive into acquiring data for a variety of assets, including stocks, options, futures (both continuous and individual contracts), and Fama-French factors.

One crucial point to remember is that data can vary across different sources. For instance, prices from two sources might differ due to distinct data sourcing methods or different adjustment methods for corporate actions. Some of the libraries we'll cover might download data for the same asset from the same source. However, libraries vary in how they return that data based on options that help you preprocess the data in preparation for research.

Lastly, while we'll focus heavily on mainstream financial data in this chapter, financial data is not limited to prices. The concept of "alternative data," which includes non-traditional data sources such as satellite images, web traffic data, or customer reviews, can be an important source of information for developing trading strategies. The Python tools to acquire and process this type of data are outside the scope of this book. We've intentionally left out the methods of acquiring and processing this type of data since it's covered in other resources dedicated to the topic.

In this chapter, we'll cover the following recipes:

- Working with stock market data with the OpenBB Platform
- Fetching historical futures data with the OpenBB Platform
- Navigating options market data with the OpenBB Platform
- Harnessing factor data using `pandas_datareader`

Technical requirements

This book relies on the Anaconda distribution of Python. We'll use Jupyter Notebook and Python script files to write the code. Unless specified otherwise, all the code should be written in Jupyter Notebooks.

Download and install the Anaconda distribution of Python. You can do this by going to `https://www.anaconda.com/download`. Depending on your operating system, the instructions for downloading and installing will vary. Please refer to the Anaconda documentation for detailed instructions.

Anaconda ships with a package manager called `conda`. Package managers make it easy to install, remove, and update Python packages. There's a great cheat sheet for the conda package manager available at `https://docs.conda.io/projects/conda/en/4.6.0/_downloads/52a95608c49671267e40c689e0bc00ca/conda-cheatsheet.pdf`.

Once you've installed the Anaconda distribution, open your Terminal on Mac or Linux or the Anaconda Prompt on Windows. If you're a Windows user, make sure to use the Command Prompt instead of the PowerShell prompt. Then follow these steps:

1. Update the `conda` package manager and follow any instructions to accept license agreements:

```
conda update -n base conda -y
```

2. Create a virtual environment:

```
conda create -n my-quant-stack python=3.11 -y
```

3. After the installation process is complete, activate the environment:

```
conda activate my-quant-stack
```

4. Install Jupyter Notebook using the package manager that ships with Python, pip:

```
pip install notebook matplotlib
```

This will set up a virtual environment using Python 3.11 and install Jupyter Notebook.

This chapter will use two Python libraries to acquire financial market data: the OpenBB Platform and `pandas_datareader`. The good news is that installing the OpenBB Platform installs many of the libraries you will need to acquire financial market data, including `pandas_datareader`. As such, there is no need to install the libraries separately.

Install the OpenBB Platform with all extensions and providers (both officially supported and community-maintained ones) using `pip`:

```
pip install openbb[all]
```

This is the easiest way to set up the OpenBB Platform for this book.

> Note
>
> **Important**
>
> In a macOS `zsh` Terminal shell, add quotation marks around the library name: `"openbb[all]"`.

To install a single extension:

```
pip install openbb[charting]
pip install openbb[ta]
```

Or install a single provider:

```
pip install openbb[yfinance]
```

To install the Nightly distribution (this installs all extras by default):

```
pip install openbb-nightly
```

> Note
>
> **Important**
>
> At the time of writing, installing the OpenBB Platform using pip isn't compatible with environments such as Google Colab and Kaggle since they come with preinstalled packages that can conflict with the ones used by the OpenBB Platform. If you run into trouble installing the OpenBB Platform, please check the online documentation for the most up-to-date instructions.

This book makes extensive use of Jupyter Notebooks. You can review instructions for using Jupyter Notebook here: `https://docs.jupyter.org/en/latest/`

> Note
>
> **Your purchase includes a free PDF copy + exclusive extras**
>
> Your purchase includes a DRM-free PDF copy of this book, 7-day trial to the Packt+ library (no credit card required), and additional exclusive extras. See the *Free benefits with your book* section in the *Preface* to unlock them instantly and maximize your learning.

Working with stock market data on the OpenBB platform

You may remember the **meme stock** hysteria that sent GameStop's stock up 1,744% in January 2021. One of the good things that came from that episode was the GameStonk terminal, now rebranded as OpenBB. OpenBB is one of the most popular open-source finance projects on GitHub for good reason: it provides a single interface to access hundreds of data feeds from one place in a standard way. OpenBB has a command-line interface that is great for manual investment research. But when it's time to get data into Python, you want the OpenBB Platform. This recipe will guide you through the process of using the OpenBB Platform to fetch stock market data.

Getting ready

By now, you should have the OpenBB Platform installed in your virtual environment. If not, go back to the beginning of this chapter and get it set up. The OpenBB Platform is free to use and offers a web-based UI to manage your configuration files, store API keys, and get code walkthroughs and examples. Sign up for a free Hub account at `https://my.openbb.co/login`. The popular course, *Getting Started with Python for Quant Finance*, uses the OpenBB Platform exclusively for all the code. Check out `https://www.pyquantnews.com/getting-started-with-python-for-quant-finance` for information on how to join.

How to do it...

Using the OpenBB Platform involves one import:

1. Import the OpenBB Platform:

```
from openbb import obb
obb.user.preferences.output_type = "dataframe"
```

2. Use the historical method to download price data for the SPY ETF:

```
data = obb.equity.price.historical("SPY", provider="yfinance")
```

3. Inspect the resulting DataFrame:

```
print(data)
```

4. Running the preceding code generates a pandas DataFrame and prints the data to the screen:

date	open	high	low	close	volume	dividend
2024-11-25	599.520020	600.859985	595.200012	597.530029	42441400	0.0
2024-11-26	598.799988	601.330017	598.070007	600.650024	45621300	0.0
2024-11-27	600.460022	600.849976	597.280029	598.830017	34000200	0.0
2024-11-29	599.659973	603.349976	599.380005	602.549988	30177400	0.0
2024-12-02	602.969971	604.320007	602.469971	603.630005	31746000	0.0
2024-12-03	603.390015	604.159973	602.340027	603.909973	26906600	0.0
2024-12-04	605.630005	607.909973	604.950012	607.659973	42787600	0.0
2024-12-05	607.659973	608.479980	606.299988	606.659973	28762200	0.0
2024-12-06	607.440002	609.070007	607.020020	607.809998	31241500	0.0
2024-12-09	607.690002	607.859985	604.080017	604.679993	34742700	0.0

Figure 1.1: Historic price data for SPY

How it works...

The OpenBB Platform follows an easy-to-understand namespace convention. All the methods for acquiring stock price data are methods on `openbb.equity`.

The `historical` method accepts a ticker symbol and returns the open, high, low, close, adjusted close, volume, and dividend in a pandas DataFrame. The additional parameters you can specify are as follows:

- `start_date`: Start date to get data from with
- `interval`: Interval (in minutes) to get data—that is, 1, 5, 15, 30, 60, or 1,440
- `end_date`: End date to get data from with
- `provider`: Source of data extracted

There's more...

An important benefit of using the OpenBB Platform is choosing your data source. By default, the OpenBB Platform will attempt to download data from free sources such as Yahoo! Finance. In most OpenBB Platform calls, you can indicate a different source. To use a source that requires an API key (either free or paid), you can configure it in the OpenBB Hub.

> **Note**
>
> Check out the OpenBB Platform documentation for the latest functionality: `https://docs.openbb.co/python`.

Let's look at some more of the functions of the OpenBB Platform.

Comparison of fundamental data

Not only can the OpenBB Platform download fundamental data in an organized and usable way, but it can also concatenate it in a single Pandas DataFrame for further analysis.

We can use the following code to see the balance sheet metrics from AAPL and MSFT:

```
obb.equity.fundamental.metrics(
    "AAPL,MSFT",
    provider="yfinance"
)
```

The output of the preceding snippet is a pandas DataFrame with fundamental data for each ticker that was passed:

	0	1
symbol	AAPL	MSFT
market_cap	2913325809664.0	3198271619072.0
pe_ratio	29.593458	37.32177
forward_pe	26.27801	32.452488
peg_ratio	2.75	2.25
peg_ratio_ttm	2.2528	2.1289
enterprise_to_ebitda	22.762	25.749
earnings_growth	0.007	0.2
earnings_growth_quarterly	-0.022	0.199
revenue_per_share	24.537	31.834
revenue_growth	-0.043	0.17
enterprise_to_revenue	7.732	13.624
quick_ratio	0.875	1.132
current_ratio	1.037	1.242
debt_to_equity	140.968	41.963
gross_margin	0.45586	0.69894
operating_margin	0.30743	0.44588
ebitda_margin	0.33968	0.52912
profit_margin	0.26306	0.36427
return_on_assets	0.22074	0.15295
return_on_equity	1.4725	0.38488
dividend_yield	0.0053	0.007
dividend_yield_5y_avg	0.0073	0.0094
payout_ratio	0.1493	0.2478
book_value	4.837	34.058
price_to_book	39.27848	12.634917
enterprise_value	2950608977920	3223296671744
overall_risk	1.0	1.0
audit_risk	6.0	3.0
board_risk	1.0	5.0
compensation_risk	2.0	2.0
shareholder_rights_risk	1.0	2.0
beta	1.264	0.893
price_return_1y	0.071517	0.298753
currency	USD	USD

Figure 1.2: Balance sheet data for MSFT and AAPL

Building stock screeners

One of the most powerful features of the OpenBB Platform is the custom stock screener. A stock screener allows you to use filters to identify stocks that might be interesting to trade. It uses the Finviz stock screener under the hood and surfaces metrics across a range of stocks based on either pre-built or custom criteria. See the documentation for more on how to use the OpenBB screener functions (`https://docs.openbb.co/python/reference/equity/screener`):

1. Create an overview screener based on a list of stocks using the default view:

```
obb.equity.compare.groups(
    group="industry",
    metric="valuation",
    provider="finviz"
)
```

The output of the preceding snippet is the following pandas DataFrame:

	name	market_cap	performance_1D	pe	forward_pe	...	volume	price_to_sales	price_to_book	price_to_cash	price_to_free_cash_flow
0	Pharmaceutical Retailers	13580000000	-0.0394	NaN	4.99	...	20580000	0.09	0.99	17.30	829.95
1	Airlines	122270000000	-0.0182	10.97	6.83	...	70720000	0.47	2.22	2.31	43.65
2	REIT - Mortgage	53670000000	-0.0068	15.94	6.98	...	40160000	1.69	0.81	3.60	4.73
3	Insurance - Reinsurance	53050000000	-0.0063	7.66	7.53	...	2049999	0.90	1.21	NaN	3.03
4	Insurance - Life	269430000000	-0.0107	12.25	8.11	...	16079999	1.10	1.48	4120.41	4.41
...	...	...	...	...	...	...	...	...	...	...	...
140	REIT - Healthcare Facilities	123940000000	-0.0028	94.22	46.31	...	27280000	5.51	1.68	25.46	22.11
141	Uranium	36590000000	0.0248	112.12	46.58	...	36490000	15.51	4.90	28.10	143.86
142	Shell Companies	26350000000	0.0185	44.08	133.74	...	10560000	46.71	2.10	36.15	105.00
143	Infrastructure Operations	34110000000	-0.0041	57.81	146.15	...	1160000	3.40	7.22	6.25	28.37
144	Real Estate - Diversified	6760000000	-0.0141	75.91	NaN	...	549690	4.54	1.74	6.63	58.78

Figure 1.3: Results of a comparison screener between F, GE, and TSLA

2. Create a screener that returns the top gainers from the technology sector based on a preset:

```
obb.equity.compare.groups(
    group="technology",
    metric="performance",
    provider="finviz"
)
```

The output of the preceding snippet is the following pandas DataFrame:

	name	performance_1d	performance_1w	performance_1m	performance_3m	performance_6m	performance_1y	performance_ytd
0	Entertainment	-0.0061	-0.0554	-0.0471	-0.0970	-0.0493	0.1120	0.1257
1	Oil & Gas Refining & Marketing	0.0042	-0.0420	-0.0115	0.0826	0.2394	0.1273	0.2957
2	Coking Coal	0.0223	-0.0390	-0.0632	0.0858	0.5051	-0.1220	0.1244
3	Software - Infrastructure	0.0043	-0.0358	-0.1335	-0.0678	0.0530	0.1395	0.1482
4	Oil & Gas Integrated	-0.0045	-0.0318	-0.0032	0.0043	0.1273	0.0090	0.1092
...	...	...	...	...	...	...	...	...
139	Residential Construction	0.0488	0.0984	0.0053	-0.0457	0.2490	-0.1016	0.0512
140	Internet Content & Information	0.0168	0.1030	0.0594	0.2329	0.4553	0.5648	0.4425
141	Textile Manufacturing	0.0537	0.1233	-0.2062	-0.2455	-0.2695	-0.4146	-0.4019
142	Mortgage Finance	0.0727	0.1330	0.0428	0.0782	0.4660	0.3890	0.6100
143	Department Stores	0.0878	0.1347	0.1536	0.2820	0.5519	0.3178	0.2591

Figure 1.4: Results of a screener showing the day's top-gaining stocks

3. Create a screener that presents an overview grouped by sector:

```
obb.equity.compare.groups(
    group="sector",
    metric="overview",
    provider="finviz"
)
```

The output of the preceding snippet is the following pandas DataFrame:

	name	stocks	market_cap	performance_1D	dividend_yield	pe	forward_pe	peg	float_short	volume
0	Gambling	18	78550000000	-0.0602	0.0038	88.00	20.37	3.28	0.0257	55830000
1	Pharmaceutical Retailers	8	13580000000	-0.0394	0.0979	NaN	4.99	NaN	0.0634	20600000
2	Staffing & Employment Services	23	172120000000	-0.0224	0.0230	26.15	22.45	2.46	0.0245	9700000
3	Lumber & Wood Production	6	21290000000	-0.0222	0.0102	25.55	13.97	1.53	0.0249	846080
4	Airports & Air Services	9	29420000000	-0.0213	0.0338	17.29	15.19	4.46	0.1007	5530000
...	...	...	...	...	...	...	...	...	...	...
140	Other Precious Metals & Mining	18	18040000000	0.0320	0.0052	64.77	23.81	3.51	0.0249	32460000
141	Copper	8	180650000000	0.0338	0.0185	42.89	25.63	1.75	0.0183	27360000
142	Oil & Gas Drilling	11	29580000000	0.0371	0.0190	18.99	9.75	0.37	0.1092	30250000
143	Semiconductors	67	6048100000000	0.0380	0.0065	49.71	26.46	1.63	0.0202	308940000
144	Silver	3	4370000000	0.0488	0.0023	46.11	24.66	1.28	0.0436	10710000

Figure 1.5: Results of a screener grouped by sector

See also

For more on OpenBB and the **Finviz** stock screener, check out the following resources:

- The OpenBB Platform documentation, which contains details on dozens of functions to acquire stock market data for free: `https://docs.openbb.co/python/reference/equity`
- The **Finviz** home page, which includes free access to the web-based screener `https://finviz.com/`
- The top-selling cohort-based course to help beginners get up and running with Python for quant finance, algorithmic trading, and data analysis: `https://www.pyquantnews.com/getting-started-with-python-for-quant-finance`

Fetching historical futures data with the OpenBB platform

Traders use continuous futures data for backtesting trading strategies. Futures traders use the roll from one contract to another as a potential opportunity for profit. The roll is the process of exiting a position in a contract as it expires and entering a position into a contract that expires in the future. Some traders simply pick an expiration date to roll to the next contract, while others use sophisticated techniques involving open interest. This **basis trade** is persistently one of the most popular trading strategies for futures traders. These traders want control over the data that's used to compute the basis trade, so acquiring individual contract data is important. This recipe will guide you through the process of using the OpenBB Platform to fetch individual futures contract data.

Getting ready

By now, you should have the OpenBB Platform installed in your virtual environment. If not, go back to the beginning of this chapter and get it set up.

How to do it...

We'll use the futures functionality in the OpenBB Platform to download individual futures data for free:

1. Import pandas and the OpenBB Platform:

```
import pandas as pd
from openbb import obb
obb.user.preferences.output_type = "dataframe"
```

2. Download the current futures curve for the VIX futures contract from the **Chicago Board Options Exchange** (**CBOE**):

```
data = obb.derivatives.futures.curve(symbol="VX_EOD")
```

3. Inspect the resulting DataFrame:

```
print(data)
```

4. Running the preceding code generates the futures curve for the VIX futures contract:

	expiration	price
0	2025-12	19.90
1	2026-01	21.10
2	2026-02	21.85
3	2026-03	22.15
4	2026-04	22.45
5	2026-05	22.55
6	2026-06	22.55
7	2026-07	22.70
8	2026-08	15.60

Figure 1.6: Settlement prices for the forward VIX index futures contracts

5. Update the DataFrame index to the expiration dates and plot the settlement prices:

```
data.index = pd.to_datetime(data.expiration)
data.plot()
```

6. By running the preceding code, we plot the VIX futures curve:

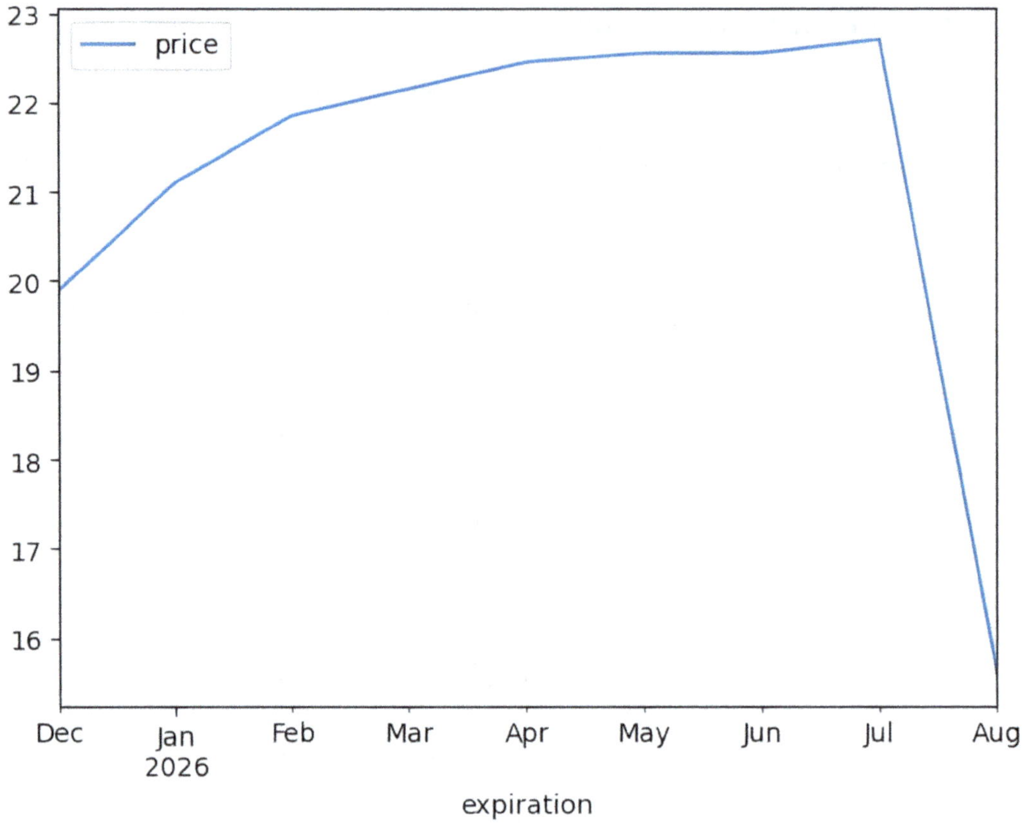

Figure 1.7: VIX futures curve

There's more...

You can use the `obb.derivatives.futures.historical` method to get historical data for an individual expiration. Stitching together data across a range of years can provide insight into the market's expectation of supply and demand of the underlying commodity:

1. First, create a list containing the year and month expirations you're interested in:

```
expirations = [
    "2026-12",
    "2027-12",
    "2028-12",
    "2029-12",
```

```
    "2030-12",
]
```

The preceding code creates a Python list of expiration years and dates in string format.

2. Now, loop through each of the expirations to download the data:

```
contracts = []
for expiration in expirations:
    df = (
        obb
        .derivatives.futures.historical(
            symbol="CL",
            expiration=expiration,
            start_date="2020-01-01",
            end_date="2022-12-31",
            provider="yfinance"
        )
    ).rename(columns={
        "close": expiration
    })
    contracts.append(df[expiration])
```

3. For each of the contracts, use the OpenBB Platform to download historical futures data for the CL contract between January 1, 2020, and December 31, 2022. Using the pandas `rename` method, change the column name from `"close"` to the expiration date. Finally, append the newly created pandas DataFrame to a list of DataFrames:

```
historical = (
    pd
    .DataFrame(contracts)
    .transpose()
    .dropna()
)
```

4. Concatenate the DataFrames together, swap the columns and rows using the transpose method, and drop any with no data using the `dropna` method. Inspect the resulting DataFrame:

```
print(historical)
```

5. By printing the DataFrame, we will see the historical settlement prices:

date	2026-12	2027-12	2028-12	2029-12	2030-12
2020-01-02	53.130001	53.180000	53.180000	53.180000	53.180000
2020-01-03	52.910000	52.959999	52.959999	52.959999	52.959999
2020-01-06	52.840000	52.889999	52.889999	52.889999	52.889999
2020-01-07	53.169998	53.240002	53.240002	53.240002	53.240002
2020-01-08	52.770000	52.840000	52.840000	52.840000	52.840000
...	...	...	...	...	...
2022-12-23	64.669998	62.119999	59.990002	58.139999	56.389999
2022-12-27	64.730003	62.180000	60.049999	58.200001	56.450001
2022-12-28	65.339996	62.790001	60.650002	58.790001	57.040001
2022-12-29	64.599998	62.119999	59.980000	58.119999	56.369999
2022-12-30	65.620003	63.110001	60.919998	58.970001	57.220001

Figure 1.8: Historic settlement prices for the December CL futures contract

The result is the data between January 2020 and December 2022 for each of the December expirations between 2023 and 2030.

To visualize the market's expectation of the future supply and demand of the December contract, you can plot the last price:

```
historical.iloc[-1].plot()
```

Here's the output:

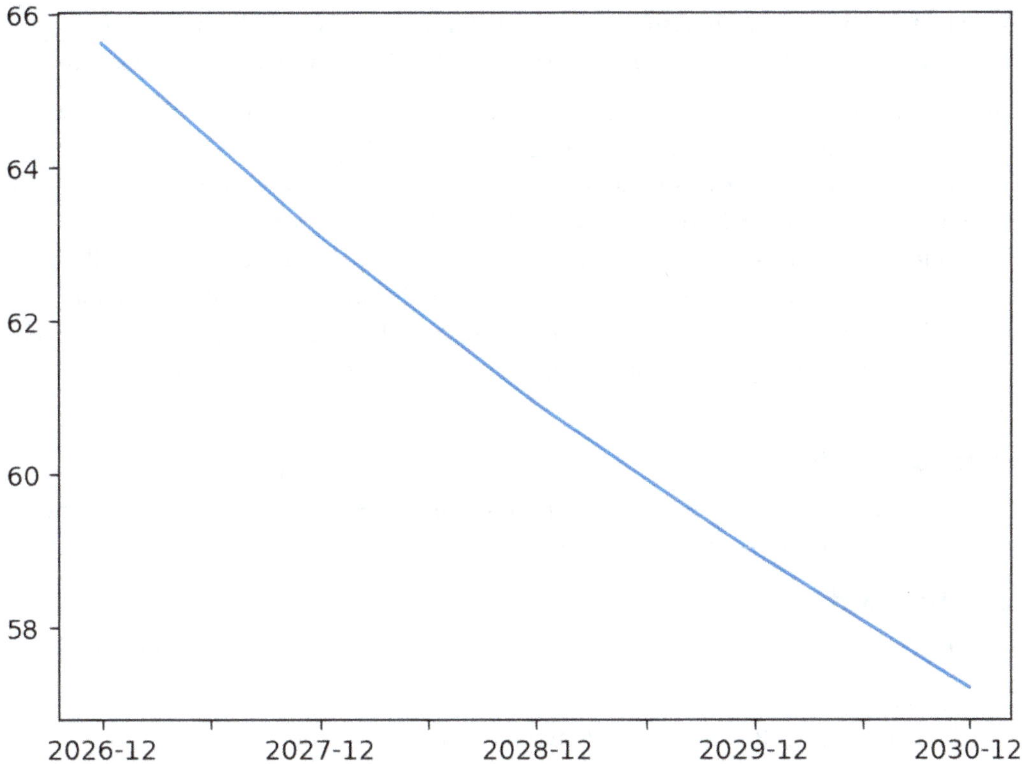

Figure 1.9: Futures curve for the December CL contract

See also

For more on the Platform futures functionality, you can browse the following documentation:

- Documentation on the OpenBB Platform's futures curve method: `https://docs.openbb.co/python/reference/derivatives/futures/curve`
- Documentation on the OpenBB Platform's historical curve method: `https://docs.openbb.co/python/reference/derivatives/futures/historical`

Navigating options market data with the OpenBB platform

Options are exchange-listed derivative contracts that convey the right (but not the obligation) to buy or sell the underlying stock at a certain price on or before a certain expiration date. Options are among the most versatile financial instruments in the market. They allow traders to define their risk profiles before entering trades and express market views not only on the direction of the underlying but also the volatility. While options offer a high degree of flexibility for trading, this feature complicates data collection for research and backtesting.

A single underlying stock can have an array of options contracts with different combinations of strike prices and expiration dates. Collecting and manipulating this data is a challenge. The combination of options contracts for all strikes and expiration dates is commonly referred to as an options chain. There can be thousands of individual options contracts at a given time for a single underlying stock. Not only does the number of individual contracts pose a challenge, but getting price data has historically been expensive. With the introduction of the OpenBB Platform, it is now only a few lines of Python code to download options chains into a pandas DataFrame. This recipe will walk you through acquiring options data using the OpenBB Platform.

Getting ready

By now, you should have the OpenBB Platform installed in your virtual environment. If not, go back to the beginning of this chapter and get it set up.

How to do it...

Similar to how we used the OpenBB Platform for futures data, we can use it for options data too:

1. Import the OpenBB Platform and Matplotlib for visualization:

```
from openbb import obb
obb.user.preferences.output_type = "dataframe"
```

2. Use the chains method to download the entire options chain:

```
chains = obb.derivatives.options.chains(symbol="SPY")
```

3. Inspect the resulting DataFrame:

```
chains.info()
```

4. By running the preceding code, we'll see the details of the options chain data:

```
<class 'pandas.core.frame.DataFrame'>
RangeIndex: 10364 entries, 0 to 10363
Data columns (total 29 columns):
 #   Column               Non-Null Count  Dtype
---  ------               --------------  -----
 0   underlying_symbol    10364 non-null  object
 1   underlying_price     10364 non-null  float64
 2   contract_symbol      10364 non-null  object
 3   expiration           10364 non-null  object
 4   dte                  10364 non-null  int64
 5   strike               10364 non-null  float64
 6   option_type          10364 non-null  object
 7   open_interest        10364 non-null  int64
 8   volume               10364 non-null  int64
 9   theoretical_price    10364 non-null  float64
 10  last_trade_price     10364 non-null  float64
 11  last_trade_time      8599 non-null   object
 12  tick                 10364 non-null  object
 13  bid                  10364 non-null  float64
 14  bid_size             10364 non-null  int64
 15  ask                  10364 non-null  float64
 16  ask_size             10364 non-null  int64
 17  open                 10364 non-null  float64
 18  high                 10364 non-null  float64
 19  low                  10364 non-null  float64
 20  prev_close           10364 non-null  float64
 21  change               10364 non-null  float64
 22  change_percent       10364 non-null  float64
 23  implied_volatility   10364 non-null  float64
 24  delta                10364 non-null  float64
 25  gamma                10364 non-null  float64
 26  theta                10364 non-null  float64
 27  vega                 10364 non-null  float64
 28  rho                  10364 non-null  float64
dtypes: float64(18), int64(5), object(6)
memory usage: 2.3+ MB
None
```

Figure 1.10: Preview of the data downloaded for the SPY options chains

Note that at the time of writing, there are 10,364 options contracts for the **SPY Exchange Traded Fund** (**ETF**) that can be downloaded from CBOE (for free).

How it works...

The `obb.derivatives.options.chains` method downloads the entire options chain and stores it in a pandas DataFrame. The `obb.derivatives.options.chains` has an additional optional parameter:

- `provider`: The source from which the data should be downloaded. The default is CBOE. You can also select Tradier, Intrinio, or TMX. Note that for Tradier, Intrinio, and TMX, you need to provide your API key, which can be configured in the OpenBB Hub.

There's more...

You can use the OpenBB Platform to download historical options data for a single contract. To do this, you need the option symbol.

We'll use the `obb.equity.price.historical` method to get the historical options data for an SPY call option with a strike price of $675 expiring on December 18, 2026:

```
data = obb.equity.price.historical(
    symbol="SPY261218C00675000",
    provider="yfinance"
)[["close", "volume"]]
```

Note

Hint

The option contract may have expired by the time you run this code. If you get an error from OpenBB saying the contract cannot be found, you'll need to select an option contract that is actively trading.

The result is a pandas DataFrame with the closing price and volume of the options contract:

date	close	volume
2025-11-14	62.279999	48
2025-11-17	60.599998	22
2025-11-18	58.049999	13
2025-11-19	57.549999	1
2025-11-20	53.419998	38
2025-11-21	56.709999	26
2025-11-24	59.020000	7
2025-11-25	62.099998	11

Figure 1.11: Closing prices and volume of the SPY options contract

Option Greeks

Options Greeks measures how options prices change given a change in one of the inputs to an options pricing model. For example, **delta** measures how an option's price changes given a change in the underlying stock price.

Using `obb.derivatives.options.chains`, the OpenBB Platform returns the most used Greeks, including Delta, Gamma, Theta, Vega, and Rho.

See also

Options are a fascinating and deep topic that is rich with opportunities for trading. You can learn more about options, volatility, and how to analyze both via the OpenBB Platform:

- Free articles, code, and other resources for options trading: `https://pyquantnews.com/free-python-resources/options-trading-with-python/`
- Learn more about financial options if you're unfamiliar with them: `https://en.wikipedia.org/wiki/Option_(finance)`
- Documentation on the OpenBB Platform's options methods: `https://docs.openbb.co/python/reference/derivatives/options`

Harnessing factor data using pandas_datareader

Diversification is great until the entire market declines in value. That's because the overall market influences all assets. Factors can offset some of these risks by targeting drivers of return not influenced by the market. Common factors are size (large-cap versus small-cap) and style (value versus growth). If you think small-cap stocks will outperform large-cap stocks, then you might want exposure to small-cap stocks. If you think value stocks will outperform growth stocks, then you might want exposure to value stocks. In either case, you want to measure the risk contribution of the factor. Eugene Fama and Kenneth French built the Fama-French three-factor model in 1992. The three Fama-French factors are constructed using six value-weighted portfolios formed on capitalization and book-to-market.

The three factors are as follows:

- **Small Minus Big**, which represents the differential between the average returns of three small-cap portfolios and three large-cap portfolios
- **High Minus Low**, which quantifies the difference in average returns between two value-oriented portfolios and two growth-oriented portfolios
- **Rm-Rf**, which denotes the market's excess return over the risk-free rate

We'll explore how to measure and isolate alpha in *Chapter 7, Build Alpha Factors for Stock Portfolios*. This recipe will guide you through the process of using pandas_datareader to fetch historical factor data for use in your analysis.

Getting ready

You can install pandas_datareader with pip either in a terminal with this command:

```
pip install pandas_datareader
```

Or directly in a Jupyter Notebook cell:

```
!pip install pandas_datareader
```

You'll need pandas_datareader to follow along with this recipe.

Note that you'll need pandas version 2 to use pandas_datareader. You can install it with the following command:

```
pip install --upgrade "pandas<3" "pandas-datareader==0.10.0"
```

How to do it...

Using the pandas_datareader library, we have access to dozens of investment research factors:

1. Import pandas_datareader:

```
import pandas_datareader as pdr
```

2. Download the monthly factor data starting in January 2000:

```
factors = pdr.get_data_famafrench("F-F_Research_Data_Factors")
```

3. Get a description of the research data factors:

```
print(factors["DESCR"])
```

4. The result is an explanation of the data included in the DataFrame:

```
F-F Research Data Factors
-------------------------

This file was created by CMPT_ME_BEME_RETS using the 202306 CRSP database. The 1-month TBill return is from Ibbotso
n and Associates, Inc. Copyright 2023 Kenneth R. French

  0 : (59 rows x 4 cols)
  1 : Annual Factors: January-December (5 rows x 4 cols)
```

Figure 1.12: Preview of the description that is downloaded with factor data

5. Inspect the monthly factor data:

```
print(factors[0].head())
```

6. By running the preceding code, we get a DataFrame containing monthly factor data:

Date	Mkt-RF	SMB	HML	RF
2018-08	3.44	1.13	-3.98	0.16
2018-09	0.06	-2.28	-1.69	0.15
2018-10	-7.68	-4.77	3.44	0.19
2018-11	1.69	-0.68	0.28	0.18
2018-12	-9.57	-2.37	-1.85	0.20

Figure 1.13: Preview of the monthly data downloaded from the Fama-French Data Library

7. Inspect the annual factor data:

```
print(factors[1].head())
```

8. By running the preceding code, we get a DataFrame containing annual factor data:

Date	Mkt-RF	SMB	HML	RF
2018	-6.95	-3.21	-9.73	1.83
2019	28.28	-6.11	-10.34	2.15
2020	23.66	13.18	-46.56	0.45
2021	23.56	-3.89	25.53	0.04
2022	-21.60	-6.82	25.81	1.43

Figure 1.14: Preview of the annual data downloaded from the Fama-French Data Library

How it works...

Under the hood, `pandas_datareader` fetches data from the Fama-French Data Library by downloading a compressed CSV file, uncompressing it, and creating a pandas DataFrame.

There are 297 different datasets with different factor data available from the Fama-French Data Library. Here are some popular versions of the Fama-French 3-factor model for different regions:

- `Developed_3_Factors`
- `Developed_ex_US_3_Factors`
- `Europe_3_Factors`
- `Japan_3_Factors`
- `Asia_Pacific_ex_Japan_3_Factors`

You can use these in the `get_data_famafrench` method just like `F-F_Research_Data_Factors`.

Some datasets return a dictionary with more than one DataFrame representing data for different time frames, portfolio weighting methodologies, and aggregate statistics. Data for these portfolios can be accessed using numerical keys. For example, the `5_Industry_Portfolios` dataset returns eight DataFrames in the dictionary. The first can be accessed using the `0` dictionary key, the second using the `1` dictionary key, and so on. Each dictionary includes a description of the dataset, which can be accessed using the `DESCR` dictionary key.

There's more...

`pandas_datareader` can be used to access data from many remote online sources. These include Tiingo, IEX, Alpha Vantage, FRED, Eurostat, and many more. Review the full list of data sources on the documentation page here: `https://pandas-datareader.readthedocs.io/en/latest/remote_data.html`.

See also

For more details on the factors available in the investment factor research library, take a look at the following resources. For another example of using the Fama-French 3-factor model, see the resources on the PyQuant News website:

- Documentation for all the Fama-French factor data: `https://mba.tuck.dartmouth.edu/pages/faculty/ken.french/data_library.html`
- Details on the Fama-French 3-factor model: `https://mba.tuck.dartmouth.edu/pages/faculty/ken.french/Data_Library/f-f_factors.html`
- Code walkthrough for using the Fama-French 3-factor model: `https://www.pyquantnews.com/past-pyquant-newsletter-issues`

2

Analyze and Transform Financial Market Data with pandas

The pandas library was invented by Wes McKinney while at the investment management firm **AQR Capital Management**, where he researched macro and credit trading strategies. He built pandas to provide flexible, easy-to-use data structures for data analysis. Since it was open-sourced in 2009, pandas has become the standard tool to analyze and transform data using Python.

pandas is well-suited for working with tabular data, like that stored in spreadsheets or databases, and it integrates well with many other data analysis libraries in the Python ecosystem. Its capabilities extend to handling missing data, reshaping datasets, and merging and joining datasets, and it also provides robust tools for loading data from flat files, Excel files, databases, and HDF5 file formats. It's widely used in academia, finance, and many areas of business due to its rich features and ease of use.

This chapter will begin by covering recipes to help you build pandas data structures, primarily focusing on DataFrames and Series, the two primary data structures of pandas. You will learn how these structures allow for a wide variety of operations, such as slicing, indexing, and subsetting large datasets, all of which are crucial in algorithmic trading. From there, you will learn how to inspect and select data from DataFrames.

After you have a firm understanding of manipulating data using pandas, we'll cover recipes for analyses that are common in algorithmic trading, including how to compute asset returns and the volatility of a return series. The chapter will teach you how to generate a cumulative return series and resample data to different time frames, providing you with the flexibility to analyze data at various granularities. You will also learn how to handle missing data, a common issue in real-world datasets.

Lastly, this chapter will show you how to apply custom functions to time series data. Throughout this chapter, you will see how pandas integrates with other libraries in the scientific Python ecosystem, such as Matplotlib for data visualization, NumPy for numerical operations, and Scikit-Learn for machine learning.

In this chapter, we'll cover the following recipes:

- Diving into pandas index types
- Building pandas Series and DataFrames
- Manipulating and transforming DataFrames
- Examining and selecting data from DataFrames
- Calculating asset returns using pandas
- Measuring the volatility of a return series
- Generating a cumulative return series
- Resampling data for different time frames
- Addressing missing data issues
- Applying custom functions to analyze time series data

Diving into pandas index types

The Index is an immutable sequence that's used for indexing and alignment that serves as the label or key for rows in the DataFrame or elements in a series. It allows for fast lookup and relational operations and as of pandas version 2, it can contain values of any type, including integers, strings, and even tuples. Indexes in pandas are immutable, which makes them safe to share across multiple DataFrames or Series. They also have several built-in methods for common operations, such as sorting, grouping, and set operations such as union and intersection. pandas supports multiple indexes, allowing for complex, hierarchical data organization. This feature is particularly useful when dealing with high-dimensional data such as option chains. We'll see examples of MultiIndexes later in this chapter.

There are seven types of pandas indexes. The differences are dependent on the type of data used to create the index. For example, an Int64Index is an index that's made up of 64-bit integers. pandas is smart enough to create the right type of index, depending on the data used to instantiate it.

How to do it...

We'll start by creating a simple index with a series of integers:

1. Import pandas as the common alias, pd:

```
import pandas as pd
```

2. Instantiate the Index class:

```
idx_1 = pd.Index([0, 1, 2, 3, 4, 5, 6, 7, 8, 9])
```

3. Inspect the index:

```
print(idx_1)
```

4. Running the preceding code generates the index and prints out its type:

```
Index([0, 1, 2, 3, 4, 5, 6, 7, 8, 9], dtype='int64')
```

Figure 2.1: A pandas Int64Index index with 10 values

How it works...

This is the simplest example of creating a pandas index. You can instantiate the `Index` class with a one-dimensional, array-like data structure containing the values you want in the index.

There's more...

pandas has several Index types to support many use cases, including those related to time series analysis. We'll cover examples of the most often-used index types.

DatetimeIndex

A more interesting index type is `DatetimeIndex`. This type of index is extremely useful when dealing with time series data:

```
days = pd.date_range("2016-01-01", periods=6, freq="D")
```

This creates an index with six incremental datetime objects starting from `2016-01-01`.

You can use many different frequencies, including seconds:

```
seconds = pd.date_range("2016-01-01", periods=100, freq="s")
```

By default, DatetimeIndexes are "timezone naive." This means they have no time zone information attached. To "localize" DatetimeIndex, use tz_localize:

```
seconds_utc = seconds.tz_localize("UTC")
```

Localizing DatetimeIndex just appends time zone information to the object. It does not adjust the time from one time zone changes. To do that, you can use tz_convert:

```
seconds_utc.tz_convert("US/Eastern")
```

PeriodIndex

It's possible to create ranges of periods, such as quarters, using the pandas period_range method:

```
prng = pd.period_range("1990Q1", "2000Q4", freq="Q-NOV")
```

period_range returns a PeriodIndex object that has special labels that represent periods. In this case, the period starts in 1990Q1 and extends through to 2000Q4 at quarterly increments, with the year ending in November.

MultiIndex

MultiIndex, also known as a hierarchical index, is a data structure that allows for complex data organization within pandas DataFrames and Series. It allows data spanning multiple dimensions to be represented, even within the inherently two-dimensional structure of a DataFrame, by allowing multiple levels of indices. We'll look at MultiIndex in detail later in this book, so don't worry if it's not exactly clear how they work yet.

To create a MultiIndex object, pass a list of tuples to the from_tuples method:

```
tuples = [
    (pd.Timestamp("2023-07-10"), "WMT"),
    (pd.Timestamp("2023-07-10"), "JPM"),
    (pd.Timestamp("2023-07-10"), "TGT"),
    (pd.Timestamp("2023-07-11"), "WMT"),
    (pd.Timestamp("2023-07-11"), "JPM"),
    (pd.Timestamp("2023-07-11"), "TGT"),
]
midx = pd.MultiIndex.from_tuples(tuples, names=("date", "symbol"))
```

There are several ways to create a `MultiIndex` object. In this example, we use a list of tuples. Each tuple contains a pandas timestamp and a ticker symbol. Using the list of tuples, you can call the `from_tuples` method to create the `MultiIndex` object. The result is a two-dimensional index that supports hierarchical DataFrames.

> Note
>
> **Important**
>
> Giving the names argument to the from_tuples method is done to give names to the index columns for label-based indexing. This is optional.

See also

The pandas documentation is very thorough. To learn more about the index types we covered in this recipe, take a look at the following resources:

- Documentation on pandas indexes: `https://pandas.pydata.org/docs/reference/api/pandas.Index.html`
- Documentation on pandas `DatatimeIndexes`: `https://pandas.pydata.org/docs/reference/api/pandas.DatetimeIndex.html`
- Documentation on pandas `MultiIndexes`: `https://pandas.pydata.org/docs/reference/api/pandas.MultiIndex.html`

Building pandas Series and DataFrames

A Series is a one-dimensional labeled array that can hold any data type, including integers, floats, strings, and objects. The axis labels of a Series are collectively referred to as the index, which allows for easy data manipulation and access. A key feature of the pandas Series is its ability to handle missing data, represented as a NumPy **nan** (Not a Number).

> Note
>
> **Important**
>
> NumPy's nan is a special floating-point value. It is commonly used as a marker for missing data in numerical datasets. The nan value a float is useful because it can be used in numerical computations and included in arrays of numbers without changing their data type, which aids in maintaining consistent data types in numeric datasets. Unlike other values, nan doesn't equal anything, which is why we need to use functions such as `numpy.isnan()` to check for nan.

Furthermore, the Series object provides a host of methods for operations such as statistical functions, string manipulation, and even plotting.

A DataFrame is a two-dimensional data structure that can be thought of as a spreadsheet with rows and columns. It's essentially a table of data with rows and columns. The data is aligned in a tabular fashion in rows and columns, and it can be of different types (for example, numbers and strings). DataFrames make manipulating data easy, allowing for operations such as aggregation, slicing, indexing, subsetting, merging, and reshaping. They also handle missing data gracefully and provide convenient methods for filtering out, filling in, or otherwise manipulating null values.

Getting ready

Before building a Series and DataFrame, make sure you have completed the previous recipe and have the indexes stored in memory.

How to do it...

Execute the following steps to construct a DataFrame out of several Series.

1. Import NumPy to create an array of normally distributed random numbers:

```
import numpy as np
```

2. Create a function that returns a NumPy array of randomly distributed numbers with the same length as the DatetimeIndex object you created earlier:

```
def rnd():
    return np.random.randn(100,)
```

The return value is a NumPy array of length 100. It's filled with random samples from a normal distribution. Creating a function allows you to return a different set of values each time the function is called.

> **Tip**
>
> When working with pandas, it's common to use random numbers to populate Series and DataFrames for testing.

3. Create three pandas Series that you'll use to create the DataFrame:

```
s_1 = pd.Series(rnd(), index=seconds)
s_2 = pd.Series(rnd(), index=seconds)
s_3 = pd.Series(rnd(), index=seconds)
```

   We use the same DatetimeIndex object we created in the previous recipe as the index for each of the Series. This lets pandas align each of the columns along the common index.

4. Create the DataFrame using a dictionary:

```
df = pd.DataFrame({"a": s_1, "b": s_2, "c": s_3})
```

   The result is a DataFrame with a DatetimeIndex object of second resolution and three columns all with samples from a normal distribution:

	a	b	c
2016-01-01 00:00:00	-1.075846	2.547374	0.415277
2016-01-01 00:00:01	-0.457549	0.498616	-0.574556
2016-01-01 00:00:02	-0.644713	1.843763	0.388706
2016-01-01 00:00:03	-0.268644	1.186620	0.857448
2016-01-01 00:00:04	-0.590639	-0.421629	-1.244135
...	...	...	...
2016-01-01 00:01:35	-1.996332	-0.625641	-0.173174
2016-01-01 00:01:36	-1.502497	1.172084	-0.238044
2016-01-01 00:01:37	-0.572685	0.106536	0.499070
2016-01-01 00:01:38	-0.905668	0.382154	-0.221563
2016-01-01 00:01:39	0.548253	-1.149373	-0.257776

Figure 2.2: DataFrame with a DatetimeIndex object and three columns of random data

How it works...

pandas Series and DataFrames have several ways of being constructed. Series can take any array-like, iterable (for example, list or tuple), dictionary, or scalar value to be created. In this example, you created a NumPy array-like object called an array. We passed in the `DatetimeIndex` object created in the previous recipe, which is the same length as the array that was used to create the Series.

DataFrames accept any multidimensional structured or homogenous objects, be they iterable, dictionaries, or other DataFrames. In this example, you passed in a Python dictionary, which is a list of key-value pairs. Each key represents the column name and each value represents the data for that column. DataFrames also accept an index argument in case the input data is not structured with an index. DataFrames can also accept a columns argument, which names the columns. Since the Series included indexes, pandas automatically used them to create the DataFrame index and aligned the values appropriately. If there were missing data for an index, pandas would still include the index but include nan as the value.

There's more...

A `MultiIndex` object is a multidimensional index that provides added flexibility to DataFrames. You can create a `MultiIndex` DataFrame from scratch or "reindex" an existing DataFrame to make it a `MultiIndex` DataFrame.

Building a MultiIndex DataFrame from scratch

Here are the steps to create it from scratch:

1. Use the same MultiIndex object you created in the previous recipe:

```
tuples = [
    (pd.Timestamp("2023-07-10"), "WMT"),
    (pd.Timestamp("2023-07-10"), "JPM"),
    (pd.Timestamp("2023-07-10"), "TGT"),
    (pd.Timestamp("2023-07-11"), "WMT"),
    (pd.Timestamp("2023-07-11"), "JPM"),
    (pd.Timestamp("2023-07-11"), "TGT"),
]
midx = pd.MultiIndex.from_tuples(tuples, names=("date", "symbol"))
```

2. Now that we have the index, we can create the DataFrame:

```
df_2 = pd.DataFrame(
    {
```

```
        "close":[158.11,144.64,132.55,158.20,146.61,134.86],
        "factor_1": [0.31, 0.24, 0.67, 0.29, 0.23, 0.71],
    },
    index=midx,
)
```

We create the DataFrame using a dictionary. The keys are the column names and the values are the data for the columns. Note that we use the index argument while passing in the `MultiIndex` object. The result is a DataFrame that contains records for each of the three symbols for each date:

		close	factor_1
date	symbol		
2023-07-10	WMT	158.11	0.31
	JPM	144.64	0.24
	TGT	132.55	0.67
2023-07-11	WMT	158.20	0.29
	JPM	146.61	0.23
	TGT	134.86	0.71

Figure 2.3: MultiIndex DataFrame

Reindexing an existing DataFrame with a MultiIndex object

It's common to add a `MultiIndex` object to a DataFrame. Let's consider an example of reindexing options data for a `MultiIndex` object:

1. Import the OpenBB Platform:

```
from openbb import obb
obb.user.preferences.output_type = "dataframe"
```

2. Download option chains using the OpenBB Platform:

```
chains = obb.derivatives.options.chains(
    "SPY",
```

```
    provider="cboe"
)
```

The result is a DataFrame with a RangeIndex object starting at 0:

	contract_symbol	expiration	strike	option_type	open_interest	...	theta	vega	rho	last_trade_timestamp	dte
0	SPY240703C00445000	2024-07-03	445.0	call	2	...	0.0000	0.000	0.0000	2024-07-01 14:02:04	0
1	SPY240703P00445000	2024-07-03	445.0	put	5	...	0.0000	0.000	0.0000	2024-07-02 09:50:35	0
2	SPY240703C00450000	2024-07-03	450.0	call	5	...	0.0000	0.000	0.0000	2024-07-03 12:43:35	0
3	SPY240703P00450000	2024-07-03	450.0	put	30	...	0.0000	0.000	0.0000	2024-07-02 11:59:56	0
4	SPY240703C00455000	2024-07-03	455.0	call	0	...	0.0000	0.000	0.0000	NaT	0
...	...	...	...	...	...	...	...	...	...	...	...
8641	SPY261218P00810000	2026-12-18	810.0	put	0	...	-0.0692	0.000	-0.0001	NaT	898
8642	SPY261218C00815000	2026-12-18	815.0	call	0	...	-0.0077	1.309	0.9418	NaT	898
8643	SPY261218P00815000	2026-12-18	815.0	put	0	...	-0.0692	0.000	-0.0001	NaT	898
8644	SPY261218C00820000	2026-12-18	820.0	call	8	...	-0.0074	1.262	0.8956	2024-07-02 13:57:35	898
8645	SPY261218P00820000	2026-12-18	820.0	put	0	...	-0.0692	0.000	-0.0001	NaT	898

Figure 2.4: DataFrame with SPY options data

Options are derivatives that are frequently grouped by expiration date, strike price, option type, and any combination of those three. Using the `set_index` method takes the arguments in the list and uses those columns as indexes, converting `RangeIndex` into a `MultiIndex` object. In this example, we use the expiration date, strike price, and option type as the three indexes:

```
df_3 = chains.set_index(["expiration", "strike", "option_type"])
```

The result is a hierarchical DataFrame with a three-dimensional MultiIndex:

expiration	strike	option_type	contract_symbol	open_interest	...	last_trade_timestamp	dte
2024-05-28	**444.0**	**call**	SPY240528C00444000	1	...	2024-05-24 12:00:01	0
		put	SPY240528P00444000	498	...	2024-05-24 15:59:58	0
	445.0	**call**	SPY240528C00445000	3	...	2024-05-28 14:21:58	0
		put	SPY240528P00445000	201	...	2024-05-23 15:44:44	0
	446.0	**call**	SPY240528C00446000	0	...	NaT	0
...	**...**	**...**	...	...	...	...	...
2026-12-18	**785.0**	**put**	SPY261218P00785000	0	...	2024-04-03 09:36:19	934
	790.0	**call**	SPY261218C00790000	0	...	2024-05-28 13:07:31	934
		put	SPY261218P00790000	0	...	NaT	934
	795.0	**call**	SPY261218C00795000	4	...	2024-05-23 11:42:10	934
		put	SPY261218P00795000	0	...	NaT	934

Figure 2.5: A DataFrame with a three-dimensional MultiIndex

You can inspect the index using dot notation:

```
df_3.index
```

As you can see, the `MultiIndex` object is a list of tuples. Each tuple contains the elements of the `MultiIndex` object. We also have a property called names, which includes a list of the `MultiIndex` level names:

```
MultiIndex([('2023-07-12', 372.0, 'call'),
            ('2023-07-12', 372.0,  'put'),
            ('2023-07-12', 373.0, 'call'),
            ('2023-07-12', 373.0,  'put'),
            ('2023-07-12', 374.0, 'call'),
            ('2023-07-12', 374.0,  'put'),
            ('2023-07-12', 375.0, 'call'),
            ('2023-07-12', 375.0,  'put'),
            ('2023-07-12', 376.0, 'call'),
            ('2023-07-12', 376.0,  'put'),
            ...
            ('2025-12-19', 645.0, 'call'),
            ('2025-12-19', 645.0,  'put'),
            ('2025-12-19', 650.0, 'call'),
            ('2025-12-19', 650.0,  'put'),
            ('2025-12-19', 655.0, 'call'),
            ('2025-12-19', 655.0,  'put'),
            ('2025-12-19', 660.0, 'call'),
            ('2025-12-19', 660.0,  'put'),
            ('2025-12-19', 665.0, 'call'),
            ('2025-12-19', 665.0,  'put')],
           names=['expiration', 'strike', 'optionType'], length=7306)
```

Figure 2.6: Inspecting the MultiIndex object

See also

To learn more about the Series and DataFrame objects, take a look at the following resources:

- Documentation on pandas Series: `https://pandas.pydata.org/docs/reference/api/pandas.Series.html`
- Documentation on pandas DataFrames: `https://pandas.pydata.org/docs/reference/api/pandas.DataFrame.html`

Manipulating and transforming DataFrames

Before moving on to more advanced recipes, it's important to understand the fundamentals of working with data. DataFrames are the most common pandas data structures you'll work with. Despite the existence of hundreds of methods for DataFrame manipulation, only a subset of these are regularly used.

In this recipe, we will show you how to manipulate a DataFrame using the following common methods:

- Creating new columns using aggregates, Booleans, and strings
- Concatenating two DataFrames together
- Pivoting a DataFrame such as Excel
- Grouping data on a key or index and applying an aggregate
- Joining options data together to create straddle prices

Getting ready

We'll start by importing the necessary libraries and downloading market price data:

1. Start by importing NumPy, pandas, and the OpenBB Platform:

```
import numpy as np
import pandas as pd
from openbb import obb
obb.user.preferences.output_type = "dataframe"
```

2. Load some stock price data to work with:

```
asset = obb.equity.price.historical(
    "AAPL",
    provider="yfinance"
)
benchmark = obb.equity.price.historical(
    "SPY",
    provider="yfinance"
)
```

How to do it...

Creating new columns is a common operation when dealing with DataFrames. Let's learn how to do this.

Creating new columns using aggregates, Booleans, and strings

Here's how to create new columns using aggregates, Booleans, strings:

1. Start by renaming the columns so that they follow Python conventions:

```
columns = [
    "open",
```

```
    "high",
    "low",
    "close",
    "volume",
    "dividend"
]
asset.columns = columns
benchmark.columns = columns
```

2. Add a new column with values from an aggregate:

```
asset["price_diff"] = asset.close.diff()
benchmark["price_diff"] = benchmark.close.diff()
```

> **Tip**
>
> When adding a new column to a DataFrame, the data you provide is automatically aligned by the DataFrame's index. This means that if you add a Series as a new column, pandas matches each value to its corresponding row in the DataFrame using the Series's index. If any index values in the DataFrame don't exist in the new Series, pandas will fill them with nan values, signifying missing data.

3. Add a new column with a Boolean:

```
asset["gain"] = asset.price_diff > 0
benchmark["gain"] = benchmark.price_diff > 0
```

4. Add a new column with a string value:

```
asset["symbol"] = "AAPL"
benchmark["symbol"] = "SPY"
```

5. Three new columns of data are to each DataFrame – `returns`, `gain`, and `symbol`:

	open	high	low	close	volume	dividend	price_diff	gain	symbol	returns
date										
2024-11-25	231.460007	233.250000	229.740005	232.869995	90152800	0.0	NaN	False	AAPL	NaN
2024-11-26	233.330002	235.570007	233.330002	235.059998	45986200	0.0	2.190002	True	AAPL	0.009404
2024-11-27	234.470001	235.690002	233.809998	234.929993	33498400	0.0	-0.130005	False	AAPL	-0.000553
2024-11-29	234.809998	237.809998	233.970001	237.330002	28481400	0.0	2.400009	True	AAPL	0.010216
2024-12-02	237.270004	240.789993	237.160004	239.589996	48137100	0.0	2.259995	True	AAPL	0.009523
...	...	...	...	...	...	...	...	...	...	...
2025-11-19	265.529999	272.209991	265.500000	268.559998	40424500	0.0	1.119995	True	AAPL	0.004188
2025-11-20	270.829987	275.429993	265.920013	266.250000	45823600	0.0	-2.309998	False	AAPL	-0.008601
2025-11-21	265.950012	273.329987	265.670013	271.489990	59030800	0.0	5.239990	True	AAPL	0.019681
2025-11-24	270.899994	277.000000	270.899994	275.920013	65585800	0.0	4.430023	True	AAPL	0.016317
2025-11-25	275.269989	280.380005	275.269989	276.970001	40124777	0.0	1.049988	True	AAPL	0.003805

Figure 2.7: Result of adding new columns to the asset DataFrame

6. Set a single value based on the aggregate of values:

```
asset_2 = asset.copy()
asset_2.at[
    asset_2.index[10],
    "volume"
] = asset_2.volume[asset_2.index[5:10]].mean().astype(int)
```

7. You can inspect the value by using the `iat` method on the `asset_2` DataFrame:

```
asset_2.iat[10, 4]
```

The result is a scalar value corresponding to the mean of the `'volume'` column, assigned to the cell located at row 10 and column 4.

Concatenating two DataFrames together

In the simplest case, concatenating two DataFrames together either stacks one on top of the other (row-wise concatenation) or lines them up next to each other (column-wise concatenation). You can control this through the axis argument.

Call the pandas `concat` method, leaving axis as the default (0 for row-wise concatenation):

```
pd.concat([asset, asset_2]).drop_duplicates()
```

Here are the concatenated DataFrames:

	open	high	low	close	volume	dividend	price_diff	gain	symbol	returns
date										
2024-11-25	231.460007	233.250000	229.740005	232.869995	90152800	0.0	NaN	False	AAPL	NaN
2024-11-26	233.330002	235.570007	233.330002	235.059998	45986200	0.0	2.190002	True	AAPL	0.009404
2024-11-27	234.470001	235.690002	233.809998	234.929993	33498400	0.0	-0.130005	False	AAPL	-0.000553
2024-11-29	234.809998	237.809998	233.970001	237.330002	28481400	0.0	2.400009	True	AAPL	0.010216
2024-12-02	237.270004	240.789993	237.160004	239.589996	48137100	0.0	2.259995	True	AAPL	0.009523
...	...	...	...	...	...	...	...	...	...	...
2025-11-20	270.829987	275.429993	265.920013	266.250000	45823600	0.0	-2.309998	False	AAPL	-0.008601
2025-11-21	265.950012	273.329987	265.670013	271.489990	59030800	0.0	5.239990	True	AAPL	0.019681
2025-11-24	270.899994	277.000000	270.899994	275.920013	65585800	0.0	4.430023	True	AAPL	0.016317
2025-11-25	275.269989	280.380005	275.269989	276.970001	40124777	0.0	1.049988	True	AAPL	0.003805
2024-12-10	246.889999	248.210007	245.339996	247.770004	40959720	0.0	1.020004	True	AAPL	0.004134

Figure 2.8: Two DataFrames concatenated row-wise (stacked on top of each other)

The method takes a list of DataFrames to concatenate. In this example, we concatenated two identical DataFrames before then dropped duplicate values using the `drop_duplicates` method.

Pivoting a DataFrame such as Excel

Pivot tables are ubiquitous in Excel. They're used to aggregate data along a defined set of columns. They work the same way in pandas. In this example, we'll aggregate the returns using three methods – `sum`, `mean`, and `std`:

Call the `pivot_table` method:

```
asset["returns"] = asset["close"].pct_change()
pd.pivot_table(
    data=asset,
    values="returns",
    columns="gain",
    aggfunc=["sum", "mean", "std"]
)
```

The result is a pivoted DataFrame with `MultiIndex` column labels:

	sum		mean		std	
gain	**False**	**True**	**False**	**True**	**False**	**True**
returns	-745.20977	809.867065	-2.025027	2.076582	1.832028	1.773361

Figure 2.9: A pivoted DataFrame

Grouping data on a key or index and applying an aggregate

Grouping lets you aggregate different sections of your data. This is useful when you're working with market data and single DataFrame contains prices for multiple assets:

Concatenate asset data and benchmark data into the same DataFrame:

```
concated = pd.concat([asset, benchmark])
```

Group the resulting DataFrame by the symbol column, return the `close` column, and apply the `ohlc` aggregate:

```
concated.groupby("symbol").close.ohlc()
```

The result is a DataFrame with open, high, low, and close properties for the asset symbol (**AAPL**) and the benchmark symbol (**SPY**):

	open	high	low	close
symbol				
AAPL	112.572701	196.185074	104.943108	177.229996
SPY	323.008636	466.563324	309.646606	438.149994

Figure 2.10: Grouped DataFrame

> **Tip**
>
> The `ohlc` aggregate is a pandas Resampler. open is the first value of the group, `high` is the maximum value of the group, `low` is the minimum value of the group, and `close` is the last value of the group.

Joining options data together to create straddle prices

DataFrame joins are similar to SQL joins. It combines two DataFrames based on a matching key. A great use case for joins is combining two DataFrames containing options chains to price straddles. A straddle is a complex options position made up of a long call and long put with the same strike and expiration:

1. Download option chains data using the OpenBB Platform:

```
chains = obb.derivatives.options.chains("AAPL", provider="cboe")
```

2. Filter out the call options and the put options for a specific expiration:

```
expirations = chains.expiration.unique()
calls = chains[
    (chains.option_type == "call")
    & (chains.expiration == expirations[10])
]

puts = chains[
    (chains.option_type == "put")
    & (chains.expiration == expirations[10])
]
```

> **Tip**
>
> The pandas `unique` method returns an array of unique values from the Series. In this case, it returns a unique set of expiration dates. From there, we select the expiration at index 5, which is sufficiently into the future and is where there will be trading activity.

3. Set the index to the strike prices:

```
calls_strike = calls.set_index("strike")
puts_strike = puts.set_index("strike")
```

4. Then, join the call DataFrame on the put DataFrame using a `left join`:

```
joined = calls_strike.join(
    puts_strike,
    how="left",
```

```
        lsuffix="_call",
        rsuffix="_put"
)
```

Since both DataFrames have a column named `last_trade_price`, we add the `lsuffix` and `rsuffix` arguments to distinguish the `last_trade_price` columns from each other.

5. Use only the price columns from the joined DataFrame:

```
prices = joined[["last_trade_price_call", "last_trade_price_put"]]
```

6. Sum up the call and put prices by using the axis argument in the `sum` method:

```
prices["straddle_price"] = prices.sum(axis=1)
```

The result is a DataFrame with the strike prices as the index, and the call, put, and straddle prices as columns for each strike:

	last_trade_price_call	last_trade_price_put	straddle_price
strike			
210.0	64.44	0.17	64.61
215.0	59.56	0.17	59.73
220.0	52.74	0.22	52.96
225.0	55.07	0.38	55.45
230.0	42.65	0.42	43.07
235.0	41.40	0.54	41.94
240.0	39.00	0.59	39.59
245.0	36.08	0.84	36.92
250.0	31.00	1.10	32.10
255.0	26.62	1.57	28.19
260.0	22.80	2.28	25.08
265.0	16.90	3.12	20.02

Figure 2.11: DataFrame containing call, put, and straddle prices

How it works...

In this recipe, we covered four ways of manipulating DataFrames.

DataFrames supports column addition via the `df["new_col"] = value` assignment syntax. For aggregates, methods such as `groupby` and `agg` compute summary metrics, which can be joined to the original DataFrame. By using Boolean indexing, such as `df["new_col"] = df["existing_col"] > threshold`, we can create new columns based on conditions.

The `pivot_table` method reshapes data, providing a multidimensional analysis tool similar to pivot tables in Excel. By specifying the index and columns parameters, we can set row and column keys, respectively. The values parameter denotes which DataFrame columns to aggregate, and `aggfunc` defines the aggregation function, such as sum or mean. This method then constructs a new DataFrame, where rows and columns are determined by unique combinations of key values.

The `groupby` method enables data segmentation based on column values. By passing one or multiple column names to `groupby`, we create a `GroupBy` object, segmenting the data. This object allows aggregation, transformation, or filtering of these groups using methods such as sum, mean, or apply. The result is a DataFrame with an index based on the grouping columns and aggregated or transformed values.

Finally, we covered the `join` method, which combines two DataFrames based on their indexes. Specifying the on parameter can alter the default behavior, using a particular column as the join key. The `how` parameter determines the type of join: `left`, `right`, `inner`, or `outer`. This method appends columns from the joining DataFrame to the calling DataFrame based on matching index or column values.

There's more...

The pandas `groupby` method is one of the most used transforms since it lets you aggregate and perform analysis on different chunks of data in the same DataFrame. Here are a few more ways to use it.

Grouping by multiple columns

`groupby` can be used with multiple columns, providing a detailed view of your data. This is useful when you want to group data based on a combination of values from different columns. For example, let's say you want to aggregate the open interest for each contract:

```
(
    chains
    .groupby(
```

```
        ["option_type", "strike", "expiration"]
    )
    .open_interest
    .sum()
)
```

The result is a Series with a `MultiIndex` object composed of `option_type`, `strike`, and `expiration`. The values are the sum of the `open_interest` aggregate for each group:

```
option_type  strike  expiration
call         5.0     2024-03-15      2.0
                     2024-06-21    341.0
                     2024-09-20    128.0
             10.0    2024-03-15      0.0
                     2024-06-21     12.0
                                    ...
put          330.0   2024-08-16      0.0
             340.0   2024-08-16      0.0
             350.0   2024-08-16      0.0
             360.0   2024-08-16      0.0
             370.0   2024-08-16      0.0
Name: open_interest, Length: 2086, dtype: float64
```

Figure 2.12: Option chains grouped by option_type, strike, and expiration with the open_interest aggregate

Applying different methods to different columns

You can use agg to apply specific methods to specific columns after grouping. For example, let's say you want to find the maximum `last_trade_price` and the total `open_interest` for each `option_type`:

```
(
    chains
    .groupby(
        ["option_type", "strike", "expiration"]
    )
    .agg({
        "last_trade_price": "max",
        "open_interest": "sum"
    })
)
```

This provides a DataFrame with `option_type`, strike, and expiration as the indexes and two columns: onewith the maximum `last_trade_price` and the other with the sum of `open_interest` for each option type. It offers a snapshot of the highest option price and total open interest for the call and put options:

option_type	strike	expiration	last_trade_price	open_interest
call	5.0	2024-06-21	185.05	31
		2024-07-19	164.00	0
		2024-08-16	182.23	1
		2024-09-20	179.30	2
		2024-10-18	172.06	0
...	...	...	...	...
put	370.0	2024-08-16	0.00	0
		2024-10-18	0.00	0
		2024-11-15	187.00	0
		2025-03-21	0.00	0
	380.0	2025-03-21	189.89	0

Figure 2.13: Maximum price and aggregate open interest for each combination of option type, strike, and expiration

Applying custom functions

You can apply your own functions using the `apply` method. For example, let's say you want to calculate the average spread (difference between ask and bid) for each group of `option_type`:

```
(
    chains
    .groupby(["option_type"])
    .apply(lambda x: (x["ask"] - x["bid"]).mean(),
        include_groups=False)
)
```

The result is a Series with `option_type` as the index, where the values represent the average spread for each option type:

```
option_type
call     1.274094
put      1.260757
dtype: float64
```

Figure 2.14: Average spread for calls and puts (not very liquid options!)

> **Tip**
>
> A `lambda` function can't be defined using the `def` keyword. It can accept any number of input arguments and returns any number of outputs. Lambda functions must exist on a single line and are useful for logic that can be written concisely.

Grouping and transforming data

The `transform` method can be used after `groupby` to return a Series with the same shape as the original, where each group is replaced with the value from a method applied to that group. For example, let's say you want to compute the z-score of `last_trade_price` within each expiration date:

```
(
    chains
    .groupby("expiration")
    .last_trade_price
    .transform(lambda x: (x - x.mean()) / x.std())
)
```

This results in a Series of the same length as `chains`, where `last_trade_price` is replaced with its z-score value within each expiration date. The z-score can be useful for comparisons as it puts all the prices on the same scale relative to their specific expiration date group:

```
0        3.552798
1       -0.646571
2        3.226523
3       -0.646871
4        3.142709
           ...
1855     1.456281
1856    -0.917640
1857     1.613997
1858    -0.942438
1859    -1.048326
Name: lastPrice, Length: 1860, dtype: float64
```

Figure 2.15: Creating a standardized price within each expiration

See also

For more on option straddles, Investopedia offers a high-quality description. To learn more about the methods that were used in this recipe, take a look at the following documentation:

- Understanding option straddles: `https://www.investopedia.com/terms/s/straddle.asp`
- Documentation on concatenating pandas data structures: `https://pandas.pydata.org/docs/reference/api/pandas.concat.html`
- Documentation on pivoting pandas DataFrames: `https://pandas.pydata.org/docs/reference/api/pandas.DataFrame.pivot.html`
- Documentation on grouping pandas DataFrames: `https://pandas.pydata.org/docs/reference/api/pandas.DataFrame.groupby.html`
- Documentation on joining pandas DataFrames: `https://pandas.pydata.org/docs/reference/api/pandas.DataFrame.join.html`

Examining and selecting data from DataFrames

Once you've loaded, manipulated, and transformed data in DataFrames, the next step is retrieving the data from DataFrames. This is where indexing and selecting data come into play. This functionality allows you to access data using methods such as `iloc` and `loc` and techniques such as Boolean indexing or query functions. These methods can target data based on its position, labels, or condition based on whether you're after a specific row, column, or combination. Inspection enables potential issues to be identified, such as missing values, outliers, or inconsistencies, that can affect analysis and modeling. Additionally, an initial inspection provides insights into the nature of data, helping determine appropriate preprocessing steps and analysis methods.

How to do it...

Let's start by downloading stock price data:

1. Start by importing pandas and the OpenBB Platform:

```
import pandas as pd
from openbb import obb
obb.user.preferences.output_type = "dataframe"
```

2. Then, we load some data:

```
df = obb.equity.price.historical(
    "AAPL",
    start_date="2021-01-01",
    provider="yfinance"
)
```

3. Display the first 5 records:

```
df.head(5)
```

4. Display the last 5 records:

```
df.tail(5)
```

5. Return the DataFrame as a NumPy array:

```
df.values
```

6. Get descriptive statistics:

```
df.describe()
```

7. Rename the columns so that they follow Python conventions:

```
df.columns = [
    "open", "high", "low", "close",
    "volume", "dividends", "splits",
]
```

8. Select one column of data:

```
df["close"]
```

> Note
>
> **Important**
>
> When selecting one column from a DataFrame, the return type is a Series. If you try to apply a DataFrame method on Series, this results in an exception. To select one column while returning a DataFrame instead of a Series, slice the DataFrame using a list by using `df[["close"]]`.

9. Select rows by index:

```
df[0:3]
```

> Note
>
> **Important**
>
> When slicing Python objects using indexes, the result is not inclusive of the last index. For example, when slicing using indexes 0:3, the values at index locations 0, 1, and 2 are returned, but not the value at index location 3.

10. `pandas` is smart enough to turn strings into `DatetimeIndex` values and use them to return a range of data between two dates:

```
df.index = pd.to_datetime(df.index)
df["2021-01-02":"2021-01-11"]
```

Note

Important

When slicing Python objects using labels, the result is inclusive of the last label. For example, when slicing using labels `"2021-01-02":"2021-01-11"`, the value at label `location` `"2021-01-11"` is included in the return value.

Selection by label using loc

The `loc` method is a method that's used for data selection based on label-based indexing. It allows data to be selected by row, column, or both, using labels of rows or list-like objects. This method is useful when the index of a DataFrame is a label other than a numerical series:

1. Selecting a single row transposes the Series and puts the DataFrame columns as row labels:

```
df.loc[df.index[0]]
```

2. Selecting a single row and single column returns a scalar:

```
df.loc[df.index[0], "close"]
```

3. Selecting a range of rows and a list of columns returns a subsection of the data:

```
df.loc[df.index[0:6], ["high", "low"]]
```

4. Selecting a range of labels and a list of columns returns a subsection of the data:

```
df.loc["2021-01-02":"2021-01-11", ["high", "low"]]
```

Selection by position using iloc

The pandas `iloc` method is a data selection method that's used for indexing based on integer locations. `iloc` works independently of the DataFrame's index labels:

1. Selecting a single row by index location transposes the Series and puts the DataFrame columns as row labels:

```
df.iloc[3]
```

2. Selecting a range of rows by index and a range of columns by index returns a subset of the data:

```
df.iloc[3:5, 0:2]
```

3. Selecting a combination of specific rows and columns by index works too:

```
df.iloc[[1, 2, 4], [0, 2]]
```

Selection by Boolean indexing

Boolean indexing involves generating a Boolean Series that corresponds to the rows in the DataFrame, where True indicates that the row meets the condition and False denotes it does not. By passing thisBoolean Series to the DataFrame, it returns only the rows where the condition is True, thereby allowing for conditional selection and manipulation of data:

1. Inspect where a condition is True for each row:

```
df.close > df.close.mean()
```

2. Using single-column values to select data:

```
df[df.close > df.close.mean()]
```

3. Use the result to return all the rows and the data at column index location 0:

```
df[df.close > df.close.mean()].iloc[:, 0]
```

4. Use label-based indexing with Boolean indexing to create query-like slicing:

```
df.loc[
    (df.close > df.close.mean())
&(df.close.mean()> 100)
&(df.volume> df.volume.mean())
]
```

How it works...

The `loc` method is for label-based data selection within a DataFrame or Series. We can reference rows and columns using their labels, defining both the row index and column name in `df.loc[row, column]` format. It supports slicing, as we saw previously, enabling multiple rows and columns to be selected based on label ranges.

The `iloc` method is for integer-location-based indexing. We use the index positions referencing rows and columns in `df.iloc[row, column]` format. It also supports slicing, allowing multiple rows and columns to be selected based on integer ranges. Unlike `loc`, `iloc` disregards index or column labels and strictly operates on integer positions.

Boolean indexing allows for data filtering based on condition evaluations. Within a DataFrame or Series, a condition that's applied to a column or the entire structure returns a Boolean array, where True values indicate rows meeting the condition. By placing this Boolean array within the DataFrame's square brackets, for example, `df[boolean_array]`, only the rows with `True` values are extracted. Multiple conditions can be combined using the `&` (and), | (or), and ~ (not) operators. Additionally, the `query` method can be used as an alternative to achieve the same result in a more readable syntax. Boolean indexing can return results from full DataFrames considerably faster than looping or enumerating through DataFrame rows.

There's more...

Indexing is one of the most important aspects of working with pandas. Let's look at some advanced examples of how to slice data.

Partial string indexing

You can select data using a DatetimeIndex object based on a partial string:

```
df["2023"]
```

The preceding code will return a DataFrame containing all records from 2023. The resulting DataFrame maintains the same columns as the original DataFrame but only includes rows where the index falls within 2023.

You can also include the month:

```
df["2023-07"]
```

The preceding code will return a DataFrame with all records from July 2023.

Using at for fast access to a scalar

If we want to quickly access the value of a specific cell, we can use the `at` accessor. For example, to get the close price on July 12, 2023, we can run the following command:

```
df.at["2023-07-12", "close"]
```

The result is the closing price on July 12, 2023. The `at` accessor provides a fast way to access a single value at a specific row-column pair.

Using nsmallest and nlargest

pandas provides handy methods to get rows with the smallest or largest values in a column. For instance, to get the five rows with the highest volume, we can use the following command:

```
df.nlargest(5, "volume")
```

The result is a DataFrame with the five rows with the highest volume values.

Using the query method to query DataFrames

The `query` method allows you to query a DataFrame in a more readable way. For instance, to get all rows where the close price is higher than the open price, you can use the following command:

```
df.query("close > open")
```

The resulting DataFrame will contain all rows where the close price was higher than the open price.

See also

Indexing can be a complex topic that takes practice to master. This recipe covers many use cases that are common in algorithmic trading. For more details, take a look at the following documentation on indexing and slicing pandas DataFrames: `https://pandas.pydata.org/docs/user_guide/indexing.html`.

Calculating asset returns using pandas

Returns are integral to understanding the performance of a portfolio. There are two types: simple returns and compound (or log) returns.

Simple returns, which are calculated as the difference in price from one period to the next divided by the price at the beginning of the period, are beneficial in certain circumstances. They aggregate across assets, meaning the simple return of a portfolio is the aggregate of the returns of the individual assets, weighted according to their proportions. This trait makes simple returns practical for comparing assets and evaluating portfolio performance over short-term intervals.

Simple returns are defined as follows:

$$R_t = \frac{P_t - P_{t-1}}{P_{t-1}} = \frac{P_t}{P_{t-1}} - 1$$

On the other hand, **compound returns**, which are calculated using the natural logarithm of the price-relative change, are additive over time. This quality makes them suitable for multi-period analyses as the compound return for a given period is the sum of the log returns within that period.

Compound returns are defined as follows:

$$r_t = \log\left(\frac{P_t}{P_{t-1}}\right) = \log(P_t) - \log(P_{t-1})$$

Compound returns are generally preferred in practice since they have mathematical properties that make them easier to use in analytics. They're less influenced by extreme values, which might skew the analysis. A major price change in a single period will have a large effect on simple returns but a moderated effect on log returns.

The additive nature of compound returns across time is mathematically convenient. If you need to calculate the total return over a sequence of periods, you simply sum up the log returns, whereas for simple returns, you would need to calculate the product of (1 plus each period's return) and then subtract one.

Given a daily compounded return, r_t, it is straightforward to solve back for the corresponding simple net return, R_t:

$$R_t = e^{r_t} - 1$$

The difference between simple and log returns becomes evident when we look into the statistical properties. If we assume that asset prices follow a log-normal distribution, which may not always be the case, the log returns would be normally distributed. This assumption is beneficial because the normal distribution is a cornerstone in statistical modelling. For daily or intraday data, the difference between simple and log returns is usually minimal, with log returns generally being slightly smaller.

How to do it...

Let's start building returns using stock data from the OpenBB Platform:

1. Import pandas, NumPy, and the OpenBB Platform:

```
import numpy as np
import pandas as pd
from openbb import obb
obb.user.preferences.output_type = "dataframe"
```

2. Download stock price data for AAPL:

```
data = obb.equity.price.historical(
    "AAPL",
    provider="yfinance"
)
```

3. Select the close data:

```
df = data.loc[:, ["close"]]
```

4. Add a new column with simple returns and compound returns using the adjusted closing price:

```
df["simple"] = df["close"].pct_change()
df["compound"] = np.log(df["close"] / df["close"].shift())
```

The resulting DataFrame now has two additional columns:

date	close	simple	compound
2023-05-30	177.300003	NaN	NaN
2023-05-31	177.250000	-0.000282	-0.000282
2023-06-01	180.089996	0.016023	0.015896
2023-06-02	180.949997	0.004775	0.004764
2023-06-05	179.580002	-0.007571	-0.007600
...	...	...	...
2024-05-21	192.350006	0.006857	0.006834
2024-05-22	190.899994	-0.007538	-0.007567
2024-05-23	186.880005	-0.021058	-0.021283
2024-05-24	189.979996	0.016588	0.016452
2024-05-28	189.990005	0.000053	0.000053

Figure 2.16: The resulting DataFrame with daily simple and compound returns

How it works...

First, we imported NumPy for numerical operations, pandas for data manipulation, and the OpenBB Platform for financial data retrieval.

Then, we used the OpenBB Platform's `obb.equity.price.historical` method to fetch the stock price data for AAPL. The data was stored in a DataFrame.

Next, we created a new DataFrame containing only the close column. We did this using the loc function, a label-based data selector.

After, we used the `pct_change` method to calculate simple returns, which represent the percentage change in the adjusted close price from the previous day. The result was stored in a new column called simple.

For compound returns, we calculated the ratio of the current day's adjusted close price to the previous day's price using the shift method. This shifted the DataFrame index by one period. Then, we took the natural logarithm of these ratios with log, reflecting the formula for compound returns. The results were stored in another new column called compound.

There's more...

The `pct_change` method accepts a periods argument that will shift the input data by that number before computing the simple return. This is useful for computing returns that are multiple periods, such as 3 days:

```
df["close"].pct_change(periods=3)
```

The result is a new Series, where each element represents a three-period simple return. Note that the first three elements of the resulting Series will be nan because there aren't enough prior periods for the calculation. (We'll learn how to fill in missing data in the *Addressing missing data issues* recipe in this chapter.)

You can also do the same with compound returns by passing an argument to the shift method:

```
np.log(df["close"] / df["close"].shift(3))
```

The `pct_change` method also accepts a `freq` parameter, which lets you resample the return to an aligned period. For example, instead of passing in 22 to the periods argument (since not all months have 22 trading days), you can pass in ME:

```
df.index = pd.to_datetime(df.index)
df["close"].pct_change(freq="ME").dropna()
```

The result is a DataFrame with monthly returns:

```
date
2020-07-31    0.109736
2020-08-31    0.216569
2020-09-30   -0.102526
2020-11-30    0.096400
2020-12-31    0.114574
2021-03-31   -0.044135
2021-04-30    0.076218
2021-06-30    0.102028
2021-08-31    0.044925
2021-09-30   -0.068037
2021-11-30    0.111313
2021-12-31    0.074228
2022-01-31   -0.015712
2022-02-28   -0.054066
2022-03-31    0.057473
2022-05-31   -0.056352
2022-06-30   -0.081430
2022-08-31   -0.025210
2022-09-30   -0.120977
2022-10-31    0.109551
2022-11-30   -0.033027
2023-01-31    0.153674
2023-02-28    0.023183
2023-03-31    0.118649
2023-05-31    0.046613
2023-06-30    0.094330
Name: Adj Close, dtype: float64
```

Figure 2.17: Series with simple returns resampled to a monthly frequency

See also

For more on the `pct_change` method, see the following documentation: `https://pandas.pydata.org/docs/reference/api/pandas.DataFrame.pct_change.html`.

Measuring the volatility of a return series

Volatility plays an integral role in finance, as a key indicator of risk linked to a particular asset. A higher degree of volatility suggests a greater risk associated with the asset as it indicates more significant price changes and, therefore, a less predictable investment outcome.

Standard deviation is widely used as a measure of asset return volatility. It statistically quantifies the dispersion of asset returns from their mean, thus providing an effective metric for risk. When asset returns exhibit a larger standard deviation, it signifies more pronounced volatility, pointing to a higher risk level. Conversely, a lower standard deviation implies that the asset returns are more stable and less likely to deviate significantly from their average, indicating a lower risk.

The standard deviation's value as a risk measure extends beyond its ability to quantify risk alone. It is a common component in calculating risk-adjusted returns that provides a more nuanced evaluation of investment performance by considering the risk taken to achieve the returns. The Sharpe ratio, for instance, is a popular risk-adjusted return measure that divides the excess return of an investment (over the risk-free rate) by its standard deviation.

How to do it...

We'll use AAPL's historic stock price to compute the volatility. Here's how it's done:

1. Import the necessary libraries:

```
import numpy as np
import pandas as pd
from openbb import obb
obb.user.preferences.output_type = "dataframe"
```

2. Load stock price data from the OpenBB Platform:

```
df = obb.equity.price.historical(
    "AAPL",
    start_date="2020-01-01",
    provider="yfinance"
)
```

3. Grab the series of adjusted close prices:

```
close = df["close"]
```

4. Compute the daily simple return:

```
returns = close.pct_change()
```

5. Calculate the daily standard deviation of returns:

```
std_dev = returns.dropna().std()
```

6. Annualize the standard deviation assuming 252 trading days in a year:

```
annualized_std_dev = std_dev * np.sqrt(252)
```

The result is a float that represents the annualized volatility over the entire period.

How it works...

The multiplication that's done by the square root of 252 in the calculation of standard deviation is based on the concept of scaling in statistics. Scaling is used when transferring a data point from one timescale to another. The number 252 is used because there are typically 252 trading days in a year. In statistical terms, variance, which is the square of standard deviation, is additive over time. This means that if you want to calculate the variance over a certain period, you can add up the variances for each sub-period. However, the standard deviation is not additive, but its square (that is, variance) is. To convert daily standard deviation into annual standard deviation, we must square it to get the variance, multiply this variance by 252 (the typical number of trading days in a year) to annualize, and then take the square root to revert to standard deviation. This process ensures we respect the additive property of variance while transitioning from daily to annual measure. By taking the square root of 252, we're essentially projecting the daily volatility over a yearly timeframe under the assumption of independent daily returns.

There's more...

Depending on the frequency of returns, we can annualize the volatility measure to match. For example, if you're looking over a long period, you may be dealing with monthly or quarterly returns. Alternatively, you may be working with daily data and want to resample to a monthly or quarterly period:

```
close.index = pd.to_datetime(close.index)
(
    close
    .pct_change(freq="ME")
    .dropna()
```

```
    .std()
    * np.sqrt(12)
)
```

You can pass the freq argument to the pct_change method to generate monthly returns. Then, instead of multiplying the standard deviation by the square root of 252, you can multiply it by the square root of 12.

Similarly, for quarters, you can pass the freq argument and multiply the standard deviation by the square root of 4:

```
(
    close
    .pct_change(freq="QE")
    .dropna()
    .std()
    * np.sqrt(4)
)
```

In both cases, the result is a float that represents the annualized volatility.

Looking at historical price changes, rather than just one moment, is important to get a broader picture of how much and how often the price has moved in the past. We'll use the pandas rolling method to plot the annualized volatility through time:

```
(
    close
    .pct_change()
    .rolling(window=22)
    .std()
    * np.sqrt(252)
).plot()
```

This results in the following plot:

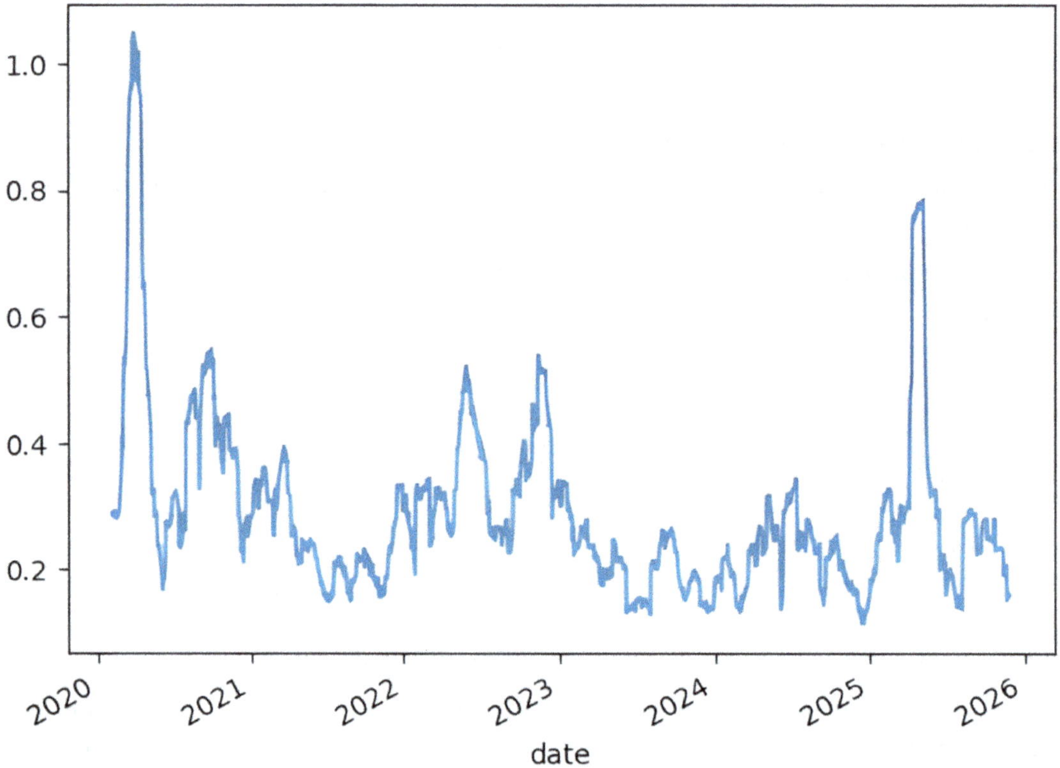

Figure 2.18: Rolling annualized volatility based on a 22-day lookback window

> **Tip**
>
> Rolling a method in pandas involves taking a range of data, applying a function or method that returns a single value, moving that range of data forward one step, applying the function, and repeating this. The result is a method being applied over a window of data that extends through the entire range of data.

See also

Volatility is a critical part of algorithmic trading. To learn more about volatility, take a look at the following article, which describes how investors think about volatility for risk management: `https://www.investopedia.com/terms/v/volatility.asp`.

Generating a cumulative return series

Cumulative returns quantify the total change in the value of an investment over a specific period. To compute the cumulative return of a series of simple single-period returns, you need to add 1 to each return, then multiply these results together, and finally subtract 1 from the product. Recall the formula for the simple return:

$$R_t = \frac{P_t - P_{t-1}}{P_{t-1}} = \frac{P_t}{P_{t-1}} - 1$$

Writing $\left(\frac{P_t}{P_{t-2}}\right) = \left(\frac{P_t}{P_{t-1}}\right)\left(\frac{P_{t-1}}{P_{t-2}}\right)$, the two-period return can be expressed as:

$$R(2) = \left(\frac{P_t}{P_{t-1}}\right)\left(\frac{P_{t-1}}{P_{t-2}}\right) - 1 = (1 + R_t)(1 + R_{t-1}) - 1$$

To compute the cumulative return of a series of continuously compounded single-period returns, you need to sum up all the single-period returns. This is because, in the case of continuously compounded returns, the logarithmic returns are additive. To illustrate, consider the two-period compound return defined as:

$$r_t(2) = \ln\big(1 + R_t(2)\big) = \ln\left(\frac{P_t}{P_{t-1}}\right) = \ln(P_t) - \ln(P_{t-1}) = p_t - p_{t-1}$$

Taking the exponent of both sides and rearranging gives:

$$p_t = P_{t-2}e^{r_t(2)}$$

so that $r_t(2)$is the compounded growth rate of prices between periods $t - 2$ and t. Using $\frac{P_t}{P_{t-2}} = \left(\frac{P_t}{P_{t-1}}\right)\left(\frac{P_{t-1}}{P_{t-2}}\right)$ and the fact that $\ln(xy) = \ln(x) + \ln(y)$ it follows that:

$$r(2) = \ln\left(\left(\frac{P_t}{P_{t-1}}\right)\left(\frac{P_{t-1}}{P_{t-2}}\right)\right) = ln\left(\frac{P_t}{P_{t-1}}\right) + ln\left(\frac{P_{t-1}}{P_{t-}}\right) = r_t + r_{t-1}$$

Getting ready

We assume that you've followed the instructions from the previous recipes and have a Series called `close` with a `DatetimeIndex` object as the index.

How to do it...

We'll use pandas to compute the cumulative sum of simple and compound returns.

The cumulative sum of simple returns

We'll start with the cumulative sum of simple returns:

1. Compute the single period daily simple returns:

```
returns = close.pct_change()
```

2. Replace all nan values with zeros by using NumPy's `isnan` method as a mask:

```
returns[np.isnan(returns)] = 0
```

3. Note that this is equivalent to using pandas:

```
returns.fillna(0.0, inplace=True)
```

4. Now, add 1 to each of the daily simple returns:

```
returns += 1
```

5. Use the `cumprod` method to build the cumulative product of returns and subtract 1:

```
cumulative_returns = returns.cumprod() - 1
```

6. Plot the result:

```
cumulative_returns.plot()
```

The result is the following plot:

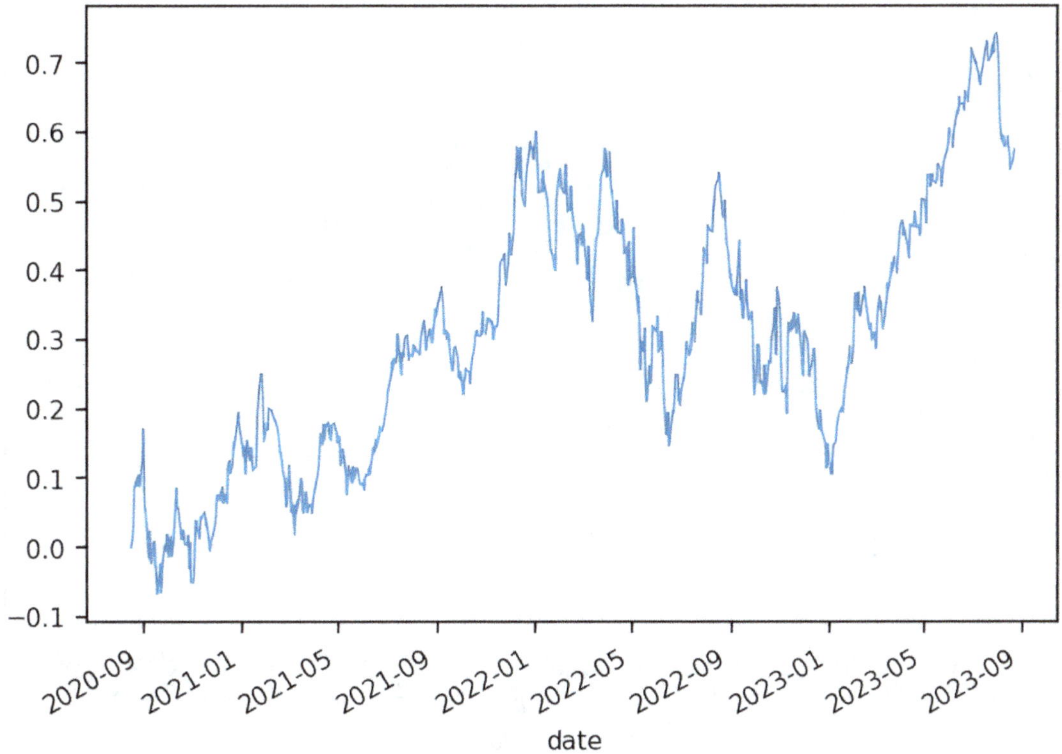

Figure 2.19: Cumulative simple returns of AAPL

The cumulative sum of compound returns

Next, we'll build the cumulative sum of compound returns:

1. Compute the single-period compound returns:

```
log_returns = np.log(close / close.shift())
```

2. Use the pandas `cumsum` method to build the cumulative product of returns:

```
cumulative_log_returns = log_returns.cumsum()
```

3. Plot the result:

```
cumulative_log_returns.plot()
```

The result is the following plot:

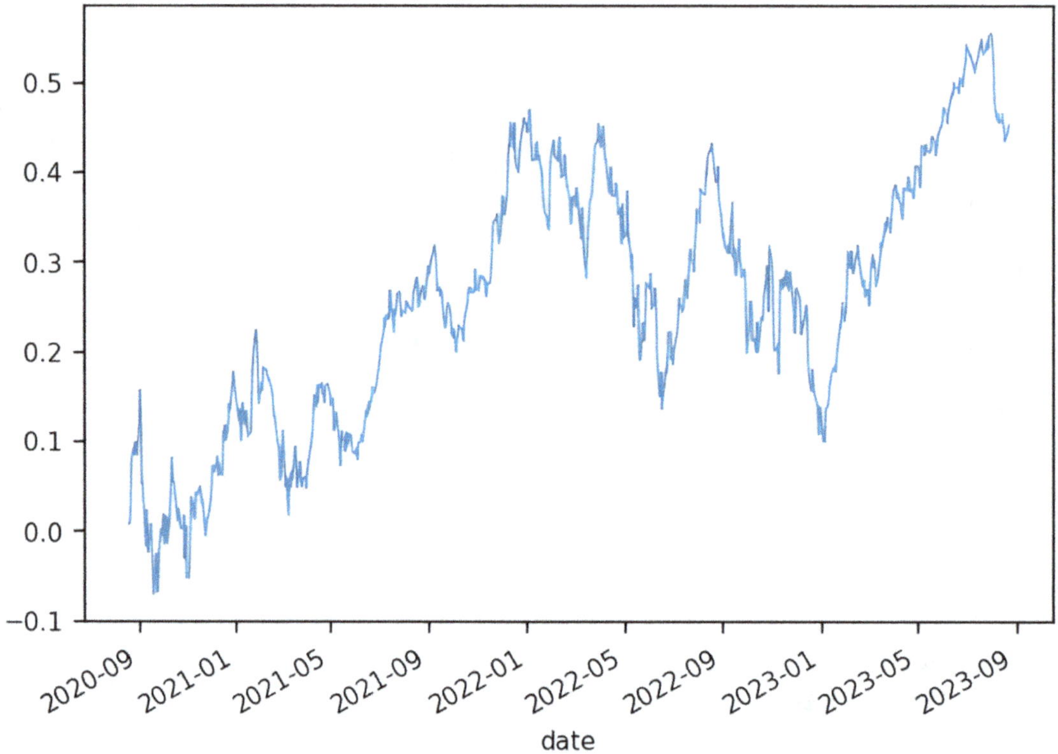

Figure 2.20: Cumulative compound returns of AAPL

Note that simple returns and compound returns will not be equal. Compound returns take into consideration returns earned on prior returns, while simple returns do not.

How it works...

`isnan` checks each value in the returns Series to see if it is a nan value.

`returns[np.isnan(returns)] = 0` takes all the positions in the returns Series where the value is nan and replaces those nan values with `0`. To compute cumulative simple returns, we first need to add 1 to every single period return. This can be accomplished by incrementing every value in the returns Series by 1 with `returns += 1`. Finally, we generate the cumulative product using the `cumprod`. It calculates the cumulative product of the Series, meaning it multiplies the values in the Series together and keeps track of the result. For example, if you have a Series with the numbers 1, 2, 3, and 4, the `cumprod` method will create a new Series with the values *1*, *2 (1 x 2)*, *6 (1 x 2 x 3)*, and *24 (1 x 2 x 3 x 4)*. Finally, we subtract 1 from each value in the cumulative series, compute the compound returns, and call `cumsum` to generate the cumulative sum of the values. Instead of multiplying the values together via `cumprod`, `cumsum` adds them.

See also

While computing returns may seem trivial, it's important to understand the difference between simple returns and compound returns. You can learn more about them, along with the methods we used to compute them, by taking a look at the following documentation:

- A deep dive into the mathematics behind simple and compound returns (and a lot more): `https://bookdown.org/compfinezbook/introcompfinr/AssetReturnCalculations.html#continuously-compounded-returns`
- Documentation on the pandas `cumsum` method: `https://pandas.pydata.org/docs/reference/api/pandas.Series.cumsum.html`
- Documentation on the pandas `cumprod` method: `https://pandas.pydata.org/docs/reference/api/pandas.Series.cumprod.html`

Resampling data for different time frames

Two types of resampling are **upsampling**, where data is converted into a higher frequency (such as daily data to hourly data), and **downsampling**, where data is converted into a lower frequency (such as daily data to monthly data). In financial data analysis, resampling can help in various ways. For instance, if you have daily stock prices, you can resample this data to calculate monthly or yearly average prices, which can be useful for long-term trend analysis. A common use case is when aligning trade and quote data. There are a lot more quotes than trades – often an order of magnitude more – and we may need to align the open, high, low, and closing quote prices to the open, high, low, and closing trade data. Since the quotes and trades will have different timestamps, resampling to a 1-second resolution is a great way to align these disparate data sources.

How to do it...

We'll work on resampling stock price data from one period to another:

1. Import the necessary libraries:

```
import numpy as np
import pandas as pd
from openbb import obb
obb.user.preferences.output_type = "dataframe"
```

2. Use the OpenBB Platform to download intraday data at 1-minute intervals:

```
df = obb.equity.price.historical(
    "AAPL",
    interval="1m",
    provider="yfinance"
)
```

3. Resample the 1-minute resolution adjusted close data to hourly:

```
resampled = df.resample(rule="h")["close"]
```

4. Grab the first value within the resampled time interval:

```
resampled.first()
```

Here's the output:

```
date
2023-07-12 09:00:00    189.910004
2023-07-12 10:00:00    190.619995
2023-07-12 11:00:00    189.716003
2023-07-12 12:00:00    188.897293
2023-07-12 13:00:00    189.429993
                          ...
2023-07-18 11:00:00    193.489899
2023-07-18 12:00:00    193.130005
2023-07-18 13:00:00    192.660004
2023-07-18 14:00:00    192.985001
2023-07-18 15:00:00    193.669907
Freq: H, Name: Adj Close, Length: 151, dtype: float64
```

Figure 2.21: Resampled Series with the first value in the interval

5. Now, grab the last value:

```
resampled.last()
```

Here's the output:

```
date
2023-07-12 09:00:00    190.710007
2023-07-12 10:00:00    189.669907
2023-07-12 11:00:00    188.639893
2023-07-12 12:00:00    189.360992
2023-07-12 13:00:00    189.919998
                          ...
2023-07-18 11:00:00    193.199997
2023-07-18 12:00:00    192.520004
2023-07-18 13:00:00    192.985001
2023-07-18 14:00:00    193.789902
2023-07-18 15:00:00    193.729996
Freq: H, Name: Adj Close, Length: 151, dtype: float64
```

Figure 2.22: Resampled Series with the last value in the interval

6. Compute the mean value within the resampled time interval:

```
resampled.mean()
```

Here's the output:

```
date
2023-07-12 09:00:00    190.771767
2023-07-12 10:00:00    190.389116
2023-07-12 11:00:00    189.314387
2023-07-12 12:00:00    189.224929
2023-07-12 13:00:00    189.812174
                          ...
2023-07-18 11:00:00    193.254420
2023-07-18 12:00:00    192.732713
2023-07-18 13:00:00    192.905636
2023-07-18 14:00:00    193.604533
2023-07-18 15:00:00    193.984174
Freq: H, Name: Adj Close, Length: 151, dtype: float64
```

Figure 2.23: Resampled Series with the mean value in the interval

7. Generate the open, high, low, and closing values for the resampled time interval:

```
resampled.ohlc()
```

Here's the output:

date	open	high	low	close
2023-07-12 09:00:00	189.910004	191.625000	189.570007	190.710007
2023-07-12 10:00:00	190.619995	190.914993	189.662003	189.669907
2023-07-12 11:00:00	189.716003	189.889999	188.489899	188.639893
2023-07-12 12:00:00	188.897293	189.759995	188.580002	189.360992
2023-07-12 13:00:00	189.429993	190.009995	189.379898	189.919998
...	...	...	...	...
2023-07-18 11:00:00	193.489899	193.637802	192.825302	193.199997
2023-07-18 12:00:00	193.130005	193.130005	192.434998	192.520004
2023-07-18 13:00:00	192.660004	193.160004	192.585007	192.985001
2023-07-18 14:00:00	192.985001	193.949905	192.985001	193.789902
2023-07-18 15:00:00	193.669907	194.229996	193.570007	193.729996

Figure 2.24: Resampled Series with the open, high, low, and closing values in the interval

How it works...

The resample method is used for time series data resampling and alters the frequency. By specifying a time frequency string, such as D for daily or M for monthly, we can decide on the new sampling rate. This method creates a `Resampler` object, upon which aggregation or transformation functions such as mean or sum can be applied. The resulting DataFrame or Series reflects the data that's consolidated or redistributed to the desired frequency. There's also a choice in how the boundaries of the bins are defined. The closed parameter can dictate which side of the bin interval is closed, either right or left. Moreover, the label parameter specifies which bin edge label to use for labelling the aggregation result.

The resample method has several useful arguments:

- `rule`: This is the offset string or object representing target conversion.
- `axis`: This specifies the axis to be resampled. By default, it's 0 (index).
- `closed`: This specifies which side of the bin interval is closed. The options are right or left.

- `label`: This specifies which bin edge label to label the bucket with. The options are right or left.
- `convention`: This is used when resampling period data (a time series with PeriodIndex) with the start or end option. The default is end.
- `kind`: This is used when upsampling from low to high frequency. The options are `timestamp` or period. By default, `timestamp` is used.
- `loffset`: This adjusts the resampled time labels.
- `base`: This is used for adjusting the start of the bins to a different timestamp.
- `on`: This is used for a DataFrame, to resample based on the time of a particular column rather than the DataFrame index.
- `level`: This is used for a `MultiIndex` DataFrame, to resample based on the time of a particular level of the `MultiIndex` object.
- `origin`: This defines the origin of the adjusted timestamps.
- `offset`: This adjusts the start of the bins based on this time delta.

There's more...

The resample and `asfreq` methods in pandas are both used to change the frequency of time series data, but they serve slightly different purposes and can be used in different scenarios. The resample method is primarily used for **downsampling**, where it provides different ways to aggregate the data for the new frequency (such as taking the mean, sum, maximum, minimum, and so on). When **upsampling**, resample can also interpolate the missing values by passing an arbitrary function to perform binning over a Series or DataFrame object in bins of arbitrary size.

The `asfreq` method is used when you want to convert a time series into a specified frequency. It does not provide any aggregation or transformation – it simply changes the frequency of the data. If you're **upsampling** (increasing the frequency), `asfreq` will introduce nan values for the newly created data points. If you're **downsampling** (decreasing the frequency), `asfreq` will drop the data points that don't fit into the new frequency.

pandas offers over 40 offsets that we can use with both resample and `asfreq`. They allow for even more flexibility than passing in D or H (for day or minute). You can see a full list by running `pd.offsets.__all__`.

Downsample the minute data to daily and adjust the labels in the index so that they match the frequency.

```
df.asfreq("D").to_period()
```

The result is a DataFrame. Note that the time portion of the index is dropped. Also, note the nan values on the days when there is no market data:

date	Open	High	Low	Close	Adj Close	Volume
2023-08-16	177.130005	177.639999	177.000000	177.494995	177.494995	3608898.0
2023-08-17	177.139999	177.505402	177.070007	177.339996	177.339996	2969302.0
2023-08-18	172.300003	173.089996	171.960007	172.945007	172.945007	4147338.0
2023-08-19	NaN	NaN	NaN	NaN	NaN	NaN
2023-08-20	NaN	NaN	NaN	NaN	NaN	NaN
2023-08-21	175.070007	175.119995	174.660004	174.731995	174.731995	1938994.0
2023-08-22	177.059998	177.085007	176.580002	176.602997	176.602997	1789325.0

Figure 2.25: DataFrame with frequency changed from 1 minute to calendar days

The `asfreq` method incorporates a method argument, directing pandas on how to handle nan values. This argument permits either backfill to populate nan values using the preceding valid observation or pad to populate with the subsequent valid observation. Additionally, the `fill_value` parameter lets us specify a custom value for filling in missing entries during the **upsampling** process.

If we want to avoid including days with no market prices, we can use the business day offset:

```
df.asfreq(pd.offsets.BDay())
```

The result is a DataFrame that only includes valid business days in the index:

	Open	High	Low	Close	Adj Close	Volume
date						
2023-08-16 09:30:00	177.130005	177.639999	177.000000	177.494995	177.494995	3608898
2023-08-17 09:30:00	177.139999	177.505402	177.070007	177.339996	177.339996	2969302
2023-08-18 09:30:00	172.300003	173.089996	171.960007	172.945007	172.945007	4147338
2023-08-21 09:30:00	175.070007	175.119995	174.660004	174.731995	174.731995	1938994
2023-08-22 09:30:00	177.059998	177.085007	176.580002	176.602997	176.602997	1789325

Figure 2.26: DataFrame with frequency changed from 1 minute to business days

Note

Important

resample applies an aggregate to the data within the selected interval (for example, ohlc), whereas asfreq changes the index and does not aggregate the data. This is apparent in *Figure 2.23*, where the time portion of the index is displayed. The values that match the given index (for example, **2023-07-12 09:30:00**) are selected for inclusion in the returned DataFrame. We can see this by selecting data from the first row using `df.loc["2023-07-12 09:30:00"]`. The result is a Series with values that match those in the first row.

See also

See the documentation for more about the differences between `resample` and *asfreq*:

- Documentation on the pandas `resample` method: `https://pandas.pydata.org/docs/reference/api/pandas.DataFrame.resample.html`
- Documentation on the pandas `asfreq` method: `https://pandas.pydata.org/docs/reference/api/pandas.DataFrame.asfreq.html`

Addressing missing data issues

pandas is well-suited to handling missing data in time series data. In the context of financial market data, missing data can occur for various reasons:

- **Market closures**: Most financial markets aren't open 24/7. They operate on specific days and hours, closing for weekends, public holidays, or special events. If a data source tries to retrieve data when the market is closed, it might represent this as a missing value.

- **Data availability**: Not all historical data is available for every market or every security. Some markets may only have data available from a certain date, or some data may be missing due to technological issues, glitches, or errors during data recording and transmission.
- **Delisting of securities**: If a security gets delisted from a market (for example, a company going out of business), no new data is produced for that security. If your timeframe extends beyond the delisting date, missing data will be encountered.
- **Data granularity**: The level of detail in the dataset might also influence the existence of missing data. For example, if you're looking for minute-by-minute data but your source only provides hourly data, you'll have missing data for each minute that isn't the start of a new hour.

pandas has ways of handling missing data. This recipe presents those most common for algorithmic trading.

Getting ready

We'll demonstrate several ways of filling in missing data. We'll start with AAPL's stock price data:

1. Import the necessary libraries:

```
import numpy as np
import pandas as pd
from openbb import obb
obb.user.preferences.output_type = "dataframe"
```

2. Download the stock price data:

```
df = obb.equity.price.historical(
    "AAPL",
    start_date="2020-07-01",
    end_date="2023-07-06",
    provider="yfinance",
)
```

3. `df` only contains the trading days for AAPL, so we'll reindex the DataFrame so that it includes all calendar days between the start and end date of the time series. First, create a DatetimeIndex object with calendar days:

```
calendar_dates = pd.date_range(
    start=df.index.min(),
    end=df.index.max(),
    freq="D"
)
```

4. Then, reindex the DataFrame:

```
calendar_prices = df.reindex(calendar_dates)
```

The resulting DataFrame is populated with nan values for dates where there is no data:

	open	high	low	close	volume	split_ratio	dividend
2020-07-01	91.279999	91.839996	90.977501	91.027496	110737200.0	0.0	0.0
2020-07-02	91.962502	92.617500	90.910004	91.027496	114041600.0	0.0	0.0
2020-07-03	NaN	NaN	NaN	NaN	NaN	NaN	NaN
2020-07-04	NaN	NaN	NaN	NaN	NaN	NaN	NaN
2020-07-05	NaN	NaN	NaN	NaN	NaN	NaN	NaN
...	...	...	...	...	...	...	...
2023-07-02	NaN	NaN	NaN	NaN	NaN	NaN	NaN
2023-07-03	193.779999	193.880005	191.759995	192.460007	31458200.0	0.0	0.0
2023-07-04	NaN	NaN	NaN	NaN	NaN	NaN	NaN
2023-07-05	191.570007	192.979996	190.619995	191.330002	46920300.0	0.0	0.0
2023-07-06	189.839996	192.020004	189.199997	191.809998	45094300.0	0.0	0.0

Figure 2.27: A DataFrame of stock prices with missing data on non-trading days

How to do it...

We'll demonstrate several examples of filling in the missing values:

Use the pandas `fillna` method with the method argument set to `bfill` to replace nan values with the next valid observation:

```
calendar_prices.bfill()
```

The result is a filled DataFrame:

	open	high	low	close	volume	split_ratio	dividend
2020-07-01	91.279999	91.839996	90.977501	91.027496	110737200.0	0.0	0.0
2020-07-02	91.962502	92.617500	90.910004	91.027496	114041600.0	0.0	0.0
2020-07-03	92.500000	93.945000	92.467499	93.462502	118655600.0	0.0	0.0
2020-07-04	92.500000	93.945000	92.467499	93.462502	118655600.0	0.0	0.0
2020-07-05	92.500000	93.945000	92.467499	93.462502	118655600.0	0.0	0.0
...	...	...	...	...	...	...	...
2023-07-02	193.779999	193.880005	191.759995	192.460007	31458200.0	0.0	0.0
2023-07-03	193.779999	193.880005	191.759995	192.460007	31458200.0	0.0	0.0
2023-07-04	191.570007	192.979996	190.619995	191.330002	46920300.0	0.0	0.0
2023-07-05	191.570007	192.979996	190.619995	191.330002	46920300.0	0.0	0.0
2023-07-06	189.839996	192.020004	189.199997	191.809998	45094300.0	0.0	0.0

Figure 2.28: A DataFrame with missing data backfilled to the previous nan

Use `ffill` to propagate the last valid observation forward:

```
calendar_prices.ffill()
```

The result is a filled DataFrame:

	open	high	low	close	volume	split_ratio	dividend
2020-07-01	91.279999	91.839996	90.977501	91.027496	110737200.0	0.0	0.0
2020-07-02	91.962502	92.617500	90.910004	91.027496	114041600.0	0.0	0.0
2020-07-03	91.962502	92.617500	90.910004	91.027496	114041600.0	0.0	0.0
2020-07-04	91.962502	92.617500	90.910004	91.027496	114041600.0	0.0	0.0
2020-07-05	91.962502	92.617500	90.910004	91.027496	114041600.0	0.0	0.0
...	...	...	...	...	...	...	...
2023-07-02	191.630005	194.479996	191.259995	193.970001	85213200.0	0.0	0.0
2023-07-03	193.779999	193.880005	191.759995	192.460007	31458200.0	0.0	0.0
2023-07-04	193.779999	193.880005	191.759995	192.460007	31458200.0	0.0	0.0
2023-07-05	191.570007	192.979996	190.619995	191.330002	46920300.0	0.0	0.0
2023-07-06	189.839996	192.020004	189.199997	191.809998	45094300.0	0.0	0.0

Figure 2.29: A DataFrame with missing data backfilled to the next nan

How it works...

The `fillna` method in pandas has several arguments that provide different ways to handle missing values:

- `value`: This specifies the value to use to fill na/nan values. It could be a scalar, dictionary, or Series.
- `axis`: This determines whether to fill missing values along rows (0 or index) or columns (1 or columns).
- `inplace`: If set to `True`, the operation modifies the data in place. The default is False.
- `limit`: Limits the number of consecutive forward/backward filled values.
- `downcast`: A dictionary of item->dtype that specifies the type of data for each item.

There's more...

Sometimes, simple forward-filling or back-filling techniques may not suffice, especially in more complex scenarios, such as generating implied volatility surfaces for derivatives pricing. Backfilling data can also introduce lookahead bias in some cases. In these cases, we need a more sophisticated method of dealing with missing data. The pandas `interpolate` method uses various interpolation techniques to fill missing values, including linear, polynomial, time, and spatial interpolations. The choice of interpolation method can be adapted based on the characteristics of the data, allowing for more accurate handling of missing values in complex structures such as implied volatility surfaces.

Here's an example of using linear interpolation to fill in the missing values in the DataFrame:

```
calendar_prices.interpolate(method="linear")
```

Here's an example of using cubic spline interpolation to fill in the missing values in the DataFrame:

```
calendar_prices.interpolate(method="cubicspline")
```

In both cases, the result is a DataFrame with filled values.

See also

For more about the `fillna` method and interpolation, take a look at the following documentation:

- Documentation on the pandas `fillna` method: `https://pandas.pydata.org/docs/reference/api/pandas.DataFrame.fillna.html`

- Documentation on the pandas `interpolate` method: `https://pandas.pydata.org/docs/reference/api/pandas.DataFrame.interpolate.html`
- More on interpolation: `https://en.wikipedia.org/wiki/Interpolation`

Applying custom functions to analyze time series data

Custom functions let us apply transformations and computations to data beyond the standard pandas methods. This flexibility becomes important when dealing with unique or complex analytical tasks. The apply function accepts a custom or built-in function as an argument and applies this function across the DataFrame or Series, returning an output containing the results.

> Note
>
> **Important**
>
> The `apply` function is notoriously slow since it operates on every row or column in a loop. Use this with caution when dealing with large DataFrames!

Getting ready

We assume that you've followed the instructions from the previous recipes and have a DataFrame called `df` with a `DatetimeIndex` object as the index.

How to do it...

We'll use the range as our custom function for this recipe:

1. Determine the range (high price minus low price) of the stock prices using an anonymous lambda function:

```
df.apply(lambda x: x["high"] - x["low"], axis=1)
```

2. Apply a user-defined function that does the same thing:

```
def fcn(row):
    return row["high"] - row["low"]
df.apply(fcn, axis=1)
```

The result in both cases is a Series with the high minus low price:

```
date
2020-07-01    0.846799
2020-07-02    1.676423
2020-07-06    1.450613
2020-07-07    1.568424
2020-07-08    1.261619
                 ...
2023-06-29    1.130005
2023-06-30    3.220001
2023-07-03    2.120010
2023-07-05    2.360001
2023-07-06    2.807999
Length: 758, dtype: float64
```

Figure 2.30: Series with the range of AAPL stock

3. Test the validity of the data by flagging where the closing price is less than the low price or greater than the high price:

```
df["valid"] = df.apply(
    lambda x: x["low"] <= x["close"] <= x["high"], axis=1)
df[df.valid == False]
```

The result is an empty DataFrame since no values were invalid:

	Open	High	Low	Close	Adj Close	Volume	Dividends	Stock Splits	valid
date									

Figure 2.31: Empty DataFrame showing now records where the closing price is outside the high and low of the day

How it works...

The pandas apply function can accept an anonymous lambda function or a user-defined function. The code for computing the range of stock prices using a lambda is equivalent to the code using a user-defined function. We pass a 1 to the axis argument to apply the calculation along each row.

You can expand the use of the apply function with its other arguments:

- `func`: The function to apply to each row or column of the DataFrame
- `axis`: Whether to apply the function to each row (0 or index) or column (1 or columns)
- `broadcast`: Whether to broadcast the output of the function back onto the DataFrame
- `raw`: If `True`, the function receives arrays instead of Series objects or DataFrames
- `reduce`: If `True`, try to apply reduction procedures
- `result_type`: Controls the type of output: expand, reduce, broadcast, or None
- `args`: Additional positional arguments to pass to `func`

There's more...

The function that's passed to the `apply` method may accept additional arguments. Let's say we're interested in calculating the price range between two columns but we want to ignore the price ranges that are below a certain threshold. Our user-defined function needs to accept the two columns for which we compute the range and the threshold value.

First, we'll define the function that calculates the price range. This function will take four arguments: a row from the DataFrame, a high column, a low column, and a threshold for the minimum range:

```
def calculate_range(row, high_col, low_col, threshold):
    range = row[high_col] - row[low_col]
    return range if range > threshold else np.nan
```

> Note
>
> **Important**
>
> When the pandas `apply` function is invoked with axis=1, it applies the specified function to each row of the DataFrame. Each row is treated as a pandas Series object, with the index of the Series being the column names of the DataFrame. This Series object, representing the entire row, is passed as an argument to the function you've defined.

This function computes the difference between the high and low prices. If this difference is greater than the threshold, it returns the difference; otherwise, it returns nan.

Next, we can use the apply method to apply this function to the DataFrame. The args parameter of apply allows us to pass extra arguments to the function:

```
threshold = 1.5
df["range"] = df.apply(
    calculate_range,
    args=("high", "low", threshold),
    axis=1
)
df.range
```

The result of this operation is a new column in the DataFrame that contains the computed price range if it's above the threshold, or nan otherwise:

```
date
2020-07-17          NaN
2020-07-20     2.437500
2020-07-21     2.507500
2020-07-22          NaN
2020-07-23     5.067497
                 ...
2023-07-17     2.510010
2023-07-18     1.910004
2023-07-19     5.580002
2023-07-20     3.970001
2023-07-21     3.740005
Name: range, Length: 758, dtype: float64
```

Figure 2.32: Series with nan *values where the difference between the high and low price does not exceed a threshold*

See also

See the following documentation for more on the apply method:

Join our community on Discord

Join our community's Discord space for discussions with the authors and other readers:
`https://discord.gg/G4YmB6DQvf`

3

Accelerate Financial Market Data Analysis with Polars and DuckDB

In this chapter, we will explore the Python tools that form a modern, high-performance data stack that aligns well with the demands of algorithmic trading. Quantitative research often requires scanning millions of rows of price, volume, fundamentals, and alternative data. Traditional CSV- and pandas-based workflows can become slow as datasets grow. These newer tools address those limitations with columnar storage, vectorized execution, and efficient memory usage.

Parquet provides a compact, columnar file format that compresses data efficiently and supports predicate pushdown, so you read only the columns and rows needed for a query. Polars is a fast DataFrame library written in Rust that uses Apache Arrow memory structures. For algorithmic trading, this means you can filter, aggregate, and transform time series at speeds much faster than pandas, while still writing clear, expressive code. Its lazy execution engine optimizes entire query plans, which is valuable when chaining complex factor computations or generating research features across many assets. Finally, DuckDB is an in-process analytical SQL engine often called the *SQLite for analytics*. It can query Parquet files directly without loading them fully into memory. This makes it ideal for joining large datasets, running factor screens, or performing exploratory research using SQL. DuckDB complements Polars by allowing you to blend DataFrame expressions with SQL queries in the same workflow.

In this chapter, you'll learn how to accelerate financial market data analysis using modern, columnar technologies built for speed and scalability. You'll convert raw CSV files into efficient Parquet datasets, then use Polars to manipulate time series with fast, expression-based operations. From there, you'll combine Polars with DuckDB to blend SQL and DataFrame-style analytics in a single workflow. You'll finish by organizing a high-performance data lake with

DuckLake to manage DuckDB catalogs on top of Parquet storage. These tools help you build robust pipelines that scale with the growing data demands of algorithmic trading research.

This chapter includes the following recipes:

- Converting CSV files into Parquet for efficient storage
- Using asynchronous Python to speed up processing
- Manipulating financial market data with Polars
- Integrating Polars with DuckDB for analysis
- Building a high-performance DataLake over Parquet files with DuckLake

Technical requirements

This chapter relies on Parquet files, Polars, DuckDB, **asynchronous** Python libraries, and a progress bar library. We also use a nice utility library called `python-dotenv`, which loads variables stored in local `.env` files into environment variables. Using this method is best practice for keeping APIs secure. You can install everything at the command line with `pip`:

```
pip install polars pyarrow duckdb python-dotenv nest_asyncio aiohttp tqdm
```

Converting CSV files to parquet for efficient storage

Algorithmic trading workflows depend on fast, reliable access to large volumes of historical market data. As datasets grow in size and complexity, inefficient storage formats can slow analysis and hinder research productivity. In this recipe, you'll learn how to convert raw CSV files into the Parquet format with Polars to improve storage efficiency and accelerate data analysis. CSV is simple and universal, but it becomes slow and unwieldy as datasets grow. Parquet provides compressed, columnar storage that is significantly faster to load and query, especially for large financial time series. By the end of this recipe, you'll have a reproducible workflow for transforming CSV data into Parquet so you can build scalable pipelines for quantitative research.

Getting ready

For this recipe, we'll use FMP to download bulk price data and historical financial statements. Fundamental data gives algorithmic traders an edge because most retail traders rely only on prices. Adding financial statement data to your strategies provides information that many others overlook.

The `premium` package gets you bulk data downloads for 58,000+ tickers over 30 years. Readers can get a 30% discount with this link: `https://site.financialmodelingprep.com/developer/docs/pricing?couponCode=quantscience`.

After signing up, copy your FMP API key. In the directory where you'll run the code, create a file named `.env` and add the following line:

```
FMP_API_KEY=YOUR_API_KEY_HERE
```

Replace `YOUR_API_KEY_HERE` with your API key, save, and close the file.

We'll use some helper functions to download price and fundamental data as CSVs. Since CSVs are so common in the industry, you may find yourself having to deal with this exact scenario.

1. Import the libraries we need for the helper functions:

```
import os
from pathlib import Path
from datetime import date
import requests
import pandas as pd
import polars as pl

from dotenv import load_dotenv
load_dotenv()
```

2. Set the FMP API base URL and get the API key from the `.env` file:

```
FMP_BASE_URL = "https://financialmodelingprep.com/api/"
API_KEY = os.environ.get("FMP_API_KEY")
```

3. Build the helper function that downloads and stores price data for a list of symbols:

```
def download_prices(symbols, start_date, end_date):
    data_dir = Path("prices")
    data_dir.mkdir(parents=True, exist_ok=True)
    for symbol in symbols:
        url = f"{FMP_BASE_URL}v3/historical-price-full/{symbol}?"
              f"from={start_date}&to={end_date}&apikey={API_KEY}"
        response = requests.get(url)
        data = response.json()
        today_str = date.today().strftime("%Y_%m_%d")
```

```
        prices_path = data_dir / f"{symbol.lower()}_{today_str}.csv"
        if "historical" in data:
            df = pd.DataFrame(data["historical"])
            df["symbol"] = symbol
            df["date"] = pd.to_datetime(df["date"])
            df.to_csv(prices_path, index=False)
```

4. Build the helper function that downloads and stores fundamental data for a financial statement type:

```
def download_bulk_fundamentals(statement_type, year, period):
    data_dir = Path("fundamentals")
    data_dir.mkdir(parents=True, exist_ok=True)
    url = f"{FMP_BASE_URL}v4/{statement_type}-bulk?"
          f"year={year}.={period}&apikey={API_KEY}"
    response = requests.get(url)
    today_str = date.today().strftime("%Y_%m_%d")
    fundamentals_path = (
        data_dir / f"{statement_type}_{year}_{period}_{today_str}.csv"
    )
    df = pd.read_csv(pd.io.common.StringIO(response.text))
    df.to_csv(fundamentals_path, index=False)
```

5. Run the two functions:

```
download_prices(
    ["AAPL", "MSFT", "PLTR", "NVDA"],
    "2020-01-01",
    "2024-12-31"
)
for year in [2020, 2021, 2022, 2023, 2024]:
    download_bulk_fundamentals("income-statement", year, "quarter")
```

You should have four CSVs in the local `prices/` directory and five CSVs in the local `fundamentals/` directory.

How to do it...

We will get our first exposure to both Polars and Parquet with a simple function that reads the CSV files and converts them to Parquet files:

1. Write a function to read the CSVs and convert them to Parquet files:

```
def replace_csv_with_parquet(csv_dir):
    for csv_path in sorted(csv_dir.glob("*.csv")):
        df = pl.read_csv(csv_path)
        parquet_path = csv_dir / f"{csv_path.stem}.parquet"
        df.write_parquet(parquet_path)
```

2. Define the paths to the price and fundamental data:

```
prices_dir = Path("prices")
fundamentals_dir = Path("fundamentals")
```

3. Run a simple test to gauge how long it takes to process one of the CSV files (replace the date in the file name with the date you run the code):

```
%timeit df_pd = pd.read_csv("prices/
aapl_2025_11_25.csv").close.rolling(22).mean()
```

4. Run the functions:

```
replace_csv_with_parquet(prices_dir)
replace_csv_with_parquet(fundamentals_dir)
```

5. Now run the speed testing using Polars and Parquet. On my Mac Studio, the Polars and Parquet combination is three times as fast:

```
%timeit df_pd = pl.read_parquet(
    "prices/aapl_2025_11_25.parquet"
).select(pl.col("close").rolling_mean(window_size=22))
```

How it works...

The function walks through every CSV file in the directory you pass to it, converts each one into a Parquet file, and then removes the original CSV. It begins by using `csv_dir.glob("*.csv")` to find all CSV files and processes them in sorted order. For each file, Polars reads the CSV into a DataFrame, automatically inferring the schema and loading the data. The function then constructs a new file path in the same directory using the original filename without its extension and appending `.parquet`. By the time the loop completes, every CSV in the directory has been converted to its Parquet equivalent.

There's more...

Polars has the concept of lazy loading, which allows you to build up a query plan without immediately executing it. Instead of reading data into memory right away, Polars records the operations you want to perform and defers execution until absolutely necessary. This enables powerful optimizations such as predicate pushdown, projection pruning, and parallel query execution.

Write a function that scans all CSV files and streams them into a combined Parquet file without first loading to memory:

```
def csv_dir_to_single_parquet(csv_dir, parquet_path):
    lazy_frames = []
    for csv_path in sorted(csv_dir.glob("*.csv")):
        lf = pl.scan_csv(csv_path)
        lf = lf.with_columns(pl.lit(csv_path.stem).alias("source_file"))
        lazy_frames.append(lf)
    combined_lf = pl.concat(lazy_frames, how="vertical")
    combined_lf.sink_parquet(parquet_path)
```

Then you can run the function:

```
parquet_path = Path("prices") / "combined_prices.parquet"
csv_dir_to_single_parquet(prices_dir, parquet_path)
```

See also

Polars and Parquet are part of the toolkit that makes up the modern data analytics stack. Polars follows a different style of programming than you may be used to with Python or even pandas. Here is the documentation: `https://docs.pola.rs`

Using asynchronous python to speed up processing

The process we followed in the last recipe for downloading and storing price data was done in a **synchronous** manner. This means each file is downloaded and processed sequentially. This is fine for dealing with a small number of processing tasks. However, when processing large volumes of data for many thousands of symbols, we prefer **asynchronous** processing. In this case, it means we process multiple files simultaneously. Following this approach significantly accelerates processing. For this recipe, we will build a series of asynchronous functions to download and process up to 50 files at the same time. We include simple rate-limiting functionality to respect the 3,000 API calls per second limit. We also introduce a library called `tqdm`, which displays a graphic progress bar. Instead of downloading data for a few ticker symbols and converting each to Parquet like in the last recipe, we'll download 25 years of historical data for all ticker symbols in FMP's database—more than 87,800 symbols at the time of writing. The result will be a single (large) Parquet file with 25 years of historical price data.

How to do it...

We'll need two helper functions and three main functions to support the asynchronous file processing pipeline.

1. Import the libraries for asynchronous Python and data processing:

```
import os
from pathlib import Path
import requests
import polars as pl
import pyarrow.parquet as pq

import asyncio
import nest_asyncio
import aiohttp
from tqdm.auto import tqdm

from dotenv import load_dotenv
load_dotenv()
```

2. Set global variables and configurations we'll use throughout the notebook:

```
API_KEY = os.environ["FMP_API_KEY"]

# 2700/min = 45/sec
RPS = 45
DELAY = 1 / RPS
CONCURRENCY = 50  # max inflight requests

# shared concurrency limiter
sem = asyncio.Semaphore(CONCURRENCY)

# shared rate limiter
```

```
rate_lock = asyncio.Lock()
next_request_time = 0.0
```

3. Make sure we have a directory for storing the historical data file:

```
data_dir = Path("prices")
data_dir.mkdir(parents=True, exist_ok=True)
```

4. Create a helper function that returns the historical price data as JSON:

```
def _request(url):
    response = requests.get(url)
    response.raise_for_status()
    return response.json()
```

5. Create a helper function that downloads a list of all stock symbols in the FMP database:

```
def get_symbol_list(api_key):
    base = "https://financialmodelingprep.com/stable"
    url = f"{base}/stock-list?apikey={api_key}"
    response = _request(url)
    return [
        d.get("symbol") for d in response if d.get("symbol") is not None
    ]
```

6. Create an asynchronous function that throttles requests to FMP. This is used to make sure we don't exceed the 3,000 requests per minute API limit:

```
async def throttle():
    """Ensure global 50 requests/sec max."""
    global next_request_time
    async with rate_lock:
        now = asyncio.get_event_loop().time()
        if now < next_request_time:
            await asyncio.sleep(next_request_time - now)
            now = next_request_time
        next_request_time = now + DELAY
```

7. Create an asynchronous function that fetches and processes a single data file with simple rate limiting:

```
async def _fetch_one(session, symbol, start_date, end_date, api_key):
    base = "https://financialmodelingprep.com/api"
    url = f"{base}/v3/historical-price-full/{symbol}?"
          f"from={start_date}&to={end_date}&apikey={api_key}"

    async with sem:
        await throttle()
        try:
            async with session.get(url) as resp:
                resp.raise_for_status()
                data = await resp.json()
        except(asyncio.TimeoutError, aiohttp.ClientError) as e:
            print(f"skip {symbol}: {e}")
            return None

    if "historical" not in data or not data["historical"]:
        return None

    return pl.DataFrame(
        data["historical"],
        schema_overrides={  # keep overflow problems away
            "open": pl.Float64,
            "high": pl.Float64,
            "low": pl.Float64,
            "close": pl.Float64,
            "adjClose": pl.Float64,
            "vwap": pl.Float64,
            "change": pl.Float64,
            "changePercent": pl.Float64,
            "changeOverTime": pl.Float64,
            "volume": pl.Float64,
            "unadjustedVolume": pl.Float64,
        },
        strict=False,
    ).with_columns(
        pl.lit(symbol).alias("symbol"),
    )
```

8. Create an asynchronous function that builds a list of the asynchronous tasks to process and tracks status:

```
async def _download_prices_to_parquet(
    symbols, start_date, end_date, api_key, out_path
):
    timeout = aiohttp.ClientTimeout(
        total=None,
        sock_connect=10,
        sock_read=60
    )
    connector = aiohttp.TCPConnector(
        limit=CONCURRENCY,
        limit_per_host=CONCURRENCY,
    )
    writer = None

    async with aiohttp.ClientSession(
        timeout=timeout, connector=connector
    ) as session:
        tasks = [
            _fetch_one(session, symbol, start_date, end_date, api_key)
            for symbol in symbols
        ]

        with tqdm(
            total=len(tasks), desc="Fetching prices", unit="Symbol"
        ) as pbar:
            for coro in asyncio.as_completed(tasks):
                df = await coro
                if df is None or df.height == 0:
                    continue
                table = df.to_arrow()
                if writer is None:
                    writer = pq.ParquetWriter(str(out_path), table.schema)
                writer.write_table(table)
                pbar.update(1)

    if writer is not None:
        writer.close()
```

9. Build the simple wrapper function that calls the asynchronous function:

```
def download_prices(symbols, start_date, end_date, api_key, out_path):
    nest_asyncio.apply()
    return asyncio.run(
        _download_prices_to_parquet(
            symbols, start_date, end_date, api_key, out_path
        )
    )
```

10. Run the code to start the download process:

```
symbols = get_symbol_list(API_KEY)

download_prices(
    symbols=symbols,
    start_date="2000-01-01",
    end_date="2025-12-31",
    api_key=API_KEY,
    out_path=data_dir / "historical-prices.parquet"
)
```

11. Processing still takes about 35 minutes. While the files are being downloaded and processed, you'll see the `tqdm` status bar showing the progress of symbol downloads:

Figure 3.1: The TQDM status bar showing the rate of concurrent downloads

The result is a single Parquet file that is about 12.5 GB.

How it works...

Let's understand how this works. The goal of this pipeline is to overlap network I/O across many symbols while still honoring Financial Modeling Prep's request limits, and to write results to Parquet incrementally so you do not need to hold the full dataset in memory.

The synchronous helper `_request()` is a small convenience wrapper around `requests.get()`. It calls `raise_for_status()` so HTTP errors fail fast, and it returns parsed JSON for any endpoints that are called only once. `get_symbol_list()` uses `_request()` to download the universe of tickers from the `/stable/stock-list` endpoint, then extracts the symbol field into a Python list. That list becomes the workload for the asynchronous portion of the recipe.

The concurrency controls are implemented with two shared primitives. The `sem = asyncio.Semaphore(CONCURRENCY)` limits how many requests can be in flight at once, which prevents your machine from opening too many simultaneous connections. The rate limiter is implemented with `rate_lock`, `DELAY`, and `next_request_time`. The `throttle()` coroutine serializes access to the timing state by acquiring `rate_lock`, then compares the current event-loop time against `next_request_time`. If the loop is "ahead" of the allowed schedule, it sleeps just long enough to align with the next permitted slot, and then it advances `next_request_time` by `DELAY`. Because every request awaits `throttle()`, the effective global rate is capped near `RPS`, even though many tasks are running concurrently.

> Note
>
> **Important**
>
> A semaphore is a concurrency control mechanism that limits how many operations can run at the same time. It works by maintaining a fixed number of "permits," where each task must acquire a permit before proceeding and releases it when finished. In asynchronous Python, a semaphore is commonly used to prevent too many concurrent tasks from accessing a shared or limited resource, such as network connections or API endpoints.

The `_fetch_one()` coroutine does the work for a single symbol. It constructs the URL for the historical endpoint and then enters async with `sem` so the request counts against the global concurrency limit. Inside the semaphore, it awaits `throttle()` to enforce the global requests-per-second limit. The call to `session.get()` is wrapped in a `try` block so timeouts and network-level client errors can be handled gracefully. When an error happens, the function prints a message and returns `None`, which lets the overall job continue instead of failing the entire run.

After a successful response, `_fetch_one()` validates the payload by checking that the JSON contains a non-empty historical key. If the payload is empty, it returns `None` so the caller can skip writing. Otherwise, it converts the historical list of dictionaries into a Polars DataFrame. The `schema_overrides` argument forces numeric-like columns such as open, close, and volume into `pl.Float64`, which reduces the odds of type inference issues across different symbols and avoids overflow problems from large integer volumes. The call to `with_columns(pl.lit(symbol).alias("symbol"))` appends the ticker so each row is self-identifying after all symbols are appended into a single Parquet dataset.

The coordinator `_download_prices_to_parquet()` sets up the HTTP client with `aiohttp.ClientTimeout` and a `TCPConnector`. The connector limits are aligned to `CONCURRENCY` so the connection pool does not exceed your intended number of simultaneous requests. It then builds a list of tasks, one per symbol, by calling `_fetch_one(...)` for each ticker.

The key to keeping the pipeline responsive is `asyncio.as_completed(tasks)`. Instead of awaiting tasks in the original order (which would stall on slow symbols), `as_completed` yields coroutines in the order they finish. As each completed result arrives, the function converts the Polars DataFrame to an Arrow table with `df.to_arrow()`. On the first successful table, it initializes a `pyarrow.parquet.ParquetWriter` using that table's schema. This is why the schema must be consistent across symbols: Parquet is written as a sequence of row groups with a fixed schema, so the writer needs a stable schema up front. Each subsequent table is appended with `writer.write_table(table)`. This pattern streams results to disk as they arrive, which keeps memory usage bounded even for large universes.

The `tqdm` progress bar is updated after each successful write. Note that the progress bar total is set to the number of tasks, but the bar advances only when a symbol produces data that is written. Symbols that error out or return no history are skipped, so it is normal for the bar not to represent "successful symbols" versus "attempted symbols" perfectly unless you track those separately.

Finally, `download_prices()` is a small synchronous wrapper around the async coordinator. `nest_asyncio.apply()` is included to make `asyncio.run(...)` usable in notebook environments that may already have an event loop running. The call to `asyncio.run(_download_prices_to_parquet(...))` creates and runs the event loop for the duration of the download, then returns when all tasks have completed and the Parquet writer has been closed.

There's more...

You can take this further by abstracting the rate limiter that enforces a semaphore-based implementation. This approach smooths bursts that can still occur under high concurrency and provides more predictable request timing. It is especially useful when working with strict APIs or when scaling the pipeline to thousands of concurrent tasks.

1. Implement a class called `SmoothRateLimiter`:

```
class SmoothRateLimiter:
    """Smooth rate limiter that enforces even distribution
       of calls over time."""
```

```
    def __init__(self, calls_per_minute: int, max_concurrent: int = 10):
        """Configure smooth limiter with pacing interval
           and concurrency cap."""
        self.calls_per_minute = calls_per_minute
        self.max_concurrent = max_concurrent
        self.semaphore = asyncio.Semaphore(max_concurrent)
        self.min_interval = 60.0 / calls_per_minute # eg., 0.06s for
                                                    #      1000/min
        self.last_call_time = 0
        self._lock = asyncio.Lock()

    async def acquire(self):
        """Acquire permission to make a request with smooth timing."""
        async with self.semaphore:  # Control concurrency
            async with self._lock:  # Control rate limiting
                now = time.time()

                # Calculate time since last call
                time_since_last = now - self.last_call_time

                if time_since_last < self.min_interval:
                    # We need to wait to maintain smooth timing
                    wait_time = self.min_interval - time_since_last
                    await asyncio.sleep(wait_time)
                    self.last_call_time = time.time()
                else:
                    # We can proceed immediately
                    self.last_call_time = now

    def release(self):
        """Release method for compatibility
           (no-op for this implementation)."""
        pass
```

2. Now instantiate the class:

```
rate_limiter = SmoothRateLimiter(RPS * 60, CONCURRENCY)
```

3. Refactor the `_fetch_one` function to acquire a token from your new class:

```
async def _fetch_one(session, symbol, start_date, end_date, api_key):
    base = "https://financialmodelingprep.com/api"
    url = f"{base}/v3/historical-price-full/{symbol}?"
          f"from={start_date}&to={end_date}&apikey={api_key}"

    await rate_limiter.acquire()
    try:
        async with session.get(url) as resp:
            resp.raise_for_status()
            data = await resp.json()
    except(asyncio.TimeoutError, aiohttp.ClientError) as e:
        print(f"skip {symbol}: {e}")
        return None
    if "historical" not in data or not data["historical"]:
        return None
    return pl.DataFrame(
        data["historical"],
        schema_overrides={  # keep overflow problems away
            "open": pl.Float64,
            "high": pl.Float64,
            "low": pl.Float64,
            "close": pl.Float64,
            "adjClose": pl.Float64,
            "vwap": pl.Float64,
            "change": pl.Float64,
            "changePercent": pl.Float64,
            "changeOverTime": pl.Float64,
            "volume": pl.Float64,
            "unadjustedVolume": pl.Float64,
        },
        strict=False,
    ).with_columns(
        pl.lit(symbol).alias("symbol"),
    )
```

Now run the same `download_prices` as you did before. You should see a consistent number of files being processed per second in the `tqdm` progress bar.

See also

Understanding how to process large volumes of data asynchronously is important for algorithmic traders. As data becomes larger and larger, coupling this technique with powerful tools like Polars and Parquet will accelerate your analysis.

- Refer to the official aiohttp documentation for deeper coverage of connection pooling, timeouts, and connector tuning for high-throughput async HTTP workloads: `https://docs.aiohttp.org/en/stable/client_advanced.html`
- The asyncio library documentation explains how semaphores, locks, and other primitives work together to safely coordinate concurrent `tasks: https://docs.python.org/3/library/asyncio-sync.html`
- PyArrow's Parquet writer documentation covers incremental writes, schema management, and performance considerations when appending large datasets: `https://arrow.apache.org/docs/python/parquet.html`

Manipulating financial market data with polars

Once we have our raw financial market data, it's time to manipulate it. On small data sets, pandas works well. However, when data begins to balloon in size to multiple gigabytes (common when dealing with higher frequency prices), Polars is the right tool for the job. In this recipe, you'll learn how to manipulate financial market data using Polars, a fast, expressive DataFrame library built on Rust. Polars' lazy execution engine, powerful expression syntax, and columnar memory model make it an efficient choice for working with time series and large tabular datasets. You'll load price data, filter observations, compute transformations, and generate derived columns using concise, high-performance queries.

Getting ready

For this recipe, we assume you have a Parquet file called `historical-prices.parquet` in the `prices/` directory.

How to do it...

In this section, we'll chain together several logical transformation steps using a Polars `LazyFrame` to clean and prepare stock price data efficiently. By deferring execution until the final step, Polars can optimize the full computation graph before any data is materialized. Here are the steps:

1. Import Polars and scan the Parquet file into a LazyFrame. Note: no data is loaded at this step:

```
import time
import polars as pl
UINT32_MAX = 2**32 - 1
```

2. Set a variable for the maximum integer size to cap the volume in case of bad data:

```
lf = pl.scan_parquet("prices/historical-prices.parquet")
```

3. Rename `camelCase` Parquet columns to Python-friendly `snake_case` names for consistency and readability across the pipeline:

```
def rename_to_snake_case(df: pl.LazyFrame) -> pl.LazyFrame:
    """Rename columns to Python snake_case."""
    return df.rename(
        {
            "adjClose": "adj_close",
            "unadjustedVolume": "unadjusted_volume",
            "changePercent": "change_percent",
            "changeOverTime": "change_over_time",
        }
    )
```

4. Remove non-common equity instruments such as warrants, rights, ADRs, preferred shares, test symbols, and venture exchange listings:

```
def filter_us_tradeable_equities_and_etfs(df: pl.LazyFrame) ->
pl.LazyFrame:
    """
    Keep only US-tradeable equities and ETFs.

    Assumptions:
      - Common equities and ETFs share the same symbol grammar
      - 1-5 uppercase letters
      - Optional single-letter class suffix (e.g. BRK.B)
      - Excludes mutual funds, derivatives, prefs, ADRs, units, etc.
```

```
    """
    s = pl.col("symbol")
    n = s.str.len_chars()

    standard = s.str.contains(r"^[A-Z]{1,5}(\.[A-Z])?$")

    excluded = (
        # warrants
        s.str.ends_with("W") | s.str.ends_with(".W")
        | s.str.ends_with(".WS") | s.str.ends_with(".WT")
        # rights
        | s.str.ends_with("R") | s.str.ends_with(".R")
        # units
        | s.str.ends_with("U") | s.str.ends_with(".U")
        | s.str.ends_with(".UN")
        # ADR / foreign ords conventions (provider-specific)
        | ((s.str.ends_with("Y") | s.str.ends_with("F"))&(n>= 5))
        # mutual funds convention
        | (s.str.ends_with("X")&(n>= 4))
        # preferreds / special issues
        | s.str.contains(r"[\$\-\^#]")
    )

    return df.filter(standard & ~excluded)
```

Note

Important

There is a lot of nuance in working with financial market data. This function is a fairly naïve approach to including only US tradeable corporate equities and ETFs. In practice, you would instead track the lifecycle of the economic entity. For example, corporations change their ticker symbol, go bankrupt, acquire other companies, spin off business units, and many other corporate actions. Bankrupt companies will often have a `.Q` suffix at the end of the ticker symbol to allow liquidating trades from creditors. When cleaning financial market data, it's important to align your process with the purpose of your analysis. For example, you would want to know if a company you hold in a backtest goes bankrupt.

5. Cast dates, numeric fields, and volumes into consistent, analysis-ready data types while capping invalid volume values:

```
def standardize_types(df: pl.LazyFrame) -> pl.LazyFrame:
    """Standardize column types from raw Parquet schema."""
    return df.with_columns(
        [
            # Date conversion (source is String)
            pl.col("date").str.strptime(
                pl.Date, strict=False).cast(pl.Datetime("ns")),

            # String columns
            pl.col("symbol", "label").cast(pl.Utf8),

            # Numeric columns (kept explicit)
            pl.col(
                "open",
                "high",
                "low",
                "close",
                "adj_close",
                "unadjusted_volume",
                "change",
                "change_percent",
                "vwap",
                "change_over_time",
            ).cast(pl.Float64),

            # Volume: clip to valid range then cast
            pl.when(pl.col("volume") < 0)
            .then(0)
            .when(pl.col("volume") > UINT32_MAX)
            .then(UINT32_MAX)
            .otherwise(pl.col("volume"))
            .cast(pl.Int64)
            .alias("volume"),
        ]
    )
```

6. Convert all ticker symbols to uppercase to ensure consistent symbol matching and grouping:

```
def normalize_symbol_case(df: pl.LazyFrame) -> pl.LazyFrame:
    """Normalize symbol case to uppercase."""
    return df.with_columns(
        [
            pl.col("symbol").str.to_uppercase().alias("symbol"),
        ]
    )
```

7. Drop records where all open, high, low, and close values are missing, indicating no usable price information:

```
def remove_all_null_ohlc(df: pl.LazyFrame) -> pl.LazyFrame:
    """Remove rows where all OHLC values are null."""
    return df.filter(
        ~(
            pl.col("open").is_null()
            & pl.col("high").is_null()
            & pl.col("low").is_null()
            & pl.col("close").is_null()
        )
    )
```

8. Drop incomplete records for liquid stocks, forward-fill prices for illiquid stocks by symbol, and replace remaining missing volumes with zero:

```
def handle_missing_data(df: pl.LazyFrame) -> pl.LazyFrame:
    """Handle missing price/volume data - VECTORIZED."""
    df = df.with_columns(
        [((pl.col("close") > 5)
        & (pl.col("volume") > 100000)).alias("is_liquid")]
    )

    has_missing_ohlc = (
        pl.col("open").is_null()
        | pl.col("high").is_null()
        | pl.col("low").is_null()
        | pl.col("close").is_null()
    )
```

```
    # For liquid stocks, drop missing OHLC
    df = df.filter(~(pl.col("is_liquid") & has_missing_ohlc))

    # For illiquid stocks, forward-fill within each symbol
    df = df.sort(["symbol", "date"])

    price_cols = ["open", "high", "low", "close"]
    df = df.with_columns([pl.col(col).forward_fill().over("symbol")
                          for col in price_cols])

    # Fill any remaining nulls in volume with 0
    df = df.with_columns([pl.col("volume").fill_null(0)])

    # Drop temporary column
    df = df.drop("is_liquid")

    return df
```

9. Chain the steps into a single lazy pipeline (nothing is executed yet):

```
lf_clean = (
    lf.pipe(rename_to_snake_case)
      .pipe(filter_us_tradeable_equities_and_etfs)
      .pipe(standardize_types)
      .pipe(normalize_symbol_case)
      .pipe(remove_all_null_ohlc)
      .pipe(handle_missing_data)
)
```

10. Finally, trigger execution when you actually need the data:

```
start = time.time()
df_clean = lf_clean.collect(engine="streaming")
print(f"Took {time.time() - start} seconds")
```

The result is a Polars DataFrame with 65 million records which was reduced from 221 million records before the cleaning process. On my Mac Studio M5, the pipeline processed in 9 seconds. Pandas would not be able to process a 12.5GB DataFrame of 221 million records:

shape: (65_862_393, 14)

date	open	high	low	close	adj_close	volume	unadjusted_volume	change	change_percent	vwap	label	change_over_time	symbol
datetime[ns]	f64	f64	f64	f64	f64	i64	f64	f64	f64	f64	str	f64	str
2000-01-03 00:00:00	53.06	53.18	45.39	48.51	40.44	4962189	4.962189e6	-4.55	-8.58	50.035	"January 03, 00"	-0.0858	"A"
2000-01-04 00:00:00	45.9	46.4	43.63	44.17	36.82	5058514	5.058514e6	-1.73	-3.77	45.025	"January 04, 00"	-0.0377	"A"
2000-01-05 00:00:00	44.64	44.64	40.64	42.03	35.04	6113793	6.113793e6	-2.61	-5.85	42.9875	"January 05, 00"	-0.0585	"A"
2000-01-06 00:00:00	41.52	41.77	39.16	39.75	33.14	2690591	2.690591e6	-1.77	-4.26	40.55	"January 06, 00"	-0.0426	"A"
2000-01-07 00:00:00	39.79	44.43	39.75	43.79	36.51	2993521	2.993521e6	4.0	10.05	41.94	"January 07, 00"	0.1005	"A"
…	…	…	…	…	…	…	…	…	…	…	…	…	…
2025-09-19 00:00:00	30.84	30.84	30.83	30.83	30.83	1335	1335.0	-0.01	-0.032425	30.83	"September 19, 25"	-0.000324	"ZZZ"
2025-09-22 00:00:00	30.93	30.93	30.7	30.75	30.75	1184	1184.0	-0.18	-0.58196	30.83	"September 22, 25"	-0.00582	"ZZZ"
2025-09-23 00:00:00	30.84	30.84	30.57	30.57	30.57	438	438.0	-0.27	-0.87549	30.7	"September 23, 25"	-0.008755	"ZZZ"
2025-09-24 00:00:00	30.62	30.62	30.62	30.62	30.62	232	232.0	0.0	0.0	30.62	"September 24, 25"	0.0	"ZZZ"
2025-09-25 00:00:00	30.61	30.61	30.24	30.24	30.24	2242	2242.0	-0.37	-1.21	30.43	"September 25, 25"	-0.0121	"ZZZ"

Figure 3.2: A 12.5GB Polars DataFrame with 221 million records

11. As a final step, save the resulting cleaned DataFrame as a Parquet file for further analysis later:

```
df_clean.write_parquet("prices/historical-prices-clean.parquet")
```

How it works...

This recipe builds a single Polars `LazyFrame` pipeline that cleans raw historical prices without materializing data until the final `collect()` call.

The pipeline starts by scanning the Parquet file into a `LazyFrame`. A `scan` is metadata-first: Polars builds a logical plan but does not load rows yet.

Next, `rename_to_snake_case` normalizes column names from `camelCase` to `snake_case` so downstream code stays consistent and readable across the full pipeline.

`filter_us_tradeable_equities_and_etfs` then reduces the universe to US-tradeable common equities and ETFs. It first identifies "standard" symbols using a strict symbol grammar (1–5 uppercase letters with an optional single-letter class suffix like BRK.B). It then removes known non-equity conventions (warrants, rights, units, ADR/foreign conventions, mutual funds, and preferred/special issues) by applying a single excluded expression and filtering on standard and ~excluded. Note this also removes non-US symbols.

After the universe filter, `standardize_types` converts raw strings and floats into analysis-ready `dtypes`. It parses dates into a timestamp type, enforces numeric columns as `Float64`, and caps `volume` to a maximum integer value to protect downstream analytics from bad ticks.

`normalize_symbol_case` forces all symbols to uppercase so grouping and joins behave deterministically, regardless of source quirks.

`remove_all_null_ohlc` drops rows where all OHLC fields are null since those rows have no usable price information.

Finally, `handle_missing_data` applies a two-path missing-data policy. It flags "liquid" rows using a simple price/volume heuristic, drops liquid rows with missing OHLC (because the gaps are more likely bad data), and forward-fills OHLC within each symbol for illiquid names to produce continuous time series. It then fills remaining missing volume with zero and removes the temporary liquidity flag.

The last step calls `collect(engine="streaming")`, which triggers execution of the entire optimized plan and returns a materialized Polars DataFrame.

There's more...

On a GPU-enabled system, Polars can execute the same lazy pipeline using NVIDIA RAPIDS by calling `.collect(engine="gpu")`. In this mode, Polars offloads supported operations such as filters, projections, string predicates, and aggregations to the GPU, allowing thousands of rows to be processed in parallel. This can significantly reduce end-to-end runtime for large datasets, especially when the workload is compute-bound rather than I/O-bound. Aside from installing the RAPIDS stack and running on compatible NVIDIA hardware, the pipeline code itself does not need to change other than the argument in the `collect` method.

Install GPU support with `pip`:

```
pip install polars[gpu] -U --extra-index-url=https://pypi.nvidia.com
```

When I run the same code on my NVIDIA DGX Spark, the entire end-to-end process runs in 3 seconds.

See also

Polars is not yet at feature parity with pandas—and pandas is still the day-to-day workhorse for data manipulation. But when you start working with big data sets, Polars is an exceptionally fast and powerful DataFrame library.

- **Polars Lazy API documentation**: Explains lazy execution, query optimization, and streaming vs. in-memory engines: `https://docs.pola.rs/user-guide/concepts/lazy-api/`.
- **Polars GPU engine (RAPIDS) documentation**: Covers GPU acceleration, supported operations, and setup requirements for `engine="gpu"`..
- **NVIDIA RAPIDS documentation**: Official guides for cuDF, GPU DataFrames, and configuring RAPIDS on CUDA-enabled systems: `https://docs.rapids.ai/`.
- **Financial Modeling Prep API documentation**: Reference for symbol metadata, security types, and exchange-specific nuances needed beyond symbol heuristics: `https://site.financialmodelingprep.com/developer/docs`.

Integrating polars with DuckDB for analysis

In this recipe, you'll explore DuckDB, an in-process analytical database designed for fast, ad hoc analytics directly on columnar data files. DuckDB brings the power of a full SQL engine to local workflows, making it especially well suited for financial market research where complex aggregations, joins, and window functions are common. Unlike traditional databases, DuckDB runs embedded in your Python process and can query data without requiring a separate server or ingestion step.

When combined with Parquet and Polars, DuckDB becomes an especially powerful tool for accelerating market data analysis. Parquet provides efficient, compressed, columnar storage for large historical datasets, Polars enables fast and expressive transformations with lazy execution, and DuckDB adds flexible SQL-based analytics on top of the same data. Together, these tools allow you to work interactively with millions of rows of market data, choosing the most efficient abstraction—expressions or SQL—at each stage of your research workflow.

Getting ready

This recipe assumes you have the parquet file `historical-prices-clean.parquet` in the `prices/` directory.

1. We'll start by demonstrating more examples of using Polars to manipulate data. Start with the imports and a scan of the `historical-prices-clean.parquet` file:

```
import polars as pl
import duckdb
lf = pl.scan_parquet("prices/historical-prices-clean.parquet")
```

2. Next, expand the Polars query plan to derive per-symbol return and volatility metrics, and compose these transformations into a single optimized execution graph before any data is materialized:

```
lf_with_metrics = (
    lf
    # Force a consistent dtype for `date`
    # no matter how it is stored in Parquet fragments
    .with_columns(
        pl.col("date").cast(pl.Utf8, strict=False).alias("date"),
        pl.col("symbol").str.to_uppercase().alias("symbol"),
    )
    # Create a parsed date column for sorting/window logic
    .with_columns(
        pl.col("date").alias("date_dt"),
    )
    .sort(["symbol", "date_dt"])
    .with_columns(
        (
            pl.col("close") / pl.col("close")
            .shift(1).over("symbol") - 1.0
        ).alias("daily_ret")
    )
    .with_columns(
        pl.col("daily_ret")
        .rolling_std(window_size=21, min_samples=21)
        .over("symbol")
        .alias("ret_std_21")
```

```
    )
)
```

3. Group by symbol and add a flag column where the closing price is between $5 and $100:

```
price_ok_by_symbol = (
    lf_with_metrics
    .group_by("symbol")
    .agg(
        (
            (pl.col("close") >= 5.0)
            & (pl.col("close") <= 100.0)
        ).all().alias("price_ok")
    )
)
```

4. Find where the 21-day standard deviation of returns is present and less than 100%:

```
vol_ok_by_symbol = (
    lf_with_metrics
    .filter(pl.col("ret_std_21").is_not_null())
    .group_by("symbol")
    .agg((pl.col("ret_std_21") < 1.0).all().alias("vol_ok"))
)
```

5. Join the query plan and filter where prices are between $5 and $100 and volatility is below 100%:

```
qualified_symbols = (
    price_ok_by_symbol
    .join(vol_ok_by_symbol, on="symbol", how="inner")
    .filter(pl.col("price_ok") & pl.col("vol_ok"))
    .select("symbol")
    .sort("symbol")
)
```

6. Finally, materialize the query and get the list of symbols that match the complex filter:

```
symbols_df = qualified_symbols.collect()
```

7. The result is a list of 8,148 symbols that meet the filter criteria:

shape: (8_148, 1)

symbol
str
"AAA"
"AAC"
"AACB"
"AACI"
"AACT"
…
"ZVOL"
"ZWRK"
"ZWS"
"ZYN"
"ZZZ"

Figure 3.3: List of symbols as a result of the complex Polars query plan

How to do it...

We'll start by registering the Polars DataFrames with DuckDB and writing SQL statements against the registered tables.

1. Connect to a DuckDB in-process database and register two tables, `prices` and `qualified_symbols`, populating the tables with data from the DataFrames:

```
con = duckdb.connect()
con.register("prices", lf_with_metrics.collect())
con.register("qualified_symbols", symbols_df)
```

2. Execute a SQL statement that generates a data summary of trading days per symbol:

```
symbol_stats = con.execute("""
    SELECT
        symbol,
        COUNT(*) AS trading_days,
```

```
    FROM prices
    GROUP BY symbol
    HAVING COUNT(*) > 1000
    ORDER BY trading_days DESC
    LIMIT 20
""").pl()
```

3. The result is a Polars DataFrame with the count of trading days per symbol:

shape: (20, 2)

symbol	trading_days
str	i64
"CNA.L"	6610
"JZCP.L"	6608
"ADIG.L"	6608
"PCT.L"	6606
"JFJ.L"	6606
…	…
"TTG.L"	6606
"FSTA.L"	6606
"NXT.L"	6606
"CWK.L"	6606
"SNR.L"	6606

Figure 3.4: Polars DataFrame with number of trading days per symbol

4. Execute a SQL statement that computes a 20-day moving average for AAPL:

```
rolling_stats = con.execute("""
    SELECT
        symbol,
        date,
        close,
        AVG(close) OVER (
            PARTITION BY symbol
            ORDER BY date
            ROWS BETWEEN 19 PRECEDING AND CURRENT ROW
        ) AS ma_20
    FROM prices
    WHERE symbol = 'AAPL'
    ORDER BY date
""").pl()
```

5. The result is a Polars DataFrame with AAPL's 20-day moving average:

shape: (6_527, 4)

symbol	date	close	ma_20
str	datetime[ns]	f64	f64
"AAPL"	2000-01-03 00:00:00	0.99944	0.99944
"AAPL"	2000-01-04 00:00:00	0.91518	0.95731
"AAPL"	2000-01-05 00:00:00	0.92857	0.94773
"AAPL"	2000-01-06 00:00:00	0.84821	0.92285
"AAPL"	2000-01-07 00:00:00	0.88839	0.915958
…	…	…	…
"AAPL"	2025-12-08 00:00:00	277.89	275.2405
"AAPL"	2025-12-09 00:00:00	277.18	275.628
"AAPL"	2025-12-10 00:00:00	278.78	275.8045
"AAPL"	2025-12-11 00:00:00	278.03	276.0325
"AAPL"	2025-12-12 00:00:00	278.28	276.299

Figure 3.5: Polars DataFrame with AAPL's 20-day moving average

6. Write an SQL join statement that joins the two registered DuckDB tables. This statement returns the data from the original clean data frame only for those symbols that match our complex filter for symbols within our desired price and volatility ranges:

```
filtered_prices = con.execute("""
    SELECT p.*
    FROM prices p
    INNER JOIN qualified_symbols q
        ON p.symbol = q.symbol
    ORDER BY p.symbol, p.date
""").pl()
```

7. The result is a Polars DataFrame that returns the data for the symbols that match the complex filter from the beginning of the recipe:

shape: (14_997_938, 14)

date	open	high	low	close	adj_close	volume	unadjusted_volume	change	change_percent	vwap	label	change_over_time	symbol
datetime[ns]	f64	f64	f64	f64	f64	i64	f64	f64	f64	f64	str	f64	str
2020-09-09 00:00:00	25.1	25.12	25.07	25.07	20.27	17327	17327.0	-0.0301	-0.11952	25.09	"September 09, 20"	-0.001195	"AAA"
2020-09-10 00:00:00	25.06	25.07	25.05	25.07	20.27	23500	23500.0	0.008	0.039904	25.0625	"September 10, 20"	0.000399	"AAA"
2020-09-11 00:00:00	25.04	25.05	25.02	25.04	20.24	33400	33400.0	-0.005	0.0	25.0375	"September 11, 20"	0.0	"AAA"
2020-09-14 00:00:00	25.01	25.06	25.01	25.02	20.23	13146	13146.0	0.01	0.039984	25.025	"September 14, 20"	0.0004	"AAA"
2020-09-15 00:00:00	25.02	25.03	25.01	25.01	20.22	12100	12100.0	-0.01	-0.039968	25.0175	"September 15, 20"	-0.0004	"AAA"
…	…	…	…	…	…	…	…	…	…	…	…	…	…
2025-09-19 00:00:00	30.84	30.84	30.83	30.83	30.83	1335	1335.0	-0.01	-0.032425	30.83	"September 19, 25"	-0.000324	"ZZZ"
2025-09-22 00:00:00	30.93	30.93	30.7	30.75	30.75	1184	1184.0	-0.18	-0.58196	30.83	"September 22, 25"	-0.00582	"ZZZ"
2025-09-23 00:00:00	30.84	30.84	30.57	30.57	30.57	438	438.0	-0.27	-0.87549	30.7	"September 23, 25"	-0.008755	"ZZZ"
2025-09-24 00:00:00	30.62	30.62	30.62	30.62	30.62	232	232.0	0.0	0.0	30.62	"September 24, 25"	0.0	"ZZZ"
2025-09-25 00:00:00	30.61	30.61	30.24	30.24	30.24	2242	2242.0	-0.37	-1.21	30.43	"September 25, 25"	-0.0121	"ZZZ"

Figure 3.6: Polars DataFrame with the data for the filtered symbols

How it works...

DuckDB runs as an in-process analytical database, so `duckdb.connect()` creates a database connection without requiring a server. When you call `con.register("prices", lf_with_metrics.collect())` and `con.register("qualified_symbols", symbols_df)`, you expose your existing Polars objects to DuckDB as queryable tables (more precisely, DuckDB treats them as relations/views). This lets you keep Polars in your primary workflow while using SQL for analysis and joins.

Next, `con.execute(...).pl()` runs the SQL query inside DuckDB and then converts the result back into a Polars DataFrame. This pattern mirrors how other recipes return their final objects for analysis and display, keeping the workflow consistent across tools.

The first query builds a quick "coverage" summary by symbol. `COUNT(*) AS trading_days` counts the number of rows per symbol. The `GROUP BY` symbol aggregates to one row per symbol, and the `HAVING COUNT(*) > 1000` clause filters out thin histories so you only keep symbols with enough trading sessions to be useful in research.

The second query computes a rolling statistic using a SQL window function. `AVG(close) OVER (...)` calculates a moving average without collapsing rows. `PARTITION BY` symbol ensures the moving average is computed independently per ticker, and `ORDER BY date ROWS BETWEEN 19 PRECEDING AND CURRENT ROW` defines a 20-row rolling window ending on each row's date.

Filtering with `WHERE symbol = 'AAPL'` limits the output to one symbol so you can validate the calculation and inspect the result easily.

Finally, the join query uses the symbol universe you built earlier. `INNER JOIN qualified_symbols q ON p.symbol = q.symbol` keeps only the rows in prices whose symbols appear in `qualified_symbols`, which is an efficient way to apply a complex, multi-step filter. The `ORDER BY p.symbol, p.date` sorts the final DataFrame so it is ready for downstream tasks such as indicator computation, factor construction, or writing to disk for later analysis.

There's more...

You can also run ad hoc SQL queries directly against the filtered dataset without explicitly managing a DuckDB connection object. DuckDB exposes a convenience interface through `duckdb.sql()`, which executes a SQL statement against any registered relations in the current process and returns the result immediately.

For example, the following query selects a subset of columns from the already filtered price data and applies an additional condition on **volume-weighted average price** (**VWAP**):

```
duckdb.sql("""
    SELECT
        date,
        symbol,
        open,
        high,
        low,
        adj_close
    FROM filtered_prices
    WHERE vwap > 15
    ORDER BY symbol, date
""").show()
```

The result is the display of data from DuckDB:

date timestamp_ns	symbol varchar	open double	high double	low double	adj_close double
2020-09-09 00:00:00	AAA	25.1	25.12	25.07	20.27
2020-09-10 00:00:00	AAA	25.06	25.07	25.05	20.27
2020-09-11 00:00:00	AAA	25.04	25.05	25.02	20.24
2020-09-14 00:00:00	AAA	25.01	25.06	25.01	20.23
2020-09-15 00:00:00	AAA	25.02	25.03	25.01	20.22
2020-09-16 00:00:00	AAA	24.97	24.98	24.97	20.19
2020-09-17 00:00:00	AAA	24.99	25.0	24.98	20.2
2020-09-18 00:00:00	AAA	24.97	24.98	24.97	20.2
2020-09-21 00:00:00	AAA	24.99	24.99	24.98	20.2
2020-09-22 00:00:00	AAA	24.98	24.99	24.98	20.2
.	.	.	.	.	.
.	.	.	.	.	.
.	.	.	.	.	.
2023-12-22 00:00:00	AAT	22.96	23.3	22.64	20.04
2023-12-26 00:00:00	AAT	22.75	23.07	22.59	20.39
2023-12-27 00:00:00	AAT	23.07	23.13	22.79	20.24
2023-12-28 00:00:00	AAT	22.68	23.01	22.65	20.33
2023-12-29 00:00:00	AAT	22.98	22.98	22.51	19.92
2024-01-02 00:00:00	AAT	22.51	23.13	22.44	20.3
2024-01-03 00:00:00	AAT	22.86	22.86	22.2	19.7
2024-01-04 00:00:00	AAT	22.3	22.66	22.19	19.87
2024-01-05 00:00:00	AAT	22.17	22.98	22.11	20.16
2024-01-08 00:00:00	AAT	22.74	23.31	22.71	20.56
? rows (>9999 rows, 20 shown)					6 columns

Figure 3.7: Data displayed from DuckDB

Here, `filtered_prices` is treated as a virtual table, even though it originated as a Polars DataFrame earlier in the recipe. DuckDB resolves the name automatically and executes the query in memory. The `WHERE vwap > 15` clause adds a lightweight, SQL-based refinement on top of your existing filters, which is often more convenient than rewriting the logic in Python.

Calling `.show()` prints the result in a tabular form, making this pattern useful for quick validation, exploratory analysis, or debugging. You can `replace .show()` with `.pl()` to return the result as a Polars DataFrame if you want to continue the analysis using Polars expressions. This hybrid approach lets you switch seamlessly between SQL and DataFrame-style workflows depending on which is clearer or more expressive for a given task.

See also

The following listed resources provide additional context and deeper references for combining Polars and DuckDB in hybrid analytical workflows. They are useful when you want to extend the patterns in this recipe to more advanced SQL features, performance tuning, and alternative execution models.

- **DuckDB SQL Window Functions documentation**: Use this reference to explore additional rolling, ranking, and analytical window functions beyond simple moving averages: `https://duckdb.org/docs/sql/window_functions.html`
- **DuckDB Python API documentation**: Consult this guide to learn more about `duckdb.sql()`, relation registration, and returning results as Pandas or Polars DataFrames: `https://duckdb.org/docs/api/python/overview.html`
- **Polars Lazy API documentation**: This resource explains how Polars' lazy execution model complements DuckDB when building efficient, end-to-end analytical pipelines: `https://pola.rs/python/user-guide/lazy/`

Building a high-performance data lake over parquet files with DuckLake

A data lake is a storage architecture designed to hold large volumes of structured and semi-structured data in its raw or lightly processed form, typically using open file formats such as Parquet. For quantitative research and trading systems, data lakes are critical because they decouple storage from compute, allowing you to scale analytics without migrating or rewriting data. DuckLake is a very new and cutting-edge project that brings data lake semantics—such as table abstractions, schema management, and transactional metadata—directly to DuckDB, while continuing to operate over plain Parquet files on disk.

DuckLake works by layering lightweight metadata and table definitions on top of Parquet datasets, giving you SQL-native access, schema evolution, and query optimization without the operational overhead of a traditional data warehouse. Because it is tightly integrated with DuckDB's vectorized execution engine, it enables extremely fast analytical queries directly against your local or cloud-backed Parquet data. This recipe shows how to create and query a DuckLake-backed data lake suitable for large-scale financial time series analysis.

Getting ready

For this recipe, you need DuckDB with DuckLake support installed. DuckLake is evolving rapidly, so make sure you are using a recent DuckDB build. We assume you already have the directory of Parquet files on disk, such as historical market data stored under a prices/ directory.

How to do it...

Follow these steps to create a DuckLake catalog, register Parquet files as managed tables, and query them through DuckDB.

1. Import DuckDB and set your local paths to create a dedicated folder for your DuckLake catalog and define the Parquet location you want to manage:

```
import duckdb
con = duckdb.connect()
catalog_path = "catalog.duckdb"
parquet_glob = "fundamentals/*.parquet"
```

2. Create a DuckDB connection and load the DuckLake extension to enable DuckLake inside your DuckDB session so you can attach and manage a lake catalog:

```
con.execute("INSTALL ducklake;")
con.execute("LOAD ducklake;")
```

3. Attach a DuckLake catalog to your session. After this step, DuckDB will treat `lake` as a catalog-backed namespace where you can create and manage lake tables.

```
con.execute(f"ATTACH 'ducklake:{catalog_path}' AS lake;")
con.execute("USE lake;")
```

4. Create a schema for your market data tables to keep lake objects organized as your dataset grows beyond a single table:

```
con.execute("CREATE SCHEMA IF NOT EXISTS market;")
```

5. Register your Parquet files as a managed DuckLake table. This turns your Parquet dataset into a catalog-managed table you can query consistently without rewriting file paths everywhere:

```
con.execute("DROP TABLE IF EXISTS market.fundamentals;")

con.execute(f"""
CREATE TABLE market.fundamentals AS
SELECT *
```

```
FROM read_parquet('{parquet_glob}', union_by_name=True);
""")
```

6. Verify the table exists and inspect its shape:

```
con.execute("SET schema 'market';")
con.execute("SHOW TABLES;").fetchall()
```

7. Run an analytics query that computes the quarter-over-quarter change in AAPL's earnings before interest taxes and depreciation which benefits from DuckDB's vectorized execution:

```
df = con.execute("""
    SELECT
      CAST(date AS DATE) AS report_date,
      period,
      calendarYear,
      EBITDA AS ebitda,
      (EBITDA / LAG(EBITDA) OVER (
        PARTITION BY symbol
        ORDER BY CAST(date AS DATE)
      ) - 1) AS ebitda_qoq_pct_change
    FROM market.fundamentals
    WHERE symbol = 'AAPL'
      AND EBITDA IS NOT NULL
    ORDER BY report_date;
""").pl()
```

The result is a Polars DataFrame with the data:

shape: (8, 5)

report_date	period	calendarYear	ebitda	ebitda_qoq_pct_change
date	str	i64	f64	f64
2009-12-26	"Q1"	2010	4.9340e9	null
2010-03-27	"Q2"	2010	4.1950e9	-0.149777
2010-06-26	"Q3"	2010	4.5070e9	0.074374
2010-09-25	"Q4"	2010	5.7760e9	0.281562
2019-12-28	"Q1"	2020	2.9519e10	4.11063
2020-03-28	"Q2"	2020	1.6678e10	-0.435008
2020-06-27	"Q3"	2020	1.6586e10	-0.005516
2020-09-26	"Q4"	2020	1.8237e10	0.099542

Figure 3.8: Polars DataFrame queries from DuckLake

How it works...

DuckLake adds a catalog layer on top of DuckDB so Parquet datasets can be managed and queried like tables. The recipe begins by opening a DuckDB connection and loading the DuckLake extension, which enables `ducklake:` URIs inside the session.

Attaching `'ducklake:{catalog_path}' AS lake` mounts a local DuckLake catalog and makes it the active namespace with `USE lake;`. From this point on, schemas and tables are created inside the catalog instead of directly against raw files. Creating the market schema is simply an organizational step that keeps related datasets grouped as the catalog grows.

The `CREATE TABLE market.fundamentals AS SELECT * FROM read_parquet(...)` statement registers all matching Parquet files as a single managed table. The `union_by_name=True` option aligns columns by name, which prevents schema mismatches across files. Dropping the table first makes the workflow repeatable during development.

The final query demonstrates why this setup is useful. DuckDB scans the Parquet-backed table using vectorized execution, computes a quarter-over-quarter EBITDA change with a `LAG` window function, and returns the result. Calling `.pl()` converts the output directly into a Polars DataFrame, letting you continue analysis in Polars without copying or rewriting data paths.

You now have a catalog-managed Parquet table that can be queried consistently and efficiently using standard SQL.

There's more...

DuckLake can also be combined with partitioned Parquet layouts to dramatically reduce query times for time-series data. For example, partitioning price data by year or symbol allows DuckDB to skip entire directories during query execution. As DuckLake matures, features such as schema evolution, multi-table joins, and transactional updates are expected to further close the gap between traditional warehouses and file-based data lakes.

See also

DuckLake and DuckDB are moving quickly, and the ecosystem is evolving fast. The following resources provide deeper technical background and updates:

- **DuckDB documentation**: Official documentation covering DuckDB's execution engine, SQL support, and file formats: `https://duckdb.org/docs`
- **DuckLake introduction**: An introduction to DuckLake's functionality: `https://ducklake.select/docs/stable/duckdb/introduction`
- **Parquet file format specification**: Background on the columnar storage format that underpins most modern data lakes: `https://parquet.apache.org`
- **DuckDB blog**: Technical articles and announcements about new features, performance improvements, and lake-style analytics: `https://duckdb.org/blog/`

Get this book's PDF version and more

Scan the QR code (or go to `packtpub.com/unlock`). Search for this book by name, confirm the edition, and then follow the steps on the page.

UNLOCK NOW

Note: Keep your invoice handy. Purchases made directly from Packt don't require an invoice.

4

Visualize Financial Market Data with Matplotlib, Seaborn, and Plotly Dash

The first step when working with data is to visualize and explore it. This is especially true when dealing with financial market data we rely on for trading. This chapter sets the stage by introducing five powerful data visualization libraries: pandas, Matplotlib, Seaborn, Plotly, and Plotly Dash.

Each tool has advantages and disadvantages and should be selected based on the use case. pandas has built-in plotting functionality using both Matplotlib and Plotly to render the charts. Matplotlib offers advanced functionality for building 3-dimensional surfaces and animated charts. Seaborn offers an array of statistical data visualizations. Plotly works with JavaScript for interactive charting. Plotly Dash is a framework for building interactive web apps with Python.

By the end of the chapter, you'll have a wide range of tools and chart types to visually inspect the financial market data required to research and build algorithmic trading applications.

In this chapter, we present the following recipes:

- Quickly visualizing data using pandas
- Animating the evolution of the yield curve with Matplotlib
- Plotting options implied volatility surfaces with Matplotlib
- Visualizing statistical relationships with Seaborn
- Creating an interactive PCA analytics dashboard with Plotly Dash

Quickly visualizing data using pandas

pandas is an all-purpose data manipulation library. Not only can you use it for data acquisition and manipulation, as we saw in *Chapter 1, Acquire Free Financial Market Data with Cutting-Edge Python Libraries* and *Chapter 2, Analyze and Transform Financial Market Data with pandas*, but you can use it for plotting too. pandas offers various "backends" that are used while plotting through a common method. In this recipe, you'll learn how to use the default backend, Matplotlib, to quickly plot financial market data using a line plot, bar chart, histogram, and others.

How to do it...

Here are the steps to perform this recipe:

You can use the Matplotlib plots through pandas by importing them.

1. Import the libraries:

```
import matplotlib.pyplot as plt
import pandas as pd
from openbb import obb
from pandas.plotting import bootstrap_plot, scatter_matrix
obb.user.preferences.output_type = "dataframe"
```

2. Download stock price data:

```
df = obb.equity.price.historical("AAPL", provider="yfinance")
```

3. Create a line chart that plots the closing price:

```
df.close.plot()
```

The result is the following chart:

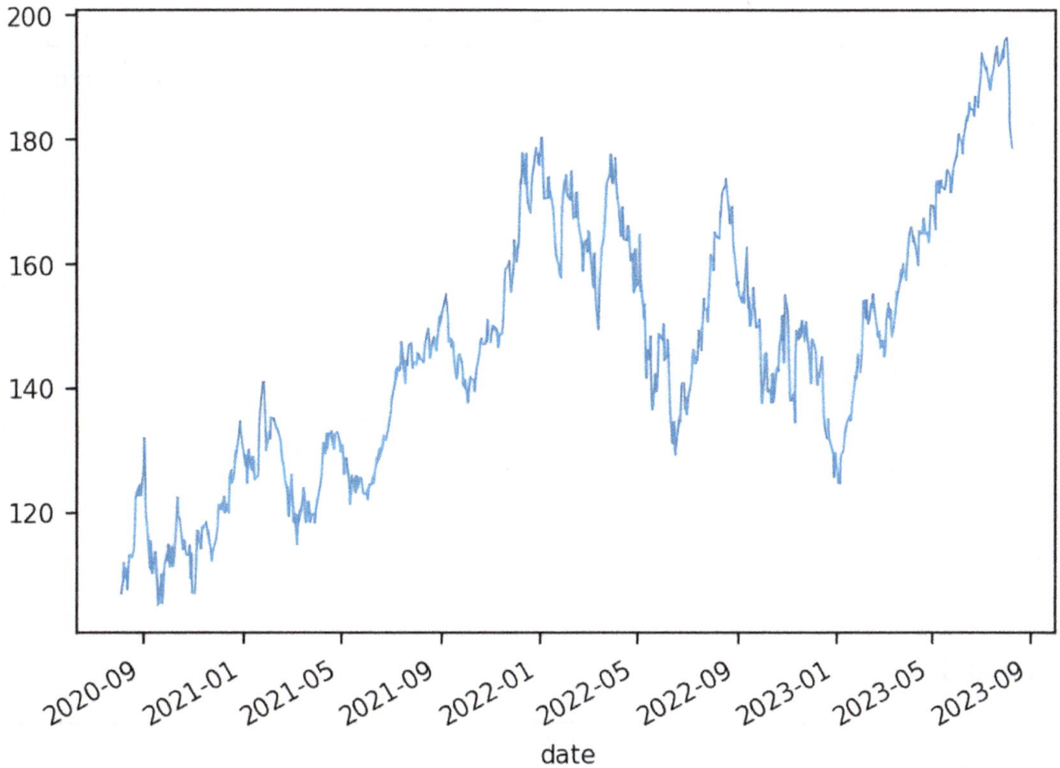

Figure 4.1: Line chart plotting AAPL's unadjusted closing price between 2020 and 2023

4. Plot the daily returns as a bar chart using additional options to style the chart:

```
returns = df.close.pct_change()
returns.name = "return"
returns.plot.bar(
    title="AAPL returns",
    grid=False,
    legend=True,
    xticks=[]
)
```

The result is the following chart:

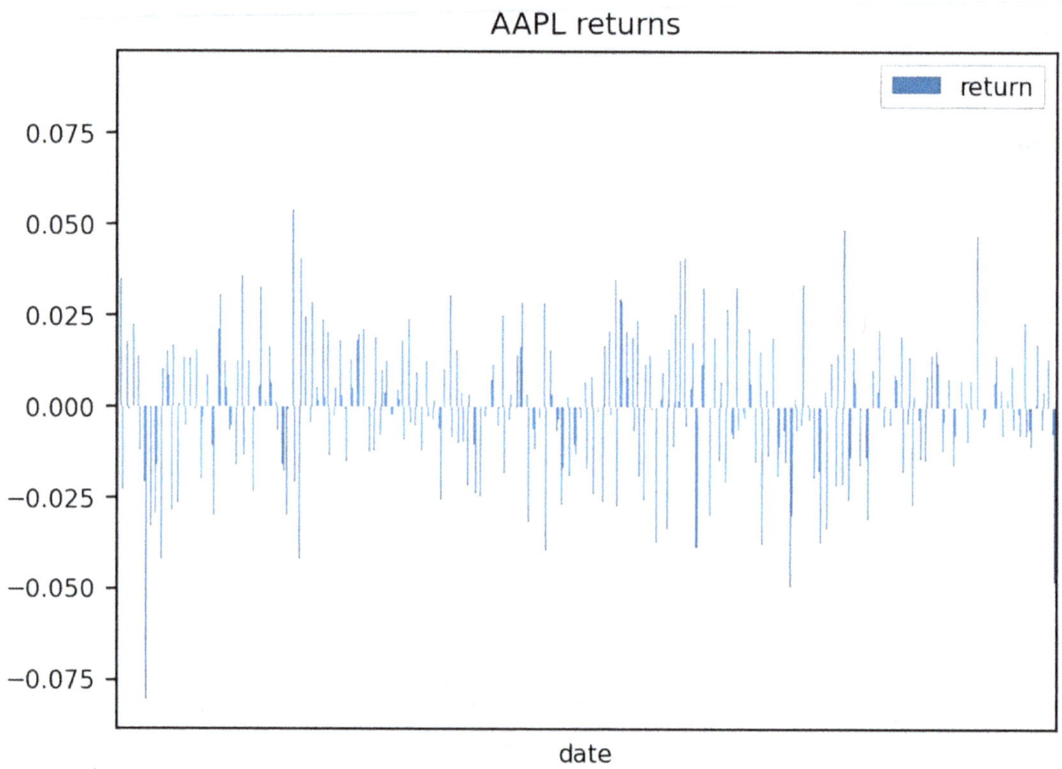

Figure 4.2: Bar chart plotting AAPL's daily returns without the x-axis labels, grid, or legend

5. Create a histogram of returns with 50 bins:

```
returns.plot.hist(bins=50)
```

The result is the following chart:

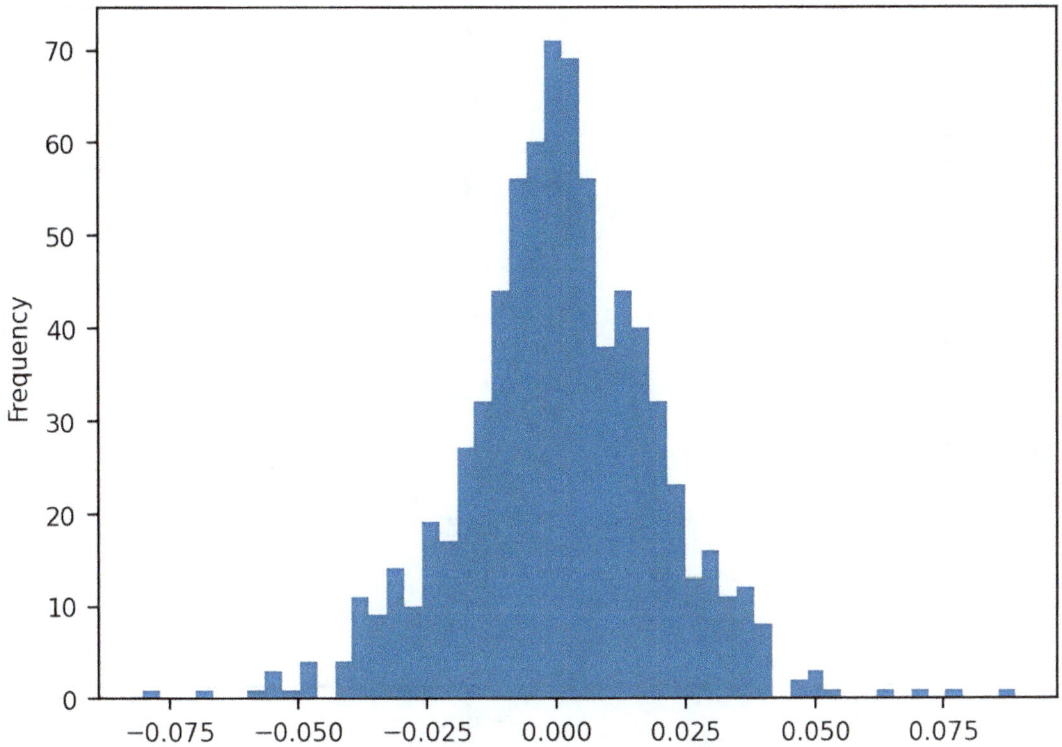

Figure 4.3: Histogram of AAPL daily returns with 50 bins

6. Create a box-and-whisker plot:

```
returns.plot.box()
```

The result is the following chart:

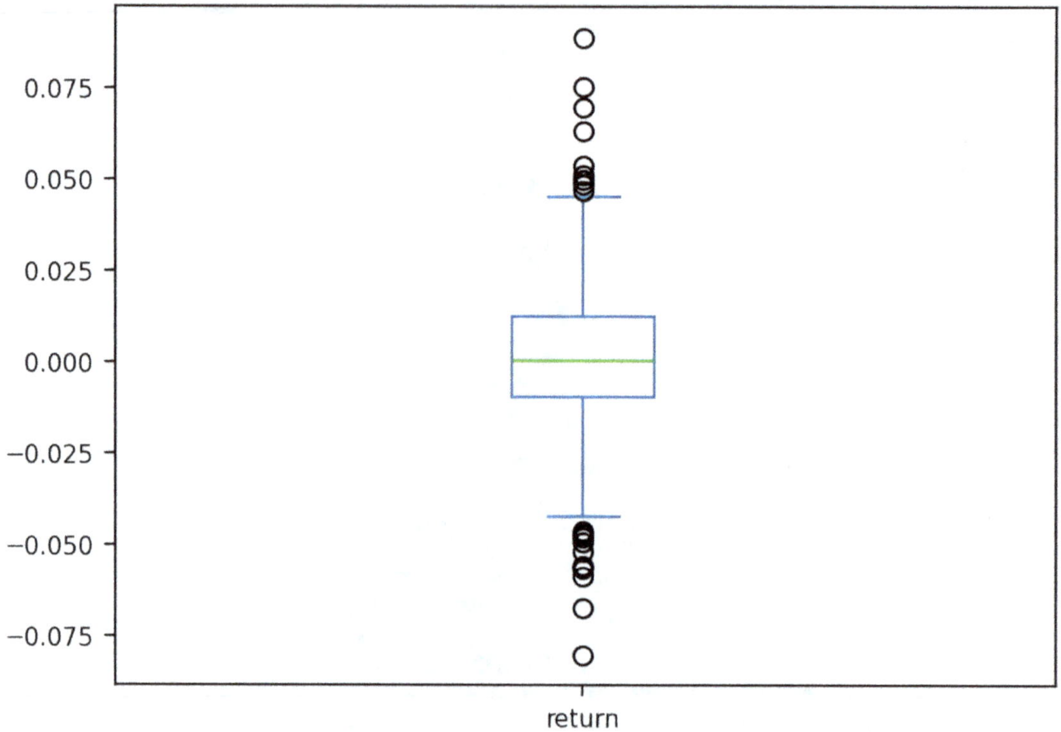

Figure 4.4: Box-and-whisker plot showing the median, quartiles, and outliers of AAPL daily returns

> Note
>
> **Important**
>
> A box plot serves as a graphical representation for displaying numerical data distributions via their quartiles. The box itself spans from the first quartile (Q1) to the third quartile (Q3), with a line indicating the median (Q2). Whiskers extend from the box boundaries to illustrate the data's range, and their default position is determined by 1.5 times the **interquartile range** (**IQR**), where IQR equals Q3 minus Q1. Data points beyond the whiskers are considered outliers.

How it works...

The pandas `plot` method lets you create various types of plots using DataFrames and Series. Under the hood, pandas uses the defined backend (Matplotlib by default) to generate these visualizations. To use this method, you first create a DataFrame or Series, then call the plot method on the object, optionally specifying the type of plot and other parameters that control the plot's appearance, such as color, size, title, and axes labels.

> Note
>
> **Important**
>
> Using the `plot` method, we can generate bar plots, density plots, scatter plots, and many others. We can define the type of plot using the kind parameter. Not all backends support all plot types. For example, the plot type `hexbin` does not work with the Plotly backend. See the pandas documentation for details.

There's more...

A common step in quantitative portfolio construction and risk management is analyzing the relationship between two or more assets. Scatter plots are a type of visual representation that can be used to explore the relationship between two stocks. Each dot on the scatter plot represents a pair of values for the two stocks at a specific point in time. The x-coordinate of the dot represents the value of one stock, and the y-coordinate represents the value of the other stock.

If the dots form a pattern that slants upwards from left to right, it suggests a positive relationship between the stocks, meaning that as one stock's price increases, the other's tends to as well. If the plot forms a pattern slanting downwards, it suggests a negative correlation, meaning that as one stock's price increases, the other's tends to decrease. If the dots appear randomly scattered with no discernible pattern, it indicates no or a weak correlation.

Compare AAPL with the Nasdaq tracking ETF, QQQ. Note that if `yfinance` returns an error, most of the time you can just wait a short time and retry.

```
qqq = obb.equity.price.historical("QQQ", provider="yfinance")
qqq_returns = qqq.close.pct_change()
asset_bench = pd.concat([returns, qqq_returns], axis=1)
asset_bench.columns = ["AAPL", "QQQ"]
asset_bench.plot.scatter(x="QQQ", y="AAPL", s=0.25)
```

The result is a scatter plot that shows the seemingly positive relationship between AAPL returns and QQQ returns.

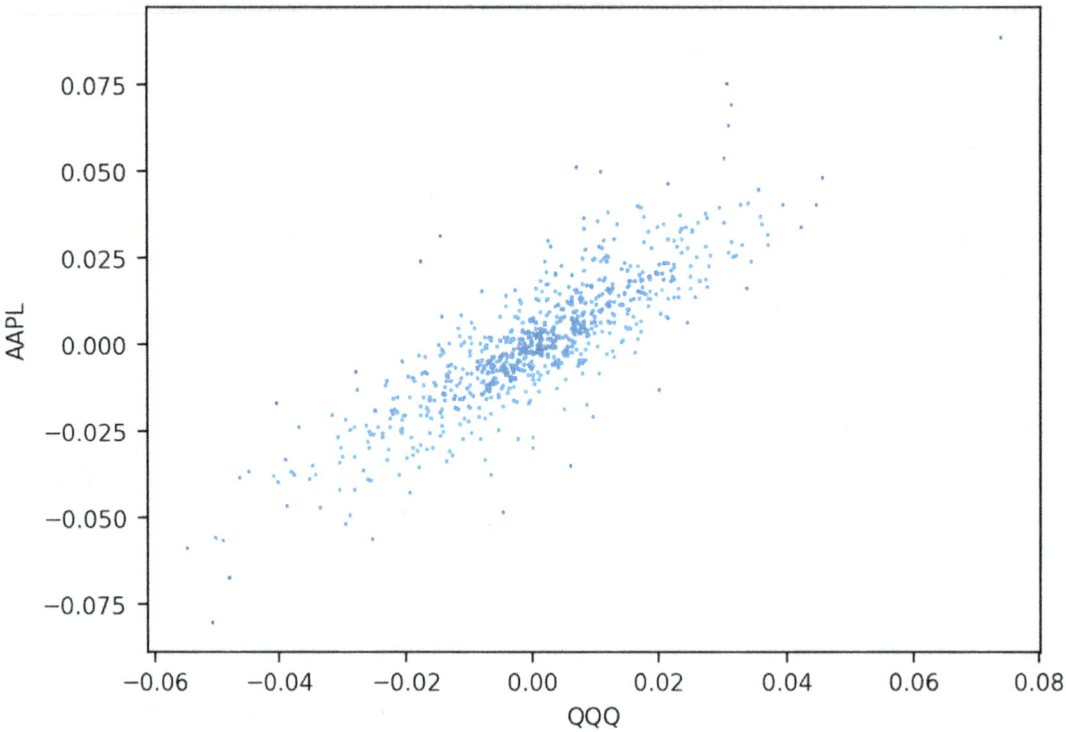

Figure 4.5: Scatter plot of AAPL daily returns and QQQ daily returns showing a positive linear relationship

The pandas `scatter_matrix` method visualizes pairwise relationships. It generates a matrix of scatter plots, each plotting a pair of columns against each other. This allows for a quick visual inspection of potential correlations or patterns within your data. Additionally, the main diagonal (from top left to bottom right) shows the histogram of each column, which helps to visualize data distribution.

```
scatter_matrix(asset_bench)
```

The result is the scatter matrix:

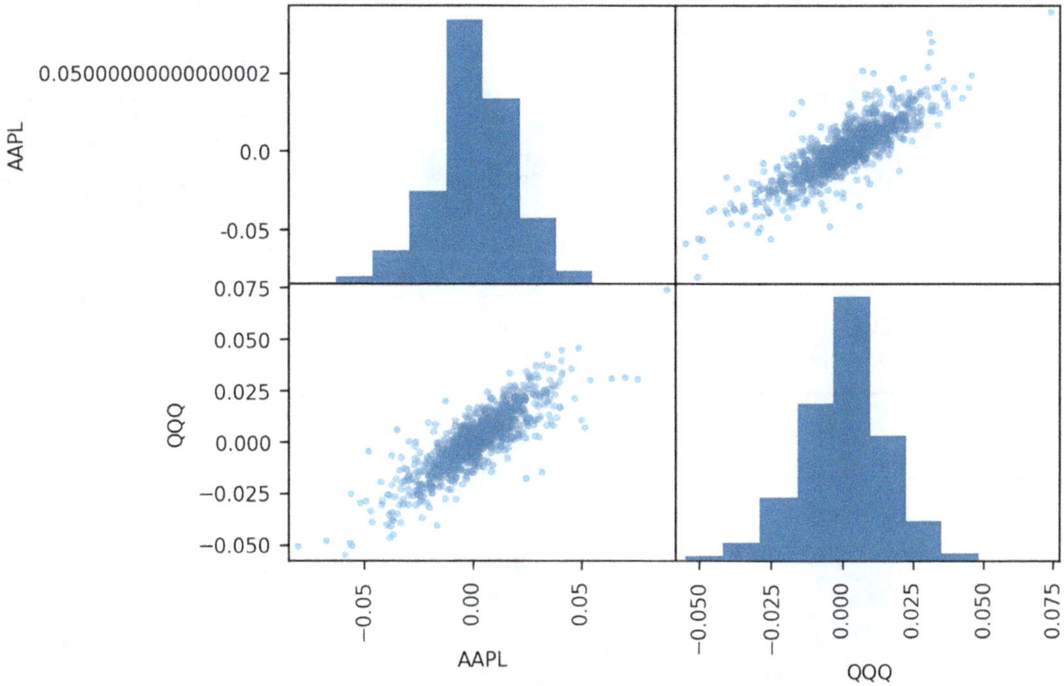

Figure 4.6: A scatter matrix plot summarizing AAPL and QQQ returns in one chart

Bootstrap plots serve to graphically evaluate the variability associated with a particular statistic, including the mean, median, and midrange. A designated subset size is randomly sampled from the data set, and the target statistic is calculated for this subset. This procedure is iteratively performed a predetermined number of times. The plots and histograms collectively form the bootstrap plot:

```
bootstrap_plot(returns)
```

By default, `bootstrap_plot` selects 50 data points to consider during each sampling. The result is a `bootstrap_plot`.

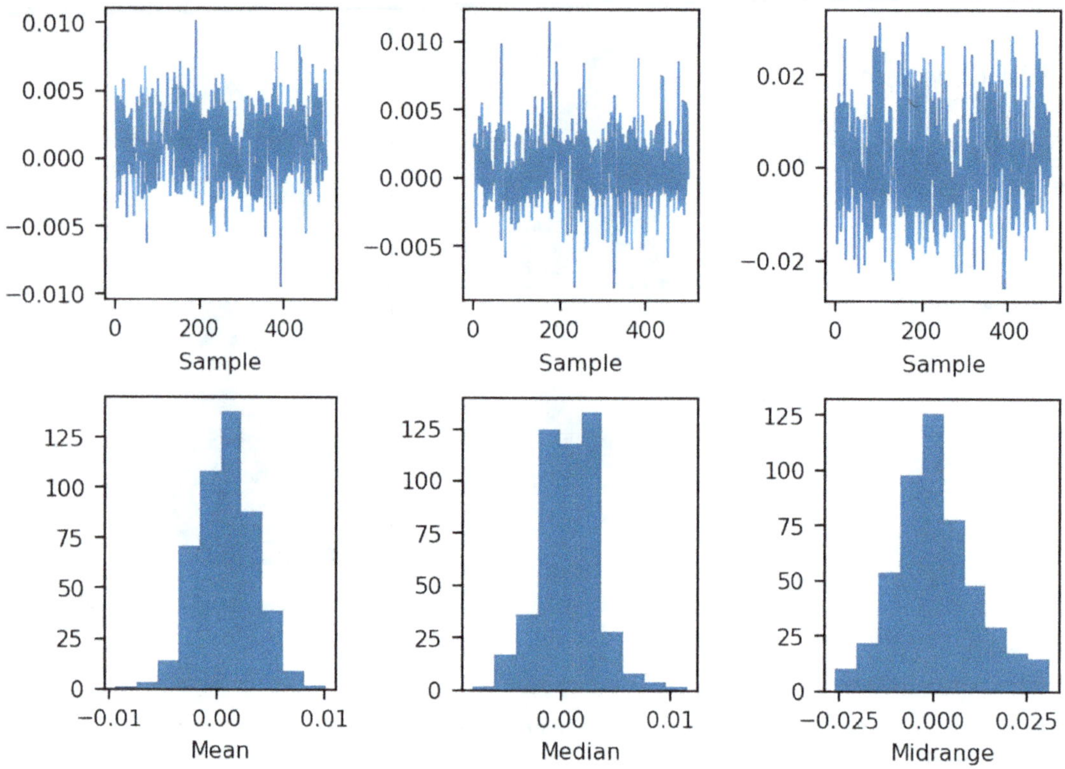

Figure 4.7: A bootstrap plot that depicts random subsets of data

See also

pandas has detailed documentation on its plots. You can read more here:

- Pandas `plot` documentation: `https://pandas.pydata.org/docs/reference/api/pandas.DataFrame.plot.html`
- Pandas `scatter_matrix` documentation: `https://pandas.pydata.org/docs/reference/api/pandas.plotting.scatter_matrix.html`
- Pandas `bootstrap_plot` documentation: `https://pandas.pydata.org/docs/reference/api/pandas.plotting.bootstrap_plot.html`

To see more practical examples of using pandas plotting, you can check out past issues of the PyQuant Newsletter here: .

Animating the evolution of the yield curve with matplotlib

Even though pandas uses Matplotlib as its backend, there are times you need to go deeper. One such case is when you want to visualize changes in data over time, such as when analyzing the evolution of the yield curve. The yield curve, which charts the yields of bonds of the same quality across different maturities, typically slopes upward. This means that longer-term bonds have higher yields than shorter-term bonds, which makes sense given the additional risks associated with holding a bond for a longer time (e.g., inflation, higher interest rate volatility). However, there are times when the yield curve inverts, meaning that shorter-term bonds yield more than longer-term ones. Many traders and economists view an inverted yield curve as a precursor to a recession.

An inverted yield curve has historically preceded U.S. recessions, suggesting traders' anticipation of lower future interest rates and a coming economic slowdown. The inversion can constrict bank profitability, leading to reduced lending and a potential economic deceleration. Additionally, the expectation of a recession can become a self-fulfilling prophecy as businesses and consumers curtail spending. Investors may also shift toward safer assets, limiting funding for riskier ventures.

How to do it...

Creating an animated plot requires a specialized method called `animation`, which is imported from Matplotlib. Here are the steps for it:

1. Import the libraries:

```
import numpy as np
import pandas as pd
import matplotlib.pyplot as plt
from matplotlib import animation
from IPython.display import HTML
import matplotlib as mpl
from openbb import obb
mpl.rcParams["animation.embed_limit"] = 100
obb.user.preferences.output_type = "dataframe"
%matplotlib inline
```

2. Define the maturities and download the data:

```
maturities = ["3m", "6m", "1y", "2y", "3y", "5y", "7y", "10y", "30y"]
data = (
    obb.fixedincome.government.treasury_rates(
        start_date="1985-01-01",
        provider="federal_reserve",
    )
    .dropna(how="all")
    .drop(columns=["month_1", "year_20"])
)
data.columns = maturities
data.index = pd.to_datetime(data.index)
```

3. Use boolean indexing to mark where the yield curve is inverted:

```
data["inverted"] = data["30y"] < data["3m"]
```

4. Precompute arrays, manipulate data for display, and cap the frames per second to speed up generation:

```
M = len(maturities)
n = len(data)

x = np.arange(M)
Y = data.loc[:, maturities].to_numpy(dtype=float) * 100.0
dates = data.index.strftime("%Y-%m-%d").to_numpy()
inv = data["inverted"].to_numpy(dtype=bool)

max_frames = 500
step = max(1, n // max_frames)
frames = np.arange(0, n, step, dtype=int)
```

5. Create the helper functions to generate the animations:

```
def init():
    line.set_data([], [])
    title.set_text("U.S. Treasury Bond Yield Curve")
    return line, title


def update(fi):
```

```
    line.set_data(x, Y[fi])
    line.set_color("r" if inv[fi] else "y")
    title.set_text(f"U.S. Treasury Bond Yield Curve ({dates[fi]})")
    return line, title
```

6. Set up and display the animated chart:

```
fig, ax = plt.subplots(figsize=(7.5, 4.5))

(line,) = ax.plot([], [], lw=2, animated=True)

ax.set_xlim(-0.25, M - 0.75)
ax.set_ylim(0, 20)
ax.set_xticks(x)
ax.set_xticklabels(maturities, rotation=0)
ax.set_yticks([2, 4, 6, 8, 10, 12, 14, 16, 18])
ax.set_xlabel("Time to maturity")
ax.set_ylabel("Yield (%)")

title = ax.text(
    0.5, 1.02, "", transform=ax.transAxes,
    ha="center", va="bottom", animated=True
)

ani = animation.FuncAnimation(
    fig,
    update,
    frames=frames,
    init_func=init,
    interval=100,
    blit=True,
    repeat=True,
)

html = ani.to_jshtml()
plt.close(fig)
HTML(html)
```

7. The result is an animated, interactive chart that displays the shape of the yield curve through time:

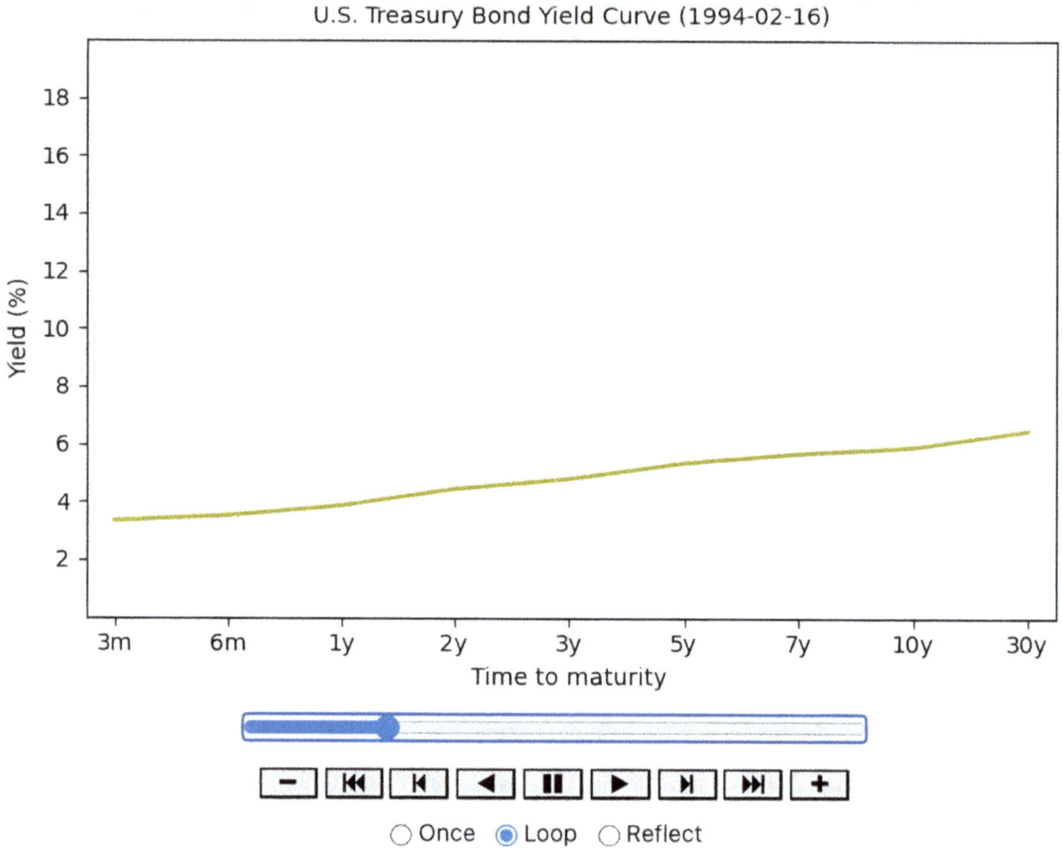

Figure 4.8: One frame from the animated plot of the US yield curve. This frame depicts the shape of the yield curve on 27 February 1985

How it works...

The recipe begins by importing Matplotlib's `animation` module, which provides the machinery for generating frame-by-frame updates of a figure. Unlike static plots, animated charts rely on repeatedly updating artists rather than redrawing the entire figure each time.

Treasury yields are downloaded with the OpenBB Platform and reshaped so that each column represents a maturity and each row a single date.

An inverted yield curve is identified in advance by comparing the 30-year and 3-month yields. This boolean flag is later used to change the line color during the animation. For performance, the yield values, dates, and inversion flags are converted to NumPy arrays, and the number of frames is capped to keep rendering fast.

The animation is driven by two functions. The `init` function prepares empty plot elements, while the `update` function redraws the yield curve for each date, updates the title, and sets the color based on whether the curve is inverted. `FuncAnimation` coordinates these updates, and the result is exported to HTML so it can be displayed interactively in a Jupyter Notebook.

There's more...

`FuncAnimation` is a versatile class. Apart from the arguments used above, it also accepts the following:

- `repeat`: A boolean value indicating if the animation should repeat once all frames have been displayed.
- `repeat_delay`: The delay, in milliseconds, between consecutive repetitions of the animation.
- `fargs`: Any additional arguments to pass to the func (i.e., the animation function).
- `save_count`: The number of values from frames to cache, to improve performance when saving the animation. If None, then the entirety of frames is cached.
- `cache_frame_data`: If True, the return values of the animate function are cached, which can be useful for speeding up the saving of long animations. If you set it to False, the frames will be recreated via the animation function during the save process.
- `event_source`: An instance of `EventSource` or None. If None, a new instance of `TimerBase` will be created. This is useful when you want to synchronize multiple animations.

These are some of the main arguments you can use with `FuncAnimation`. There are also some internal and base class arguments available, but they're less commonly used in most applications.

You can also save the animation to an MP4 file. To do so, replace this code:

```
html = ani.to_jshtml()
plt.close(fig)
HTML(html)
```

With this code:

```
from IPython.display import Video
ani.save("yieldcurve.mp4", writer="ffmpeg", dpi=140, fps=20)
Video("yieldcurve.mp4", embed=True)
```

This will generate and save an MP4 file called `yieldcurve.mp4` and display it in the Notebook.

See also

The animation API is very rich, offering many animation options. You can read more here (this is the documentation for Matplotlib's animation API):

`https://matplotlib.org/stable/api/animation_api.html`

Plotting options implied volatility surfaces with matplotlib

Traders use Matplotlib to visualize complex data, such as **options implied volatility surfaces**. These visuals illustrate how the implied volatility of options varies across different expiration dates and strike prices. Implied volatility surfaces are important for traders for information on the market's expectations of future volatility.

These surfaces show two main features: skew and term structure. Skew refers to how implied volatility varies at different strike prices for the same expiration date. It can indicate the market's expectation of significant price shifts. The term structure shows how implied volatility varies across options with the same strike price but different expiration dates. The term structure shows how volatility is expected to evolve over time.

Although a detailed explanation of skew and term structure is beyond the scope of this book, it's important to note that these aspects of the volatility surface are important for making informed trading decisions. They also play a significant role in selecting appropriate hedging strategies and in fine-tuning pricing and risk assessment models for more complex financial instruments.

Getting ready

We'll start with a fresh Jupyter Notebook to avoid plotting the surface plot on the same axes as the animated plot.

How to do it...

As with the animated charts, to create three-dimensional surfaces, we need to import the Axes3D class from the `mpl_toolkits` module.

1. Import the libraries:

```
import matplotlib.pyplot as plt
import numpy as np
from mpl_toolkits.mplot3d import Axes3D
```

```
from openbb import obb
obb.user.preferences.output_type = "dataframe"
```

2. Download options data using the OpenBB SDK:

```
chains = obb.derivatives.options.chains(
    "AAPL",
    provider="cboe",
)
```

3. Filter the options data to include only call options:

```
calls = chains[chains.option_type == "call"]
```

4. Filter the calls with days to expiration under three months and with a strike price greater than 100. Then drop any duplicates:

```
calls = calls[
    (calls.dte < 100)
&(calls.strike>= 100)
]
calls.drop_duplicates(subset=["strike", "dte"], keep=False, inplace=True)
```

5. Pivot the DataFrame to put strikes in the index, days to expiration along the columns, and the implied volatility within the cells. Then drop rows where all values in a column are nan:

```
vol_surface = (
    calls
    .pivot(
        index="strike",
        columns="dte",
        values="implied_volatility"
    )
    .dropna(how="all", axis=1)
)
```

6. Use NumPy's `meshgrid` method to create a two-dimensional grid using the strike price and days to expiration for use in the plot:

```
strike, dte = np.meshgrid(
    vol_surface.columns,
    vol_surface.index
)
```

7. Finally, plot the surface:

```
fig = plt.figure(figsize=(15, 15))
ax = fig.add_subplot(111, projection='3d')
ax.set_xlabel("Days to Expiration")
ax.set_ylabel("Strike Price")
ax.set_zlabel("Implied Volatility")
ax.plot_surface(
    strike,
    dte,
    vol_surface.values,
    cmap="viridis"
)
```

8. The result is a three-dimensional surface plot with the strike price on the x-axis, the days to expiration on the y-axis, and the implied volatility on the z-axis:

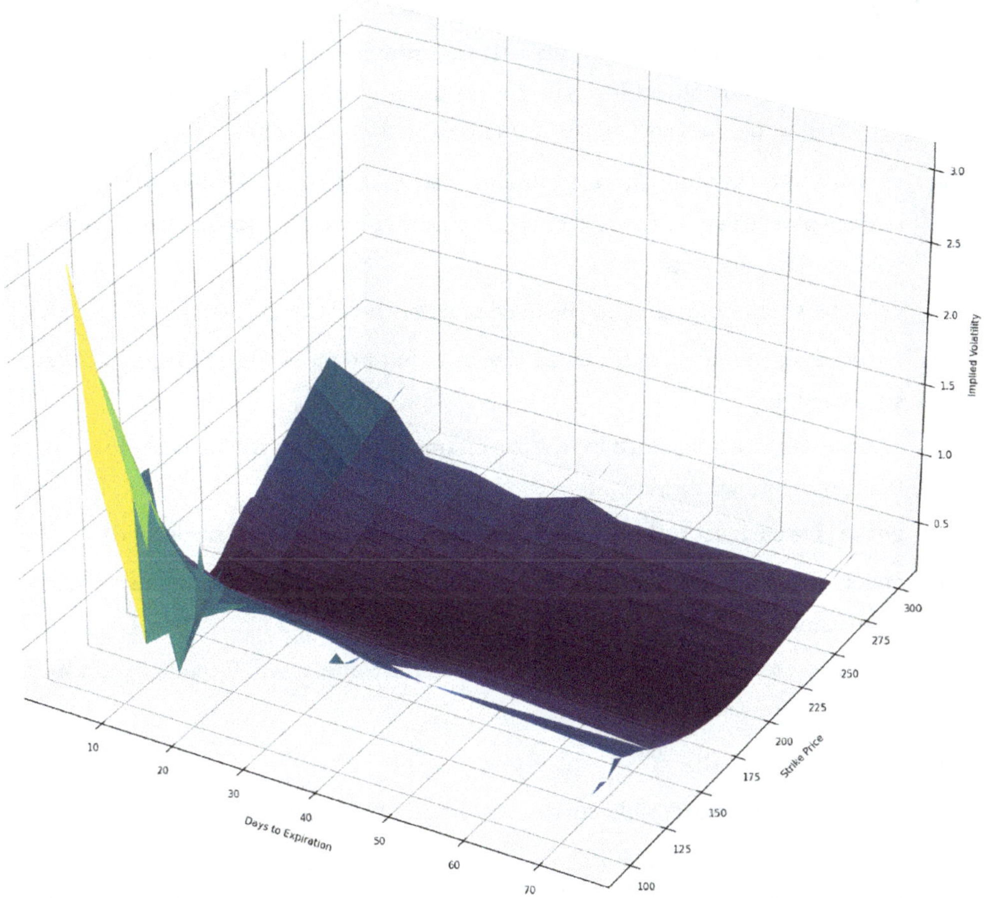

Figure 4.9: Options implied volatility surface shown for AAPL call options

How it works...

We download options data and narrow down the dataset to options expiring in less than 90 days with a strike price of $100 or more. It then cleans the data by removing any entries with identical strike prices and expiration periods to ensure uniqueness. The core of the process involves reorganizing the data into a DataFrame where each row and column represent different strike prices and expiration times. We then use the NumPy `meshgrid` method to build two-dimensional grids corresponding to the strike prices and expiration times. The grid is the same structure as the `vol_surface` DataFrame. The culmination of this process is the generation of a 3D plot, where the axes denote the strike price, days to expiration, and implied volatility, respectively.

There's more...

The `plot_surface` method of Matplotlib's 3D axes provides an easy way to create three-dimensional surface plots. In addition to the arguments we used in the preceding section, there are several other arguments commonly used in algorithmic trading:

- `rstride` and `cstride`: These arguments control the stride (step size) used to create the surface plot. The `rstride` and `cstride` parameters set the stride size for row and column data, respectively.
- `color`: A single color that can be used to color the entire surface.
- `facecolors`: A matrix of the same size as Z that provides the colors for each face of the surface plot.
- `linewidth`: The line width for the wireframe is drawn on the surface plot. The default is 0, meaning no wireframe.
- `antialiased`: If set to `True`, the surface will be `antialiased` (smoothed).
- `shade`: If `True`, the surface plot will be shaded, giving it a gradient effect based on light source and orientation.
- `vmin` and `vmax`: The `colorbar` range. If either is None, it will be computed using min(Z) or max(Z), respectively.

See also

To learn more about plotting, yield curves, and implied volatility surfaces, see the resources below:

- Documentation for Matplotlib's `plot_surface` method: `https://matplotlib.org/stable/api/_as_gen/mpl_toolkits.mplot3d.axes3d.Axes3D.plot_surface.html`
- More about the history of inverted yield curves: `https://www.investopedia.com/terms/i/invertedyieldcurve.asp`
- More about how the implied volatility surface is used in practice: `https://www.investopedia.com/articles/stock-analysis/081916/volatility-surface-explained.asp`

Visualizing statistical relationships with Seaborn

A major part of algorithmic trading is engineering factors. Factor engineering involves creating predictors for algorithmic trading models, often called **alpha factors**. These factors represent patterns or anomalies in the market. They aim to predict future price movements based on historical and real-time data. Factor engineering is increasingly reliant on machine learning and statistical methods. These tools help in automatically extracting patterns from vast datasets. Machine learning models, such as neural networks, can identify non-linear relationships missed by traditional methods. Feature selection techniques aid in determining the most relevant predictors. Regularization techniques prevent overfitting, ensuring model robustness. Clustering and dimensionality reduction help manage complex datasets.

The seaborn library is tailor-made for visualizing statistical relationships, making it an important tool for factor engineering. Seaborn is built on Matplotlib and integrates with pandas making it familiar to users of those tools (which we now are).

How to do it...

We'll import Seaborn for the statistical plots. Here are the steps to try this recipe:

1. Import the libraries:

```
import matplotlib.pyplot as plt
import numpy as np
import pandas as pd
import seaborn as sns
from openbb import obb
obb.user.preferences.output_type = "dataframe"
```

2. Download stock price history using the OpenBB SDK:

```
data = obb.equity.price.historical(
    ["AAPL", "SPY"],
    start_date="2020-01-01",
    provider="yfinance"
).pivot(columns="symbol", values="close")
```

3. Compute the daily returns:

```
returns = (
    data
    .pct_change(fill_method=None)
    .dropna()
)
```

4. Reshape the data to a long format using the pandas `melt` method:

```
returns = returns.reset_index()
melted = pd.melt(
    returns,
    id_vars=["date"],
    value_vars=["AAPL"],
    var_name="stock",
    value_name="returns",
)
```

5. Add a new column for the month:

```
melted["month"] = pd_todatetime(melted["date"]).dt.to_period("M")
```

6. Generate the box plot:

```
g = sns.boxplot(
    x="month",
    y="returns",
    hue="stock",
    data=melted
)
g.set_xticklabels(
    melted["month"].unique(),
    rotation=45
)
```

The result is a box plot summarizing the monthly returns:

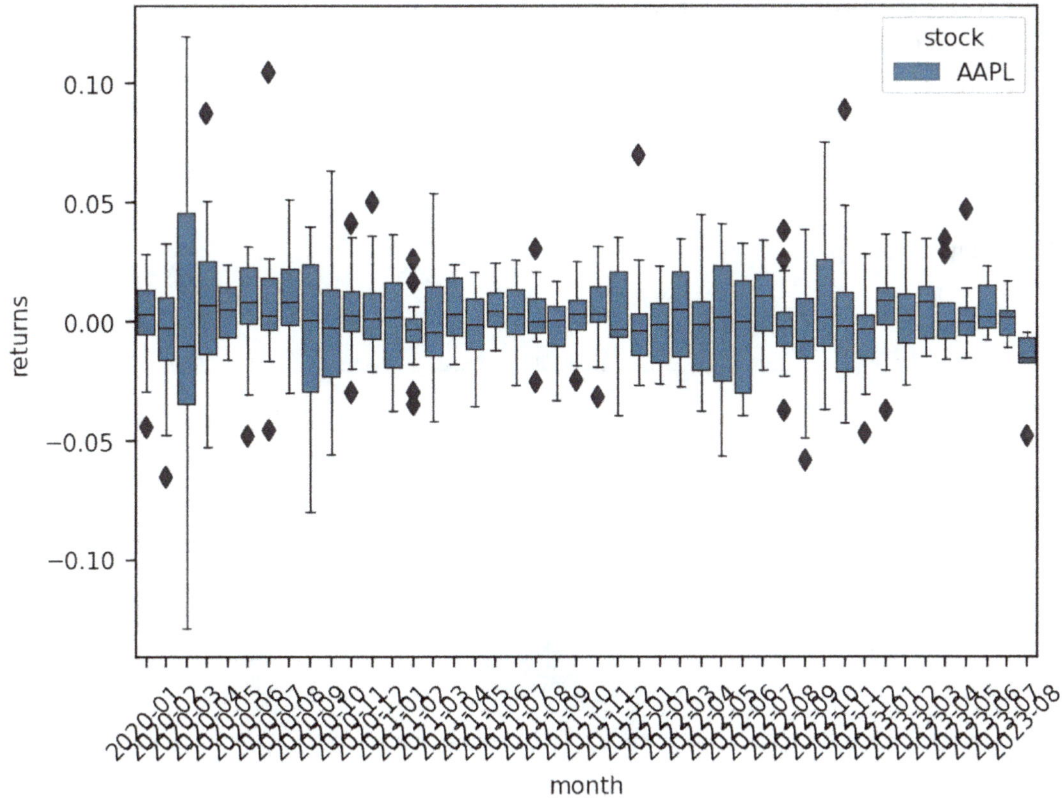

Figure 4.10: Box plot showing monthly summary statistics for AAPL returns

How it works...

The code computes daily percentage changes in AAPL's closing prices and removes any `nan` values. This Series of returns is then transformed into a DataFrame with two columns: the date and the respective return for that date. Using `melt`, the DataFrame is reshaped to be compatible with Seaborn's `boxplot` function. It also extracts the month from each date and adds it as a new column. Lastly, the `boxplot` method creates a box plot with months on the x-axis and returns on the y-axis. The x-axis labels (months) are set with a 45-degree rotation to help with readability. The final visualization shows the distribution of AAPL's daily returns for each month in the data.

There's more...

Another popular chart type is the `jointplot`, which is a combination of a scatter plot and histograms for each variable along the margins. Traders use joint plots to visually assess the correlation between assets, aiding in diversification, pairs trading, and risk management. The plots help in identifying linear relationships, distribution patterns, and potential outliers. Here is a sample code:

```
g = sns.jointplot(
    x="SPY", y="AAPL", data=returns, kind="reg", truncate=False,
)
```

The result is a joint plot.

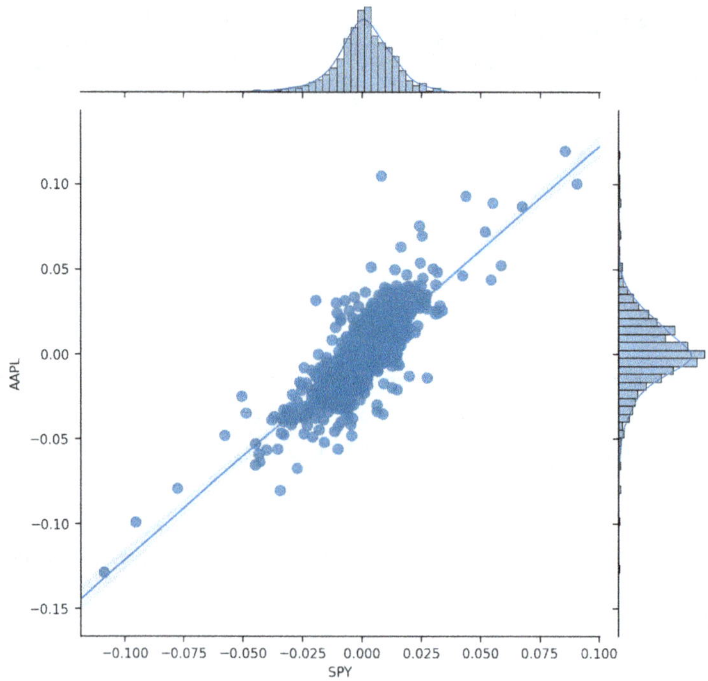

Figure 4.11: Joint plot demonstrating a positive linear relationship between AAPL and SPY returns

Tip

Note the `reg` argument passed to the kind parameter. This indicates the type of plot to draw. The value "reg" stands for regression, meaning Seaborn will not only plot the scatter points of SPY vs. AAPL returns but also compute and display a linear regression fit to the data.

Traders use correlation matrices to understand the linear relationships between multiple assets simultaneously. Let's build a correlation matrix for the stocks in the Dow Jones Industrial Average.

The first step is to grab the list of companies and their ticker symbols from the DJIA Wikipedia page:

```
dji = pd.read_html(
    "https://en.wikipedia.org/wiki/Dow_Jones_Industrial_Average",
    storage_options={"User-Agent": "Mozilla/5.0"}
)[1]
```

The read_html method is a convenient function in pandas that extracts tables from a given webpage. We're interested in the third table (indexed as [2]), which has details about the companies in the Dow Jones Industrial Average.

Now that we have the ticker symbols, let's use them to get the historical stock price data and calculate the daily returns:

```
dji_data = (
    obb.equity.price.historical(
        dji.Symbol, start_date="2020-01-01", provider="yfinance"
    )
).pivot(columns="symbol", values="close")
dji_returns = dji_data.pct_change(fill_method=None).dropna()
```

To understand the relationship between different stocks, we compute the pairwise correlation between all of them using the pandas corr method:

```
corr = dji_returns.corr()
```

Before visualizing the correlation, we'll make some tweaks to make our heatmap more intuitive. First, we'll create a mask to hide the upper triangle of the correlation matrix, as it mirrors the lower triangle:

```
mask = np.triu(
    np.ones_like(corr, dtype=bool)
)
```

Next, we'll generate a color palette that will help visually distinguish positive from negative correlations in our heatmap:

```
cmap = sns.diverging_palette(230, 20, as_cmap=True)
```

Set the font size to 4 points to include more of the labels and plot the heatmap:

```
plt.rcParams["font.size"] = 4
sns.heatmap(
    corr, mask=mask, cmap=cmap,
    vmin=-1.0, vmax=1.0,
    center=0, square=True, linewidths=0.5,
)
```

The result is a correlation heatmap:

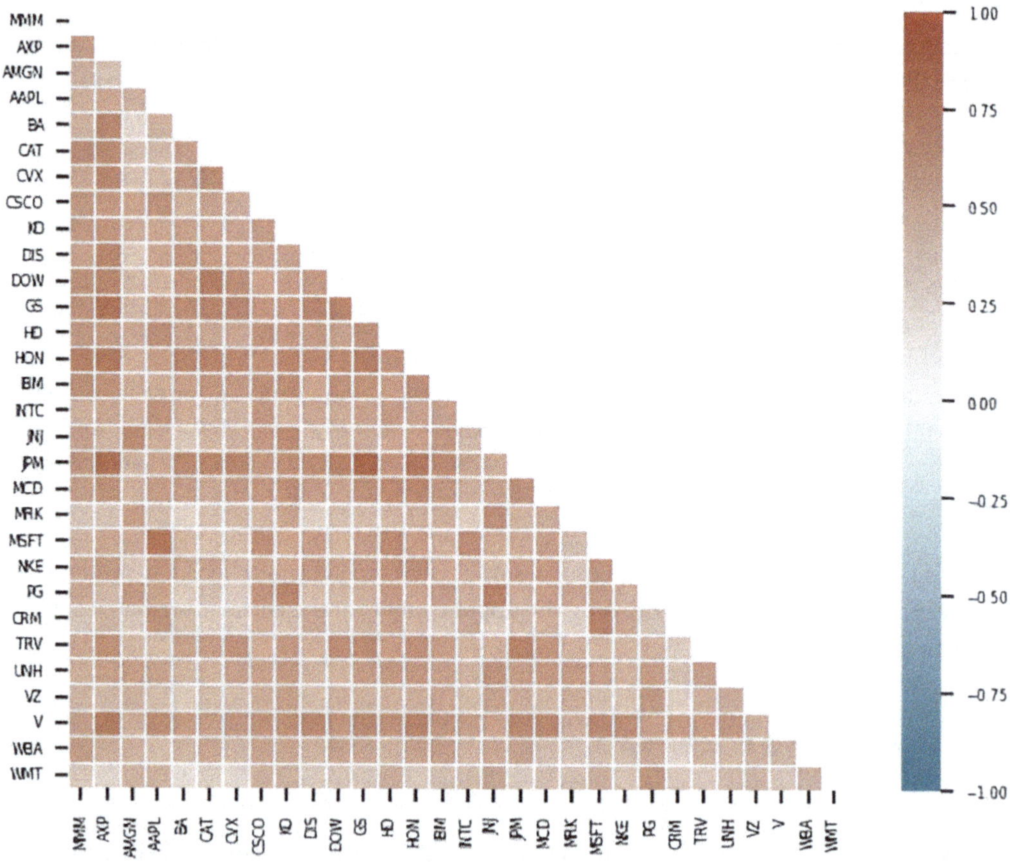

Figure 4.12: Heatmap shaded with the correlations between the constituents of the Dow Jones Industrial Average

See also

Seaborn is a popular charting library with many unit types. Read more here:

- Documentation for the Seaborn boxplot: `https://seaborn.pydata.org/generated/seaborn.boxplot.html`
- Documentation for the Seaborn joint plot: `https://seaborn.pydata.org/generated/seaborn.jointplot.html`
- Documentation for the Seaborn heatmap: `https://seaborn.pydata.org/generated/seaborn.heatmap.html`

Creating an interactive PCA analytics dashboard with Plotly Dash

Principal component analysis is used widely in data science. It's a way to reduce the number of dimensions in a data set. In a stock portfolio, a dimension might be a column of returns for one of the stocks. In a portfolio of 100 stocks, there are 100 dimensions. PCA converts those 100 dimensions into the few that explain the most variance in the data.

PCA isolates the statistical return drivers of a portfolio. These drivers are called **alpha factors** (or just **factors**) because they create returns that are not explained by a benchmark. Quants use factors in trading strategies. First, they isolate the components. Then they buy the stocks with the largest exposure to a factor and sell the stocks with the smallest exposure to a factor. We'll look at PCA in a later recipe. For now, we'll use it to create a Plotly Dash app.

Instead of changing the dates, number of components, and ticker symbols in code, we can do it in an interactive web app. In this recipe, we'll create a Plotly Dash app that accepts a list of ticker symbols, identifies the principal components of their returns, and generates plots to visualize the top factors.

Getting ready

So far, we've been writing code in Jupyter Notebook. For this recipe, you'll create a Python script called `app.py` and run it from the command line. Our aim is to highlight some of the intriguing features of Plotly Dash, even if they aren't essential for a basic app for conducting principal component analysis on stock returns.

You'll need to install a few new libraries. Make sure your virtual environment is active and run the following command:

```
pip install dash plotly dash-bootstrap-components scikit-learn
```

Plotly and scikit-learn may already be installed through the OpenBB Platform installation.

How to do it...

Here are the steps to try this recipe (all the code below should be written in the `app.py` script file):

1. Begin by importing all necessary libraries to create the web application:

```
import datetime
import numpy as np
import pandas as pd
import dash
from dash import dcc, html
import dash_bootstrap_components as dbc
from dash.dependencies import Input, Output
import plotly.graph_objs as go
import plotly.io as pio
from sklearn.decomposition import PCA
from openbb import obb
obb.user.preferences.output_type = "dataframe"
```

2. Set the default styling, templates, and initialize the app:

```
pio.templates.default = "plotly"
app = dash.Dash(__name__, external_stylesheets=[dbc.themes.BOOTSTRAP])
```

3. Construct the components of the user interface starting with the text field to enter the list of ticker symbols, the dropdown to select the number of components, the date picker to select the range of data, and the submit button to run the app:

```
ticker_field = [
    html.Label("Enter Ticker Symbols:"),
    dcc.Input(
        id="ticker-input",
        type="text",
        placeholder="Enter Tickers separated by commas(e.g. AAPL,MSFT)",
        style={"width": "50%"}
    ),
]
components_field = [
    html.Label("Select Number of Components:"),
```

```
        dcc.Dropdown(
            id="component-dropdown",
            options=[{"label": i,"value": i} for i in range(1,6)],
            value=3,
            style={"width": "50%"}
        ),
    ]
    date_picker_field = [
        html.Label("Select Date Range:"),  # Label for date picker
        dcc.DatePickerRange(
            id="date-picker",
            start_date=datetime.datetime.now() - datetime.timedelta(365 * 3),
            end_date=datetime.datetime.now(),
            # Default to today's date
            display_format="YYYY-MM-DD",
        ),
    ]
    submit = [
        html.Button("Submit", id="submit-button"),
    ]
```

4. Combine the form elements and placeholders for visualizations to form the app layout:

```
    app.layout = dbc.Container(
        [
            html.H1("PCA on Stock Returns"),
            dbc.Row([dbc.Col(ticker_field)]),
            dbc.Row([dbc.Col(components_field)]),
            dbc.Row([dbc.Col(date_picker_field)]),
            dbc.Row([dbc.Col(submit)]),
            dbc.Row(
                [
                    dbc.Col([dcc.Graph(id="bar-chart")], width=4),
                    dbc.Col([dcc.Graph(id="line-chart")], width=4),
                    dbc.Col([dcc.Graph(id="scatter-plot")], width=4),
                ]
            ),
        ]
    )
```

5. Implement the function that updates the charts upon user input:

Note

Important

All the code between steps 5 and 13 belongs to the same function. Make sure you properly indent the code after the definition.

```
@app.callback(
    [
        Output("bar-chart", "figure"),
        Output("line-chart", "figure"),
        Output("scatter-plot", "figure"),
    ],
    [Input("submit-button", "n_clicks")],
    [
        dash.dependencies.State("ticker-input", "value"),
        dash.dependencies.State("component-dropdown", "value"),
        dash.dependencies.State("date-picker", "start_date"),
        dash.dependencies.State("date-picker", "end_date"),
    ],
)
def update_graphs(n_clicks, tickers, n_components, start_date, end_date):
    if not tickers:
        return {}, {}, {}
```

6. Parse inputs from the user:

```
    tickers = tickers.split(",")
    start_date = datetime.datetime.strptime(
        start_date, "%Y-%m-%dT%H:%M:%S.%f").date()
    end_date = datetime.datetime.strptime(
        end_date, "%Y-%m-%dT%H:%M:%S.%f").date()
```

7. Download stock data:

```
    data = obb.equity.price.historical(
        tickers,
        start_date=start_date,
        end_date=end_date,
        provider="yfinance"
```

```
).pivot(columns="symbol", values="close")
daily_returns = data.pct_change().dropna()
```

8. Fit the principal component model:

```
pca = PCA(n_components=n_components)
pca.fit(daily_returns)
explained_var_ratio = pca.explained_variance_ratio_
```

9. Generate the bar chart for individual explained variance:

```
bar_chart = go.Figure(
    data=[
        go.Bar(
            x=["PC" + str(i + 1) for i in range(
                n_components)],
            y=explained_var_ratio,
        )
    ],
    layout=go.Layout(
        title="Explained Variance by Component",
        xaxis=dict(title="Principal Component"),
        yaxis=dict(title="Explained Variance"),
    ),
)
```

10. Generate the line chart for cumulative explained variance:

```
cumulative_var_ratio = np.cumsum(explained_var_ratio)
line_chart = go.Figure(
    data=[
        go.Scatter(
            x=["PC" + str(i + 1) for i in range(
                n_components)],
            y=cumulative_var_ratio,
            mode="lines+markers",
        )
    ],
    layout=go.Layout(
        title="Cumulative Explained Variance",
        xaxis=dict(title="Principal Component"),
```

```
            yaxis=dict(title="Cumulative Explained Variance"),
        ),
    )
```

11. Compute factor exposures:

```
    X = np.asarray(daily_returns)
    factor_returns = pd.DataFrame(
        columns=["f" + str(i + 1) for i in range(
            n_components)],
        index=daily_returns.index,
        data=X.dot(pca.components_.T),
    )
    factor_exposures = pd.DataFrame(
        index=["f" + str(i + 1) for i in range(n_components)],
        columns=daily_returns.columns,
        data=pca.components_,
    ).T
    labels = factor_exposures.index
    data = factor_exposures.values
```

12. Generate the chart for factor exposures:

```
    scatter_plot = go.Figure(
        data=[
            go.Scatter(
                x=factor_exposures["f1"],
                y=factor_exposures["f2"],
                mode="markers+text",
                text=labels,
                textposition="top center",
            )
        ],
        layout=go.Layout(
            title="Scatter Plot of First Two Factors",
            xaxis=dict(title="Factor 1"),
            yaxis=dict(title="Factor 2"),
        ),
    )
```

13. Return the charts to the app:

```
    return bar_chart, line_chart, scatter_plot
```

14. To run the app, open the terminal, navigate to the directory where the app.py script is located, and run the following command:

```
python app.py
```

15. Running the code starts the app and prints the URL where it is running. Navigate to the URL, enter a list of tickers and press submit. The result will look something like this:

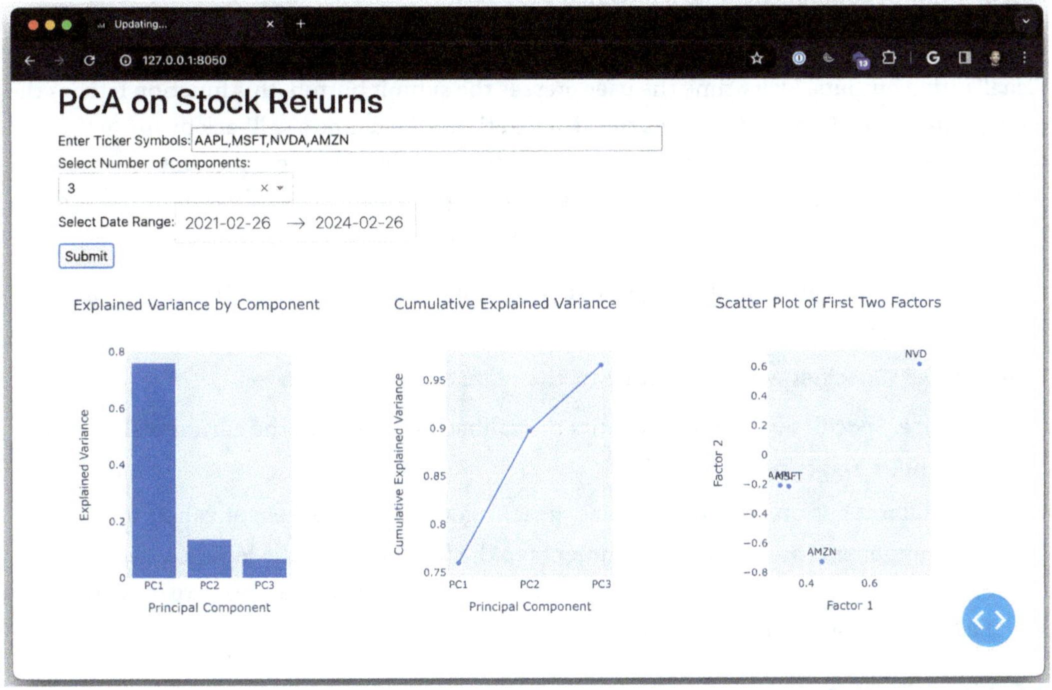

Figure 4.13: Screenshot of our new PCA analytics app

How it works...

Callbacks in Plotly Dash define the logic that connects the components in the application. These callbacks are what enable user interactions. A callback refers to a Python function that gets automatically executed by Dash whenever an input component's property changes. In our app, the callback is defined as `update_graphs`.

First, we import the necessary libraries we need for the analysis and web app. We import datetime for handling dates, NumPy for numerical operations, and pandas for data manipulation. Dash, its extensions, and other related packages provide the backbone for our web application. Specifically, `dash_bootstrap_components` assists in styling, and OpenBB fetches the stock data. Lastly, PCA from sklearn will help us perform the principal component analysis.

We then select a default template for chart styling and initialize our Dash app with a Bootstrap theme. Next, we construct the components the user will interact with, like a text field for entering ticker symbols, a dropdown to choose the number of principal components, a date picker for specifying the data range, and a submit button to start the analysis. Next, we organize our UI components into a layout.

Next, we implement the callback function, `update_graphs`, which ties our user inputs to the visualization outputs. Every time the user presses the submit button, this function fetches the data, performs the PCA, and updates the visualizations. We define a callback by using the callback decorator provided by Dash. This decorator specifies which component properties to watch (Input) and which to update (Output). In our app, clicking the submit button triggers the `callback` function. The decorator takes three inputs:

- `Output`: Specifies which components will be updated once the callback function is executed
- `Input`: Specifies which components the callback should listen to
- `State`: Specifies which components the callback should read the current value from without triggering the function

When the submit button is clicked, `update_graphs` gets called, the current values of the specified components are passed as arguments to the function, and the logic inside `update_graphs` executes. The function returns the visualizations, and these are rendered in the specified `Output` components in the app.

There's more...

Plotting with different Python libraries has distinct advantages depending on the context. pandas, while inherently great for data manipulation, offers basic plotting capabilities that are mainly suited for quick and simple visualizations directly from DataFrames. Matplotlib, one of the most widely used plotting libraries for Python, provides a greater degree of flexibility and customization but generally lacks interactive features. Seaborn, which is built on top of Matplotlib, enhances visual aesthetics and has functions tailored for statistical visualizations, making it more intuitive for certain analyses. Plotly Express, on the other hand, is a more modern library designed for interactivity from the ground up, making it well-suited for dynamic environments like Plotly Dash apps.

See also

PCA is common in all data sciences and is especially useful in algorithmic trading. Read more about the technical details of PCA at Wikipedia.

- Description of PCA: `https://en.wikipedia.org/wiki/Principal_component_analysis`
- Plotly Dash user guide: `https://dash.plotly.com`

Join our community on Discord

Join our community's Discord space for discussions with the authors and other readers: `https://discord.gg/G4YmB6DQvf`

5

Build a Quantamental Research Database with Hedge Fund Tools

Modern quantitative research breaks down when datasets grow too large, too slow, or too biased to trust. In this chapter, you'll learn how to use ArcticDB, a high-performance DataFrame database developed by Man Group, to build a professional-grade research data layer that scales to millions of rows while preserving point-in-time correctness. Man Group is one of the world's largest publicly listed systematic hedge fund managers, and ArcticDB reflects decades of institutional experience operating data-intensive trading strategies where performance, reproducibility, and data integrity are critical. Originally built as an internal system to replace fragile flat files and ad hoc databases, ArcticDB is designed specifically for financial time series and point-in-time analytics, making it a foundational tool for serious quantitative research. If you're newer to Python or databases, this chapter rewards careful reading. Each section targets a specific problem you'll hit in real research—slow queries, corrupted data, lookahead bias—so the effort pays off the moment you start building strategies. Treat the code here as scaffolding you'll reuse for years, not a one-time exercise.

Building on earlier chapters that focused on data acquisition, transformation, and performance, this chapter shows how professional systematic firms store, query, and analyze data at scale. These skills form the foundation for robust factor research, backtesting, and live trading systems in later chapters.

In this chapter, we present the following recipes:

- Creating bias-free historical datasets with versioned data and time travel
- Computing rolling metrics against millions of rows of historical price data
- Building a Warren Buffett value stock screener with historical fundamental data
- Building an options data analytics query tool with millions of rows of options data

Technical requirements

To install ArcticDB, use the `pip` package manager:

```
pip install arcticdb
```

Creating bias-free historical datasets with versioned data and time travel

ArcticDB's time travel and versioning features solve a core problem in quantitative research: the same analysis should produce the same dataset, even after you correct bad prices or ingest late-arriving data. Instead of overwriting files and losing provenance, ArcticDB stores each change as a new, immutable version, so you can reproduce results exactly as they existed "as of" a point in time. ArcticDB is particularly effective when working with very wide, highly sparse DataFrames, which are common in financial research when prices are pivoted by symbol or factor. In practice, systematic trading firms routinely work with DataFrames containing tens of thousands of columns, where over 99% of values may be missing on any given date, and ArcticDB is designed to store and query these efficiently without material performance degradation. When this sparse, column-oriented storage model is combined with ArcticDB's low-latency reads and writes, it becomes a powerful tool for algorithmic traders who need both speed and strict point-in-time correctness.

Getting ready

We assume you have access to the `historical-prices-clean.parquet` file that we created in *Chapter 3, Accelerate Financial Market Data Analysis with Polars and DuckDB*, in the `prices/` directory.

How to do it...

We'll load historical prices from a Parquet file, pivot the data into a wide, sparse DataFrame with one column per symbol, and store it in ArcticDB. Here are the steps for it:

1. Import the libraries required for the recipe:

```
from pathlib import Path
import pandas as pd
import polars as pl
import arcticdb as adb
import numpy as np
import datetime as dt
```

2. Read the Parquet file using Polars:

```
parquet_path = Path("prices") / "historical-prices-clean.parquet"
lf = pl.scan_parquet(parquet_path)
df = (
    lf.with_columns(
        pl.col("date").cast(pl.Datetime)
    )
    .collect()
)
```

3. Pivot the data so that each symbol becomes a column and closing prices form a wide, sparse DataFrame. Even using a high-performance library like Polars, this will take a few minutes:

```
wide_df = (
    df
    .pivot(values="close", index="date", on="symbol")
    .sort("date")
)

pdf = (
    wide_df
    .to_pandas(use_pyarrow_extension_array=False)
    .set_index("date")
    .sort_index()
)
```

4. Create an ArcticDB library and write the initial dataset with metadata. Note this operation will consume 10GB+ of storage space on your computer:

```
arctic = adb.Arctic("lmdb://equities")
lib = arctic.get_library("prices", create_if_missing=True)
adb_symbol = "close"

item = lib.write(
    adb_symbol,
    pdf,
    metadata={
        "ingested_at": "2025-12-10",
        "source": "prices/historical-prices-clean.parquet",
```

```
            "structure": "wide_sparse_by_symbol",
            "notes": "Initial pivoted close price dataset",
        },
    )
    snapshot_v1_version = item.version
    print(snapshot_v1_version)
    print(item)
```

5. The result is the version number and metadata of the ArcticDB item, including the custom metadata we added in the previous step:

```
Version: 3
VersionedItem(symbol='close', library='prices', data=n/a, version=3, metadata={'ingested_at': '2025-12-10', 'sourc
e': 'prices/historical-prices-clean.parquet', 'structure': 'wide_sparse_by_symbol', 'notes': 'Initial pivoted clos
e price dataset'}, host='LMDB(path=/Users/jason/Work/book/2nd Edition/Algorithmic-Trading-with-Python-Cookbook-2e/
05. Build a Quantamental Research Database with ArcticDB/equities)', timestamp=1766148749003215000)
```

Figure 5.1: Version number and details of the ArcticDB item

6. Read the data that was written:

```
snapshot_v1 = lib.tail(adb_symbol).data
print(snapshot_v1)
```

The result is a pandas DataFrame with 23,337 columns of closing prices.

```
                 A     AA    AAA   AAAC      AABB  AAC   AACB    AACG  AACI  \
date                                                                          
2025-12-08  142.44  44.46  24.97    NaN  0.013250  NaN  10.34  1.0000   NaN   
2025-12-09  140.64  43.47  25.02    NaN  0.012800  NaN  10.34  0.9510   NaN   
2025-12-10  143.47  44.64  25.01    NaN  0.013000  NaN  10.32  0.9000   NaN   
2025-12-11  142.87  47.24  25.05  20.02  0.012395  NaN  10.32  0.9790   NaN   
2025-12-12  139.68  46.14  25.03  20.02  0.013200  NaN  10.30  0.9419   NaN   

              AACS  ...  ZXZZT  ZY  ZYBT   ZYME  ZYN  ZYNE  ZYT.L    ZYXI  \
date                ...                                                     
2025-12-08  0.0001  ...  12.15 NaN  2.15  26.41  NaN   NaN    NaN  0.8099   
2025-12-09  0.0001  ...  12.15 NaN  2.12  25.81  NaN   NaN    NaN  0.8501   
2025-12-10  0.0001  ...  18.01 NaN  2.02  25.87  NaN   NaN    NaN  0.8723   
2025-12-11     NaN  ...    NaN NaN  2.03  24.94  NaN   NaN    NaN  0.8625   
2025-12-12     NaN  ...  17.98 NaN  2.01  25.48  NaN   NaN    NaN  0.7400   

            ZZLL  ZZZ  
date                   
2025-12-08   NaN  NaN  
2025-12-09   NaN  NaN  
2025-12-10   NaN  NaN  
2025-12-11   NaN  NaN  
2025-12-12   NaN  NaN  

[5 rows x 23337 columns]
```

Figure 5.2: A pandas DataFrame with 23,337 columns of closing prices

7. Synthesize new closing prices across all the symbols:

```
symbols = snapshot_v1.columns
random_data = np.random.rand(3, len(symbols)) * 100
df_append = pd.DataFrame(random_data, columns=symbols)
df_append.index = pd.DatetimeIndex(
    pd.date_range(dt.datetime(2025, 12, 13), periods=3, freq="D"),
    dtype="datetime64[ns]",
    name="date"
)
```

8. Append the new data to the item that was already written:

```
lib.append(adb_symbol, df_append)
```

The result is the details of the appended item. Note that the `version` is incremented.

```
VersionedItem(symbol='close', library='prices', data=n/a, version=1, metadata=None, host='LMDB(path=/Users/jason/W
ork/book/2nd Edition/Algorithmic-Trading-with-Python-Cookbook-2e/05. Build a Quantamental Research Database with A
rcticDB/equities)', timestamp=1766147848665145000)
```

Figure 5.3: Details of the appended item with the `version` incremented

9. Review the appended data:

```
lib.tail(adb_symbol).data
```

The result is a pandas DataFrame with three additional rows of synthesized data appended in the last step:

date	A	AA	AAA	AAAC	AABB	AAC	AACB	AACG	AACI	AACS	...
2025-12-11	142.870000	47.240000	25.050000	20.020000	0.012395	NaN	10.320000	0.979000	NaN	NaN	...
2025-12-12	139.680000	46.140000	25.030000	20.020000	0.013200	NaN	10.300000	0.941900	NaN	NaN	...
2025-12-13	23.131501	22.146034	82.544556	89.942670	80.690183	17.592798	15.869025	33.005602	85.470776	56.372190	...
2025-12-14	2.918685	63.732119	68.298154	62.651552	44.471155	67.254594	54.560267	5.919311	51.507123	32.387770	...
2025-12-15	2.233899	82.607946	99.649054	66.251311	24.936344	98.028183	1.548889	49.256031	50.863364	41.898536	...

5 rows × 23337 columns

Figure 5.4: A pandas DataFrame with three additional rows of synthesized data appended in the last step

10. Time-travel to retrieve the dataset as it existed in a prior version:

```
item = lib.tail(adb_symbol, as_of=snapshot_v1_version)
print(f"Version: {item.version}")
print(item.data)
```

11. The result is the prior version of the item before the append was made. Note the appended rows do not appear since it is the prior version:

```
Version: 0
                 A     AA    AAA   AAAC      AABB  AAC   AACB    AACG  AACI  \
date
2025-12-08  142.44  44.46  24.97    NaN  0.013250  NaN  10.34  1.0000   NaN
2025-12-09  140.64  43.47  25.02    NaN  0.012800  NaN  10.34  0.9510   NaN
2025-12-10  143.47  44.64  25.01    NaN  0.013000  NaN  10.32  0.9000   NaN
2025-12-11  142.87  47.24  25.05  20.02  0.012395  NaN  10.32  0.9790   NaN
2025-12-12  139.68  46.14  25.03  20.02  0.013200  NaN  10.30  0.9419   NaN

              AACS  ...  ZXZZT  ZY  ZYBT   ZYME  ZYN  ZYNE  ZYT.L    ZYXI  \
date                ...
2025-12-08  0.0001  ...  12.15 NaN  2.15  26.41  NaN   NaN    NaN  0.8099
2025-12-09  0.0001  ...  12.15 NaN  2.12  25.81  NaN   NaN    NaN  0.8501
2025-12-10  0.0001  ...  18.01 NaN  2.02  25.87  NaN   NaN    NaN  0.8723
2025-12-11     NaN  ...    NaN NaN  2.03  24.94  NaN   NaN    NaN  0.8625
2025-12-12     NaN  ...  17.98 NaN  2.01  25.48  NaN   NaN    NaN  0.7400

            ZZLL  ZZZ
date
2025-12-08   NaN  NaN
2025-12-09   NaN  NaN
2025-12-10   NaN  NaN
2025-12-11   NaN  NaN
2025-12-12   NaN  NaN

[5 rows x 23337 columns]
```

Figure 5.5: The prior version of the item before the append was made

12. Create a DataFrame of zeros, which we will use to overwrite the data. This is for demonstration. In practice, updates are used to revise data previously stored with updated prices:

```
symbols = snapshot_v1.columns
zeros = np.zeros((5, len(symbols)))
df_update = pd.DataFrame(zeros, columns=symbols)

df_update.index = pd.DatetimeIndex(
```

```
        pd.date_range(dt.datetime(2025, 12, 11), periods=5, freq="D"),
        dtype="datetime64[ns]",
        name="date"
    )
```

13. Update the new data to the item that has already been written:

```
lib.update(adb_symbol, df_update)
```

Review the updated data:

```
lib.tail(adb_symbol).data
```

14. The result is a pandas DataFrame with the last five rows updated to zero across all columns. Note this includes two rows from the original data and three rows of data we appended in the previous step.

	A	AA	AAA	AAAC	AABB	AAC	AACB	AACG	AACI	AACS	...	ZXZZT	ZY	ZYBT	ZYME	ZYN	ZYNE	ZYT.L	ZYXI
date																			
2025-12-11	0.0	0.0	0.0	0.0	0.0	0.0	0.0	0.0	0.0	0.0	...	0.0	0.0	0.0	0.0	0.0	0.0	0.0	0.0
2025-12-12	0.0	0.0	0.0	0.0	0.0	0.0	0.0	0.0	0.0	0.0	...	0.0	0.0	0.0	0.0	0.0	0.0	0.0	0.0
2025-12-13	0.0	0.0	0.0	0.0	0.0	0.0	0.0	0.0	0.0	0.0	...	0.0	0.0	0.0	0.0	0.0	0.0	0.0	0.0
2025-12-14	0.0	0.0	0.0	0.0	0.0	0.0	0.0	0.0	0.0	0.0	...	0.0	0.0	0.0	0.0	0.0	0.0	0.0	0.0
2025-12-15	0.0	0.0	0.0	0.0	0.0	0.0	0.0	0.0	0.0	0.0	...	0.0	0.0	0.0	0.0	0.0	0.0	0.0	0.0

5 rows × 23337 columns

Figure 5.6: A pandas DataFrame with the last five rows updated to zero across all columns

15. Time-travel to retrieve the dataset as it existed in a prior version:

```
item = lib.tail(adb_symbol, as_of=snapshot_v1_version)
print(item.version)
print(item.data)
```

The result is the prior version of the item before the update was made. Note the updated rows do not appear since it is the prior version.

```
Version: 0
                 A     AA    AAA   AAAC      AABB  AAC   AACB    AACG  AACI  \
date
2025-12-08  142.44  44.46  24.97    NaN  0.013250  NaN  10.34  1.0000   NaN
2025-12-09  140.64  43.47  25.02    NaN  0.012800  NaN  10.34  0.9510   NaN
2025-12-10  143.47  44.64  25.01    NaN  0.013000  NaN  10.32  0.9000   NaN
2025-12-11  142.87  47.24  25.05  20.02  0.012395  NaN  10.32  0.9790   NaN
2025-12-12  139.68  46.14  25.03  20.02  0.013200  NaN  10.30  0.9419   NaN

              AACS  ...  ZXZZT  ZY  ZYBT   ZYME  ZYN  ZYNE  ZYT.L    ZYXI  \
date                ...
2025-12-08  0.0001  ...  12.15 NaN  2.15  26.41  NaN   NaN    NaN  0.8099
2025-12-09  0.0001  ...  12.15 NaN  2.12  25.81  NaN   NaN    NaN  0.8501
2025-12-10  0.0001  ...  18.01 NaN  2.02  25.87  NaN   NaN    NaN  0.8723
2025-12-11     NaN  ...    NaN NaN  2.03  24.94  NaN   NaN    NaN  0.8625
2025-12-12     NaN  ...  17.98 NaN  2.01  25.48  NaN   NaN    NaN  0.7400

            ZZLL  ZZZ
date
2025-12-08   NaN  NaN
2025-12-09   NaN  NaN
2025-12-10   NaN  NaN
2025-12-11   NaN  NaN
2025-12-12   NaN  NaN

[5 rows x 23337 columns]
```

Figure 5.7: The prior version of the item before the append was made

How it works...

This recipe begins by loading historical prices from a Parquet file and pivoting them into a wide, sparse DataFrame with one column per symbol and dates on the index. Even with Polars, this pivot is expensive when the universe spans tens of thousands of symbols, because it materializes a matrix where most values are missing. This structure is intentional, as it matches how price data is consumed in factor research and backtesting.

When the pivoted DataFrame is written to ArcticDB, it becomes a versioned symbol. The initial write creates the first immutable version and returns an item containing the version number and metadata. ArcticDB efficiently stores this dataset—here with more than 23,000 columns—by segmenting and compressing columns internally rather than rewriting the entire DataFrame on each change. Reading the data back with `tail` reconstructs the latest version as a pandas DataFrame.

Appending new rows shows how ArcticDB handles incremental data ingestion. The append operation adds only the new dates, creates a new version, and preserves all prior versions. This pattern mirrors daily market data ingestion and avoids costly full rewrites. Using time travel with `as_of` allows you to retrieve the dataset exactly as it existed before the append, ensuring historical analyses remain free from lookahead bias.

Finally, the `update` operation demonstrates how ArcticDB applies corrections to existing data. Unlike append, updates replace values for overlapping dates and columns, producing another version while leaving earlier versions untouched. Time travel confirms that both the pre-append and pre-update datasets remain accessible, providing a complete and auditable history of changes.

There's more...

You can combine time travel with lightweight querying to extract subsets of wide datasets efficiently. For example, you can read only a handful of symbols from a DataFrame with thousands of columns:

```
subset = lib.read(
    adb_symbol,
    columns=["AAPL", "MSFT", "AMZN"]
).data
```

Metadata also becomes increasingly valuable as your research pipeline grows. By storing ingestion dates, sources, and change notes, you create a durable audit trail that links every backtest or research result to an exact data version:

```
meta = lib.read_metadata(adb_symbol, as_of=1).metadata
print(meta)
```

This pattern scales cleanly to multi-asset universes, factor matrices, and signal stores, where wide, sparse DataFrames are the norm rather than the exception.

See also

The following resources provide deeper coverage of ArcticDB's versioning model, time travel semantics, and efficient storage of large, column-oriented datasets. Note that at the time of writing, version 6.5.0 is the latest stable version.

- Overview and introduction to ArcticDB: `https://docs.arcticdb.io/6.5.0/#what-is-arcticdb`
- ArcticDB versioning and time travel overview: `https://docs.arcticdb.io/6.5.0/#modifications-versioning-aka-time-travel`
- Python API reference: `https://docs.arcticdb.io/6.5.0/api/`

Compute rolling metrics on millions of rows of historic price data

Portfolio risk is never static. A stock's sensitivity to market movements shifts as economic conditions change, companies release earnings, and volatility spikes. The Capital Asset Pricing Model, developed in the 1960s, treats beta—a measure of how much an asset moves relative to the market—as a constant. Formally, $\beta = Cov(R\_i, R\_m) / Var(R\_m)$, where *R_i* is the asset's return and R_m is the market return. Practitioners quickly discovered this assumption breaks down in the real world. Market environments and company-specific events continuously reshape these relationships, making point-in-time beta calculations insufficient for active risk management.

Rolling beta addresses this limitation by calculating beta over a moving window of time. Instead of a single number, you get a time series that reveals how an asset's market sensitivity evolves. Portfolio managers use rolling beta to monitor real-time risk exposure, track shifting correlations, and trigger timely rebalancing or hedging decisions. During volatile periods, it provides quantifiable signals for reducing exposure or adjusting sector weights before drawdowns materialize.

This recipe will guide you through the process of computing rolling beta using Python. You'll download historical price data, store it efficiently using ArcticDB, calculate rolling covariances and variances, and visualize how beta changes across a portfolio of global stocks over time.

Getting ready

In this recipe, we'll use the excellent `yfinance` Python library to download historical price data. The library is a great, lightweight library that works well when working with only a few tickers. `yfinance` downloads data directly from Yahoo Finance, so any ticker symbol on Yahoo Finance works with `yfinance`.

You should have `yfinance` installed already, but if not, install it with `pip`:

```
pip install yfinance
```

How to do it...

We'll use ArcticDB to store historical price data and compute rolling betas for a portfolio of global stocks:

1. Import the necessary libraries:

```
import datetime as dt
import arcticdb as adb
import yfinance as yf
```

2. Create a connection to a local ArcticDB database:

```
arctic = adb.Arctic("lmdb://equities")
lib = arctic.get_library("portfolio", create_if_missing=True)
```

3. Define the time period, frequency, and stock universe:

```
start = dt.datetime(2013, 1, 1)
end = dt.datetime(2024, 12, 31)
freq = "1d"
symbols = {
    "^GSPC": "S&P 500",
    "AAPL": "Apple",
    "MSFT": "Microsoft",
    "GOOG": "Google",
    "AMZN": "Amazon",
    "NVDA": "Nvidia",
    "META": "Meta",
    "TSLA": "Tesla",
    "TSM": "TSMC",
    "TCEHY": "Tencent",
    "005930.KS": "Samsung",
    "ORCL": "Oracle",
    "ADBE": "Adobe",
    "ASML": "ASML",
    "CSCO": "Cisco",
}
```

4. Download historical price data for all symbols:

```
hist = yf.download(
    list(symbols.keys()),
    interval=freq,
    start=start,
    end=end,
    auto_adjust=True
)
```

5. Store each price type in the database:

```
for l in hist.columns.levels[0]:
    lib.write(l, hist[l])
```

6. Read the closing prices, forward-fill missing values, and compute daily returns:

```
hist_adj_close = lib.read("Close").data
hist_adj_close_clean = hist_adj_close.ffill()
hist_adj_close_clean.isnull().any().any()
hist_daily_returns = hist_adj_close_clean.pct_change(1).iloc[1:]
returns_sym = "hist/returns_Close_clean"
lib.write(returns_sym, hist_daily_returns)
```

7. Set the rolling window parameters and extract returns for the beta calculation period:

```
index_ticker = "^GSPC"
roll_days = 130
beta_start = dt.datetime(2018, 1, 1)
beta_end = dt.datetime(2024, 12, 31)
beta_returns = lib.read(
    returns_sym,
    date_range=(beta_start, beta_end)
).data
index_returns = beta_returns[index_ticker]
stock_returns = beta_returns.drop(columns=index_ticker)
```

8. Calculate rolling covariance, rolling variance, and rolling beta:

```
rolling_cov = (
    stock_returns
```

```
        .rolling(roll_days)
        .cov(index_returns)
        .iloc[roll_days - 1:]
)
rolling_index_var = (
    index_returns
    .rolling(roll_days)
    .var()
    .iloc[roll_days - 1:]
)
rolling_beta = (
    rolling_cov
    .divide(rolling_index_var, axis="index")
    .rename(columns=symbols)
)
```

9. Plot the rolling beta time series:

```
ax = rolling_beta.plot(
    grid=True,
    linewidth=0.5,
    title=f"Rolling {roll_days}-day beta"
)
ax.legend(loc="upper left")
```

10. Running the preceding code generates a chart showing how each stock's beta against the S&P 500 evolves over time:

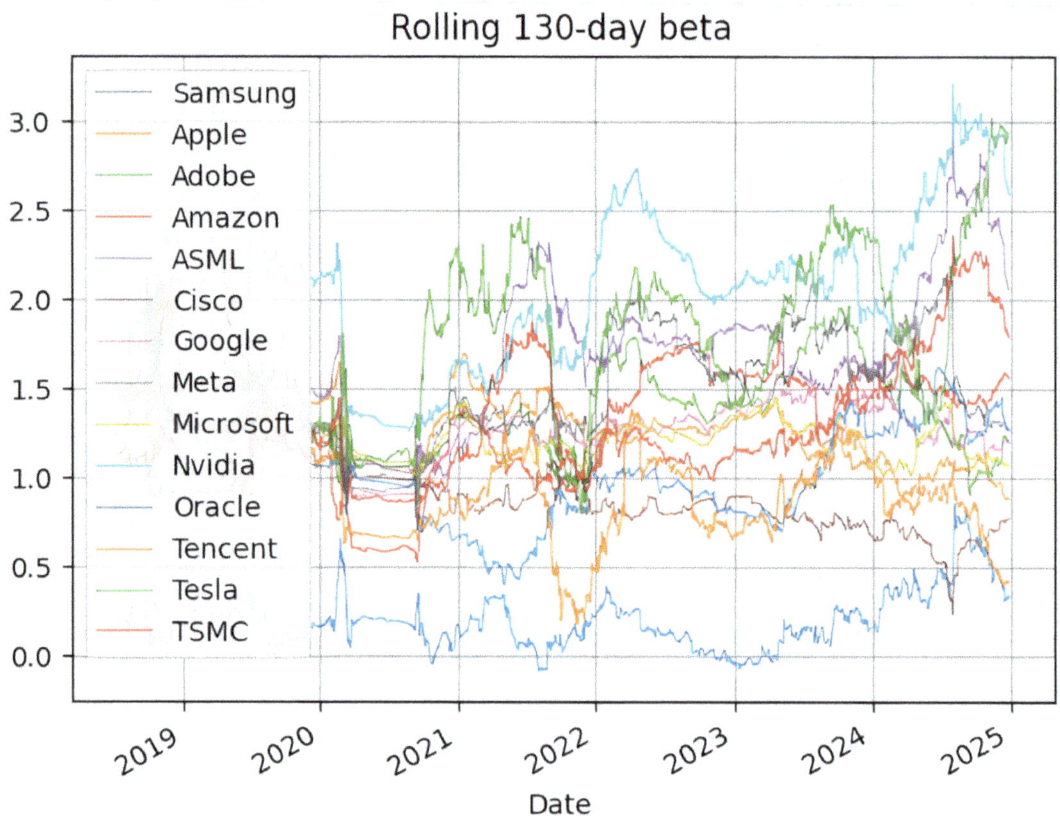

Figure 5.8: Rolling 130-day beta for global technology stocks relative to the S&P 500

How it works...

ArcticDB provides a local DataFrame database that eliminates repeated downloads between sessions. The `yf.download` function retrieves daily adjusted prices for all symbols in a single call, and forward-filling with `ffill()` handles missing values from regional market holidays.

Beta quantifies how much a stock moves relative to the broader market. The formula derives from linear regression:

```
beta = covariance(stock_returns, market_returns) / variance(market_returns)
```

The covariance term measures how the stock and market move together. When both rise or fall on the same days, covariance is positive. When they move in opposite directions, covariance is negative. The variance term in the denominator normalizes this relationship by the market's own volatility, producing a standardized sensitivity measure.

A beta of 1.0 means the stock moves in lockstep with the market. A beta of 1.5 indicates the stock tends to move 50% more than the market—if the S&P 500 rises 2%, we expect that stock to rise approximately 3%. Values below 1.0 suggest lower sensitivity, while negative betas indicate inverse correlation with market movements.

The `rolling()` method applies this calculation over a moving window of 130 trading days, roughly six months. Each day, the window shifts forward: the oldest observation drops out and the newest enters. This produces a time series of beta values rather than a single static number.

We compute `rolling_cov` by calculating the covariance between each stock's returns and the index returns within each window. The `rolling_index_var` captures the market's variance over the same periods. Dividing covariance by variance yields the rolling beta for each stock at each point in time.

The 130-day window balances responsiveness against noise. Shorter windows react quickly to regime changes but produce choppy estimates. Longer windows provide stability but lag behind genuine shifts in market relationships. Six months captures meaningful changes while smoothing out day-to-day randomness.

There's more...

You can extend this analysis by computing rolling alpha alongside rolling beta. Alpha measures the excess return a stock generates after accounting for its market exposure. Jensen's alpha uses the same regression framework, formally $\alpha = R\_i - [R\_f + \beta(R\_m - R\_f)]$, where R_f is the risk-free rate:

```
rolling_mean_stock = (
    stock_returns
    .rolling(roll_days)
    .mean()
    .iloc[roll_days - 1:]
)
rolling_mean_index = (
    index_returns
    .rolling(roll_days)
    .mean()
    .iloc[roll_days - 1:]
)
rolling_alpha = (
    rolling_mean_stock
    - rolling_beta
    .rename(columns={v: k for k, v in symbols.items()})
```

```
    .multiply(rolling_mean_index, axis="index")
)
rolling_alpha = rolling_alpha.rename(columns=symbols) * 252
```

Positive alpha indicates the stock outperformed what its beta-adjusted market exposure would predict. Negative alpha suggests underperformance relative to the risk taken.

You can also experiment with different window lengths. A 21-day window captures monthly dynamics and reacts quickly to earnings announcements or sector rotations. A 252-day window provides a full-year perspective that filters out seasonal effects. Comparing betas across multiple window lengths reveals whether a stock's market sensitivity is stable or regime-dependent. Have a look at the code here:

```
windows = [21, 63, 130, 252]
for w in windows:
    rolling_cov_w = stock_returns.rolling(w).cov(index_returns).iloc[w - 1:]
    rolling_var_w = index_returns.rolling(w).var().iloc[w - 1:]
    rolling_beta_w = rolling_cov_w.divide(rolling_var_w, axis="index")
    ax = rolling_beta_w.plot(
        grid=True,
        linewidth=0.5,
        title=f"Rolling {roll_days}-day beta"
    )
    ax.legend(loc="upper left")
```

The result is a chart of rolling betas:

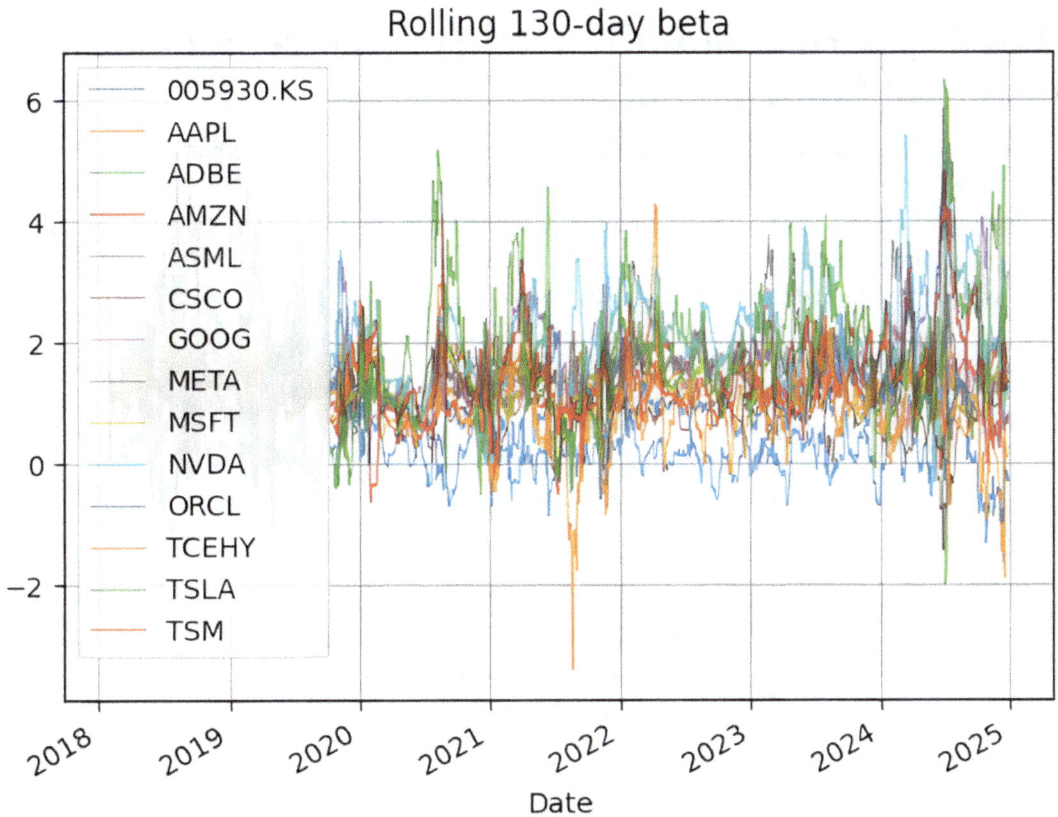

Figure 5.9: Rolling beta calculated across 21-day, 63-day, 130-day, and 252-day windows showing sensitivity to window length selection

See also

For more on rolling metrics and portfolio risk analysis, check out the following resources:

- The ArcticDB documentation for advanced storage and querying features: `https://docs.arcticdb.io/`
- Details on the Capital Asset Pricing Model and beta interpretation: `https://en.wikipedia.org/wiki/Capital_asset_pricing_model`
- The pandas documentation on rolling window calculations: `https://pandas.pydata.org/docs/reference/api/pandas.DataFrame.rolling.html`

Building a Warren Buffett value stock screener with historical fundamental data

Value investing is based on the idea that markets periodically misprice companies. This allows disciplined investors to buy strong businesses at a discount to their intrinsic value. Warren Buffett popularized this approach, combining fundamental analysis with patience and long investment horizons to achieve exceptional long-term returns. From 1965 to 2023, Berkshire Hathaway compounded capital at nearly twice the rate of the S&P 500.

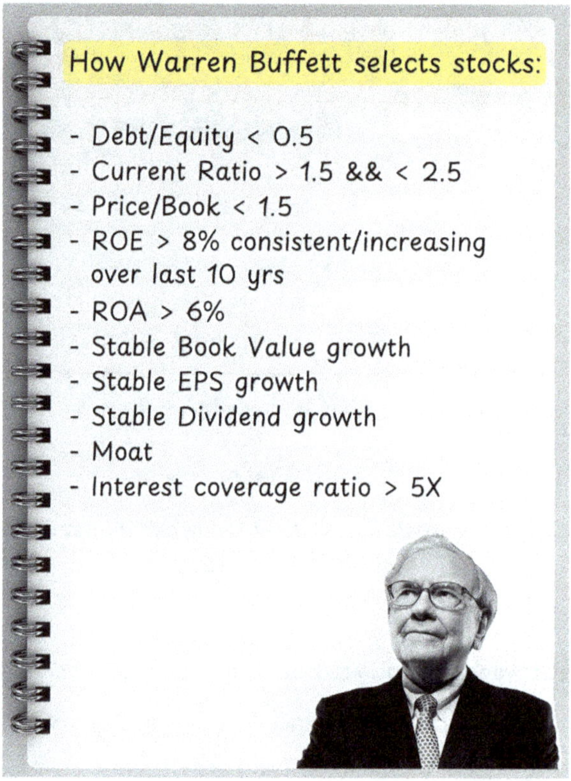

Figure 5.10: Warren Buffett's stock selection criteria

In practice, value investing relies on historical fundamental data, which are financial ratios derived from balance sheets, income statements, and cash flow statements, to identify companies that are cheap, profitable, and financially stable. For modern algorithmic traders, access to clean, point-in-time fundamental data provides an informational edge over strategies that rely solely on price and volume, because fundamentals evolve more slowly and encode structural business quality rather than short-term market noise.

This recipe shows how to use ArcticDB to store large volumes of historical fundamental data and apply database-level screening with the Query Builder, allowing you to run repeatable, bias-free value screens across market history.

How to do it...

In this recipe, we'll download bulk financial ratio data, store it in ArcticDB, and use the Query Builder to screen for value stocks using Buffett-style financial criteria. Here are the steps for it:

1. Import the libraries for the analysis:

```
import os
import requests
import pandas as pd
from io import StringIO
import arcticdb as adb
from dotenv import load_dotenv
load_dotenv()
```

2. Set the API base URL and get the API key:

```
FMP_BASE_URL = "https://financialmodelingprep.com/api"
API_KEY = os.environ.get("FMP_API_KEY")
```

3. Set the year for the download:

```
year = 2025
```

4. Construct the URL, download the bulk ratios data, and convert it into a pandas DataFrame:

```
url = f"{FMP_BASE_URL}/v4/ratios-bulk?year={year}.=annual&apikey={API_KEY}"
response = requests.get(url)
response.raise_for_status()
ratios = pd.read_csv(StringIO(response.text))
```

5. Build the ArcticDB URI and write or update the data into the ArcticDB DataFrame database:

```
arctic = adb.Arctic("lmdb://fundamentals")
lib = arctic.get_library("financial_ratios", create_if_missing=True)
adb_sym = f"financial_ratios/{year}"
```

```
adb_fcn = lib.update if lib.has_symbol(adb_sym) else lib.write
adb_fcn(adb_sym, ratios)
```

6. Use the `QueryBuilder` ArcticDB to build a simple query for stocks that meet the Warren Buffett criteria:

```
cols = [
    "symbol",
    "period",
    "date",
    "debtEquityRatio",
    "currentRatio",
    "priceToBookRatio",
    "returnOnEquity",
    "returnOnAssets",
    "interestCoverage"
]
q = adb.QueryBuilder()
filter = (
    (q["debtEquityRatio"] < 0.5)
    & ((q["currentRatio"] > 1.5) & (q["currentRatio"] < 2.5))
    & (q["priceToBookRatio"] < 1.5)
    & (q["returnOnEquity"] > 0.08)
    & (q["returnOnAssets"] > 0.06)
    & (q["interestCoverage"] > 5)
)
q = q[filter]
results = lib.read(f"financial_ratios/{year}",
query_builder=q).data[cols].set_index("symbol")
```

The result is a pandas DataFrame with the stocks that meet the criteria:

symbol	period	date	debtEquityRatio	currentRatio	priceToBookRatio	returnOnEquity	returnOnAssets	interestCoverage
000270.KS	FY	2024-12-31	0.064417	1.549352	0.708112	0.175045	0.105362	124.812926
000612.SZ	FY	2024-12-31	0.103146	1.682025	1.227622	0.094422	0.073043	28.517815
001311.SZ	FY	2024-12-31	0.008263	2.287700	1.038540	0.093175	0.071981	192.663424
002128.SZ	FY	2024-12-31	0.203229	1.660538	1.269960	0.154367	0.103451	27.655330
002154.SZ	FY	2024-12-31	0.088094	2.032302	1.469156	0.113268	0.074141	29.597882
...	...	...	...	...	...	...	...	...
WHGLY	FY	2024-12-31	0.349311	1.873833	0.930710	0.151205	0.081246	16.468531
WHGRF	FY	2024-12-31	0.349311	1.873833	0.930710	0.151205	0.081246	16.468531
WIIM.JK	FY	2024-12-31	0.221711	2.439483	0.758968	0.156011	0.098676	28.978140
WLMM3.SA	FY	2024-12-31	0.480213	2.396213	1.402010	0.167348	0.098640	10.280191
WLMM4.SA	FY	2024-12-31	0.480213	2.396213	1.402010	0.167348	0.098640	10.280191

575 rows × 8 columns

Figure 5.11: Stocks that pass the screener

How it works...

This recipe begins by retrieving bulk financial ratio data from the **Financial Modeling Prep** (**FMP**) API and converting it into a pandas DataFrame. The FMP bulk endpoint returns a large, flat dataset containing standardized financial ratios across many companies for a given reporting period, making it well suited for systematic screening. Once downloaded, the data is immediately usable for quantitative analysis without additional normalization.

The DataFrame is then written into ArcticDB, where each year's data is stored as a versioned symbol. ArcticDB's write-or-update pattern ensures that if data for a given year already exists, it can be corrected or extended without overwriting prior versions. This is especially important for fundamental data, which is frequently revised as companies restate earnings or vendors correct historical records. By persisting each revision as a new version, ArcticDB preserves a complete audit trail and enables point-in-time analysis.

Screening is performed using ArcticDB's `QueryBuilder`, which allows filtering logic to be expressed declaratively and evaluated inside the database engine. Rather than loading all financial ratios into memory and filtering them with pandas, the query builder pushes the filtering criteria—such as leverage, liquidity, valuation, and profitability thresholds—down to the storage layer. Only the rows that satisfy the Buffett-style value constraints are returned to Python, reducing memory usage and improving performance.

The result of the query is a pandas DataFrame containing only the companies that meet the defined value criteria. Because the screen operates on versioned, historical data stored in ArcticDB, it can be rerun consistently across different years or reporting periods. This makes the approach suitable not just for exploratory analysis, but for systematic value-factor research and backtesting where reproducibility and bias control are critical.

There's more...

You can extend this value screener by incorporating fundamental growth metrics, which are also available from Financial Modeling Prep. In addition to raw ratios, FMP provides tables that track the growth of key fundamentals, such as return on equity, revenue, earnings, and free cash flow, over time. These datasets allow you to move beyond static "cheapness" and evaluate whether a company's fundamentals are improving consistently, which is a hallmark of high-quality value businesses.

Using pandas or Polars, you can join historical ratio tables with their corresponding growth tables on keys such as symbol, date, and period. Once joined, the combined dataset can be written back to ArcticDB as a new, versioned symbol. From there, ArcticDB's Query Builder can be used to express more sophisticated screens, such as requiring return on equity to be positive and increasing over the last 5 or 10 years, or filtering for companies with stable balance sheets and accelerating profitability.

See also

The following resources provide additional context and tools for extending fundamental analysis workflows and value-based screening strategies:

- FMP reference for accessing financial ratios, growth metrics, and historical fundamentals: `https://site.financialmodelingprep.com/developer/docs/`
- Learn more about Warren Buffett and his investing style: `https://en.wikipedia.org/wiki/Warren_Buffett`

Building an options data analytics query tool with millions of rows of options data

In this recipe, you'll learn how to use ArcticDB to query and analyze an options dataset with 2,370,886 rows without sacrificing performance. Large options chains quickly overwhelm in-memory tools, making even simple analytics slow and unreliable as data volumes grow. You'll use ArcticDB's **query builder** functionality to express complex filters and projections declaratively, pushing computation down to the database rather than pulling entire datasets into memory. The techniques in this recipe form the foundation for scalable, exploratory derivatives research workflows used in professional quantitative trading environments.

We'll use Polars to lazy load the CSV files from the sample data download. Because ArcticDB needs a pandas DataFrame to insert data, we'll convert our Polars DataFrame before inserting it into ArcticDB. Polars reads ~100MB of options data in 350 milliseconds, whereas pandas takes 2,000 milliseconds. In both cases, inserting the data into ArcticDB takes about 75 milliseconds.

Download the sample options data we use for the recipe here: `https://pqn.kit.com/sample-options-data`

How to do it...

We'll read in the data and use it to create an ArcticDB DataFrame database.

1. Import the libraries we need for the analysis:

```
import matplotlib.pyplot as plt
import datetime as dt
import arcticdb as adb
import polars as pl
import pandas as pd
```

2. Initialize an Arctic database connection and get the `options` library:

```
arctic = adb.Arctic("lmdb://equity_options")
lib = arctic.get_library("options", create_if_missing=True)
```

3. Read all CSV files from the rut-eod directory and store their data in the Arctic database:

```
lf = (
    pl.scan_csv("rut-eod/*.csv")  # Lazy glob
    .with_columns(
        pl.col("date").str.strptime(
            pl.Date,
            "%m/%d/%Y",
            strict=True
        ).cast(pl.Datetime),
        pl.col("option_expiration").str.strptime(
            pl.Date,
            "%m/%d/%Y",
            strict=True
        ).cast(pl.Datetime),
    )
)
df = lf.collect(engine="streaming")
```

```
pdf = df.to_pandas(use_pyarrow_extension_array=False).set_index("date")

adb_sym = "options/all"
(lib.update if lib.has_symbol(adb_sym) else lib.write)(adb_sym, pdf)
```

4. Read data for the "RUT" underlying from the ArcticDB DataFrame database:

```
rut = lib.read("options/all").data
```

5. Define a function to read the volatility curve for a specific options chain:

```
def read_vol_curve(
    as_of_date, underlying, expiry, delta_low, delta_high
):
    q = adb.QueryBuilder()
    filter = (
        (q.symbol == underlying) &
        (q.option_expiration == expiry) &
        (
            (
                (q.delta >= delta_low) &
                (q.delta <= delta_high)
            ) | (
                (q.delta >= -delta_high) &
                (q.delta <= -delta_low)
            )
        )
    )
    q = (
        q[filter]
        .groupby("strike")
        .agg({"iv": "mean"})
    )

    # Read the filtered data from the Arctic database
    return lib.read(
        "options/all",
        date_range=(as_of_date, as_of_date),
        query_builder=q
    ).data
```

6. Define input parameters for querying and plotting the volatility curves:

```
as_of_date = pd.Timestamp("2006-07-28")
expiry = pd.Timestamp("2013-06-22")
underlying = "RUT"
dte = 30
delta_low = 0.05
delta_high = 0.50
```

7. Query expiration dates for the given underlying asset and date:

```
q = adb.QueryBuilder()
filter = (
    (q.symbol == underlying) &
    (q.option_expiration > as_of_date + dt.timedelta(days=dte))
)
q = q[filter].groupby("option_expiration").agg({"volume": "sum"})
expiries = (
    lib
    .read(
        "options/all",
        date_range=(as_of_date, as_of_date),
        query_builder=q
    )
    .data
    .sort_index()
    .index
)
```

8. Plot the implied volatility curves for the retrieved expiration dates:

```
_, ax = plt.subplots(1, 1)
cmap = plt.get_cmap("rainbow", len(expiries))
format_kw = {"linewidth": 0.5, "alpha": 0.85}
for i, expiry in enumerate(expiries):
    curve = read_vol_curve(
        as_of_date,
        underlying,
        expiry,
        delta_low,
        delta_high
```

```
        )
        (
            curve
            .sort_index()
            .plot(
                ax=ax,
                y="iv",
                label=expiry.strftime("%Y-%m-%d"),
                grid=True,
                color=cmap(i),
                **format_kw
            )
        )
    ax.set_ylabel("implied volatility")
    ax.legend(loc="upper right", framealpha=0.7)
```

The result is the following chart of the volatility skew across the various expirations:

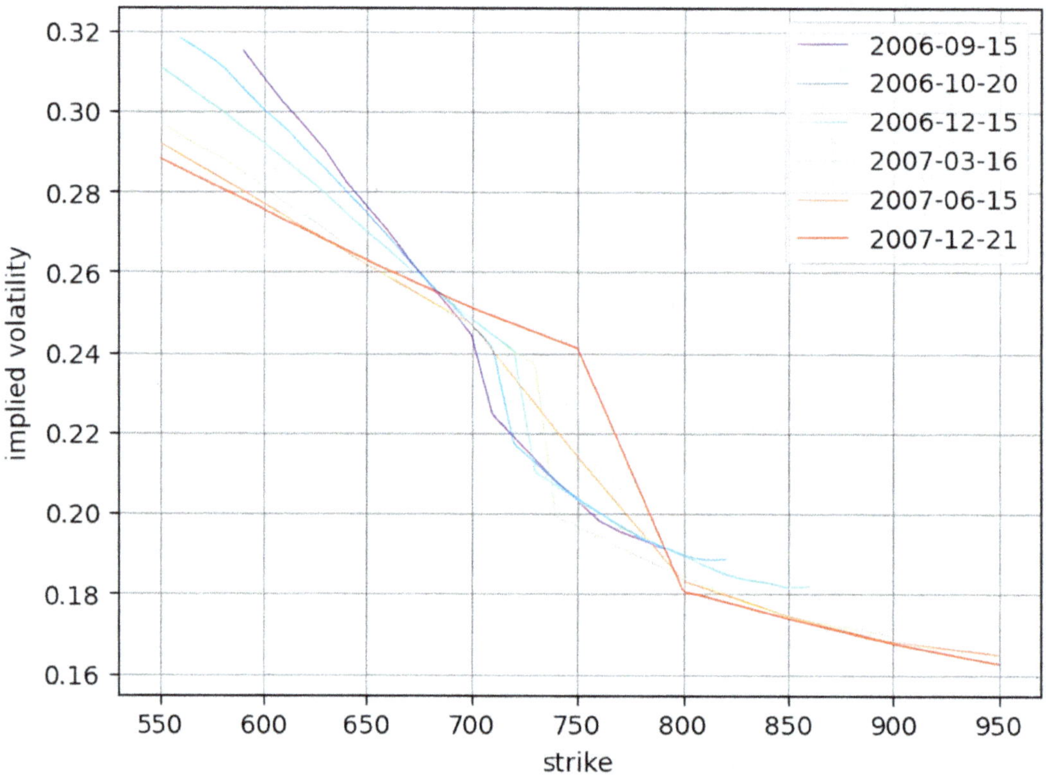

Figure 5.12: Chart of the volatility skew across expirations

How it works...

The process begins by initializing an ArcticDB instance backed by a local **LMDB** store using the `lmdb://equity_options` URI. **Lightning Memory-Mapped Database** (**LMDB**) is a fast, embedded key–value store that uses memory-mapped files, allowing ArcticDB to achieve very low-latency reads without running a separate database server. This makes LMDB well-suited for local research workflows where performance, durability, and simplicity are important.

The raw options data is ingested using Polars' lazy CSV scanning, which allows multiple files to be parsed efficiently before materializing the final DataFrame. After normalizing date columns and converting the data to pandas, the dataset is written to ArcticDB under a single symbol. ArcticDB stores the data in immutable, versioned segments, which enables fast reads, efficient updates, and fully reproducible research.

Querying is handled through ArcticDB's `QueryBuilder`, which provides a declarative interface for filtering, grouping, and aggregating data directly inside the database. The query builder constructs an execution plan that is evaluated at read time, ensuring only the minimum required data is scanned and returned. This approach avoids loading entire options chains into memory and keeps interactive analytics responsive even when working with millions of rows.

Finally, the filtered results are returned as a pandas DataFrame and plotted using Matplotlib. Because each query is scoped to a specific date, underlying, and set of option characteristics, ArcticDB efficiently reconstructs point-in-time volatility curves across multiple expirations.

There's more...

You can take this approach further by storing ArcticDB libraries remotely on **Amazon S3**, which allows you to scale storage independently of compute and share datasets across machines or teams. ArcticDB supports S3-backed storage natively, making it easy to switch from local LMDB to cloud-based object storage with minimal code changes.

For example, instead of using a local LMDB URI, you can initialize an ArcticDB instance backed by S3 as follows:

```
arctic = adb.Arctic(
    "s3://my-arcticdb-bucket",
    region="us-east-1"
)
lib = arctic.get_library("options", create_if_missing=True)
```

With this configuration, all symbols and versions are persisted directly to S3, while ArcticDB continues to provide the same query, versioning, and point-in-time guarantees. This setup is especially useful for large historical datasets, collaborative research environments, or cloud-based research notebooks where local disk space is limited.

See also

The ArcticDB documentation is rich with examples and can be found here: `https://docs.arcticdb.io/latest/`

Get this book's PDF version and more

6

Conduct Market Research with Advanced AI and Agentic Workflows

Traditional market research requires hours of manual work: reading financial statements, analyzing price patterns, comparing competitors, and synthesizing findings into actionable insights. Modern AI systems can automate much of this work, processing documents at scale and generating structured analyses that would take human analysts far longer to produce. This chapter shows you how to build AI-powered research tools that augment your trading workflow.

The recipes in this chapter progress from single-agent systems to multi-agent workflows that mirror how research teams operate. You will start by building an AI equity research analyst that answers questions about financial statements using retrieval-augmented generation. Then you will create an agent that writes and executes Python code to analyze stock price performance automatically. As the complexity increases, you will implement comparative analysis workflows that process multiple documents in parallel, multi-agent systems where specialized agents collaborate on research reports, and finally a system that converts trading strategy research papers into executable code.

These AI systems are not meant to replace human judgment in trading decisions. Instead, they accelerate the research process by handling repetitive analysis tasks, extracting key information from large documents, and generating first drafts of code and reports. You maintain control over the final output and can verify the AI's work before using it in your trading systems.

The code in this chapter uses LlamaIndex as the primary framework for building AI agents and workflows, with Claude as the language model. We introduce LangChain in the first recipe since it is commonly used in the industry, but rely on LlamaIndex for the remaining recipes because of its simpler API for agent development. LlamaIndex provides abstractions for document processing, vector storage, and agent orchestration that simplify building complex AI applications. The patterns you learn here apply broadly to any document-heavy research task in finance.

We pin all library versions because LangChain, LlamaIndex, and related packages are under active and rapid development. This recipe uses Claude Opus 4.5, but you can substitute any Anthropic model. See the full list at `https://docs.anthropic.com/en/docs/about-claude/models`. In this chapter, we will cover the following recipes:

- Building your own AI equity research analyst to analyze financial statements
- Writing Python code to analyze stock price performance automatically with AI
- Using AI agentic workflows to automate comparative analysis
- Automating equity research reports with AI
- Converting trading strategy research papers into code with LlamaIndex

Building your own AI equity research analyst to analyze financial statements

Algorithmic trading strategies often incorporate fundamental data to filter stocks or validate signals. Before deploying capital, traders need to understand a company's financial health, revenue trends, and margin stability. Traditionally, this means spending hours reading through quarterly reports, 10-K filings, and earnings transcripts. This manual process doesn't scale when you're screening dozens of potential trading candidates.

This recipe shows you how to build an AI-powered equity research analyst that automates document analysis. Using LangChain, ChromaDB, and Claude, you'll create an agent that reads PDF financial statements and answers natural language questions about them. The system uses vector embeddings to understand the semantic meaning of your questions, finding relevant information even when the exact terminology differs between your query and the document.

By the end of this recipe, you'll have a reusable tool that can quickly extract key metrics from any financial document, helping you make faster and more informed trading decisions.

Getting ready

Install the required packages with pinned versions:

```
pip install langchain==1.2.7 langchain-anthropic==1.3.1 langchain-chroma==1.1.0
langchain-community==0.4.1 langgraph==1.0.7 pypdf==6.6.2 chromadb==1.4.1 python-
dotenv==1.2.1
```

Create a `.env` file in your working directory with your Anthropic API key:

```
ANTHROPIC_API_KEY=your-api-key-here
```

You can obtain an Anthropic API key by creating an account at `https://console.anthropic.com/`. Navigate to API Keys in the dashboard and generate a new key.

Download the sample Apple financial statement PDF from the book's GitHub repository and place it in your working directory as `apple.pdf`.

How to do it...

We'll build a research agent step by step, starting with loading the PDF and ending with an interactive query system.

1. Import the required libraries and load environment variables:

```
from langchain_community.document_loaders import PyPDFLoader
from langchain_chroma import Chroma
from langchain_anthropic import ChatAnthropic
from langchain_core.tools import create_retriever_tool
from langchain.agents import create_agent
from dotenv import load_dotenv
load_dotenv()
```

2. Load the financial statement PDF and split it into pages:

```
loader = PyPDFLoader("apple.pdf")
pages = loader.load_and_split()
print(f"Loaded {len(pages)} pages from the PDF")
```

3. Create a vector store to enable semantic search over the document:

```
store = Chroma.from_documents(pages, collection_name="annualreport")
retriever = store.as_retriever()
```

4. Create a retriever tool that the agent can use to search the documents:

```
retriever_tool = create_retriever_tool(
    retriever,
    "apple_financials_search",
    "Search for information about Apple financial statements. "
    "Use this for any questions about Apple revenue, income, "
    "expenses, or other financial metrics."
)
```

5. Initialize the Claude language model with a temperature setting of 0.1. Temperature is a dial that controls how predictable or creative an LLM's responses are. Low values make it stick to the most likely answer, while high values let it take more chances and surprise you. Use low temperature when you need consistent, factual output, and higher temperature when you want variety or brainstorming:

```
llm = ChatAnthropic(
    model="claude-opus-4-20250514",
    temperature=0.1
)
```

6. Create the research agent using the ReAct pattern:

```
agent = create_agent(llm, [retriever_tool])
```

7. Query the agent about the company's financials:

```
query = "What was Apple's total revenue and how does it compare to the
previous year?"
result = agent.invoke({"messages": [("user", query)]})
print(result["messages"][-1].content)
```

8. Inspect the agent's response:

```
Based on the financial statements I found, here's Apple's revenue comparison:

## Apple's Revenue Comparison

### Quarterly Results (Q2):
- **Q2 2023** (Three months ended April 1, 2023): **$94.8 billion**
- **Q2 2022** (Three months ended March 26, 2022): **$97.3 billion**
- **Year-over-year change**: Down $2.5 billion or -2.5%

### First Half Results (Six Months):
- **First Half 2023** (Six months ended April 1, 2023): **$212.0 billion**
- **First Half 2022** (Six months ended March 26, 2022): **$221.2 billion**
- **Year-over-year change**: Down $9.2 billion or -4.2%
```

Figure 6.1: Agent response showing Apple's revenue analysis with year-over-year comparison

How it works...

The recipe combines several technologies to create an intelligent document analysis system.

The `PyPDFLoader` reads PDF files and extracts text content from each page. Financial statements often span dozens of pages, so splitting the document into smaller chunks makes it easier to find relevant information.

`ChromaDB` is a vector database that stores text as numerical embeddings. These embeddings capture the semantic meaning of the text, not just the words themselves. When you ask about "revenue growth," the system finds pages discussing revenue changes even if they use terms like "net sales increase" or "top-line expansion."

The retriever tool wraps the vector database in a format that `LangChain` agents understand. The description you provide helps the agent decide when to use this tool versus responding from general knowledge.

Claude processes natural language queries and generates responses. The low temperature setting of 0.1 makes responses more deterministic and focused, which is appropriate for financial analysis where precision matters.

The `create_ agent` function implements the ReAct pattern, where the agent reasons about what information it needs, takes actions to retrieve that information, and then synthesizes a response. This allows the agent to handle complex multi-part questions by breaking them down into smaller retrieval operations.

There's more...

The basic recipe handles single-document analysis, but real trading workflows often require comparing multiple companies or tracking financials over time. These extensions show how to scale the approach for more sophisticated research.

When screening stocks for a momentum strategy, you might want to quickly compare revenue growth across several companies in the same sector. Creating separate vector stores for each company lets the agent pull data from multiple sources to answer comparative questions. This is far more efficient than manually reading through each company's filings. Have a look at the following code:

```
apple_store = Chroma.from_documents(
    apple_pages,
    collection_name="apple_financials"
)
microsoft_store = Chroma.from_documents(
    msft_pages,
    collection_name="microsoft_financials"
)
apple_tool = create_retriever_tool(
    apple_store.as_retriever(),
    "apple_search",
    "Search Apple financial statements."
)
msft_tool = create_retriever_tool(
    microsoft_store.as_retriever(),
    "microsoft_search",
    "Search Microsoft financial statements."
)
agent = create_agent(llm, [apple_tool, msft_tool]
```

For backtesting strategies that use fundamental data, you'll want to persist the vector store to disk. This avoids reprocessing PDFs every time you run your analysis, which becomes important when working with years of historical filings:

```
store = Chroma.from_documents(
    pages,
    collection_name="annualreport",
    persist_directory="./chroma_db"
)
```

```
# Later, reload without reprocessing the PDF
store = Chroma(
    collection_name="annualreport",
    persist_directory="./chroma_db"
)
```

Some financial questions require more context than the default retrieval provides. Increasing the number of retrieved chunks helps the model synthesize information spread across multiple sections of the document, such as when calculating ratios that require data from both the income statement and the balance sheet:

```
retriever = store.as_retriever(
    search_type="similarity",
    search_kwargs={"k": 5}
)
```

See also

For more details on how to expand your use of these tools, see the documentation:

- LangChain documentation: `https://python.langchain.com/docs/`
- ChromaDB documentation: `https://docs.trychroma.com/`
- Anthropic Claude documentation: `https://docs.anthropic.com/`
- SEC EDGAR database for downloading financial statements: `https://www.sec.gov/edgar/`

Writing Python code to analyze stock price performance automatically with AI

Algorithmic traders need to analyze stock performance across multiple time frames and indicators before making trading decisions. Writing this analysis code repeatedly for different stocks is tedious and error-prone. What if you could describe what you want in plain English and have an AI write and execute the code for you?

This recipe shows you how to build an AI agent that automatically writes and runs Python code for stock analysis. Using LlamaIndex's code interpreter tool and Claude, you'll create an agent that understands natural language requests like "calculate the 20-day moving average" and generates working code to produce real results. The agent executes code in a sandboxed environment, captures the output, and can even debug errors and retry automatically.

This approach accelerates your research workflow by eliminating the gap between idea and implementation. Instead of spending time on boilerplate code for data fetching and indicator calculations, you can focus on the analysis itself and quickly iterate on trading hypotheses.

Getting ready

Install the required packages with pinned versions:

```
pip install llama-index==0.14.13 llama-index-llms-anthropic==0.10.7 llama-index-tools-code-interpreter==0.4.1 yfinance==1.1.0
```

How to do it...

We'll build an agent that can write and execute Python code for stock analysis on demand:

1. Import the required libraries and load environment variables:

```
from llama_index.llms.anthropic import Anthropic
from llama_index.core.agent import FunctionAgent, AgentWorkflow
from llama_index.tools.code_interpreter.base import CodeInterpreterToolSpec
from dotenv import load_dotenv
load_dotenv()
```

2. Initialize the code interpreter tool:

```
code_spec = CodeInterpreterToolSpec()
tools = code_spec.to_tool_list()
print(f"Created {len(tools)} tools")
```

3. Configure the Claude language model:

```
llm = Anthropic(model="claude-opus-4-20250514")
```

4. Create the code analysis agent with a system prompt:

```
agent = FunctionAgent(
    name="CodeAnalyst",
    description=(
        "An agent that writes and executes Python code for stock analysis"
    ),
    system_prompt=(
        "You are a Python code expert for financial analysis. "
        "Always use the code_interpreter tool to write and execute Python"
```

```
            "code when analyzing data. Use yfinance to fetch stock data."
        ),
        tools=tools,
        llm=llm,
    )
```

5. Set up the agent workflow:

```
workflow = AgentWorkflow(
    agents=[agent],
    root_agent="CodeAnalyst"
)
```

6. Run a stock performance analysis:

```
ticker = "PLTR"

prompt = f"""
Use the code interpreter to analyze {ticker} stock:
1. Fetch the last 30 days of historical prices using yfinance
2. Calculate the percentage change from start to end
3. Find the highest and lowest closing prices
4. Calculate the average daily trading volume
5. Print a summary of the analysis
"""
result = await workflow.run(user_msg=prompt)
print(result)
```

7. Inspect the analysis results:

```
Here's a comprehensive analysis of PLTR (Palantir Technologies) stock over the last 30 days:

## 📊 PLTR Stock Analysis Summary

### Price Analysis
| Metric | Value |
|--------|-------|
| **Starting Price** | $174.04 |
| **Ending Price** | $157.88 |
| **Percentage Change** | **-9.29%** |
| **Highest Close** | $181.68 (on 2026-01-07) |
| **Lowest Close** | $146.59 (on 2026-01-30) |
| **Price Range** | $35.09 |

### Volume Analysis
| Metric | Value |
|--------|-------|
| **Average Daily Volume** | 43.6 million shares |
| **Total Volume** | 915.7 million shares |
| **Highest Volume Day** | 112.9 million shares |
| **Lowest Volume Day** | 22.8 million shares |
```

Figure 6.2: Agent output showing PLTR stock performance analysis with price changes and volume data

How it works...

The recipe combines LlamaIndex's agent framework with a sandboxed code execution environment to create an AI-powered coding assistant.

The `CodeInterpreterToolSpec` instance creates a secure Python environment where the agent can execute code. When the agent calls this tool, it passes Python code as a string, and the tool runs it in isolation, capturing both `stdout` and `stderr`. This sandboxing prevents the AI from accidentally modifying files or running dangerous commands on your system.

The `FunctionAgent` class wraps the language model with the ability to use tools. When you send a prompt, the agent decides whether to respond directly or use a tool. The system prompt is crucial here—it instructs the agent to always use the code interpreter rather than just generating code in its text response. Without this guidance, the agent might simply show you code without executing it.

Claude Opus 4.5 excels at code generation because it can reason about programming concepts and maintain context across a multi-step analysis. Setting `max_tokens=4096` ensures Claude can generate complete code blocks without truncation. This is essential when the agent writes detailed analysis scripts with multiple calculations. When the agent encounters an error, it can read the traceback, understand what went wrong, and generate corrected code automatically.

The `AgentWorkflow` class provides the execution framework. Even with a single agent, it handles the asynchronous nature of tool calls and manages the conversation state between the user prompt, tool invocations, and final response.

There's more...

The code interpreter agent becomes more powerful when you ask it to perform complex multi-step analyses that would normally require significant coding effort.

Technical analysis often requires calculating multiple indicators and combining them into trading signals. The agent can handle this complexity because it understands both the financial concepts and the pandas operations needed to implement them. Have a look at this code:

```
prompt = f"""
Use the code interpreter to perform technical analysis on {ticker}:
1. Fetch 90 days of price data
2. Calculate the 20-day and 50-day simple moving averages
3. Determine if there's a bullish or bearish crossover
4. Calculate the RSI (Relative Strength Index) using a 14-day period
5. Print a technical analysis summary with buy/sell signals
"""

result = await workflow.run(user_msg=prompt)
print(result)
```

You can also compare multiple stocks simultaneously. This is useful for pair trading strategies or sector analysis where you need to evaluate relative performance:

```
prompt = """
Use the code interpreter to compare AAPL, MSFT, and GOOGL:
1. Fetch 60 days of price data for all three stocks
2. Normalize prices to percentage returns from the start date
3. Calculate the correlation matrix between the three stocks
4. Identify which pair has the highest correlation
5. Print the results
"""

result = await workflow.run(user_msg=prompt)
print(result)
```

For backtesting ideas, you can ask the agent to simulate simple trading rules and calculate hypothetical returns:

```
prompt = f"""
Use the code interpreter to backtest a simple strategy on {ticker}:
1. Fetch 6 months of daily price data
2. Generate buy signals when price crosses above the 20-day SMA
3. Generate sell signals when price crosses below the 20-day SMA
4. Calculate the return if you followed these signals
5. Compare to buy-and-hold return over the same period
"""

result = await workflow.run(user_msg=prompt)
print(result)
```

See also

LlamaIndex is an alternative Python library to LangChain. Read more about LlamaIndex here:

- LlamaIndex documentation: `https://docs.llamaindex.ai/`
- LlamaIndex code interpreter tool: `https://developers.llamaindex.ai/python/cloud/llamasheets/examples/coding_agent`
- `Yfinance documentation: https://github.com/ranaroussi/yfinance`

Using AI agentic workflows to automate comparative analysis

Pair trading and relative value strategies require comparing financial metrics across multiple companies. Manually extracting data from earnings reports and building comparison models is time-consuming, especially when analyzing an entire sector. An automated workflow can process multiple documents simultaneously, apply consistent modeling assumptions, and generate structured comparisons ready for trading decisions.

This recipe shows you how to build an agentic workflow that automates comparative financial analysis. Using LlamaIndex workflows and LlamaCloud's document extraction service, you'll create a system that processes earnings reports from two companies in parallel, builds financial models for each, and generates an investment recommendation. The workflow coordinates multiple AI agents, each handling a specific task, while maintaining data consistency through typed events and structured schemas.

By encoding your analysis process in a workflow, you create a repeatable, auditable system that can be applied to any pair of companies. This is particularly valuable for systematic trading strategies that need to regularly reassess relative valuations.

Getting ready

Install the required packages with pinned versions:

```
pip install llama-cloud-services==0.6.54 nest-asyncio==1.6.0
```

Add your LlamaCloud API key to the `.env` file:

```
LLAMA_CLOUD_API_KEY=your-api-key-here
```

You can obtain a LlamaCloud API key by creating an account at `https://cloud.llamaindex.ai/`. Navigate to API Keys in the dashboard and generate a new key.

Download the sample earnings report PDFs (`tsla.pdf` and `ford.pdf`) from the book's GitHub repository. Also download the `modeling_assumptions.txt` file, which contains the financial modeling parameters.

How to do it...

We'll build a workflow that extracts financial data from two earnings reports and produces a comparative analysis. Here are the steps for it:

1. Import the required libraries and set up the async environment:

```
from pydantic import BaseModel, Field
from typing import Optional
from llama_cloud_services import LlamaExtract
from llama_cloud.core.api_error import ApiError
from llama_cloud import ExtractConfig
from llama_index.core.workflow import (
    Event,
    StartEvent,
    StopEvent,
    Context,
    Workflow,
    step,
)
from llama_index.llms.anthropic import Anthropic
from llama_index.core.prompts import ChatPromptTemplate
```

```
import nest_asyncio
nest_asyncio.apply()
from dotenv import load_dotenv
load_dotenv()
```

2. Define Pydantic models for structured data extraction and output:

```
class RawFinancials(BaseModel):
    revenue: Optional[float] = Field(
        None, description="Extracted revenue (in million USD)"
    )
    operating_income: Optional[float] = Field(
        None, description="Extracted operating income (in million USD)"
    )
    eps: Optional[float] = Field(
        None, description="Extracted earnings per share"
    )

class InitialFinancialDataOutput(BaseModel):
    company_name: str = Field(..., description="Company name")
    ticker: str = Field(..., description="Stock ticker symbol")
    report_date: str = Field(..., description="Date of the report")
    raw_financials: RawFinancials = Field(
        ..., description="Structured raw financial metrics"
    )

class FinancialModelOutput(BaseModel):
    revenue_projection: float = Field(
        ..., description="Projected revenue for next year (million USD)"
    )
    growth_rate: float = Field(
        ..., description="Expected revenue growth rate (%)"
    )
    valuation_estimate: float = Field(
        ..., description="Estimated enterprise value (million USD)"
    )
    summary: str = Field(..., description="Brief summary of the analysis")

class ComparativeAnalysisOutput(BaseModel):
    comparative_analysis: str = Field(
        ..., description="Comparative analysis between companies"
```

```
    )
    overall_recommendation: str = Field(
        ..., description="Investment recommendation with rationale"
    )

class FinalEquityResearchMemoOutput(BaseModel):
    company_a_model: FinancialModelOutput
    company_b_model: FinancialModelOutput
    comparative_analysis: ComparativeAnalysisOutput
```

3. Define events for communication between workflow steps:

```
class DeckAParseEvent(Event):
    deck_content: InitialFinancialDataOutput

class DeckBParseEvent(Event):
    deck_content: InitialFinancialDataOutput

class CompanyAModelEvent(Event):
    model_output: FinancialModelOutput

class CompanyBModelEvent(Event):
    model_output: FinancialModelOutput
```

4. Build the comparative analysis workflow class:

```
class ComparativeAnalysisWorkflow(Workflow):
    def __init__(
        self, extract_agent, modeling_path: str, llm=None, **kwargs
    ):
        super().__init__(**kwargs)
        self.extract_agent = extract_agent
        self.llm = llm or Anthropic(
            model="claude-opus-4-5-20251101", max_tokens=4096)
        with open(modeling_path, "r") as f:
            self.modeling_data = f.read()

    async def _parse_deck(
        self, deck_path
    ) -> InitialFinancialDataOutput:
        result = await self.extract_agent.aextract(deck_path)
```

```
        return InitialFinancialDataOutput(**result.data)

    @step
    async def parse_deck_a(
        self, ctx: Context, ev: StartEvent
    ) -> DeckAParseEvent:
        output = await self._parse_deck(ev.deck_path_a)
        return DeckAParseEvent(deck_content=output)

    @step
    async def parse_deck_b(
        self, ctx: Context, ev: StartEvent
    ) -> DeckBParseEvent:
        output = await self._parse_deck(ev.deck_path_b)
        return DeckBParseEvent(deck_content=output)

    async def _generate_financial_model(
        self, financial_data: InitialFinancialDataOutput
    ) -> FinancialModelOutput:
        prompt_str = """You are an expert financial analyst.
Using the following raw financial data and modeling assumptions,
produce a financial model summary.

Raw Financial Data:
{raw_data}

Financial Modeling Assumptions:
{assumptions}

Return your output as JSON with fields:
- revenue_projection (float): Projected revenue for next year in million
USD
- growth_rate (float): Expected revenue growth rate as percentage
- valuation_estimate (float): Estimated enterprise value in million USD
- summary (str): Brief summary of the analysis
"""
        prompt = ChatPromptTemplate.from_messages(
            [("user", prompt_str)]
        )
        result = await self.llm.astructured_predict(
            FinancialModelOutput,
```

```
            prompt,
            raw_data=financial_data.model_dump_json(),
            assumptions=self.modeling_data,
        )
        return result

    @step
    async def refine_model_a(
        self, ctx: Context, ev: DeckAParseEvent
    ) -> CompanyAModelEvent:
        model = await self._generate_financial_model(ev.deck_content)
        return CompanyAModelEvent(model_output=model)

    @step
    async def refine_model_b(
        self, ctx: Context, ev: DeckBParseEvent
    ) -> CompanyBModelEvent:
        model = await self._generate_financial_model(ev.deck_content)
        return CompanyBModelEvent(model_output=model)

    @step
    async def compare_models(
        self, ctx: Context, ev: CompanyAModelEvent | CompanyBModelEvent
    ) -> StopEvent | None:
        events = ctx.collect_events(
            ev, [CompanyAModelEvent, CompanyBModelEvent]
        )
        if events is None:
            return None

        model_a_ev, model_b_ev = events
        model_a = model_a_ev.model_output
        model_b = model_b_ev.model_output

        prompt_str = """You are an expert investment analyst.
Compare the following financial models and provide an investment
recommendation.

Company A Model:
{company_a_model}
```

```
Company B Model:
{company_b_model}

Return your output as JSON with fields:
- comparative_analysis (str): Detailed comparison of the two companies
- overall_recommendation (str): Investment recommendation with rationale
"""
        prompt = ChatPromptTemplate.from_messages([("user", prompt_str)])
        analysis = await self.llm.astructured_predict(
            ComparativeAnalysisOutput,
            prompt,
            company_a_model=model_a.model_dump_json(),
            company_b_model=model_b.model_dump_json(),
        )

        final = FinalEquityResearchMemoOutput(
            company_a_model=model_a,
            company_b_model=model_b,
            comparative_analysis=analysis,
        )
        return StopEvent(result={"memo": final})
```

5. Create the LlamaExtract agent for document parsing:

```
llama_extract = LlamaExtract()

try:
    existing = llama_extract.get_agent(name="comparative-analysis")
    if existing:
        llama_extract.delete_agent(existing.id)

except ApiError as e:
    if e.status_code != 404:
        raise

extract_agent = llama_extract.create_agent(
    name="comparative-analysis",
    data_schema=InitialFinancialDataOutput,
    config=ExtractConfig(extraction_mode="BALANCED"),
)
```

6. Initialize and run the workflow:

```
workflow = ComparativeAnalysisWorkflow(
    extract_agent=extract_agent,
    modeling_path="modeling_assumptions.txt",
    timeout=300,
)

result = await workflow.run(
    deck_path_a="tsla.pdf",
    deck_path_b="ford.pdf",
)

memo = result["memo"]
```

7. Display the comparative analysis results:

```
print("=== EQUITY RESEARCH MEMO ===")
print(f"\nCompany A (Tesla):")
print(
    f"Revenue Projection: ${memo.company_a_model.revenue_projection:,.0f}M"
)
print(f"Growth Rate: {memo.company_a_model.growth_rate}%")
print(f"Valuation: ${memo.company_a_model.valuation_estimate:,.0f}M")
print(f"\nCompany B (Ford):")
print(
    f"Revenue Projection: ${memo.company_b_model.revenue_projection:,.0f}M"
)
print(f"Growth Rate: {memo.company_b_model.growth_rate}%")
print(f"Valuation: ${memo.company_b_model.valuation_estimate:,.0f}M")
print(f"\nRecommendation:")
print(memo.comparative_analysis.overall_recommendation)
```

8. Inspect the workflow output:

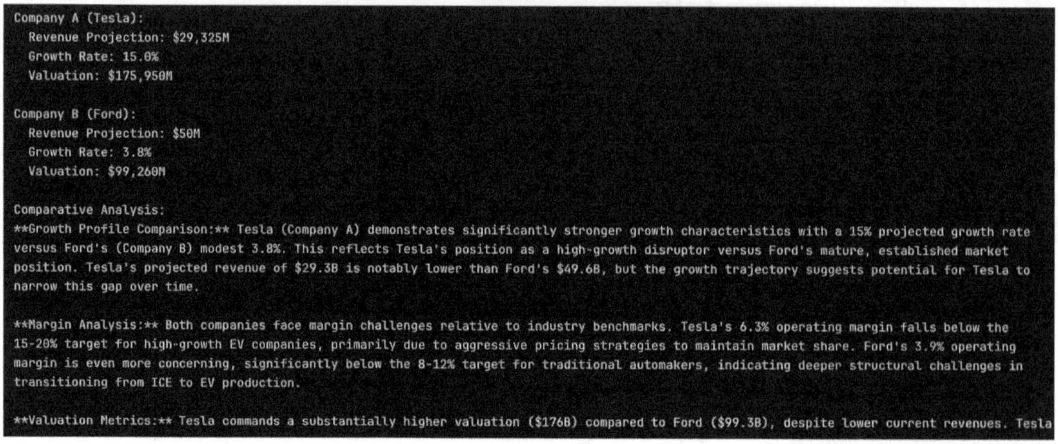

```
Company A (Tesla):
  Revenue Projection: $29,325M
  Growth Rate: 15.0%
  Valuation: $175,950M

Company B (Ford):
  Revenue Projection: $50M
  Growth Rate: 3.8%
  Valuation: $99,260M

Comparative Analysis:
**Growth Profile Comparison:** Tesla (Company A) demonstrates significantly stronger growth characteristics with a 15% projected growth rate
versus Ford's (Company B) modest 3.8%. This reflects Tesla's position as a high-growth disruptor versus Ford's mature, established market
position. Tesla's projected revenue of $29.3B is notably lower than Ford's $49.6B, but the growth trajectory suggests potential for Tesla to
narrow this gap over time.

**Margin Analysis:** Both companies face margin challenges relative to industry benchmarks. Tesla's 6.3% operating margin falls below the
15-20% target for high-growth EV companies, primarily due to aggressive pricing strategies to maintain market share. Ford's 3.9% operating
margin is even more concerning, significantly below the 8-12% target for traditional automakers, indicating deeper structural challenges in
transitioning from ICE to EV production.

**Valuation Metrics:** Tesla commands a substantially higher valuation ($176B) compared to Ford ($99.3B), despite lower current revenues. Tesla
```

Figure 6.3: Comparative analysis output showing Tesla vs. Ford financial projections and investment recommendation

How it works...

The workflow orchestrates multiple processing steps that can run in parallel where dependencies allow.

When the workflow starts, it receives paths to two earnings report PDFs. `StartEvent` triggers both `parse_deck_a` and `parse_deck_b` steps simultaneously since they have no dependencies on each other. Each step uses `LlamaExtract` to read the PDF and extract structured financial data according to the `InitialFinancialDataOutput` schema.

`LlamaExtract` is a cloud service optimized for document understanding. Unlike simple PDF text extraction, it uses AI to interpret tables, identify relevant metrics, and map them to your schema fields. The `BALANCED` extraction mode provides good accuracy without the latency of the most thorough analysis modes.

When each parse step completes, it emits an event (`DeckAParseEvent` or `DeckBParseEvent`) that triggers the corresponding financial model generation step. These steps also run in parallel, each calling Claude to analyze the extracted data and apply the modeling assumptions.

The `compare_models` step uses `collect_events` to wait for both `CompanyAModelEvent` and `CompanyBModelEvent` before proceeding. This synchronization pattern allows the workflow to parallelize work while ensuring all required data is available before the final comparison. The step returns **None** until both events arrive, at which point it generates the comparative analysis.

Pydantic models serve two purposes: they define the schema for `LlamaExtract` and they enable Claude's structured prediction. The `astructured_predict` method instructs Claude to return JSON conforming to the specified model, which is then validated and converted to a Python object automatically.

There's more...

The workflow pattern scales well to more complex analysis scenarios. You can extend it to compare entire sectors or add additional analysis steps.

For sector-wide screening, you can modify the workflow to accept a list of companies and dynamically create parse and model steps for each. This requires using workflow patterns for dynamic step creation, which LlamaIndex supports through programmatic event emission. Have a look at the code:

```
# Analyze multiple companies by running separate workflows
companies = [
    ("tsla.pdf", "Tesla"),
    ("ford.pdf", "Ford"),
    ("gm.pdf", "GM"),
]

results = []
for pdf_path, name in companies:
    single_result = await single_company_workflow.run(deck_path=pdf_path)
    results.append((name, single_result))

# Compare all results
for name, result in results:
    print(f"{name}: Growth {result.growth_rate}%,"
          f"Valuation ${result.valuation_estimate:,.0f}M")
```

You can add validation steps to cross-check extracted data against external sources. For example, comparing extracted revenue figures to known quarterly results helps catch extraction errors before they propagate through the analysis:

```
@step
async def validate_extraction(
    self, ctx: Context, ev: DeckAParseEvent
) -> ValidatedDataEvent:
    extracted = ev.deck_content.raw_financials.revenue
    # Fetch known revenue from another source
```

```
    known_revenue = await fetch_from_data_provider(ev.deck_content.ticker)

    if abs(extracted - known_revenue) / known_revenue > 0.05:
        raise ValueError(f"Extraction mismatch: {extracted} vs {known_revenue}")

    return ValidatedDataEvent(deck_content=ev.deck_content)
```

The modeling assumptions file can be customized per sector. You can create separate assumption files for technology, automotive, healthcare, and other sectors to produce more accurate projections that reflect industry-specific dynamics.

See also

Pydantic is a useful library that is used heavily in AI libraries. Read more here: `https://docs.pydantic.dev/`

Automating equity research reports with AI

Professional equity research involves multiple specialized roles working together: analysts gather data, writers synthesize findings into reports, and editors review for accuracy and clarity. Replicating this team structure with AI agents creates a system that can produce research reports autonomously while maintaining quality through built-in review cycles.

This recipe shows you how to build a multi-agent system that automates equity research report generation. Using LlamaIndex's agent workflow framework, you'll create three specialized agents that collaborate: a `ResearchAgent` that searches the web for current market news, a `WriteAgent` that synthesizes findings into structured reports, and a `ReviewAgent` that provides feedback and quality control. The agents hand off control to each other automatically based on their system prompts, mimicking how a research team operates.

This architecture is valuable for systematic trading because it can generate consistent, timely research on any topic. Whether you need daily briefings on specific stocks, sector analysis, or event-driven reports, the same workflow can be reused with different prompts.

Getting ready

Install the required packages with pinned versions:

```
pip install tavily-python==0.7.21
```

Add your Tavily API key to the `.env` file:

```
TAVILY_API_KEY=your-api-key-here
```

You can obtain a Tavily API key by creating an account at `https://tavily.com/`. The free tier provides enough searches for development and testing.

How to do it...

We'll build a three-agent system where each agent has a specialized role in producing equity research reports. Here is the code for it:

1. Import the required libraries and load environment variables:

```
import os
from llama_index.llms.anthropic import Anthropic
from llama_index.core.agent.workflow import (
    FunctionAgent,
    AgentWorkflow,
    AgentOutput,
    ToolCall,
    ToolCallResult,
)
from tavily import AsyncTavilyClient
from dotenv import load_dotenv
load_dotenv()
```

2. Initialize the language model and create shared state storage:

```
llm = Anthropic(model="claude-opus-4-5-20251101", max_tokens=4096)
research_state = {
    "research_notes": {},
    "report_content": "",
    "review": "",
}
```

3. Define the tools that agents will use:

```
async def search_web(query: str) -> str:
    """Search the web for information on a topic."""
    client = AsyncTavilyClient(api_key=os.getenv("TAVILY_API_KEY"))
    result = await client.search(query)
    return str(result)

async def record_notes(notes: str, notes_title: str) -> str:
    """Record research notes with a title."""
```

```
        research_state["research_notes"][notes_title] = notes
        return f"Notes recorded under title: {notes_title}"

    async def write_report(report_content: str) -> str:
        """Write the final report content."""
        research_state["report_content"] = report_content
        return "Report written successfully."

    async def review_report(review: str) -> str:
        """Review the report and provide feedback."""
        research_state["review"] = review
        return f"Review recorded: {review}"
```

4. Create `ResearchAgent` that gathers information:

```
research_agent = FunctionAgent(
    name="ResearchAgent",
    description="Searches the web for information and records notes.",
    system_prompt=(
        "You are the ResearchAgent. Search the web for information on the"
        "given topic and record your findings as notes using the"
        "record_notes tool. Once you have gathered enough information"
        "(at least 2-3 searches), hand off to the"
        "WriteAgent to write the report."
    ),
    llm=llm,
    tools=[search_web, record_notes],
    can_handoff_to=["WriteAgent"],
)
```

5. Create `WriteAgent` that produces reports:

```
write_agent = FunctionAgent(
    name="WriteAgent",
    description="Writes reports based on research notes.",
    system_prompt=(
        "You are the WriteAgent. Write a concise report in markdown format"
        "based on what the ResearchAgent found. Use the write_report"
        "tool to save the report. Once written,"
        "hand off to the ReviewAgent for feedback."
    ),
```

```
    llm=llm,
    tools=[write_report],
    can_handoff_to=["ReviewAgent", "ResearchAgent"],
)
```

6. Create `ReviewAgent` that ensures quality:

```
review_agent = FunctionAgent(
    name="ReviewAgent",
    description="Reviews reports and provides feedback.",
    system_prompt=(
        "You are the ReviewAgent. Review the report and use the"
        "review_report tool to record your feedback."
        "Approve the report if it's good, or request specific changes."
        "If major changes are needed, hand off to the WriteAgent."
    ),
    llm=llm,
    tools=[review_report],
    can_handoff_to=["WriteAgent"],
)
```

7. Build and run the agent workflow:

```
agent_workflow = AgentWorkflow(
    agents=[research_agent, write_agent, review_agent],
    root_agent=research_agent.name,
)

handler = agent_workflow.run(
    user_msg=(
        "Write a brief equity research report on"
        "NVIDIA's stock performance in January 2025."
        "Focus on the DeepSeek news impact and analyst reactions."
    )
)

current_agent = None
async for event in handler.stream_events():
    if (
        hasattr(event, "current_agent_name")
        and event.current_agent_name != current_agent
```

```
        ):
            current_agent = event.current_agent_name
            print(f"\n{'='*50}")
            print(f"Agent: {current_agent}")
            print(f"{'='*50}\n")
        elif isinstance(event, AgentOutput):
            if event.response.content:
                print(f"Output: {event.response.content[:200]}...")
            if event.tool_calls:
                print(f"Tools: {[call.tool_name for call"
                      f"in event.tool_calls]}")
        elif isinstance(event, ToolCallResult):
            print(f"Tool Result ({event.tool_name}):"
                  f"{str(event.tool_output)[:150]}...")
```

8. Display the final report:

```
print("\n" + "="*50)
print("FINAL EQUITY RESEARCH REPORT")
print("="*50)
print(research_state["report_content"])
```

Inspect the workflow output:

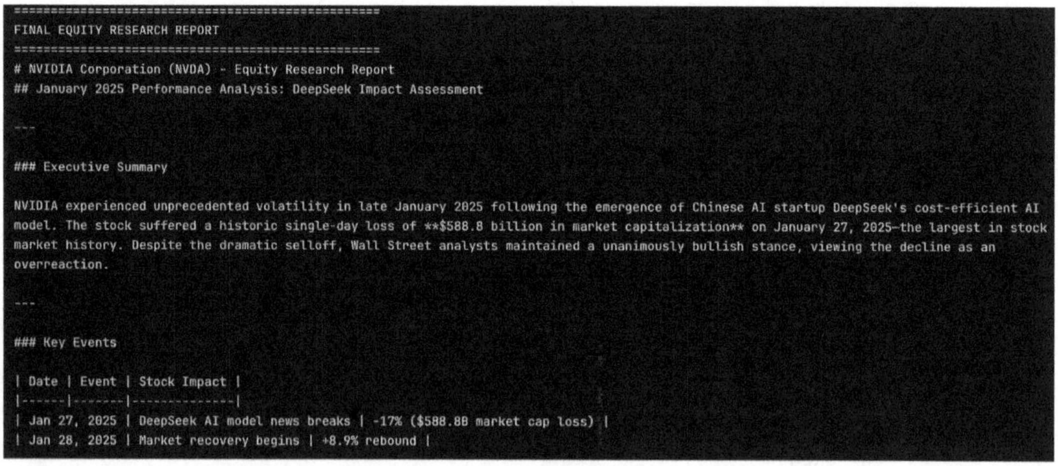

```
==================================================
FINAL EQUITY RESEARCH REPORT
==================================================
# NVIDIA Corporation (NVDA) - Equity Research Report
## January 2025 Performance Analysis: DeepSeek Impact Assessment

---

### Executive Summary

NVIDIA experienced unprecedented volatility in late January 2025 following the emergence of Chinese AI startup DeepSeek's cost-efficient AI
model. The stock suffered a historic single-day loss of **$588.8 billion in market capitalization** on January 27, 2025—the largest in stock
market history. Despite the dramatic selloff, Wall Street analysts maintained a unanimously bullish stance, viewing the decline as an
overreaction.

---

### Key Events

| Date | Event | Stock Impact |
|------|-------|--------------|
| Jan 27, 2025 | DeepSeek AI model news breaks | -17% ($588.8B market cap loss) |
| Jan 28, 2025 | Market recovery begins | +8.9% rebound |
```

Figure 6.4: Multi-agent workflow output showing agent handoffs and the final equity research report on NVIDIA

How it works...

The multi-agent architecture separates concerns into specialized roles, each with focused capabilities and clear handoff rules.

The `FunctionAgent` class creates agents that can use tools and transfer control to other agents. Each agent has a system prompt that defines its behavior, a set of tools it can call, and a list of agents it can hand off to. When an agent decides its task is complete, it uses an implicit handoff tool to transfer control.

`ResearchAgent` starts the workflow. It uses the `search_web` tool to query Tavily for current market news. Tavily is designed for AI applications and returns structured search results that are easy for language models to process. The agent makes multiple searches to gather comprehensive information, then records its findings using `record_notes`.

When `ResearchAgent` has enough information, it hands off to the `WriteAgent`. The handoff includes context about what was researched, allowing the `WriteAgent` to understand what notes are available. `WriteAgent` synthesizes this information into a markdown-formatted report and saves it using `write_report`.

After writing, the `WriteAgent` hands off to the `ReviewAgent` for quality control. `ReviewAgent` evaluates the report and can either approve it or request changes. If changes are needed, it hands back to `WriteAgent` with specific feedback. This review loop can iterate multiple times until the report meets quality standards.

The shared state dictionary allows tools to persist data across agent handoffs. This is simpler than passing large amounts of context through the handoff mechanism and ensures all agents can access the same information.

There's more...

The multi-agent pattern extends naturally to more sophisticated research workflows. You can add specialized agents for different aspects of equity research.

Adding a data agent that fetches quantitative metrics provides hard numbers to complement the qualitative research. This agent could pull price data, financial ratios, and technical indicators as shown here:

```
async def fetch_stock_data(ticker: str) -> str:
    """Fetch current stock data and key metrics."""
    import yfinance as yf
    stock = yf.Ticker(ticker)
    info = stock.info
```

```
    return f"""
    Price: ${info.get('currentPrice', 'N/A')}
    Market Cap: ${info.get('marketCap', 'N/A'):,}
    P/E Ratio: {info.get('trailingPE', 'N/A')}
    52-Week Range: ${info.get('fiftyTwoWeekLow', 'N/A')} - ${
        info.get('fiftyTwoWeekHigh', 'N/A')}
    """

data_agent = FunctionAgent(
    name="DataAgent",
    description="Fetches quantitative stock data and metrics.",
    system_prompt=(
        "You are the DataAgent. Fetch stock data for the requested ticker "
        "and provide key metrics. Hand off to WriteAgent when done."
    ),
    llm=llm,
    tools=[fetch_stock_data],
    can_handoff_to=["WriteAgent"],
)
```

For longer research tasks, you can add persistence to save and resume workflows. This is useful when research spans multiple sessions or requires human review at certain checkpoints:

```
import json

def save_state(filename: str):
    with open(filename, "w") as f:
        json.dump(research_state, f)

def load_state(filename: str):
    global research_state
    with open(filename, "r") as f:
        research_state = json.load(f)
```

You can also create specialized research agents for different domains. A `MacroAgent` instance could focus on economic indicators and interest rates, while a `SectorAgent` instance analyzes industry trends and competitive dynamics:

```
macro_agent = FunctionAgent(
    name="MacroAgent",
    description="Analyzes macroeconomic factors affecting the stock.",
```

```
    system_prompt=(
        "You are the MacroAgent. Research macroeconomic factors like:"
        "interest rates, inflation, and economic indicators that could impact"
        "the stock. Focus on factors relevant to the specific sector."
    ),
    llm=llm,
    tools=[search_web, record_notes],
    can_handoff_to=["WriteAgent"],
)
```

See also

Tavily is a commonly used Python library that makes it easy to access news programmatically. You can read more here: `https://docs.tavily.com/`.

Converting trading strategy research papers into code with LlamaIndex

Algorithmic traders frequently discover promising strategies in academic papers and research reports, but implementing those strategies requires careful translation from prose to code. This manual process is time-consuming and error-prone, especially when papers contain complex mathematical notation or ambiguous descriptions. An AI agent that can read research documents and generate working code eliminates this bottleneck and accelerates strategy development.

This recipe shows you how to build an AI agent that reads trading strategy PDFs and converts them into executable Python code. Using LlamaIndex's document processing and agent workflow framework, you'll create a system that extracts strategy descriptions through semantic search, then generates both an implementation plan and complete code. The agent uses **retrieval-augmented generation** (**RAG**) to ground its outputs in the actual document content, reducing hallucination and improving accuracy.

Getting ready

Install the required packages:

```
pip install llama-index-embeddings-huggingface==0.5.2
```

Add your HuggingFace token to the `.env` file in your working directory:

```
HF_TOKEN=your-huggingface-token-here
```

You can obtain a HuggingFace token by creating an account at `https://huggingface.co/`. Navigate to **Settings** | **Access Tokens** and generate a new token. The token enables faster model downloads and higher rate limits when using HuggingFace embedding models.

The `pairs.pdf` file containing a pairs trading strategy should be in your working directory. You can download sample trading strategy papers from academic sources like SSRN (`https://www.ssrn.com/`)or arXiv (`https://arxiv.org/`).

How to do it...

As is typical when using LLMs to write code, we'll first create an implementation plan. The LLM will then use that plan to write the code. Here are the steps for it:

1. Import the required libraries and load environment variables:

```
import warnings
warnings.filterwarnings('ignore')
from llama_index.core import (
    SimpleDirectoryReader, VectorStoreIndex, Settings)
from llama_index.embeddings.huggingface import HuggingFaceEmbedding
from llama_index.llms.anthropic import Anthropic
from llama_index.core.agent.workflow import FunctionAgent, AgentWorkflow
from dotenv import load_dotenv
load_dotenv()
```

2. Initialize the embedding model and language model:

```
Settings.embed_model = HuggingFaceEmbedding(
    model_name="BAAI/bge-small-en-v1.5")
llm = Anthropic(model="claude-opus-4-5-20251101", max_tokens=4096)
Settings.llm = llm
```

3. Load the PDF and create a searchable vector index:

```
documents = SimpleDirectoryReader(input_files=["pairs.pdf"]).load_data()
index = VectorStoreIndex.from_documents(documents, show_progress=False)
query_engine = index.as_query_engine()
print(f"Index created with {len(documents)} document chunks")
```

4. Define tools for querying the PDF:

```
async def query_pdf(question: str) -> str:
    """Query the pairs trading PDF for specific information."""
    response = query_engine.query(question)
    return str(response)

async def extract_strategy() -> str:
    """Extract the complete trading strategy description from the PDF."""
    query = (
        "Extract a detailed description of the "
        "pairs trading strategy from this document. Include: "
        "1) The assets being traded, 2) The statistical methods used, "
        "3) The entry and exit signals, 4) Any risk management rules."
    )
    response = query_engine.query(query)
    return str(response)
```

5. Create the strategy implementation agent:

````
strategy_agent = FunctionAgent(
    name="TradingStrategyAgent",
    description="Converts trading strategy PDFs into Python code.",
    system_prompt="""You are a trading strategy implementation specialist.
Your task is to:

1. First, use extract_strategy to get the trading strategy from the PDF
2. Then, use query_pdf if you need additional details about specific
aspects
3. Finally, create a complete implementation plan AND Python code

When you have gathered enough information, provide your response in this
exact format:

IMPLEMENTATION PLAN:
[Your detailed plan here]

PYTHON CODE:
```python
[Your complete, executable Python code here]
```
````

```
The Python code should be complete and runnable, including all imports,
functions,
and a main execution block. Focus on the core strategy logic - use pandas,
numpy,
and statsmodels for the implementation.
""",
    llm=llm,
    tools=[extract_strategy, query_pdf],
)

agent_workflow = AgentWorkflow(
    agents=[strategy_agent],
    root_agent=strategy_agent.name,
)
```

6. Run the workflow to generate code:

```
handler = agent_workflow.run(
    user_msg=(
        "Read the pairs.pdf file and convert the trading strategy into"
        "Python code. First extract the strategy, then create an "
        "implementation plan and generate complete,"
        "executable Python code."
    )
)

response = await handler
final_response = response.response.content
```

7. Parse and display the results:

```
if "IMPLEMENTATION PLAN:" in final_response:
    parts = final_response.split("PYTHON CODE:")
    plan = parts[0].replace("IMPLEMENTATION PLAN:", "").strip()

    if len(parts) > 1:
        code = parts[1].strip()
        if "```python" in code:
            code = code.split("```python")[1].split("```")[0].strip()
        elif "```" in code:
```

```
                code = code.split("```")[1].split("```")[0].strip()

    print("=" * 50)
    print("IMPLEMENTATION PLAN")
    print("=" * 50)
    print(plan)
```

8. Inspect the generated plan:

```
==================================================
IMPLEMENTATION PLAN
==================================================
Based on the extracted information, I can now create an implementation plan and Python code for this pairs trading strategy.


1. Data Acquisition and Preprocessing
   - Load historical price data for DJUSPR and DJUSHC indices
   - Calculate daily returns for both indices
   - Split data into training (2005-2017) and testing (2018-2022) periods

2. Copula Model Implementation
   - Fit marginal distributions (t-distributions) to each index's returns
   - Estimate copula parameters (correlation and degrees of freedom)
   - Implement daily recalibration of the copula model

3. Z-Score Calculation and Signal Generation
   - Generate simulated returns using the fitted copula
   - Calculate spread as difference between simulated returns
   - Compute Z-score: (observed_spread - mean_simulated_spread) / std_simulated_spread
   - Generate trading signals when |Z-score| > 2.58 (99% confidence)
```

Figure 6.5: AI agent output showing the implementation plan for the pairs trading strategy

Then we print the output:

```
print("\n" + "=" * 50)
print("GENERATED PYTHON CODE")
print("=" * 50)
print(code)
```

9. Inspect the generated output:

```
==================================================
GENERATED PYTHON CODE
==================================================
import numpy as np
import pandas as pd
from scipy import stats
from scipy.stats import t, norm
from scipy.optimize import minimize
import matplotlib.pyplot as plt
from datetime import datetime
import warnings
warnings.filterwarnings('ignore')

class PairsTradingStrategy:
    def __init__(self, confidence_level=0.99, lookback_window=252):
        """
        Initialize the pairs trading strategy

        Parameters:
        confidence_level: Confidence level for Z-score threshold (default 0.99)
        lookback_window: Number of days for rolling window calculations (default 252)
        """
```

Figure 6.6: AI agent output showing the generated Python code for the pairs trading strategy

How it works...

The system combines document processing with an AI agent that can query the indexed content and generate structured outputs.

`SimpleDirectoryReader` extracts text from PDF files and splits it into manageable chunks. For research papers, this typically produces 10-20 chunks depending on document length. `VectorStoreIndex` creates embeddings for each chunk using the HuggingFace BGE model, enabling semantic search that finds relevant passages based on meaning rather than keyword matching.

`FunctionAgent` is configured with two tools: `extract_strategy` performs a comprehensive query to get the main strategy description, while `query_pdf` allows follow-up questions about specific aspects like parameter values or edge cases. The system prompt instructs the agent to first gather information, then produce a structured response with both a plan and code.

When the workflow runs, the agent autonomously decides which tools to use and in what order. It typically calls `extract_strategy` first to get an overview, then may call `query_pdf` multiple times to clarify details. The agent tracks what information it has gathered and determines when it has enough context to generate the final output.

The output parsing extracts the implementation plan and code from the agent's response. The plan describes the modules, data structures, and functions needed. The code is complete and executable, including all imports and a main block. This separation allows traders to review the plan before examining the code.

There's more...

The PDF-to-code pattern extends to many document processing scenarios in algorithmic trading.

You can process multiple documents simultaneously by creating indices for each paper and giving the agent access to all of them. This is useful when implementing strategies that combine ideas from several sources. Have a look at the following code:

```
papers = ["pairs.pdf", "momentum.pdf", "mean_reversion.pdf"]
indices = {}

for paper in papers:
    docs = SimpleDirectoryReader(input_files=[paper]).load_data()
    indices[paper] = VectorStoreIndex.from_documents(docs)

async def query_paper(paper_name: str, question: str) -> str:
    """Query a specific paper for information."""
    if paper_name in indices:
        engine = indices[paper_name].as_query_engine()
        return str(engine.query(question))
    return f"Paper {paper_name} not found"
```

For complex strategies, you can add a code validation step that checks the generated code for syntax errors and runs basic tests before presenting it to the user. Here is the code for it:

```
import ast

def validate_python_code(code: str) -> dict:
    """Validate generated Python code for syntax errors."""
    try:
        ast.parse(code)
        return {"valid": True, "error": None}
```

```
    except SyntaxError as e:
        return {"valid": False, "error": str(e)}
```

The system can also be extended to generate backtesting code by providing the agent with additional context about your backtesting framework and data formats. Include examples of working backtest code in the system prompt to guide the agent toward compatible output.

See also

HuggingFace hosts thousands of pre-trained embedding models optimized for different languages and domains. The BGE models used in this recipe are among the top performers on semantic search benchmarks: `https://huggingface.co/BAAI/bge-small-en-v1.5`

Join our community on Discord

Join our community's Discord space for discussions with the authors and other readers: `https://discord.gg/G4YmB6DQvf`

7

Build Alpha Factors for Stock Portfolios

Professional traders often construct factor portfolios to target and exploit market inefficiencies, such as anomalies in value, size, or momentum, to generate better risk-adjusted returns. Firms like WorldQuant, AQR, and Dimensional Fund Advisors have built multi-billion dollar businesses on this approach, with AQR managing over $100 billion in factor-driven strategies spanning value, momentum, and quality, and WorldQuant running tens of thousands of systematic alphas across global markets. These aren't academic curiosities; they're the mechanical drivers behind some of the most successful systematic funds in the world. By systematically identifying and weighing securities based on these specific characteristics or factors, investors can create a portfolio that captures the desired exposures while minimizing unintended risks. Factors act as the fundamental building blocks of investing, being the persistent forces that influence returns across various asset classes. A trading edge is a consistent, non-random inefficiency in the market that can be exploited for profit. Factors are the inefficiencies that drive asset prices and form the basis of this edge, allowing traders to capitalize on these persistent anomalies.

Factor analysis is a broad topic but comes down to identifying the factors, determining the sensitivity of a portfolio to those factors, and taking action. That action can be hedging undesirable risk based on the factor exposure or increasing exposure to the factor. In this chapter, we explore the key elements of identifying factors, hedging out unwanted risks, and setting up forward returns to assess the predictive power of factors. We'll use Python libraries for statistical modeling to build a principal component analysis and linear regression. Then, we'll introduce the Zipline Reloaded Pipeline API, which will prepare us for analyzing factors.

In this chapter, we present the following recipes:

- Identifying latent return drivers using principal component analysis

- Finding and hedging portfolio beta using linear regression
- Analyzing portfolio sensitivities to the Fama-French factors
- Assessing market inefficiency based on volatility
- Preparing a factor ranking model using the Zipline Reloaded Pipeline API

Identifying latent return drivers using principal component analysis

Principal component analysis (**PCA**) is a dimensionality reduction technique that is widely used in data science. It transforms the original features into a new set of features, called **principal components**, which reflect the maximum variance in the data. In other words, it transforms a large set of variables into a smaller set of variables, while still containing most of the information from the larger set.

There are various sources of risk in an asset portfolio, including market risk, sector risk, and asset-specific risk. PCA helps identify and quantify these risks by breaking down the returns of the portfolio into components that explain the maximum variance. The first few principal components usually capture most of the variance, and they can be analyzed to understand the major sources of risk in the portfolio.

This recipe will use scikit-learn to run PCA on a portfolio of eight stocks made up of mining and technology companies.

Getting ready

For this recipe, we introduce scikit-learn, which provides algorithms for classification, regression, clustering, dimensionality reduction, and more. It's built on `NumPy`, `SciPy`, and `Matplotlib`, which makes it easy to integrate with other scientific Python libraries. We'll use it to conduct our analysis.

You can install scikit-learn using `pip`:

```
pip install scikit-learn
```

How to do it...

Scikit-learn makes it easy to run a PCA. Here's how to do it:

1. Import the libraries we need for the analysis:

```
import numpy as np
import pandas as pd
```

```
from openbb import obb
from sklearn.decomposition import PCA
import matplotlib.pyplot as plt
obb.user.preferences.output_type = "dataframe"
```

2. Download data for gold mining stocks and healthcare stocks and compute their daily returns:

```
symbols = ["NEM", "RGLD", "SSRM", "CDE", "LLY", "UNH", "JNJ", "MRK"]
data = obb.equity.price.historical(
    symbols,
    start_date="2020-01-01",
    end_date="2022-12-31",
    provider="yfinance",
).pivot(columns="symbol", values="close")
returns = data.pct_change().dropna()
```

3. Run the PCA using three components and fit the model:

```
pca = PCA(n_components=3)
pca.fit(returns)
```

4. Extract the explained variance ratio for each component and extract the principal components:

```
pct = pca.explained_variance_ratio_
pca_components = pca.components_
```

5. Plot the contribution of each principal component and the cumulative percent of explained variance:

```
cum_pct = np.cumsum(pct)
x = np.arange(1, len(pct) + 1, 1)
plt.subplot(1, 2, 1)
plt.bar(x, pct * 100, align="center")
plt.title("Contribution (%)")
plt.xticks(x)
plt.xlim([0, 4])
plt.ylim([0, 100])
plt.subplot(1, 2, 2)
plt.plot(x, cum_pct * 100, "ro-")
```

```
plt.title("Cumulative contribution (%)")
plt.xticks(x)
plt.xlim([0, 4])
plt.ylim([0, 100])
```

The last code block results in the following chart:

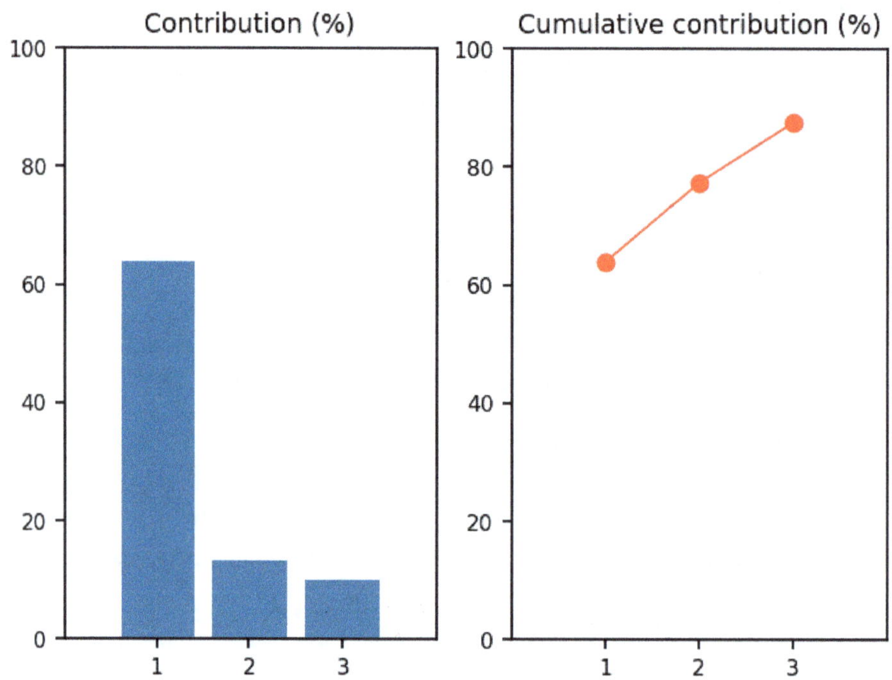

Figure 7.1: Contribution and cumulative contribution of explained variance for the first three principal components

How it works...

There is ample documentation on how PCA works so we will not cover the math behind the process. But in summary, the `PCA(n_components=3)` code creates a `PCA` object that will compute the first three principal components of the returns data. The `n_components=3` parameter specifies that we want to select the top three principal components. The call to `pca.fit` fits the PCA model to the returns data, which hides most of the complexity of PCA. Under the hood, PCA standardizes the returns and computes a covariance matrix. Next, the eigen decomposition is performed on the covariance matrix, which computes the eigenvectors and eigenvalues that indicate the directions and magnitude of data variance. Finally, eigenvectors are ordered by their eigenvalues in descending order and the top three are chosen as principal components.

There's more...

From the principal components, we can transform the original returns data into a new set of features that represent the statistical risk factors that explain the most variance in the returns, as shown in the following code:

```
X = np.asarray(returns)
factor_returns = X.dot(pca_components.T)
factor_returns = pd.DataFrame(
    columns=["f1", "f2", "f3"],
    index=returns.index,
    data=factor_returns
)
```

The preceding code will return the following `DataFrame`, containing a time series of the statistical risk factors:

Date	f1	f2	f3
2020-01-03	-0.028845	0.007909	-0.013464
2020-01-06	-0.081169	-0.006508	0.058871
2020-01-07	0.003694	0.015644	0.013973
2020-01-08	-0.105891	-0.028187	0.005725
2020-01-09	0.001918	-0.018469	-0.023525

Figure 7.2: DataFrame containing a time series of the statistical risk factors

The statistical risk factors are similar to more conventional risk factors such as the Fama-French factors we'll explore in the *Analyzing portfolio sensitivities to the Fama-French factors* recipe in this chapter. The returns data is projected onto the principal components obtained from the `PCA`. This is done by taking the dot product of `X` with the transpose of the `pca_components` matrix. The `pca_components` matrix contains the principal components of the returns data, which were previously computed using the fit method.

This step transforms the original returns data into a new set of features (the principal components or factors) that explain the most variance in the data. These factors should give us an idea of how much of the portfolio's returns come from some unobservable statistical feature.

With the principal components, we can create the exposure of each asset to the three principal components:

```
factor_exposures = pd.DataFrame(
    index=["f1", "f2", "f3"],
    columns=returns.columns,
    data=pca_components
).T
```

The resulting `factor_exposuresDataFrame` is shown in the following screenshot. It shows how much each asset in the portfolio is exposed to each of the three factors. The exposure of each asset to each of the three factors (**"f1"**, **"f2"**, **"f3"**) represents how much the returns of that asset are influenced by changes in those factors.

	f1	f2	f3
NEM	0.292250	0.091439	0.394104
RGLD	0.308669	0.125098	0.416761
SSRM	0.427029	0.227828	0.485778
CDE	0.783970	-0.030216	-0.618241
LLY	0.062208	-0.605558	0.131696
UNH	0.101891	-0.535551	0.136475
JNJ	0.061262	-0.338930	0.108649
MRK	0.065923	-0.393423	0.070823

Figure 7.3: DataFrame containing the exposure of each asset to each factor

We can visualize each asset's exposure to the first two principal components on an annotated scatter plot:

```
labels = factor_exposures.index
data = factor_exposures.values
plt.scatter(data[:, 0], data[:, 1])
plt.xlabel("factor exposure of PC1")
```

```
plt.ylabel("factor exposure of PC2")
for label, x, y in zip(labels, data[:, 0], data[:, 1]):
    plt.annotate(
        label,
        xy=(x, y),
        xytext=(-20, 20),
        textcoords="offset points",
        arrowprops=dict(
            arrowstyle="->",
            connectionstyle="arc3,rad=0"
        ),
    )
```

The result is the following scatter plot showing the exposure to the factors:

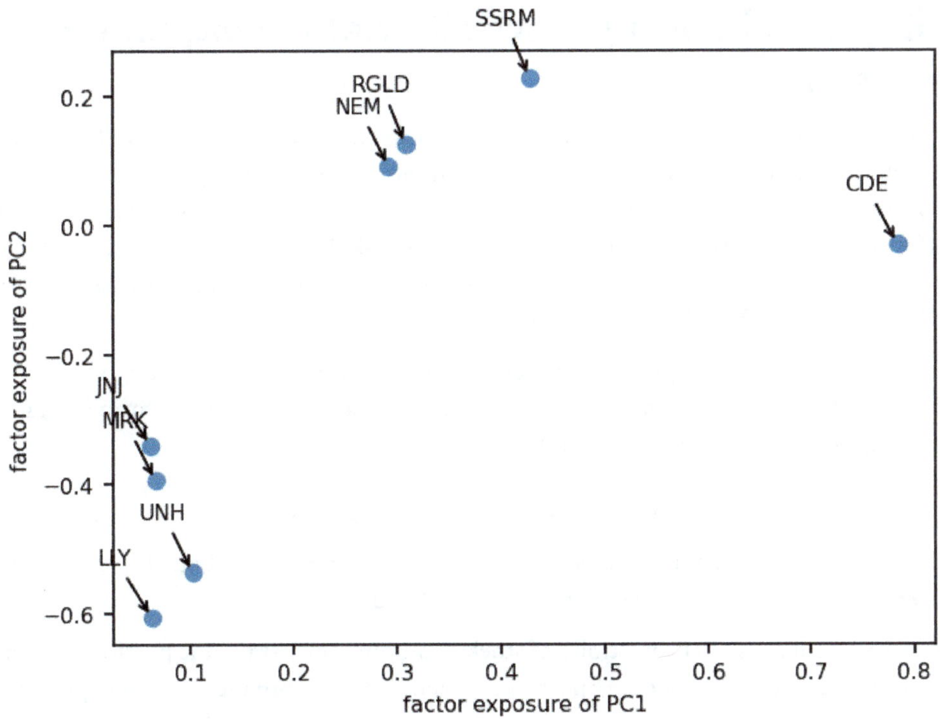

Figure 7.4: Scatter plot showing the stock exposure to the first two principal components

The gold mining stocks have higher factor exposures compared to the healthcare stocks, indicating that they are more sensitive to changes in the underlying factors. The healthcare stocks have lower and negative exposures to "**f2**", indicating that they may provide some diversification benefits in a portfolio that is highly exposed to this factor. The factors may represent different sources of systematic risk in the market, such as market risk, interest rate risk, or industry-specific risks.

See also

PCA is an important dimensionality reduction technique commonly used in portfolio management. You can visit the following links to learn more about PCA:

- More on PCA: `https://en.wikipedia.org/wiki/Principal_component_analysis`
- Documentation for scikit-learn: `https://scikit-learn.org/stable/`
- Documentation for the scikit-learn implementation of PCA used in this recipe: `https://scikit-learn.org/stable/modules/generated/sklearn.decomposition.PCA.html`

Finding and hedging portfolio beta using linear regression

Algorithmic traders often seek exposure to specific risks that they believe will yield outsized returns while hedging other risks they deem unfavorable or unnecessary. For instance, a trader might want exposure to stocks with the lowest price-to-earnings ratios, believing they will outperform while hedging against the broader market risk. This selective exposure helps traders maximize returns by capitalizing on perceived opportunities while minimizing the potential downside by hedging against certain risks.

Factor models are a way of explaining the returns of an asset or portfolio through a combination of the returns of another asset, portfolio, or factor. The general form of a factor model using a linear combination is as follows:

$$Y = \alpha + \beta 1 X1 + \beta 2 X2 + \beta n Xn$$

The sensitivity of portfolio returns to a risk factor X is described by the beta. It's the beta that must be hedged to concentrate exposure to the risk factors.

In this recipe, we'll construct a portfolio of stocks, compute the beta of the portfolio returns to SPY returns, and construct a hedging portfolio to neutralize the broader market exposure.

Getting ready

For this recipe, we introduce `Statsmodels`, which provides classes and functions for estimating many statistical models and for conducting statistical tests and statistical data exploration. We'll use it to conduct our analysis.

You can install `statsmodels` using `pip`:

```
pip install statsmodels
```

How to do it...

We'll use `statsmodels` to measure the sensitivity of a portfolio of stocks to a benchmark, then offset the portfolio with a short position to hedge beta:

1. Import the libraries for the analysis:

```
import matplotlib.pyplot as plt
import numpy as np
import pandas as pd
import statsmodels.api as sm
from IPython.display import Markdown, display
from openbb import obb
from statsmodels import regression
obb.user.preferences.output_type = "dataframe"
```

2. Define the stock symbols for the portfolio including SPY as the benchmark and download the data:

```
symbols = [
    "NEM",
    "RGLD",
    "SSRM",
    "CDE",
    "LLY",
    "UNH",
    "JNJ",
    "MRK",
    "SPY",
]
data = obb.equity.price.historical(
    symbols,
    start_date="2020-01-01",
    end_date="2022-12-31",
    provider="yfinance",
).pivot(columns="symbol", values="close")
```

3. Separate the SPY benchmark returns from the portfolio data and compute daily percentage returns:

```
benchmark_returns = data.pop("SPY").pct_change().dropna()
```

4. Calculate equal-weighted portfolio returns by summing individual stock returns:

```
portfolio_returns = data.pct_change().dropna().sum(axis=1)
portfolio_returns.name = "portfolio"
```

5. Plot the daily returns of both the portfolio and benchmark to visually compare their behavior:

```
portfolio_returns.plot()
benchmark_returns.plot()
plt.ylabel("Daily Return")
plt.legend()
plt.show()
```

6. The result is a plot of the daily returns during the analysis period:

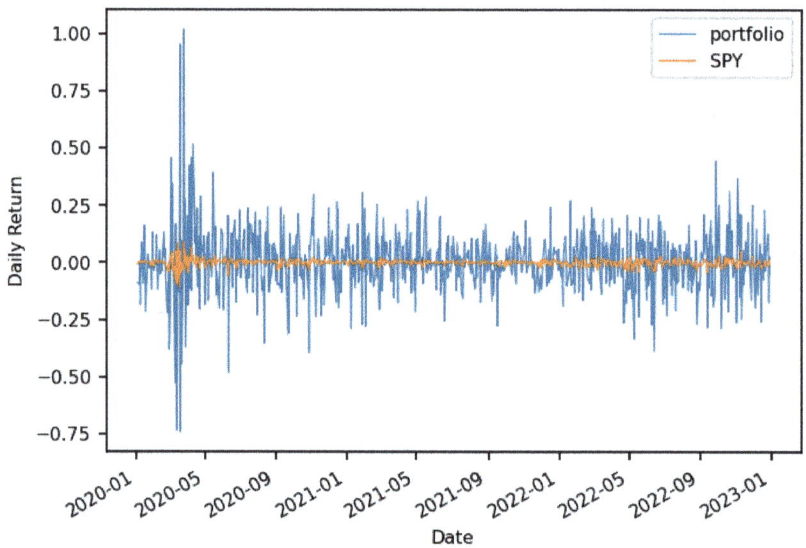

Figure 7.5: Plot of portfolio and benchmark returns

7. Create a function that returns the alpha and beta coefficients from a linear regression:

```
def linreg(x, y):
    x = sm.add_constant(x)
    model = regression.linear_model.OLS(y, x).fit()
    x = x[:, 1]
    return model.params[0], model.params[1]
```

8. Generate the alpha and beta coefficients from the regression between the portfolio and benchmark returns:

```
X = benchmark_returns.values
Y = portfolio_returns.values
alpha, beta = linreg(X, Y)
print(f"Alpha: {alpha}")  # => 0.0028
print(f"Beta: {beta}")  # => 5.5745
```

9. Create a scatter plot that visualizes the linear relationship between the portfolio and benchmark returns:

```
X2 = np.linspace(X.min(), X.max(), 100)
Y_hat = X2 * beta + alpha
plt.scatter(X, Y, alpha=0.3)
plt.xlabel("SPY daily return")
plt.ylabel("Portfolio daily return")
plt.plot(X2, Y_hat, "r", alpha=0.9)
```

The result is the following scatter plot showing the daily returns and their linear relationship:

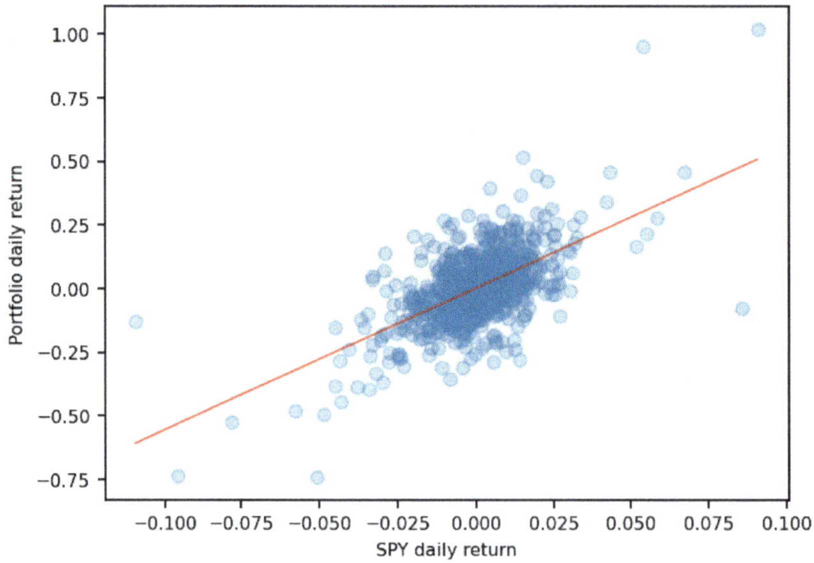

Figure 7.6: Scatter plot showing the linear relationship between the portfolio and benchmark returns

10. Finally, construct a time series of portfolio returns including the beta hedge:

```
hedged_portfolio_returns = -1 * beta * benchmark_returns +
portfolio_returns
```

11. Rerun the regression to confirm that the beta is 0:

```
P = hedged_portfolio_returns.values
_, beta = linreg(X, P)
print(f"Beta: {beta}")  => 0.0000
```

How it works...

We demonstrate the beta hedge by first constructing a portfolio of eight stocks by adding up the daily returns of each stock for each day. We use the S&P 500 tracking ETF as a proxy for the broader market. The ETF symbol is SPY. We download price data for SPY along with our portfolio for convenience, since we can use the pandas pop method on the SPY column as a separate series. We then compute the daily returns for both the portfolio and the benchmark.

The next step is running a regression that has a few lines of code. X is the independent variable representing the benchmark returns, and Y is the dependent variable representing the portfolio returns. The `linreg` function takes these returns, adds a constant term to X for the intercept, and then fits a linear model using ordinary least squares regression. It then returns the parameters of the fitted model, which are the intercept (alpha) and the slope (beta).

> Note
>
> **Important**
>
> Adding a constant term for the intercept is crucial for accurately modeling the relationship between the dependent and independent variables in a linear regression. If we do not include a constant term for the intercept, we are essentially forcing the regression line to pass through the origin (0, 0), which may not be an accurate representation of the relationship between the variables.

After we have our alpha and beta terms, we can build a hedged portfolio. As we learned in the introduction to this recipe, traders hedge exposure to risk that they don't want. If we can determine that our portfolio returns are linked to a risk factor through a linear relationship, then we can initiate a short position in that risk factor – in our case, the broader market represented by SPY. The amount we want to trade is represented by our beta. This is effective because if our returns are made up of $\alpha + \beta$ SPY, then going short β SPY will result in our new returns being $\alpha + \beta$ SPY – β SPY = α. That is, no exposure to the returns of SPY. We validate that the beta of the hedged portfolio is 0 by rerunning the regression.

There's more...

The information ratio is a measure used to evaluate the risk-adjusted performance of a trading strategy. It is calculated by dividing the portfolio's active return (the difference between the portfolio return and the benchmark return) by the active risk (the standard deviation of the active return). The information ratio is a useful way to compare two portfolios against their benchmark. Let's build a function that computes it:

```
def information_ratio(
    portfolio_returns,
    benchmark_returns
):
    active_return = portfolio_returns - benchmark_returns
    tracking_error = active_return.std()
    return active_return.mean() / tracking_error
```

Let's use the information ratio to compare the differences between our hedged and unhedged portfolios:

```
hedged_ir = information_ratio(
    hedged_portfolio_returns,
    benchmark_returns
)
unhedged_ir = information_ratio(
    portfolio_returns,
    benchmark_returns
)
print(f"Hedged information ratio: {hedged_ir}")
print(f"Unhedged information ratio: {unhedged_ir}")
```

Running the preceding code block shows us the unhedged portfolio has a lower risk-adjusted return. That's to be expected since the returns attributable to the benchmark have not been hedged.

See also

Hedging is an important part of proper risk management and successful trading. Using a simple linear relationship between the portfolio returns and the factor returns is a great way to neutralize unwanted risk. To learn more about the topic that we covered in this recipe, visit the following links:

- `Statsmodels` documentation on ordinary least squares: `https://www.statsmodels.org/stable/examples/notebooks/generated/ols.html`
- More about how beta is used in portfolio management and trading: `https://www.investopedia.com/terms/b/beta.asp`
- More about how to use the information ratio: `https://pyquantnews.com/how-to-measure-skill-portfolio-manager/`

Analyzing portfolio sensitivities to the Fama-French factors

The Fama-French factors are a set of factors identified by economists Eugene F. Fama and Kenneth R. French to explain the variation in stock returns. These factors serve as the foundation of the Fama-French three-factor model. In *Chapter 1, Acquire Free Financial Market Data with Cutting-Edge Python Libraries*, we learned how to use `pandas_datareader` to download Fama-French factor data.

In this recipe, we'll compute the exposure of our portfolio to the size and market value factors.

Getting ready

You should already have pandas_datareader installed from *Chapter 1, Acquire Free Financial Market Data with Cutting-Edge Python Libraries*. If not, you can install it using pip:

```
pip install pandas_datareader
```

We'll also assume you have the data DataFrame loaded with historic prices created in the last recipe.

How to do it...

We'll reuse what we learned in the prior recipes about using beta to compute factor sensitivities.

1. Import the libraries we need for the analysis:

```
import numpy as np
import pandas as pd
import pandas_datareader as pdr
from openbb import obb
import statsmodels.api as sm
from statsmodels import regression
from statsmodels.regression.rolling import RollingOLS
obb.user.preferences.output_type = "dataframe"
```

2. Now, resample the daily return data to monthly using asfreq and replace the row labels with monthly format using to_period. This is the format of the Fama-French factor data. A consistent format lets us align the data in the same DataFrame later:

```
monthly_returns = (
    data
    .asfreq("M")
    .dropna()
    .pct_change(fill_method=None)
    .to_period("M")
)
```

The result is a DataFrame with monthly returns suitable for alignment with the Fama-French monthly factor data:

Date	NEM	RGLD	SSRM	CDE	LLY	UNH	JNJ	MRK	SPY
2015-01	NaN	NaN	NaN	NaN	NaN	NaN	NaN	NaN	NaN
2015-02	NaN	NaN	NaN	NaN	NaN	NaN	NaN	NaN	NaN
2015-03	NaN	NaN	NaN	NaN	NaN	NaN	NaN	NaN	NaN
2015-04	0.220175	0.022500	0.203091	0.108280	-0.010736	-0.058247	-0.013917	0.036186	0.009834
2015-05	0.000000	0.000000	0.000000	0.000000	0.000000	0.000000	0.000000	0.000000	0.000000
...	...	...	...	...	...	...	...	...	...
2022-07	0.000000	0.000000	0.000000	0.000000	0.000000	0.000000	0.000000	0.000000	0.000000
2022-08	-0.306854	-0.139352	-0.188644	-0.092105	-0.067904	0.011098	-0.084986	-0.063727	0.047528
2022-09	0.029778	0.020892	0.090437	0.239130	0.073432	-0.024465	0.012520	0.017037	-0.092446
2022-10	0.006900	0.015798	-0.061863	0.105263	0.119808	0.099220	0.064949	0.175105	0.081275
2022-11	0.121692	0.182919	0.103917	-0.074074	0.027687	-0.013312	0.029769	0.088142	0.055592

Figure 7.7: DataFrame with monthly portfolio returns

3. Next, we compute the active returns and use them as the dependent variable. This will help us understand the sensitivity of the Fama-French factors to our active returns:

```
bench = monthly_returns.pop("SPY")
R = monthly_returns.mean(axis=1)
active = (R - bench).dropna()
```

4. Now, let's download the Fama-French data using `pandas_datareader`:

```
factors = pdr.get_data_famafrench(
    'F-F_Research_Data_Factors',
    start="2015-01-01",
    end="2022-12-31"
)[0][1:] / 100
SMB = factors.loc[active.index, "SMB"]
HML = factors.loc[active.index, "HML"]
```

5. Now that we have our returns and factor data, build a pandas `DataFrame` that aligns the data along the common date index:

```
df = pd.DataFrame(
    {
```

```
            "R": active,
            "SMB": SMB,
            "HML": HML,
        },
        index=active.index
    ).dropna()
```

6. Run the regression and get the beta coefficients for each factor. These coefficients represent the exposure of our active returns to the Fama-French factors:

```
b1, b2 = regression.linear_model.OLS(
    df.R,
    df[["SMB", "HML"]]
).fit().params
To see how these sensitivities evolve through time, use the Statsmodels
RollingOLS class:
exog = sm.add_constant(df[["SMB", "HML"]])
rols = RollingOLS(active, exog, window=12)
rres = rols.fit()
fig = rres.plot_recursive_coefficient(
    variables=["SMB", "HML"],
    figsize=(5.5, 6.6)
)
```

This results in the following two charts that plot the 12-month rolling regression over time along with the 95% confidence intervals:

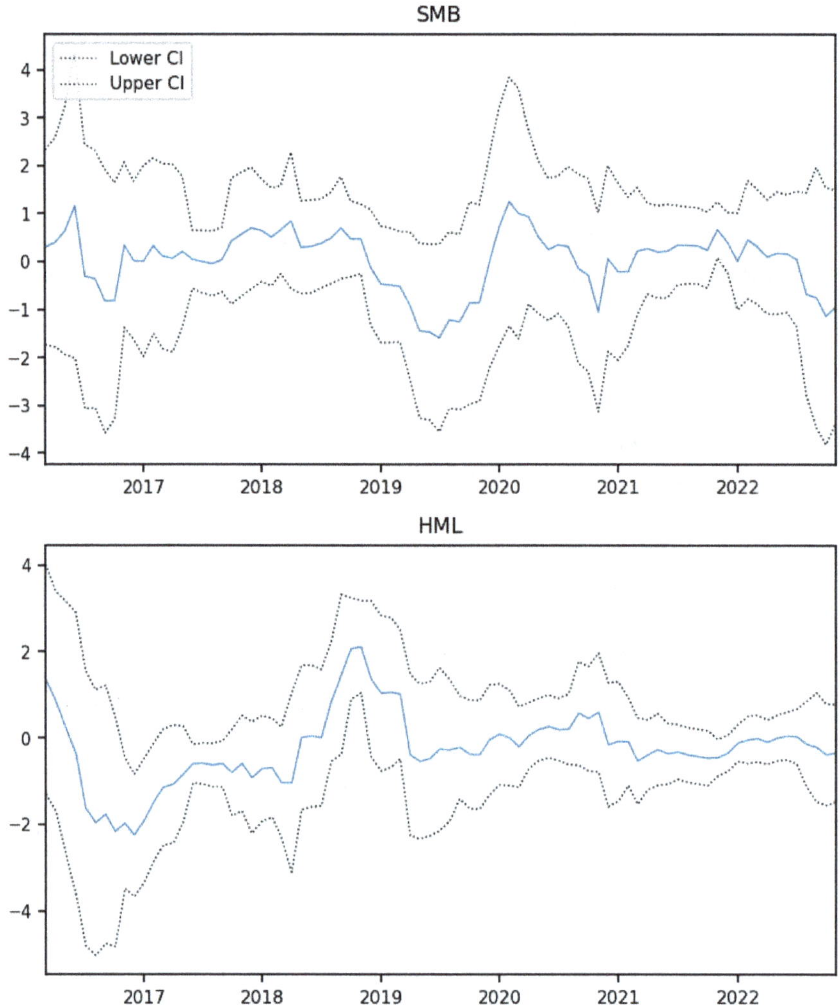

Figure 7.8: Betas for two of the Fama-French factors using a 12-month rolling window

How it works...

We follow the same procedure in downloading financial market data using `OpenBB` and computing portfolio returns as in the *Finding and hedging portfolio beta using linear regression* recipe in this chapter. The Fama-French factor data is in monthly resolution, so we use `asfreq` and `to_period` to resample our price data to monthly, then compute monthly returns.

From there, we compute active returns, which are the portion of portfolio returns that cannot be attributed to the market's overall movement and are instead a result of active portfolio management decisions. As we learned, investment factors are systematic risk factors that explain the differences in returns between different securities. A portfolio's active return can be influenced by its exposure to these factors.

To measure the exposure, we compute the beta coefficients of the factors using the `OLS` method from the `Statsmodels` library to fit a linear regression model. The dependent variable is `df.R`, which represents the active returns of our portfolio, while the independent variables are `df["SMB"]` and `df["HML"]`, representing the **Small Minus Big** (**SMB**) and **High Minus Low** (**HML**) factors of the Fama-French three-factor model, respectively. The `fit` method is used to estimate the parameters of the model, which, in this case, are the betas for the `SMB` and `HML` factors stored in b1 and b2.

To get an idea of how the exposures evolve through time, we build a rolling regression using the `RollingOLS` class. The exogenous variable is created by adding a constant column (for the intercept) to the `SMB` and `HML` factors. The `RollingOLS` class is then initialized with a window size of 12, and the `fit` method is called to compute the rolling OLS estimates. Finally, the `plot_recursive_coefficient` method is used to create a plot of the rolling estimates of the regression coefficients for `SMB` and `HML` over the 12-period window.

There's more...

Marginal Contribution to Active Risk (**MCAR**) quantifies the additional active risk each factor brings to your portfolio. Mathematically, the MCAR for factor i is expressed as MCAR_i = [β_i × Σ_j (β_j × Cov(F_i, F_j))] / σ²_a, where β_i is the sensitivity to factor i, Cov(F_i, F_j) is the covariance between factors i and j, and σ²_a is the variance of active returns. To compute the `MCAR` of the factors, we multiply the factor sensitivity by the covariance between the factors and then divide by the square of the standard deviation of the active returns. This calculation shows the amount of risk incurred by being exposed to each factor, considering the exposures to other factors already in your portfolio. The risk contribution that is not explained is the exposure to factors other than the ones being analyzed.

```
F1 = df.SMB
F2 = df.HML
cov = np.cov(F1, F2)
ar_squared = (active.std()) ** 2
mcar1 = (b1 * (b2 * cov[0, 1] + b1 * cov[0, 0])) / ar_squared
mcar2 = (b2 * (b1 * cov[0, 1] + b2 * cov[1, 1])) / ar_squared
print(f"SMB risk contribution: {mcar1}")
print(f"HML risk contribution: {mcar2}")
print(f"Unexplained risk contribution: {1 - (mcar1 + mcar2)}")
```

Running the preceding code shows only about 0.7% of the risk is explained by these two factors. Let's plot the `MCAR` for these factors over time:

1. Compute the 12-month rolling covariances between the factors:

```
covariances = (
    df[["SMB", "HML"]]
    .rolling(window=12)
    .cov()
).dropna()
```

2. Compute the 12-month rolling active return squared:

```
active_risk_squared = (
    active.rolling(window=12).std()**2
).dropna()
```

3. Combine the rolling factor betas:

```
betas = pd.concat(
    [rres.params.SMB, rres.params.HML],
    axis=1
).dropna()
```

4. Create an empty `DataFrame` to store the rolling `MCAR` data:

```
MCAR = pd.DataFrame(
    index=betas.index,
    columns=betas.columns
)
```

5. Loop through each factor and each date, computing the `MCAR` value:

```
for factor in betas.columns:
    for t in betas.index:
        s = np.sum(
            betas.loc[t] * covariances.loc[t][factor])
        b = betas.loc[t][factor]
```

```
        AR = active_risk_squared.loc[t]
        MCAR[factor][t] = b * s / AR
```

6. Finally, plot the MCAR for each factor as follows:

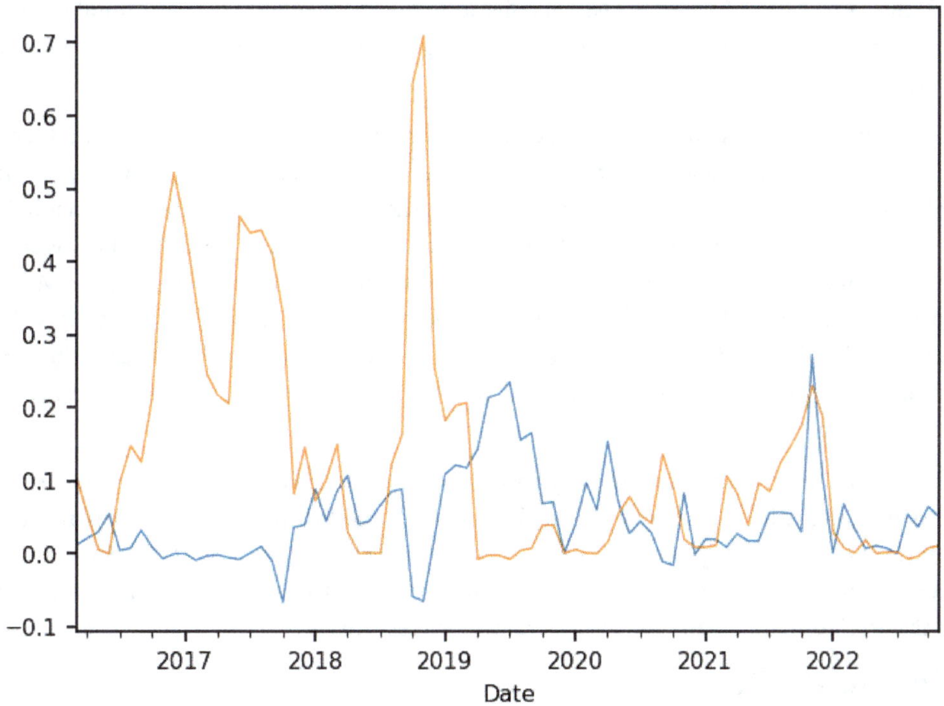

Figure 7.9: Rolling marginal contribution to risk for the two Fama-French factors

See also

By systematically selecting securities with certain factor characteristics, investors aim to achieve better risk-adjusted returns compared to the broader market or a specific benchmark. Factor investing is a broad and deep topic. To learn more about factor investing, visit the following links:

- **BlackRock's introduction to factor investing**: `https://www.blackrock.com/us/individual/investment-ideas/what-is-factor-investing`

`Advances in Active Portfolio Management` by Richard Grinold and Ronald Kahn is an advanced guide that delves deep into the quantitative aspects of active portfolio management, including topics such as portfolio construction, risk management, and implementation: `https://amzn.to/44zJeMk`

Assessing market inefficiency based on volatility

Using volatility as a factor reflects the market inefficiency related to the pricing of volatile stocks. Historically, stocks with lower volatility have tended to outperform those with higher volatility on a risk-adjusted basis. This phenomenon contradicts the traditional finance theory that higher risk should be compensated with higher return and thus represents a market inefficiency.

One of the first steps in analyzing a factor's performance is calculating forward returns. Forward returns are the returns of a security in a future period. Once the forward returns are calculated, we can use the Spearman rank correlation to understand the relationship between the factor and the forward returns. The Spearman rank correlation assesses how well the relationship between two variables can be described using a monotonic function. A high Spearman rank correlation indicates that the factor ranks securities in a way that is closely aligned with the ranking of securities by their forward returns, suggesting that the factor has predictive power. Conversely, a low Spearman rank correlation suggests that the factor is not a good predictor of forward returns.

The Parkinson estimator uses the high and low prices over a period to get a more accurate measure of volatility. The basic idea is that the high and low prices encapsulate more information about the price movement than just the closing prices. In this recipe, we'll build a factor using Parkinson volatility, compute the forward returns, and determine the Spearman rank correlation between the factor and forward returns.

How to do it...

We'll calculate Parkinson volatility and forward returns to measure the predictive power of Parkinson volatility as a tradable factor:

1. Import the libraries we'll use for the analysis:

```
import numpy as np
import pandas as pd
import seaborn as sns
import matplotlib.pyplot as plt
from openbb import obb
from scipy.stats import spearmanr
obb.user.preferences.output_type = "dataframe"
```

2. Use `OpenBB` to download data:

```
symbols = ["NEM", "RGLD", "SSRM", "CDE", "LLY", "UNH", "JNJ", "MRK"]
data = obb.equity.price.historical(
    symbols,
    start_date="2015-01-01",
    end_date="2022-12-31",
    provider="yfinance"
)
prices = data[["high", "low", "close", "volume", "symbol"]]
```

3. As a preprocessing step, let's make sure all our tickers have at least two years of data. We'll create a mask and grab the stocks that meet our criteria:

```
nobs = prices.groupby("symbol").size()
mask = nobs[nobs > 2 * 12 * 21].index
prices = prices[prices.symbol.isin(mask)]
```

4. Next, set the symbol column as an index, reorder, and drop duplicates:

```
prices = (
    prices
    .set_index("symbol", append=True)
    .reorder_levels(["symbol", "date"])
    .sort_index(level=0)
).drop_duplicates()
```

The result is the following `MultiIndex DataFrame` with symbol as the first index and date as the second:

		high	low	close	volume
symbol	**date**				
CDE	**2015-01-02**	5.30	4.96	5.30	2864400
	2015-01-05	5.45	5.14	5.44	2997000
	2015-01-06	5.73	5.45	5.69	3885200
	2015-01-07	5.94	5.47	5.61	4099700
	2015-01-08	5.85	5.51	5.60	2903300

Figure 7.10: MultiIndex DataFrame with symbol and date as indexes

5. Next, we'll create a function that returns the normalized Parkinson volatility estimate:

```
def parkinson(data, window=14, trading_days=252):
    rs = (1.0 / (4.0 * np.log(2.0))) * ((
        data.high / data.low).apply(np.log))**2.0
    def f(v):
        return (trading_days * v.mean())**0.5
    result = rs.rolling(
        window=window,
        center=False
    ).apply(func=f)
    return result.sub(result.mean()).div(result.std())
```

6. We'll apply that function to each group of stocks and add the Parkinson estimator as a new column:

```
prices["vol"] = (
    prices
    .groupby("symbol", group_keys=False)
    .apply(parkinson)
)
prices.dropna(inplace=True)
```

The result is the `MultiIndex DataFrame` with each stock's normalized Parkinson volatility added as a new column:

		high	low	close	volume	vol
symbol	**date**					
CDE	**2015-01-22**	6.43	6.15	6.31	3404900	0.502344
	2015-01-23	6.25	5.93	5.99	2234000	0.466274
	2015-01-26	6.13	5.69	6.11	2149800	0.512970
	2015-01-27	6.42	6.12	6.32	3697700	0.508157
	2015-01-28	6.36	5.89	5.99	2668300	0.488355

Figure 7.11: Updated MultiIndex DataFrame with per-stock normalized Parkinson volatility

7. Now that we have the normalized Parkinson volatility, we can compute historic and forward returns. First, compute the historic returns over 1, 5, 10, 21, 42, and 63 periods representing one day through three months:

```
lags = [1, 5, 10, 21, 42, 63]
for lag in lags:
    prices[f"return_{lag}d"] = (
        prices
        .groupby(level="symbol")
        .close
        .pct_change(lag)
    )
```

8. Compute the forward returns for the same periods:

```
for t in [1, 5, 10, 21, 42, 63]:
    prices[f"target_{t}d"] = (
        prices
        .groupby(level="symbol")[f"return_{t}d"]
        .shift(-t)
    )
```

The result is new columns in the prices `DataFrame` representing the historical and forward returns, as shown in the following screenshot:

symbol	date	high	low	close	volume	vol	return_1d	return_5d	return_10d	return_21d	return_42d	return_63d	target_1d	target_5d	target_10d	target_21d	target_42d	target_63d
CDE	2015-01-22	6.43	6.15	6.31	3404900	0.502344	NaN	NaN	NaN	NaN	NaN	NaN	-0.050713	-0.058637	0.145800	-0.083994	-0.133122	-0.118859
	2015-01-23	6.25	5.93	5.99	2234000	0.466274	-0.050713	NaN	NaN	NaN	NaN	NaN	0.020033	0.051753	0.170284	-0.083472	-0.118531	-0.136895
	2015-01-26	6.13	5.69	6.11	2149800	0.512970	0.020033	NaN	NaN	NaN	NaN	NaN	0.034370	0.045827	0.189853	-0.094926	-0.147300	-0.067103
	2015-01-27	6.42	6.12	6.32	3697700	0.508157	0.034370	NaN	NaN	NaN	NaN	NaN	-0.052215	0.036392	0.136076	-0.115506	-0.202532	-0.106013
	2015-01-28	6.36	5.89	5.99	2668300	0.488355	-0.052215	NaN	NaN	NaN	NaN	NaN	-0.008347	0.188648	0.158598	-0.025042	-0.191987	-0.086811
...	...	...	...	...	...	...	...	...	...	...	...	...	...	...	...	...	...	...
UNH	2022-12-23	531.31	522.90	531.31	1292300	-0.477275	0.008006	0.014531	-0.014633	0.003021	-0.016493	0.045145	0.001280	NaN	NaN	NaN	NaN	NaN
	2022-12-27	535.84	529.85	531.99	1596700	-0.480026	0.001280	0.016024	-0.025409	-0.010472	-0.020583	0.046462	-0.006654	NaN	NaN	NaN	NaN	NaN
	2022-12-28	538.15	527.73	528.45	1694200	-0.429141	-0.006654	0.015840	-0.018152	-0.007177	-0.024640	0.028233	0.002706	NaN	NaN	NaN	NaN	NaN
	2022-12-29	533.68	528.86	529.88	1379700	-0.450631	0.002706	0.004436	-0.015752	0.003561	-0.038749	0.041369	0.000566	NaN	NaN	NaN	NaN	NaN
	2022-12-30	530.50	524.84	530.18	1849600	-0.491593	0.000566	0.005862	0.004738	-0.032094	-0.044979	0.049778	NaN	NaN	NaN	NaN	NaN	NaN

Figure 7.12: DataFrame with historic and forward returns for each stock in our portfolio

9. Print the first 10 rows for the first symbol to inspect the historic returns for each period:

date	high	low	close	volume	vol	return_1d	return_5d	return_10d	return_21d	return_42d	return_63d	target_1d	target_5d	target_10d	target_21d	target_42d	target_63d
2015-01-22	24.69	23.98	24.29	13132700	1.021514	NaN	NaN	NaN	NaN	NaN	NaN	-0.005764	-0.004940	0.021820	0.068753	-0.058872	-0.034582
2015-01-23	24.43	23.67	24.15	12056800	0.976772	-0.005764	NaN	NaN	NaN	NaN	NaN	0.014079	0.041408	-0.004141	0.068737	-0.069151	0.034369
2015-01-26	24.63	23.35	24.49	11189200	1.059908	0.014079	NaN	NaN	NaN	NaN	NaN	0.026541	0.025316	0.004900	0.063699	-0.095141	0.044916
2015-01-27	25.25	24.53	25.14	10774500	0.948081	0.026541	NaN	NaN	NaN	NaN	NaN	-0.035004	-0.020684	-0.029037	0.046539	-0.115752	0.048130
2015-01-28	25.05	24.03	24.26	11251300	0.962112	-0.035004	NaN	NaN	NaN	NaN	NaN	-0.003710	0.023083	-0.004946	0.085326	-0.092333	0.091509
2015-01-29	24.34	23.42	24.17	8850000	1.016856	-0.003710	-0.004940	NaN	NaN	NaN	NaN	0.040546	0.026893	0.014067	0.071163	-0.101779	0.095987
2015-01-30	25.22	23.92	25.15	11594400	1.139382	0.040546	0.041408	NaN	NaN	NaN	NaN	-0.001590	-0.043738	-0.014712	0.018688	-0.096620	0.053280
2015-02-02	25.20	24.56	25.11	7497000	1.109351	-0.001590	0.025316	NaN	NaN	NaN	NaN	-0.019514	-0.019912	-0.036639	0.003186	-0.110315	0.037435
2015-02-03	25.07	24.14	24.62	9038100	0.957277	-0.019514	-0.020684	NaN	NaN	NaN	NaN	0.008123	-0.008530	0.004874	0.027620	-0.082859	0.054021
2015-02-04	25.03	24.50	24.82	7071100	0.708258	0.008123	0.023083	NaN	NaN	NaN	NaN	0.000000	-0.027397	-0.014504	-0.061241	-0.106769	0.033441

Figure 7.13: Slice of the prices DataFrame showing historic returns for stock NEM

10. Finally, use the Seaborn plotting library to visualize how the one-day forward return is related to the normalized Parkinson volatility factor:

```
target = "target_1d"
metric = "vol"
j = sns.jointplot(
    x=metric,
    y=target,
    data=prices
)
plt.tight_layout()
df = prices[[metric, target]].dropna()
r, p = spearmanr(df[metric], df[target])
```

The result is the following joint plot, which shows the relationship along with the distributions of the values:

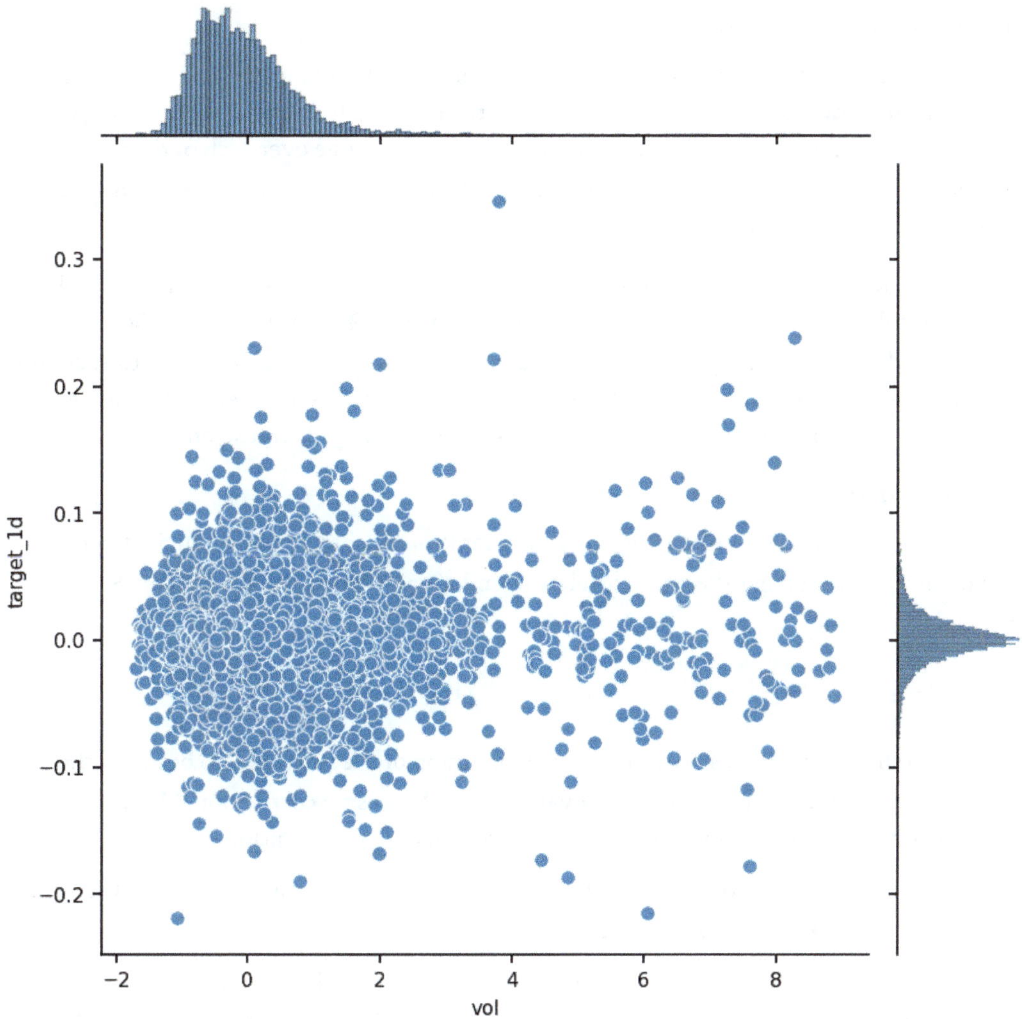

Figure 7.14: Joint plot of normalized Parkinson volatility versus one-day forward return

How it works...

In this recipe, we begin to touch on the data preprocessing required when preparing data for factor analysis.

We modify the `DataFrame` with the historical data by setting symbol as a part of a MultiIndex, reordering the levels of the index to have symbol first, and then removing any duplicate rows. This allows us to apply the normalized Parkinson volatility to each group in the next step. To do it, we group by symbol and use the apply method to apply our custom Parkinson volatility function to each chunk of data.

Finally, we compute the historic and forward returns. In the first loop, the code computes historical returns over several periods specified in the lags list. It does this by grouping the `DataFrame` by symbol and then computing the percentage change over each of the specified lags. These historical returns are then added to the `DataFrame` as new columns with the names `return_1d`, `return_5d`, and so on.

In the second loop, the code computes future returns for several periods specified in the list. It does this by taking the already computed historical returns (`return_1d`, `return_5d`, and so on) and shifting them up by the specified number of periods. This essentially assigns to each row the return that will occur *t* days in the future. These future returns are then added to the `DataFrame` as new columns with the names `target_1d`, `target_5d`, and so on.

There's more...

The `spearmanr` function computes the Spearman rank-order correlation coefficient between two data arrays. We can get the rank correlation and p-value using the `spearmanr` `SciPy` method:

```
stat, pvalue = spearmanr(df[metric], df[target])
```

The `stat` coefficient measures the strength and direction of the relationship between the two variables, with a value between -1 and 1. A value of 0 indicates no correlation, 1 indicates a perfect positive correlation, and -1 indicates a perfect negative correlation.

In this context, `stat` is the correlation between Parkinson volatility and the forward returns, which is 0.0378, a weak positive correlation.

The `pvalue` tests the null hypothesis that the data is uncorrelated. A small `pvalue` (typically ≤ 0.05) indicates that you can reject the null hypothesis. In this case, the `pvalue` is 0.0158, so we reject the null hypothesis, which suggests there is a statistically significant correlation between the Parkinson volatility and the returns of this portfolio.

See also

For more resources on the tools and techniques used in this recipe, visit the following links:

- Walk-through of Parkinson volatility: `https://www.ivolatility.com/help/3.html`
- Average true range: `https://en.wikipedia.org/wiki/Average_true_range`

- Spearman rank correlation: `https://en.wikipedia.org/wiki/Spearman%27s_rank_correlation_coefficient`
- SciPy's implementation of the Spearman rank correlation coefficient documentation: `https://docs.scipy.org/doc/scipy/reference/generated/scipy.stats.spearmanr.html`

Preparing a factor ranking model using zipline pipeline

Zipline Reloaded is an open source Python library that provides a comprehensive backtesting framework for algorithmic trading. The library provides tools to manage the algorithm's capital, set trading commissions, and simulate orders.

One of the most powerful features of Zipline Reloaded is the Pipeline API. Pipelines let us define factors from columns of data from bundles. Pipelines efficiently process large amounts of data in a single pass while also filtering down to a smaller set of assets of interest. Pipelines allow us to rank a universe of stocks based on the computed factor and output those data in a format suitable for the Alphalens library, which analyzes factor performance and risk. We'll look at Alphalens in *Chapter 10, Evaluate Factor Risk and Performance with Alphalens Reloaded.*

In this recipe, we'll build a data bundle using free stock market data, define a momentum factor, and rank a universe of stocks based on their performance in that factor.

Getting ready

Zipline Reloaded has a built-in process to download and bundle free historical market data from Nasdaq Data Link. Zipline Reloaded requires an API key to be set before using it.

Since an account is free, it makes sense to sign up. This is something you can do via the Nasdaq Data Link website (`https://data.nasdaq.com/`). Your API key is in your profile (`https://data.nasdaq.com/account/profile`).

After you get your API key set up, install Zipline Reloaded. The steps differ depending on your operating system.

For windows, Unix/Linux, and mac intel users

If you're running on an Intel x86 chip, you can use conda:

```
conda install -c conda-forge zipline-reloaded pyfolio-reloaded alphalens-reloaded
-y
```

For apple silicon users

If you have a Mac with an M-series chip, you need to install some dependencies first. The easiest way is to use Homebrew (`https://brew.sh`).

Install the dependencies with Homebrew:

```
brew install freetype pkg-config gcc openssl hdf5 ta-lib
```

Install the Python dependencies with `conda`:

```
conda install -c conda-forge pytables h5py -y
```

Install the Zipline Reloaded ecosystem:

```
pip install zipline-reloaded pyfolio-reloaded alphalens-reloaded
```

In this example, we'll use the free data bundle provided by Nasdaq Data Link. This dataset has market price data on 3,000 stocks through 2018.

The free dataset is great for getting up and running but it is limited. We'll explore more robust options in *Chapter 9, Event-Based Backtesting Factor Portfolios with Zipline Reloaded*. Make sure you have your Nasdaq Data Link API key handy.

How to do it...

To build the analysis, we'll import the required Zipline Reloaded modules:

1. Import the libraries we need for the analysis:

```
import os
import numpy as np
import pandas as pd
from zipline.data.bundles.core import load
from zipline.pipeline import Pipeline
from zipline.pipeline.data import USEquityPricing
from zipline.pipeline.engine import SimplePipelineEngine
from zipline.pipeline.factors import (
    AverageDollarVolume, CustomFactor, Returns)
from zipline.pipeline.loaders import USEquityPricingLoader
```

2. Set your API key as an environment variable and load the free Nasdaq data into a bundle:

```
os.environ["QUANDL_API_KEY"] = "YOUR_API_KEY"
bundle_data = load("quandl", os.environ, None)
```

3. Build a US equity pricing loader:

```
pipeline_loader = USEquityPricingLoader(
    bundle_data.equity_daily_bar_reader,
    bundle_data.adjustment_reader,
    fx_reader=None
)
```

4. Use the pricing loader to create a Pipeline engine:

```
engine = SimplePipelineEngine(
    get_loader=lambda col: pipeline_loader,
    asset_finder=bundle_data.asset_finder
)
```

5. Implement a custom 12 month – 1 month momentum factor, common within the industry, that returns a measure of price momentum:

```
class MomentumFactor(CustomFactor):
    inputs = [USEquityPricing.close, Returns(window_length=126)]
    window_length = 252
    def compute(self, today, assets, out, prices, returns):
        out[:] = (
            (prices[-21] -prices[-252]) / prices[-252]
            - (prices[-1] - prices[-21]) / prices[-21]
        ) / np.nanstd(returns, axis=0)
```

6. Create a that instantiates the custom momentum factor, builds a filter for average dollar volume over the last 30 days, and returns a Pipeline:

```
def make_pipeline():
    momentum = MomentumFactor()
    dollar_volume = AverageDollarVolume(window_length=30)
    return Pipeline(
        columns={
```

```
            "factor": momentum,
            "longs": momentum.top(50),
            "shorts": momentum.bottom(50),
            "rank": momentum.rank()
        },
        screen=dollar_volume.top(100)
    )
```

7. Run the Pipeline:

```
results = engine.run_pipeline(
    make_pipeline(),
    pd.to_datetime("2012-01-04"),
    pd.to_datetime("2012-03-01")
)
```

8. Clean up the resulting DataFrame by removing records with no factor data, adding names to the MultiIndex and sorting the values first by date and then by factor value:

```
results.dropna(subset="factor", inplace=True)
results.index.names = ["date", "symbol"]
results.sort_values(by=["date", "factor"], inplace=True)
```

The result is a `MultiIndex DataFrame` including the raw factor value, Boolean values indicating a short or long position, and how the stock's factor value is ranked among the universe:

		factor	longs	shorts	rank
date	**symbol**				
2012-01-04	**Equity(300 [BAC])**	-2.522045	False	False	165.0
	Equity(1264 [GS])	-2.215784	False	False	220.0
	Equity(1888 [MS])	-2.204802	False	False	225.0
	Equity(1894 [MSFT])	-1.949654	False	False	295.0
	Equity(457 [C])	-1.830819	False	False	345.0
...	**...**	...	...	...	...
2012-03-01	**Equity(3105 [WMT])**	3.409414	False	False	2607.0
	Equity(1690 [LLY])	3.809608	False	False	2642.0
	Equity(399 [BMY])	4.689588	True	False	2685.0
	Equity(1770 [MCD])	4.816880	True	False	2691.0
	Equity(1789 [MDLZ])	5.680276	True	False	2706.0

Figure 7.15: MultiIndex DataFrame with factor information and trading indicators

How it works...

The first step is to initialize a Pipeline loader for US equities. `USEquityPricingLoader` is responsible for loading pricing and adjustment data for US equities from the specified data sources. The `SimplePipelineEngine` class is used to run a pipeline. The `get_loader` parameter is a function that returns a loader to be used to load the data needed for the pipeline. In this case, it's a lambda function that always returns the previously defined `pipeline_loader`. The `asset_finder` parameter is used to do asset lookups. Here, it is set to the `asset_finder` of `bundle_data`, which is an object that knows how to look up asset metadata for the bundle.

Our code defines a custom factor, `MomentumFactor`. This factor computes momentum as the percentage change in price over the first 126 days of the 252-day window minus the percentage change in price over the last 21 days, divided by the standard deviation of the returns over the 252-day window. `inputs` is the data that the factor needs: the close prices of the US equities and the returns over a 126-day window. Window length is the number of days of data that the compute method will receive. The `compute` method is where the actual computation of the factor is done. The out array is where the computed factor values are stored. The [:] after out is used to modify the out array in place.

Next, we implement a function called `make_pipeline` that brings the factor, the universe screener, and Pipeline together. The `MomentumFactor` class is instantiated to compute momentum, and the `AverageDollarVolume` function is used with a 30-day window to calculate average dollar volume. The pipeline includes columns for the momentum factor, Boolean masks for selecting the top and bottom 50 securities based on momentum, and the momentum rank across all securities. Additionally, the pipeline employs a screen to focus on the top 100 securities by dollar volume.

There's more...

Zipline Reloaded comes with many built-in factor classes that can be used within trading algorithms. Some of the more commonly used factors are as follows:

- `ExponentialWeightedMovingAverage`: Computes the exponential weighted moving average over a specified window length
- `BollingerBands`: Computes the Bollinger Bands over a specified window length
- `VWAP`: Computes the volume-weighted average price over a specified window length

- `AnnualizedVolatility`: Computes the annualized volatility of an asset over a specified window length
- `MaxDrawdown`: Computes the maximum drawdown of an asset over a specified window length

See also

To learn more about Zipline Reloaded, see the documentation here: `https://zipline.ml4trading.io`.

Get this book's PDF version and more

Scan th QR code (or go to `packtpub.com/unlock`). Search for this book by name, confirm the edition, and then follow the steps on the page.

UNLOCK NOW

Note: Keep your invoice handy. Purchases made directly from Packt don't require an invoice.

8

Vector-Based Backtesting with VectorBT

Now that we've touched on the fundamental Python tools for algorithmic trading, we'll move to the next phase of the workflow: backtesting. Since most strategies will not consistently make money, and those that do may only make money for a short time, quickly iterating through ideas is critical. This chapter demonstrates how to use vector-based backtesting for the simulation and optimization of trading strategies.

VectorBT is a high-performance, vector-based backtesting framework that allows for efficient evaluation of trading strategies by processing entire time-series data arrays at once, rather than one data point at a time. This method significantly speeds up backtesting operations, making it ideal for rapid strategy iteration. The technique is highly customizable, enabling traders to fine-tune parameters and assess multiple strategies concurrently. We will explore the optimization of these strategies with VectorBT.

In this chapter, we will explore the following recipes:

- Building technical strategies with VectorBT
- Conducting walk-forward optimization with VectorBT
- Optimizing the SuperTrend strategy with VectorBT Pro

Building technical strategies with VectorBT

This recipe introduces you to the powerful vector-based backtesting library `VectorBT`. One of the most compelling advantages of using `VectorBT` is its speed in running simulations. Whether you are testing a single strategy or optimizing across a multi-dimensional parameter space, `VectorBT` instance's performance is optimized to deliver results in a fraction of the time traditional methods would require.

Built on top of well-established libraries such as pandas, `NumPy`, and `Numba`, `VectorBT` seamlessly integrates into the data science ecosystem. It leverages pandas for its `DataFrame` structure, which is familiar to most quants. `NumPy's` numerical computing abilities provide the mathematical backbone, ensuring that heavy calculations are performed efficiently. However, the real game-changer is `Numba`, a **Just-In-Time (JIT)** compiler that translates Python functions to optimized machine code at runtime. Thanks to `Numba`, `VectorBT` can execute loops and mathematical operations at speeds comparable to those of a low-level language, all while allowing you to write in Python. Numba can be used outside of VectorBT and should be considered when using numerical computations. This recipe introduces VectorBT by building a simple moving average crossover strategy (the `Hello World` of trading strategy development).

Getting ready

There are two versions of VectorBT: a free open-source library and a more fully featured Pro version. This recipe uses the free open-source version.

You can install it using `pip`:

```
pip install vectorbt
```

How to do it...

VectorBT can be considered an extension of pandas. Let's see it in action:

1. Import the libraries needed for the analysis:

```
import pandas as pd
import vectorbt as vbt
```

2. Download data using the built-in data downloading class:

```
start = "2016-01-01 UTC"
end = "2020-01-01 UTC"
prices = vbt.YFData.download(
    ["META", "AAPL", "AMZN", "NFLX", "GOOG"],
    start=start,
    end=end
).get("Close")
```

The result is the following pandas `DataFrame` with the closing prices for the selected symbols:

symbol	META	AAPL	AMZN	NFLX	GOOG
Date					
2016-01-04 05:00:00+00:00	102.220001	24.009066	31.849501	109.959999	37.091999
2016-01-05 05:00:00+00:00	102.730003	23.407415	31.689501	107.660004	37.129002
2016-01-06 05:00:00+00:00	102.970001	22.949339	31.632500	117.680000	37.181000
2016-01-07 05:00:00+00:00	97.919998	21.980770	30.396999	114.559998	36.319500
2016-01-08 05:00:00+00:00	97.330002	22.096996	30.352501	111.389999	35.723499

Figure 8.1: A pandas DataFrame with market data

3. Build the moving average indicators using VectorBT's built-in MA class:

```
fast_ma = vbt.MA.run(prices, 10, short_name="fast")
slow_ma = vbt.MA.run(prices, 30, short_name="slow")
```

4. Next, we'll find the entry positions. In this example, these occur when the fast-moving average crosses above the slow-moving average:

```
entries = fast_ma.ma_crossed_above(slow_ma)
```

The result is the following pandas DataFrame containing boolean values where trades should be entered:

fast_window	10				
slow_window	30				
symbol	META	AAPL	AMZN	NFLX	GOOG
Date					
2016-01-04 05:00:00+00:00	False	False	False	False	False
2016-01-05 05:00:00+00:00	False	False	False	False	False
2016-01-06 05:00:00+00:00	False	False	False	False	False
2016-01-07 05:00:00+00:00	False	False	False	False	False
2016-01-08 05:00:00+00:00	False	False	False	False	False

Figure 8.2: A pandas DataFrame with locations of entry positions

5. Do the opposite for the exit positions:

```
exits = fast_ma.ma_crossed_below(slow_ma)
```

6. Run the backtest using the entry and exit signals:

```
pf = vbt.Portfolio.from_signals(prices, entries,exits)
```

7. Visualize the mean daily return for each symbol:

```
pf.total_return().groupby("symbol").mean().vbt.barplot()
```

The result is an interactive Plotly bar chart with the mean daily returns for each symbol:

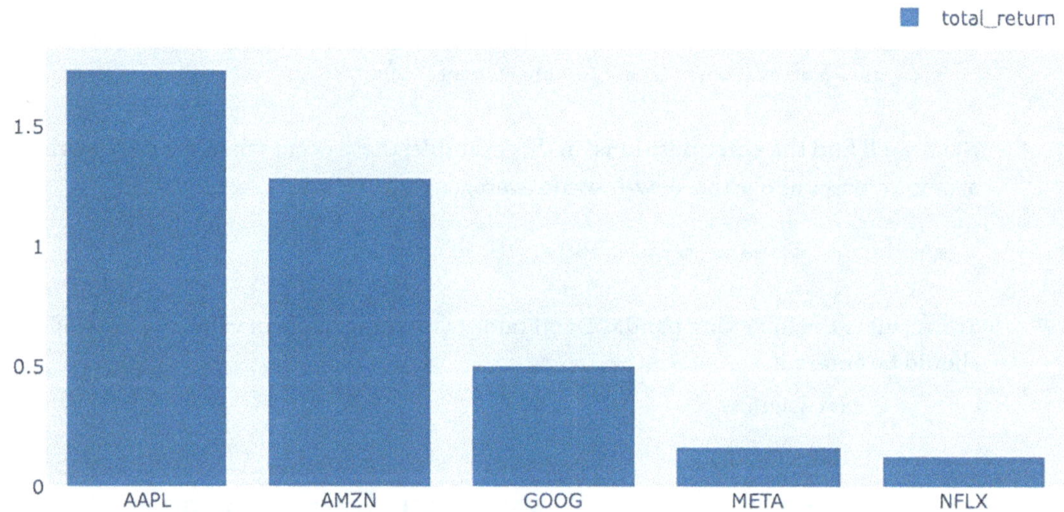

Figure 8.3: Interactive Plotly bar chart with the mean daily returns for each symbol

8. Inspect the returns for each symbol by simply holding each throughout the analysis period:

```
(
    vbt
    .Portfolio
    .from_holding(
        prices,
        freq='1d'
    )
```

```
        .total_return()
        .groupby("symbol")
        .mean()
        .vbt
        .barplot()
)
```

The result is the following bar chart with the mean daily returns for each symbol, assuming that they were simply held throughout the analysis period:

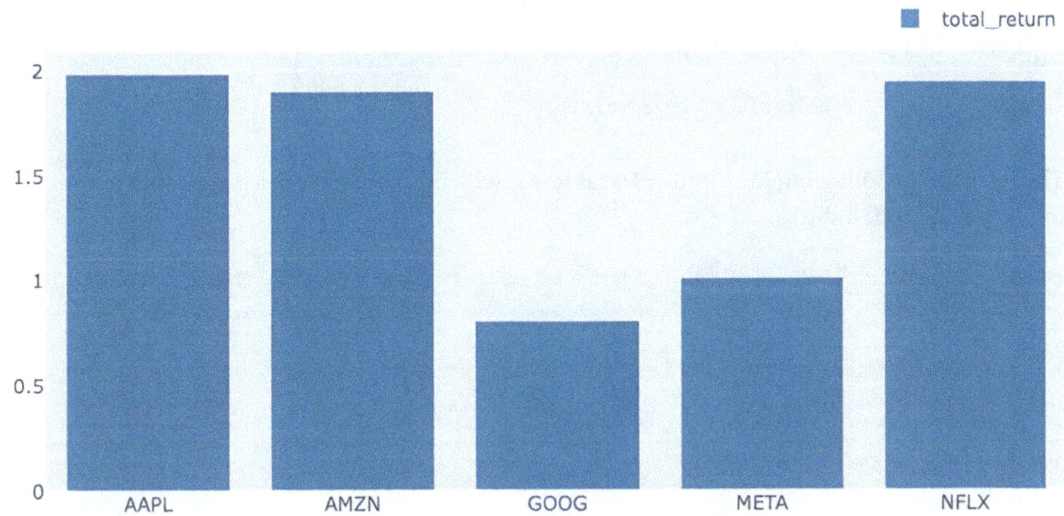

Figure 8.4: Returns from a simple holding strategy

How it works...

The code performs a simple moving average crossover strategy on the FAANG stocks to demonstrate the VectorBT backtesting framework. We download historical closing prices for the META, AAPL, AMZN, NFLX, and GOOG stocks using `YFData.download`. We then use the get method and the close key to return the closing prices from the `YFData` object.

From there, we calculate two moving averages: a fast-moving average with a 10-day window and a slow-moving average with a 30-day window. We do this using the MA class, which takes the price data, the window size, and a short name for the moving average as arguments. The `ma_crossed_above` method identifies points where the fast-moving average crosses above the slow-moving average, signaling a buy entry. Conversely, the `ma_crossed_below` method identifies points where the fast-moving average crosses below the slow-moving average, signaling a sell or exit.

Finally, the `from_signals` method is used to simulate the portfolio's performance based on these entry and exit signals and the historical price data. The resulting portfolio object, `pf`, contains various statistics and data that can be used for further analysis of the strategy's performance. We extract the total returns using the `total_returns` method, group by each symbol, and plot the mean returns.

There's more...

The power in VectorBT is not backtesting simple trading strategies. It's in VectorBT's capacity for running split tests and different iterations of parameters very quickly.

Let's split the data into four panels:

```
mult_prices, _ = prices.vbt.range_split(n=4)
```

The result is the following MultiIndex DataFrame, which has historic price data split across four separate split indexes:

split_idx	0					1				
symbol	META	AAPL	AMZN	NFLX	GOOG	META	AAPL	AMZN	NFLX	GOOG
0	102.220001	24.009066	31.849501	109.959999	37.091999	116.860001	27.059305	37.683498	127.489998	39.306999
1	102.730003	23.407412	31.689501	107.660004	37.129002	118.690002	27.029024	37.859001	129.410004	39.345001
2	102.970001	22.949341	31.632500	117.680000	37.181000	120.669998	27.166475	39.022499	131.809998	39.701000
3	97.919998	21.980772	30.396999	114.559998	36.319500	123.410004	27.469334	39.799500	131.070007	40.307499
4	97.330002	22.097000	30.352501	111.389999	35.723499	124.900002	27.720940	39.846001	130.949997	40.332500
...	...	...	...	...	...	...	...	...	...	...
246	117.400002	27.091925	38.317001	125.580002	39.563000	177.199997	41.427494	58.417999	189.940002	53.006001
247	117.269997	27.145506	38.029499	125.589996	39.495499	175.990005	40.376480	58.838001	187.759995	52.837002
248	118.010002	27.317902	38.570000	128.350006	39.577499	177.619995	40.383587	59.112999	186.240005	52.468498
249	116.919998	27.201422	38.606499	125.889999	39.252499	177.919998	40.497204	59.305000	192.710007	52.407001
250	116.349998	27.194427	38.257500	125.330002	39.139500	176.460007	40.059280	58.473499	191.960007	52.320000

split_idx	2					3				
symbol	META	AAPL	AMZN	NFLX	GOOG	META	AAPL	AMZN	NFLX	GOOG
0	181.419998	40.776524	59.450500	201.070007	53.250000	131.740005	34.163826	75.014000	271.200012	50.803001
1	184.669998	40.769421	60.209999	205.050003	54.124001	137.949997	35.622265	76.769501	297.570007	53.535500
2	184.330002	40.958790	60.479500	205.630005	54.320000	138.050003	35.542969	81.475502	315.339996	53.419498
3	186.850006	41.425125	61.457001	209.990005	55.111500	142.529999	36.220528	82.829002	320.269989	53.813999
4	188.279999	41.271263	62.343498	212.050003	55.347000	144.229996	36.835613	82.971001	319.959991	53.733002
...	...	...	...	...	...	...	...	...	...	...
246	124.059998	35.278683	67.197998	233.880005	48.811001	205.119995	69.327438	89.460503	333.200012	67.178001
247	134.179993	37.763054	73.544998	253.669998	51.973000	207.789993	70.702927	93.438499	332.630005	68.019997
248	134.520004	37.517971	73.082001	255.570007	52.194000	208.100006	70.676102	93.489998	329.089996	67.594498
249	133.199997	37.537189	73.901001	256.079987	51.854000	204.410004	71.095573	92.344498	323.309998	66.806999
250	131.089995	37.900017	75.098503	257.660004	51.780499	205.250000	71.615021	92.391998	323.570007	66.850998

Figure 8.5: A pandas DataFrame with split indexes

Within each split, we can run different combinations of our fast and slow moving average windows:

```
fast_ma = vbt.MA.run(mult_prices, [10, 20], short_name="fast")
slow_ma = vbt.MA.run(mult_prices, [30, 30], short_name="slow")
```

Rerun the methods to find entries and exits:

```
entries = fast_ma.ma_crossed_above(slow_ma)
exits = fast_ma.ma_crossed_below(slow_ma)
```

Inspect the exits DataFrame. The result is a MultiIndex DataFrame that includes each combination of moving average windows within each split:

fast_window	10																			
slow_window	30																			
split_idx	0					1					2					3				
symbol	META	AAPL	AMZN	NFLX	GOOG	META	AAPL	AMZN	NFLX	GOOG	META	AAPL	AMZN	NFLX	GOOG	META	AAPL	AMZN	NFLX	GOOG
0	False	False	False	False	False	False	False	False	False	False	False	False	False	False	False	False	False	False	False	False
1	False	False	False	False	False	False	False	False	False	False	False	False	False	False	False	False	False	False	False	False
2	False	False	False	False	False	False	False	False	False	False	False	False	False	False	False	False	False	False	False	False
3	False	False	False	False	False	False	False	False	False	False	False	False	False	False	False	False	False	False	False	False
4	False	False	False	False	False	False	False	False	False	False	False	False	False	False	False	False	False	False	False	False
...	...	...	...	...	...	...	...	...	...	...	...	...	...	...	...	...	...	...	...	...
246	False	False	False	False	False	False	False	False	False	False	True	False	False	False	False	False	False	False	False	False
247	False	False	False	False	False	True	False	False	False	False	False	False	False	False	False	False	False	False	False	False
248	False	False	False	False	False	False	False	False	False	False	False	False	False	False	False	False	False	False	False	False
249	False	False	False	False	False	False	False	False	False	False	False	False	False	False	False	False	False	False	False	False
250	True	False	False	False	False	False	False	False	False	False	False	False	False	False	False	False	False	False	False	False

fast_window	20																			
slow_window	30																			
split_idx	0					1					2					3				
symbol	META	AAPL	AMZN	NFLX	GOOG	META	AAPL	AMZN	NFLX	GOOG	META	AAPL	AMZN	NFLX	GOOG	META	AAPL	AMZN	NFLX	GOOG
0	False	False	False	False	False	False	False	False	False	False	False	False	False	False	False	False	False	False	False	False
1	False	False	False	False	False	False	False	False	False	False	False	False	False	False	False	False	False	False	False	False
2	False	False	False	False	False	False	False	False	False	False	False	False	False	False	False	False	False	False	False	False
3	False	False	False	False	False	False	False	False	False	False	False	False	False	False	False	False	False	False	False	False
4	False	False	False	False	False	False	False	False	False	False	False	False	False	False	False	False	False	False	False	False
...	...	...	...	...	...	...	...	...	...	...	...	...	...	...	...	...	...	...	...	...
246	False	False	False	False	False	False	False	False	False	False	False	False	False	False	False	False	False	False	False	False
247	True	False	False	False	False	False	False	False	False	False	False	False	False	False	False	False	False	False	False	False
248	False	False	False	False	False	False	False	False	False	False	False	False	False	False	False	False	False	False	False	False
249	False	False	True	False	False	False	False	False	False	False	False	False	False	False	True	False	False	False	False	False
250	False	False	False	False	False	False	True	False	False	False	False	False	True	False	False	False	False	False	False	False

Figure 8.6: A MultiIndex DataFrame with each combination of moving average windows within each split

Rerun the backtest analysis with the split data:

```
pf = vbt.Portfolio.from_signals(
    mult_prices,
    entries,
    exits,
    freq="1D"
)
```

Visualize the results by grouping total returns by split index and symbol, finding the mean, and plotting:

```
(
    pf
    .total_return()
    .groupby(
        ['split_idx', 'symbol']
    )
    .mean()
    .unstack(level=-1)
    .vbt
    .barplot()
)
```

The result is the following bar chart with the mean daily returns for each symbol across each split:

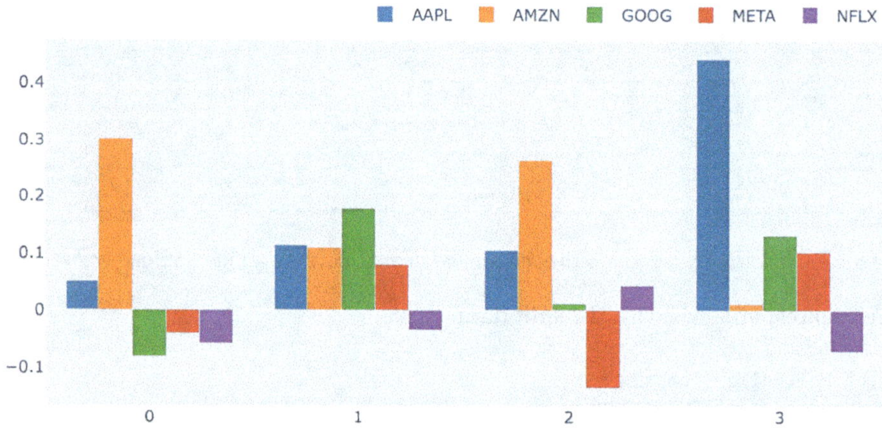

Figure 8.7: A visualization of mean daily returns grouped by split and symbol

VectorBT supports trading statistics based on the orders property on the `pf` object:

```
pf.orders.stats(group_by=True)
```

The result is a Series with various trading statistics:

```
Start                                    0
End                                    250
Period                   251 days 00:00:00
Total Records                          291
Total Buy Orders                       157
Total Sell Orders                      134
Min Size                          0.253075
Max Size                          4.677407
Avg Size                          1.629121
Avg Buy Size                      1.637868
Avg Sell Size                     1.618872
Avg Buy Price                   103.523933
Avg Sell Price                  104.650348
Total Fees                             0.0
Min Fees                               0.0
Max Fees                               0.0
Avg Fees                               0.0
Avg Buy Fees                           0.0
Avg Sell Fees                          0.0
Name: group, dtype: object
```

Figure 8.8: Trading statistics from the backtest analysis

We can also extract specific performance metrics for each combination of split, moving average window, and symbol:

```
pf.sharpe_ratio()
```

The result is the following MultiIndex Series:

```
fast_window  slow_window  split_idx  symbol
10           30           0          META     -0.472595
                                     AAPL      1.125228
                                     AMZN      1.633329
                                     NFLX     -0.470585
                                     GOOG     -0.051110
                          1          META      0.449941
                                     AAPL      1.043138
                                     AMZN      0.611364
                                     NFLX     -0.359590
                                     GOOG      1.754603
```

Figure 8.9: The Sharpe ratio for each combination of split, moving average window, and symbol

See also

The free, open-source version of VectorBT has good documentation, examples, and additional resources to help you get started. You can find it here: `https://vectorbt.dev`.

Conducting walk-forward optimization with vectorbt

Walk-forward optimization is an advanced technique in algorithmic trading that aims to address the issue of curve-fitting in strategy development. Unlike traditional backtesting, whereby a strategy is optimized once over a historical dataset and then applied to out-of-sample data, walk-forward optimization divides the entire dataset into multiple in-sample and out-of-sample periods. The strategy is optimized on each in-sample period using a timeseries split rather than the randomly shuffled folds common in machine learning workflows. This distinction matters: shuffling samples across folds, as is standard practice for cross-sectional ML problems, leaks future information into the training set and invalidates results when applied to timeseries data. A timeseries split preserves chronological order, ensuring the model only learns from data available at the point of decision. The optimized parameters are then validated on the corresponding out-of-sample period. This process is repeated, or "walked forward," through the entire dataset. The objective is to assess how well the strategy adapts to changing market conditions over time. By continually re-optimizing and validating the strategy, walk-forward optimization provides a more realistic representation of a strategy's robustness and potential for future performance. This method is computationally intensive but offers a more rigorous approach to strategy validation.

This recipe uses VectorBT's built-in `rolling_split` method to take advantage of the library's speed and lets us run thousands of simulations in seconds.

Getting ready

This recipe uses the free, open-source version of VectorBT that we installed in the last recipe.

How to do it...

We'll run the backtest analysis and test whether the out-of-sample Sharpe ratios are statistically greater than the in-sample results:

1. Import the libraries for the analysis. We'll use SciPy to run a statistical test to collect evidence of overfitting:

```
import numpy as np
import scipy.stats as stats
import vectorbt as vbt
```

2. Download market price data using the built-in downloader:

```
start = "2016-01-01 UTC"
end = "2020-01-01 UTC"
prices = vbt.YFData.download(
    "AAPL",
    start=start,
    end=end
).get("Close")
```

3. Create data splits for the walk-forward optimization. This code segments the prices into 30 splits, each two years long, and reserves 180 days for the test:

```
(in_price, in_indexes), (out_price, out_indexes) =
prices.vbt.rolling_split(
    n=30,
    window_len=365 * 2,
    set_lens=(180,),
    left_to_right=False,
)
```

4. Now create the function that returns the Sharpe ratios for all combinations of moving average windows:

```
def simulate_all_params(price, windows, **kwargs):
    fast_ma, slow_ma = vbt.MA.run_combs(
        price,
        windows,
        r=2,
        short_names=["fast", "slow"]
    )
    entries = fast_ma.ma_crossed_above(slow_ma)
    exits = fast_ma.ma_crossed_below(slow_ma)
    pf = vbt.Portfolio.from_signals(price, entries,
        exits, **kwargs)
    return pf.sharpe_ratio()
```

5. Create two helper functions that return the indexes and parameters where the performance is maximized:

```
def get_best_index(performance):
    return performance[
        performance.groupby("split_idx").idxmax()
    ].index
def get_best_params(best_index, level_name):
    return best_index.get_level_values(
        level_name).to_numpy()
```

6. Implement a function that runs the backtest given the best moving average values and returns the associated Sharpe ratio:

```
def simulate_best_params(price, best_fast_windows,
    best_slow_windows, **kwargs):
        fast_ma = vbt.MA.run(
            price,
            window=best_fast_windows,
            per_column=True
        )
        slow_ma = vbt.MA.run(
            price,
            window=best_slow_windows,
            per_column=True
```

```
        )
        entries = fast_ma.ma_crossed_above(slow_ma)
        exits = fast_ma.ma_crossed_below(slow_ma)
        pf = vbt.Portfolio.from_signals(
            price, entries, exits, **kwargs)
        return pf.sharpe_ratio()
```

7. Finally, we will run the analysis by passing in a range of moving average windows to `simulate_all_params`. This returns the Sharpe ratio for every combination of moving average windows for every data split. In other words, these are the in-sample Sharpe ratios:

```
windows = np.arange(10, 40)
in_sharpe = simulate_all_params(
    in_price,
    windows,
    direction="both",
    freq="d"
)
```

8. Next, we will get the best in-sample moving average windows and combine them into a single array:

```
in_best_index = get_best_index(in_sharpe)
in_best_fast_windows = get_best_params(
    in_best_index,
    "fast_window"
)
in_best_slow_windows = get_best_params(
    in_best_index,
    "slow_window"
)
in_best_window_pairs = np.array(
```

```
    list(zip(in_best_fast_windows, in_best_slow_windows))
)
```

9. The last step is to retrieve the out-of-sample Sharpe ratios using the optimized moving average windows:

```
out_test_sharpe = simulate_best_params(
    out_price,
    in_best_fast_windows,
    in_best_slow_windows,
    direction="both",
    freq="d"
)
```

The result is the following MultiIndex Series that identifies the optimal moving average window values for each split along with the associated Sharpe ratio:

```
ma_window  ma_window  split_idx
10         11         0            0.104954
12         13         1            0.318318
                      2            0.971219
10         11         3            1.386785
12         13         4            1.303272
10         11         5            2.133298
                      6            2.043526
```

Figure 8.10: Maximized Sharpe ratios across each data split

How it works...

The code executes a walk-forward optimization on a moving average crossover strategy for AAPL stock. We begin by fetching historical closing prices for AAPL for the period from January 1, 2016, to January 1, 2020. The data is then partitioned into in-sample and out-of-sample sets using VectorBT's `rolling_split` method. The in-sample set is designated for optimization, while the out-of-sample set is reserved for validation.

The `rolling_split` method in VectorBT is designed to split a time series into rolling in-sample and out-of-sample periods for walk-forward optimization or other time-based analyses. These are the parameters we use in the recipe:

- `n`: This refers to the number of splits. It determines how many in-sample and `out-of-sample` periods will be created.

- `window_len`: This describes the length of each rolling window in the time series. This is often specified in terms of the number of time steps (e.g., days).
- `set_lens`: This is a tuple specifying the length of each `in-sample` and `out-of-sample` set within each rolling window. The sum of these lengths should not exceed `window_len`.
- `left_to_right`: Determines whether to resolve `set_lens` from left to right. Otherwise, the first set will be variable.

In the optimization phase, the `simulate_all_params` function is responsible for strategy backtesting across a range of moving average window sizes. It calculates both fast and slow moving averages, generates entry and exit signals, and simulates the portfolio's performance, returning the Sharpe ratio as the performance metric.

> **Tip**
>
> You can select any performance metric to optimize for. The `pf` portfolio object has dozens of different metrics to choose from. You can execute `dir(pf)` to inspect the properties and methods of the object.

Next, we use the `get_best_index` and `get_best_params` functions to identify the optimal moving average window sizes based on the highest Sharpe ratios achieved during the in-sample testing.

Finally, the code proceeds to the out-of-sample testing phase. The `simulate_best_params` function takes the optimal moving average window sizes identified in the in-sample phase and applies them to the `out-of-sample` dataset. It then simulates the portfolio's performance using these parameters, again computing the Sharpe ratio as the performance metric.

The code is structured to leverage `VectorBT`'s efficient backtesting capabilities, which is particularly advantageous in a walk-forward optimization context where multiple iterations of backtesting and re-optimization are required.

```
in_sample_best = in_sharpe[in_best_index].values
out_sample_test = out_test_sharpe.values
t, p = stats.ttest_ind(
    a=out_sample_test,
    b=in_sample_best,
    alternative="greater"
)
```

First, the line `in_sample_best = in_sharpe[in_best_index].values` filters the Sharpe ratios stored in `in_sharpe` to include only those corresponding to the best-performing parameter sets. It then extracts these filtered Sharpe ratios as a NumPy array and stores them in the `in_sample_best` variable. We do the same for the out-of-sample dataset.

The `ttest_ind` function from the SciPy stats module takes the two independent `out_sample_test` and `in_sample_best` samples as its arguments. The `alternative="greater"` parameter specifies that the test is one-sided, which we use to evaluate whether the mean Sharpe ratio of the out-of-sample set is statistically greater than that of the in-sample set. The function returns the calculated t-statistic and the p-value.

The results give us a t-statistic of approximately *-1.085* and a p-value of approximately 0.859. The negative value of the t-statistic suggests that the mean of the out-of-sample Sharpe ratios is negative. Further, the high p-value tells us there is not enough statistical evidence to conclude that the out-of-sample Sharpe ratios are greater than the in-sample Sharpe ratios. The negative t-statistic and the high p-value together suggest that the strategy may not perform as well on new, unseen data as it does on the data on which it was optimized. This could be a warning sign regarding the strategy's robustness and its ability to generalize to new data. Ideally, you'd hope to see a t-statistic over 1.0 and a p-value under 0.05.

See also

Using VectorBT to quickly iterate on optimized strategies, coupled with SciPy to test the statistical significance of those strategies, is a powerful workflow. You can learn more about SciPy's stats module here: `https://docs.scipy.org/doc/scipy/reference/stats.html#module-scipy.stats`.

Optimizing the SuperTrend strategy with VectorBT Pro

The SuperTrend indicator is a trend-following indicator that is used in technical analysis to identify the direction of an asset's momentum. It is constructed using two primary components: the **Average True Range** (**ATR**) and a multiplier. The ATR measures the asset's volatility over a specified period, while the multiplier is a user-defined constant that adjusts the sensitivity of the indicator.

The SuperTrend is calculated as follows:

1. Compute the ATR for a given period
2. Calculate the basic upper band as the sum of the high and low prices, divided by 2, plus the product of the multiplier and the ATR

3. Calculate the `basic lower band` as the sum of the high and low prices, divided by 2, minus the product of the multiplier and the ATR
4. The `SuperTrend` is then defined as the upper band when the price is below it, and as the lower band when the price is above it

The indicator flips between the upper and lower bands, signaling a change in trend. When the price is above the SuperTrend line, it suggests an uptrend and a buy signal is generated. Conversely, when the price is below the SuperTrend line, it suggests a downtrend and a sell signal is generated.

To build the SuperTrend indicator, we will introduce VectorBT Pro. VectorBT Pro is a more full-featured version of VectorBT that offers enhancements such as pulling data from AlphaVantage and Polygon, as well as synthetic data generators, multi-threading, stop laddering, time stops, order delays, portfolio optimization with RiskFolio-Lib and PyPortfolioOpt, and more.

This recipe will demonstrate how to construct a custom indicator using integrations with TA-Lib and Numba.

Getting ready

We need to install a few dependencies to get VectorBT working. First is TA-Lib which is a technical analysis library. The second is H5DF which is a data storage solution.

For Windows, Unix/Linux, and Mac Intel users

If you're running on an Intel x86 chip, you can use `conda`:

```
conda install -c conda-forge pytables h5py ta-lib -y
```

For Apple Silicon users

If you have a Mac with an M-series chip, you need to install some dependencies first. The easiest way is to use Homebrew (`https://brew.sh`).

Install the dependencies with Homebrew:

```
brew install hdf5 ta-lib
```

Install the Python dependencies with `conda`:

```
conda install -c conda-forge pytables h5py ta-lib -y
```

Now we're ready to install VectorBT Pro.

VectorBT Pro has a small monthly subscription fee. Details can be found at `https://vectorbt.pro/become-a-member/`. After you've been added to the list of collaborators and have accepted the repository invitation, the next step is to create a Personal Access Token for your GitHub account to access the Pro repository. To do so, follow these steps:

1. Go to `https://github.com/settings/tokens`
2. Click on **Generate a new token**
3. Enter a name (such as `terminal`)
4. Set the expiration to a fixed number of days
5. Select the **repo** scope
6. Generate the token and save it in a safe place

Once your token has been created, you can install Pro using `pip`:

```
pip install -U "vectorbtpro[base] @ git+https://github.com/polakowo/
vectorbt.pro.git"
```

When you're prompted for a password, use the token that you generated in the previous steps. For more installation details, see the *Getting started* guide on the Pro website, which is accessible after signing up.

How to do it...

We'll examine a few key features of VectorBT Pro, including the multi-threaded data downloading and indicator factory:

1. Import the libraries we need for the analysis. Note the import of `vectorbtpro` instead of `vectorbt`:

```
import talib
import numpy as np
from numba import njit
import vectorbtpro as vbt
```

2. Use VectorBT Pro's multi-threading capability to download the market data in 517 milliseconds:

```
start = "2016-01-01 UTC"
end = "2020-01-01 UTC"
with vbt.Timer() as timer:
    prices = vbt.YFData.pull(
```

```
        ["META", "AAPL", "AMZN", "NFLX", "GOOG"],
        start=start,
        end=end,
        execute_kwargs=dict(engine="threadpool")
    )
print(timer.elapsed())
```

3. Extract the high, low, and closing prices from the prices object:

```
high = prices.get("High")
low = prices.get("Low")
close = prices.get("Close")
```

4. Implement a helper function that calculates the basic bands:

```
def get_basic_bands(med_price, atr, multiplier):
    matr = multiplier * atr
    upper = med_price + matr
    lower = med_price - matr
    return upper, lower
```

5. Implement the function that calculates the final bands. This function returns the trend and direction, as well as both the long and short positions. Note the `@njit` decorator, which compiles the code using Numba to achieve machine language-like speeds:

```
@njit
def get_final_bands(close, upper, lower):
    trend = np.full(close.shape, np.nan)
    dir_ = np.full(close.shape, 1)
    long = np.full(close.shape, np.nan)
    short = np.full(close.shape, np.nan)
    for i in range(1, close.shape[0]):
        if close[i] > upper[i - 1]:
            dir_[i] = 1
        elif close[i] < lower[i - 1]:
            dir_[i] = -1
        else:
            dir_[i] = dir_[i - 1]
            if dir_[i] > 0 and lower[i] < lower[i - 1]:
                lower[i] = lower[i - 1]
            if dir_[i] < 0 and upper[i] > upper[i - 1]:
```

```
                upper[i] = upper[i - 1]
            if dir_[i] > 0:
                trend[i] = long[i] = lower[i]
            else:
                trend[i] = short[i] = upper[i]
        return trend, dir_, long, short
```

6. Put it all together in the final function, which returns the output from the `get_final_bands` function. Note the use of TA-Lib's `MEDPRICE` and `ATR` methods, which further speed up the analysis:

```
def supertrend(high, low, close, period=7,
    multiplier=3):
        avg_price = talib.MEDPRICE(high, low)
        atr = talib.ATR(high, low, close, period)
        upper, lower = get_basic_bands(avg_price, atr, multiplier)
        return get_final_bands(close, upper, lower)
```

7. Use VectorBT Pro's indicator factory class to convert our `supertrend` function into an indicator that we can use with Pro's analysis capabilities:

```
SuperTrend = vbt.IF(
    class_name="SuperTrend",
    short_name="st",
    input_names=["high", "low", "close"],
    param_names=["period", "multiplier"],
    output_names=["supert", "superd", "superl", "supers"],
).with_apply_func(
    supertrend, takes_1d=True,
    period=7, multiplier=3,
)
```

8. We will then create a custom class that inherits the indicator that we just built using VectorBT Pro's indicator factory. This class includes a method plot that encapsulates the formatting and setup of a plot:

```
class SuperTrend(SuperTrend):
    def plot(
        self,
        column=None,
```

```
        close_kwargs=None,
        superl_kwargs=None,
        supers_kwargs=None,
        fig=None,
        **layout_kwargs
    ):
        close_kwargs = close_kwargs if close_kwargs else {}
        superl_kwargs = superl_kwargs if superl_kwargs else {}
        supers_kwargs = supers_kwargs if supers_kwargs else {}
        close = self.select_col_from_obj(
            self.close, column).rename("Close")
        supers = self.select_col_from_obj(
            self.supers, column).rename("Short")
        superl = self.select_col_from_obj(
            self.superl, column).rename("Long")
        fig = close.vbt.plot(fig=fig, **close_kwargs, **layout_kwargs)
        supers.vbt.plot(fig=fig, **supers_kwargs)
        superl.vbt.plot(fig=fig, **superl_kwargs)
        return fig
```

9. We're now ready to create an instance of our SuperTrend indicator and visualize where the indicator suggests long and short positions:

```
st = SuperTrend.run(high, low, close)
st.loc["2016-01-01":"2020-01-01", "AAPL"].plot().show()
```

The result is a Plotly chart with the closing price for AAPL and the locations of long and short signals:

Figure 8.11: A chart with the long and short signals for AAPL

10. The next step is to run the backtest. First, let's find the entry and exit signals:

```
entries = (~st.superl.isnull()).vbt.signals.fshift()
exits = (~st.supers.isnull()).vbt.signals.fshift()
```

The result is two DataFrames with boolean values for each day indicating where a long or short position exists:

symbol	META	AAPL	AMZN	NFLX	GOOG
Date					
2016-01-04 00:00:00-05:00	False	False	False	False	False
2016-01-05 00:00:00-05:00	False	False	False	False	False
2016-01-06 00:00:00-05:00	False	False	False	False	False
2016-01-07 00:00:00-05:00	False	False	False	False	False
2016-01-08 00:00:00-05:00	False	False	False	False	False

Figure 8.12: A DataFrame with entry locations

11. Finally, we can run the backtest and inspect the risk and performance results:

```
pf = vbt.Portfolio.from_signals(
    close=close,
    entries=entries, exits=exits,
```

```
    fees=0.001, freq="1d"
)
pf.stats(group_by=True)
```

The result is a Series with the consolidated statistics of the strategy:

```
Start                                    2016-01-04 00:00:00-05:00
End                                      2019-12-31 00:00:00-05:00
Period                                          1006 days 00:00:00
Start Value                                                  500.0
Min Value                                               458.811175
Max Value                                               744.719854
End Value                                               739.035201
Total Return [%]                                          47.80704
Benchmark Return [%]                                     152.73135
Total Time Exposure [%]                                  86.481113
Max Gross Exposure [%]                                       100.0
Max Drawdown [%]                                         11.348404
Max Drawdown Duration                            184 days 00:00:00
Total Orders                                                   161
Total Fees Paid                                          18.243214
Total Trades                                                    83
Win Rate [%]                                             56.410256
Best Trade [%]                                           27.086949
Worst Trade [%]                                         -22.352306
Avg Winning Trade [%]                                     7.681076
Avg Losing Trade [%]                                       -5.1919
Avg Winning Trade Duration             50 days 13:38:10.909090909
Avg Losing Trade Duration              16 days 22:35:17.647058823
Profit Factor                                             1.843733
Expectancy                                                2.132568
Sharpe Ratio                                              0.967803
Calmar Ratio                                              0.905523
Omega Ratio                                               1.177398
Sortino Ratio                                               1.3654
Name: group, dtype: object
```

Figure 8.13: A sample of the Series with the risk and performance statistics for the SuperTrend strategy

How it works...

The code fetches historical financial data on META, AAPL, AMZN, NFLX, and GOOG for the date range from January 1, 2016, to January 1, 2020. It uses the `pull` method from the `YFData` class to download this data. The `execute_kwargs=dict(engine="threadpool")` argument specifies that a thread pool should be used for concurrent execution, which speeds up the data retrieval process. The last data pre-processing step is to simply extract the high, low, and closing prices from the `YFData` object.

The `get_basic_bands` function calculates the basic upper and lower bands used in the SuperTrend indicator. It takes three arguments: `med_price`, which is the median price of the asset; `atr`, the ATR; and `multiplier`, a user-defined constant to adjust sensitivity. The function returns both the upper and lower bands.

Next, we implement the heart of the `SuperTrend` indicator. The `get_final_bands` function is JIT compiled, which is optimized using Numba's `@njit` decorator for better performance. It calculates the final upper and lower bands, as well as the trend direction for our `SuperTrend` indicator. It takes three arrays as input: `close` for closing prices, `upper` for the basic upper band, and `lower` for the basic lower band. The function returns four arrays: `trend` (final band based on trend direction), `dir_` (trend direction), `long` (lower band during uptrends), and `short` (upper band during downtrends).

`supertrend` calculates the SuperTrend indicator using high, low, and close prices. It takes five arguments: `high`; `low`; `close` for the high, low, and closing prices, respectively; `period` for the number of lookback periods to consider for the ATR; and `multiplier` to adjust the sensitivity of the bands. The `supertrend` function returns the final upper and lower bands, the trend direction, and the bands used during uptrends and downtrends, as calculated by `get_final_bands`.

Next, we define a custom indicator class, `SuperTrend`, using VectorBT Pro's `IndicatorFactory` class. This class encapsulates the `SuperTrend` indicator logic for easier reuse and integration within the Pro ecosystem. The `with_apply_func` method attaches the previously defined `supertrend` function to this custom indicator class. This function will be called when the `SuperTrend` indicator is run.

Finally, we run the backtest. We first run the custom `SuperTrend` indicator on high, low, and close price data, generating SuperTrend values, trend directions, and bands for both long and short positions. Finally, a portfolio is constructed using the entry and exit signals with VectorBT Pro's `from_signals` method. The portfolio uses the close prices for trade execution, incorporates a trading fee of 0.1%, and assumes a daily trading frequency.

There's more...

Since we encapsulated the `SuperTrend` indicator logic using Pro's indicator factory, we can optimize it. The two parameters in question are period and multiplier:

1. First, let's create ranges of values for each of the parameters:

```
periods = np.arange(4, 20)
multipliers = np.arange(20, 41) / 10
```

2. Then we call the run method on the SuperTrend indicator, passing in the market prices, as well as our arrays of periods and multipliers:

```
st = SuperTrend.run(
    high, low, close,
    period=periods,
    multiplier=multipliers,
    param_product=True,
)
```

3. Pro runs through every combination of period and multiplier. We then run through the same code as before that identifies the entries, exits, and runs the backtest. The difference is that now, our DataFrames containing entry and exit positions have a MultiIndex index for each combination of period and multiplier:

st_period	4					...	19				
st_multiplier	2.0					...	4.0				
symbol	META	AAPL	AMZN	NFLX	GOOG	...	META	AAPL	AMZN	NFLX	GOOG
Date											
2016-01-04 00:00:00-05:00	False	False	False	False	False	...	False	False	False	False	False
2016-01-05 00:00:00-05:00	False	False	False	False	False	...	False	False	False	False	False
2016-01-06 00:00:00-05:00	False	False	False	False	False	...	False	False	False	False	False
2016-01-07 00:00:00-05:00	False	False	False	False	False	...	False	False	False	False	False
2016-01-08 00:00:00-05:00	False	False	False	False	False	...	False	False	False	False	False

Figure 8.14: A DataFrame with entry locations for each stock for each combination of period and multiplier

4. Once we have created the entries and exits, we run the backtest:

```
pf = vbt.Portfolio.from_signals(
    close=close, entries=entries, exits=exits,
    fees=0.001, freq="1d"
)
```

5. To visualize the parameter hotspots (the combinations with the maximum Sharpe ratio), use a heatmap:

```
pf.sharpe_ratio.vbt.heatmap(
    x_level="st_period",
```

```
    y_level="st_multiplier",
    slider_level="symbol"
)
```

The result is an interactive heatmap that lets us select which asset to visualize. In this case, we select AAPL:

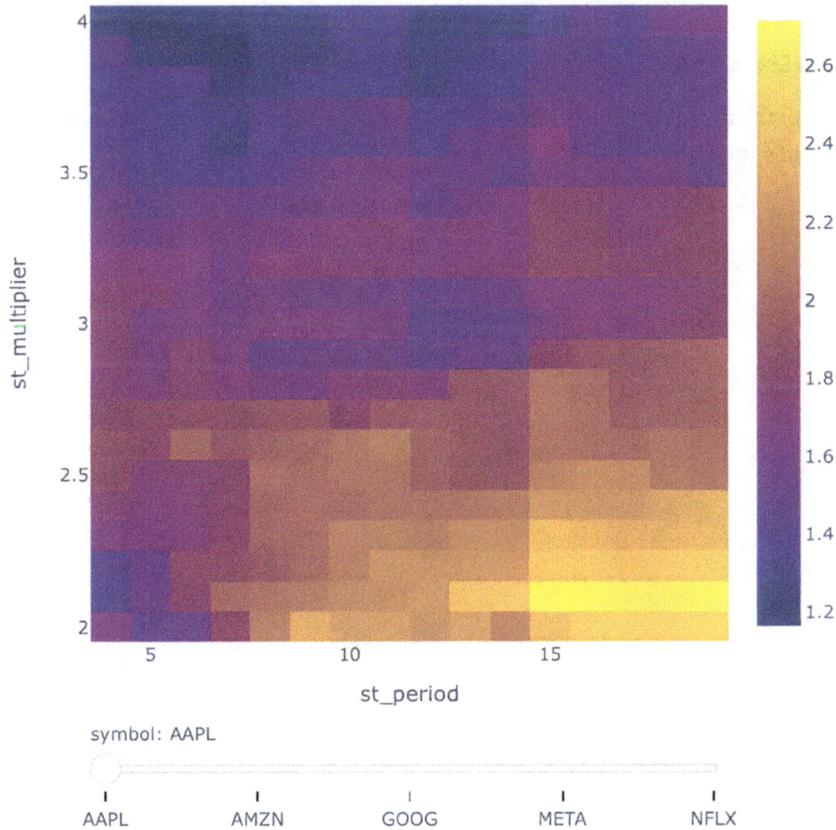

Figure 8.15: An interactive heatmap showing the Sharpe ratio at each parameter combination

Tip

The `pf` object has many risk and performance metrics available for plotting. To get an idea of what's available, `print dir(pf)` to see the object attributes. You can easily plot a different metric on a heatmap by replacing `sharpe_ratio` with whichever metric you're interested in.

See also

We've only begun to scratch the surface of VectorBT and VectorBT Pro. It's designed for speed, which is perfect for optimizing features of our trading strategies.

To learn more about the `SuperTrend` indicator, consult the VectorBT Pro information page at `https://vectorbt.pro/become-a-member/`.

Join our community on Discord

Join our community's Discord space for discussions with the authors and other readers: `https://discord.gg/G4YmB6DQvf`

9

Event-Based Backtesting Factor Portfolios with Zipline Reloaded

Zipline Reloaded is an event-driven backtesting framework that processes market events sequentially, allowing for more realistic modeling of order execution and slippage. Unlike vector-based frameworks, it accounts for the temporal sequence of market events, making it suitable for complex strategies that involve conditional orders or asset interactions. While generally slower than vector-based approaches, event-based backtesting frameworks tend to better simulate market dynamics making them helpful for path-dependent strategies requiring intricate order logic, state management, and risk management.

Zipline Reloaded is well suited for backtesting large universes and complex portfolio construction techniques. The Pipeline API is designed for high-efficiency computation of factors among thousands of securities. We'll use Zipline Reloaded to backtest portfolio factor strategies, the results of which can be analyzed with other tools in the Zipline Reloaded ecosystem.

In this chapter, we present the following recipes:

- Backtesting a momentum factor strategy with Zipline Reloaded
- Exploring a mean reversion strategy with Zipline Reloaded

Technical requirements

We installed Zipline Reloaded in *Chapter 7, Build Alpha Factors for Stock Portfolios*. In case you missed it, follow along with the instructions here. The steps to install Zipline Reloaded differ depending on your operating system.

For Windows, Unix/Linux, and Mac Intel users

If you're running on an Intel x86 chip, you can use `conda`:

```
conda install -c conda-forge zipline-reloaded pyfolio-reloaded alphalens-reloaded
-y
```

For Mac M1/M2 users

If you have a Mac with an M1 or M2 chip, you need to install some dependencies first. The easiest way is to use Homebrew (`https://brew.sh`).

Install the dependencies with Homebrew:

```
brew install freetype pkg-config gcc openssl hdf5 ta-lib
```

Install the Python dependencies with `conda`:

```
conda install -c conda-forge pytables h5py -y
```

Install the Zipline Reloaded ecosystem:

```
pip install zipline-reloaded pyfolio-reloaded alphalens-reloaded
```

In this example, we'll use the free data bundle provided by Nasdaq Data Link. This dataset has market price data on 3,000 stocks through 2018.

Backtesting a momentum factor strategy with Zipline Reloaded

Before we begin, it's important to understand the difference between vector-based backtesting frameworks and event-based backtesting frameworks. In *Chapter 8, Vector-Based Backtesting with VectorBT*, we touched on the differences between vector-based and event-based backtesting. Here is a more detailed assessment:

Feature	Vector-Based	Event-Based
Processing Method	Vectorized operations	Sequentially
Computational Efficiency	Highly efficient, especially for large datasets	Less efficient due to the need to process each event individually
Complexity in Coding	Simpler and more concise	More detailed programming to simulate market events accurately
Suitability for Strategy Type	Without complex state or path dependencies.	Ideal for complex, state-dependent, and path-dependent strategies
Order Execution Modeling	Assumes immediate order execution; less accurate for modeling real market conditions like slippage and delays.	More accurately models order execution dynamics, including delays, slippage, and partial fills.
Risk Management Simulation	Basic risk management features; may not capture dynamic risk adjustments effectively.	Detailed risk management with realistic simulations of stop-losses and other real-time adjustments.
Scalability	Highly scalable for large-scale data analysis and multiple assets.	Challenging with large-scale tick-by-tick data due to computational demands.
Risk of Overfitting	Higher risk of overfitting	Risk exists but can be better managed
Development Cycle	Faster development and testing cycles due to computational efficiency and simpler code.	Potentially slower due to increased complexity and computational demands.
Realism	Less realistic as it does not simulate the sequential flow of market events.	Higher realism in simulating real-world market conditions and trader actions.

Figure 9.1: Comparison of vector-based and event-based backtesting frameworks

In *Chapter 7, Build Alpha Factors for Stock Portfolios,* we defined a custom factor that computes a momentum score for US equities over a 252-day window. The factor's value is determined by comparing the 252-day relative price change against the 22-day relative price change. This difference is then standardized by dividing it by the standard deviation of the 126-day returns, effectively scaling the momentum score by the asset's recent volatility. The result provides a normalized momentum score for each asset, capturing both long-term and short-term price movements in relation to its recent volatility.

In this recipe, we'll incorporate the factor into the Zipline Reloaded backtesting framework and inspect the performance of the strategy.

Getting ready

We assume you ingested the free `quandl` data bundle and it's still available on your local machine. We also assume you still have your Nasdaq API key in the environment variables. If not, run the following code after the imports:

```
from zipline.data.bundles.core import load
os.environ["QUANDL_API_KEY"] = "YOUR_API_KEY"
bundle_data = load("quandl", os.environ, None)
```

The free data is limited to about 3,000 US equities and the data collection stops in 2018. If you'd like data coverage for nearly 20,000 US equities updated daily, you can consider the premium data service offered by Norgate Data.

The instructions to set up this premium data service are outlined in detail in the article *How to set up Norgate Data for Zipline Reloaded*, which you can find at this URL: `https://www.pyquantnews.com/free-python-resources/how-to-set-up-norgate-data-for-zipline-reloaded`.

If you follow the example, replace `quandl` with `norgatedata-us-equity-universe` in the `run_algorithm` function that follows.

How to do it...

In this recipe, we introduce several novel features of the Zipline Reloaded backtesting framework that require their own imports namely, the date, and time rules, the Pipeline API, custom factors, and commission and slippage models:

1. Start by importing the libraries we'll need for the backtest:

```
import pandas as pd
import numpy as np
from zipline import run_algorithm
from zipline.pipeline import Pipeline
from zipline.pipeline.data import USEquityPricing
from zipline.pipeline.factors import (
    AverageDollarVolume, CustomFactor, Returns
)
from zipline.api import (
    attach_pipeline,
    calendars,
    pipeline_output,
    date_rules,
    time_rules,
    set_commission,
    set_slippage,
    record,
    order_target_percent,
    get_open_orders,
    get_datetime,
    schedule_function
```

```
)
import pandas_datareader as web
```

2. Next, define the number of long and short stocks we want in our portfolio:

```
N_LONGS = N_SHORTS = 50
```

3. Use the same custom momentum factor we defined in the previous chapter:

```
class MomentumFactor(CustomFactor):
    inputs = [USEquityPricing.close,
        Returns(window_length=126)]
    window_length = 252
    def compute(self, today, assets, out, prices, returns):
        out[:] = (
            (prices[-21] -prices[-252]) / prices[-252]
            - (prices[-1] - prices[-21]) / prices[-21]
        ) / np.nanstd(returns, axis=0)
```

4. Use the same pipeline we defined in the previous chapter:

```
def make_pipeline():
    momentum = MomentumFactor()
    dollar_volume = AverageDollarVolume(
        window_length=30)
        return Pipeline(
            columns={
                "factor": momentum,
                "longs": momentum.top(N_LONGS),
                "shorts": momentum.bottom(N_SHORTS),
                "ranking": momentum.rank(),
            },
            screen=dollar_volume.top(100),
        )
```

5. Zipline Reloaded is an event-driven backtesting framework that allows us to "hook" into different events, including an event that fires before trading starts. We use this hook to "install" our factor pipeline:

```
def before_trading_start(context, data):
    context.factor_data = pipeline_output("factor_pipeline")
```

6. Next, we define the `initialize` function, which is run when the backtest starts:

```
def initialize(context):
    attach_pipeline(make_pipeline(), "factor_pipeline")
    schedule_function(
        rebalance,
        date_rules.week_start(),
        time_rules.market_open(),
        calendar=calendars.US_EQUITIES,
    )
```

7. Now, define a function that contains the logic to rebalance our portfolio. Here we buy the top `N_LONGS` stocks with the highest ranking factor and short the bottom `N_SHORTS` stocks with the lowest ranking factor:

```
def rebalance(context, data):
    factor_data = context.factor_data
    record(factor_data=factor_data.ranking)
    assets = factor_data.index
    record(prices=data.current(assets, "price"))
    longs = assets[factor_data.longs]
    shorts = assets[factor_data.shorts]
    divest = set(
        context.portfolio.positions.keys()) - set(
            longs.union(shorts)
        )
    exec_trades(
        data,
        assets=divest,
        target_percent=0
    )
    exec_trades(
        data,
```

```
        assets=longs,
        target_percent=1 / N_LONGS
    )
    exec_trades(
        data,
        assets=shorts,
        target_percent=-1 / N_SHORTS
    )
```

8. We abstract away the order execution in an `exec_trades` function, which loops through the provided assets and executes the orders:

```
def exec_trades(data, assets, target_percent):
    for asset in assets:
        if data.can_trade(
            asset) and not get_open_orders(asset):
                order_target_percent(asset, target_percent)
```

9. Finally, we run the backtest using the `run_algorithm` function:

```
start = pd.Timestamp("2016")
end = pd.Timestamp("2018")
perf = run_algorithm(
    start=start,
    end=end,
    initialize=initialize,
    before_trading_start=before_trading_start,
    capital_base=100_000,
    bundle="quandl",  # use norgatedata-us-equity-universe
                      # for Norgate premium data
)
```

The output is a DataFrame that contains trading, risk, and performance statistics for each day in the backtest:

```
perf.info()
```

It's this DataFrame that we use to analyze the characteristics of the backtest.

```
<class 'pandas.core.frame.DataFrame'>
DatetimeIndex: 503 entries, 2016-01-04 21:00:00+00:00 to 2017-12-29 21:00:00+00:00
Data columns (total 39 columns):
 #   Column                    Non-Null Count  Dtype
---  ------                    --------------  -----
 0   period_open               503 non-null    datetime64[ns, UTC]
 1   period_close              503 non-null    datetime64[ns, UTC]
 2   starting_value            503 non-null    float64
 3   ending_value              503 non-null    float64
 4   starting_cash             503 non-null    float64
 5   ending_cash               503 non-null    float64
 6   returns                   503 non-null    float64
 7   portfolio_value           503 non-null    float64
 8   longs_count               503 non-null    int64
 9   shorts_count              503 non-null    int64
 10  long_value                503 non-null    float64
 11  short_value               503 non-null    float64
 12  long_exposure             503 non-null    float64
 13  pnl                       503 non-null    float64
 14  short_exposure            503 non-null    float64
 15  capital_used              503 non-null    float64
 16  orders                    503 non-null    object
 17  transactions              503 non-null    object
 18  gross_leverage            503 non-null    float64
 19  positions                 503 non-null    object
 20  net_leverage              503 non-null    float64
 21  starting_exposure         503 non-null    float64
 22  ending_exposure           503 non-null    float64
 23  factor_data               503 non-null    object
 24  prices                    503 non-null    object
 25  sharpe                    502 non-null    float64
 26  sortino                   502 non-null    float64
 27  max_drawdown              503 non-null    float64
 28  max_leverage              503 non-null    float64
 29  excess_return             503 non-null    float64
 30  treasury_period_return    503 non-null    float64
 31  trading_days              503 non-null    int64
 32  period_label              503 non-null    object
 33  algorithm_period_return   503 non-null    float64
 34  algo_volatility           502 non-null    float64
 35  benchmark_period_return   503 non-null    float64
 36  benchmark_volatility      502 non-null    float64
 37  alpha                     0 non-null      object
 38  beta                      0 non-null      object
dtypes: datetime64[ns, UTC](2), float64(26), int64(3), object(8)
memory usage: 157.2+ KB
```

Figure 9.2: Output DataFrame from our Zipline Reloaded backtest

How it works...

We dove into the inner workings of the Pipeline API and custom factors in *Chapter 7, Build Alpha Factors for Stock Portfolios*, so here, we'll focus on the remaining code to run the backtest.

The `before_trading_start` function is invoked prior to the beginning of each trading day. It takes two parameters:

- `context`: A persistent namespace that allows the storage of variables between function calls. It retains its values across multiple days and can be used to store and manage data that the algorithm needs over time.
- `data`: An object that provides access to current and historical pricing and volume data, among other things.

Before every trading day, we fetch the output of a defined pipeline named `factor_pipeline`. The `pipeline_output` function retrieves the computed results of the named pipeline for the current day. These results are then stored in the `context` namespace under the `factor_data` key. This allows the algorithm to access and use the pipeline's output in subsequent functions or during the trading day.

> Note
>
> **Important**
>
> The `context` object in the Zipline Reloaded backtesting framework serves as a persistent namespace, allowing algorithms to store and manage variables across multiple function calls and trading sessions. It retains its values throughout the algorithm's execution, acting as a central repository for data, counters, flags, and other essential information that the algorithm requires for its operations and decision-making processes.

The `initialize` function is used to set up initial configurations and operations that the algorithm will use throughout its execution. Here, the function first attaches a data pipeline, created by the `make_pipeline` method, and names it `factor_pipeline`. Subsequently, the `schedule_function` method is used to schedule the `rebalance` function to run at the start of each week at the market's opening time, using the US equities trading calendar. This ensures that the algorithm will regularly adjust its portfolio based on the logic defined in the `rebalance` function following the exchange's open days.

The `rebalance` function adjusts the portfolio based on specific criteria. Initially, the function retrieves the factor data stored in the `context` object and adds the rank to the output DataFrame using the `record` function. It then fetches the current prices of the assets under consideration and adds them to the output DataFrame as well. The assets are then categorized into three groups: `longs` (assets the algorithm intends to buy), `shorts` (assets it plans to sell short), and divest (current portfolio holdings in neither the longs nor shorts list, indicating they should be sold off).

We implement a function called exec_trades to abstract away the order execution. For each asset in the list, the function first checks whether the asset is tradable and that there are no open orders for it using the can_trade and get_open_orders methods. If both conditions are met, the function places an order for the asset to adjust its position to the desired target percentage using the order_target_percent method.

Finally, we call run_algorithm to start the backtest, taking in the start and end dates, the initialize and before_trading_start functions to set up and prepare for each trading day, a starting capital of $100,000, and specifying the data bundle as quandl. The results of the backtest are stored in the perf variable for further analysis.

There's more...

The output of a Zipline Reloaded backtest provides a comprehensive overview of an algorithm's performance. It includes a time series of key metrics, such as portfolio value, returns, and specific asset positions. Additionally, it captures risk metrics, transaction logs, and other diagnostic data that help in evaluating the strategy's robustness and potential pitfalls.

The output can be used with the risk and performance libraries Pyfolio and Alphalens, which we dive into in the next two chapters. For now, we'll inspect a few of the key outputs:

```
perf.portfolio_value.plot(title="Cumulative returns")
```

The result is a plot showing the cumulative equity of your algorithm:

Figure 9.3: Cumulative equity of the algorithm

Create a histogram of daily returns:

```
perf.returns.hist(bins=50)
```

The result is a histogram showing the frequency of daily returns across 50 bins:

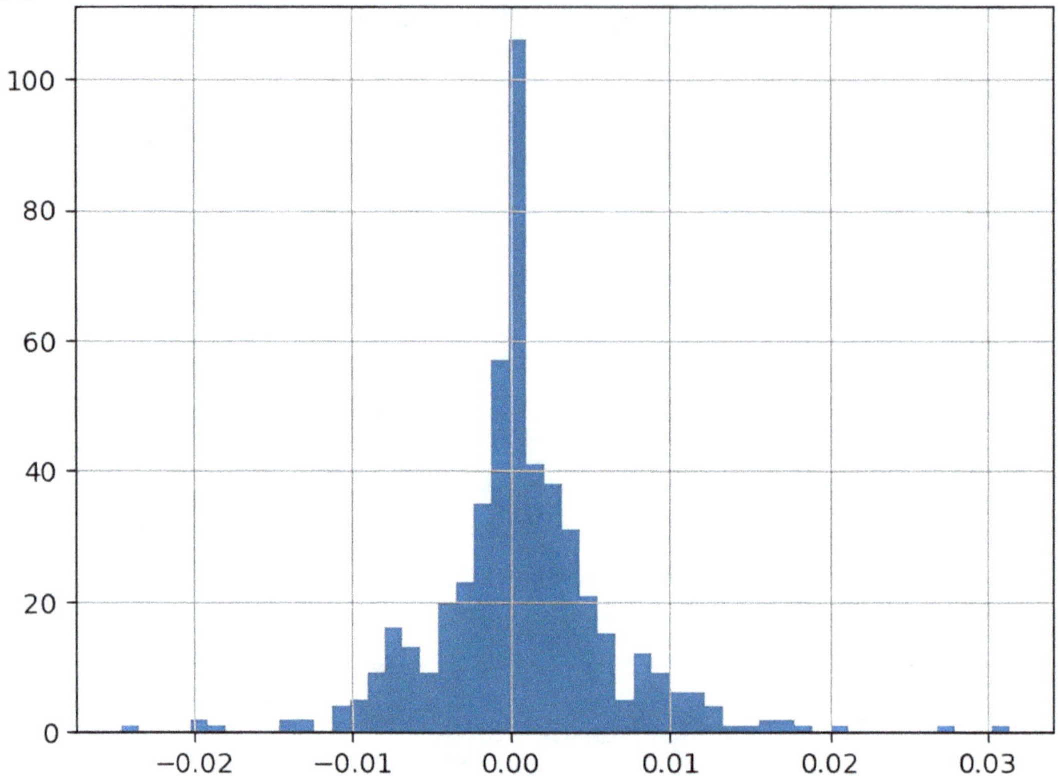

Figure 9.4: Histogram of daily portfolio returns

Plot the Sharpe ratio for the algorithm:

```
perf.sharpe.plot()
```

The result is a plot visualizing the Sharpe ratio of the algorithm:

Figure 9.5: Plot of the Sharpe ratio for the algorithm

Note

Hint

Zipline Reloaded uses an expanding window when computing the Sharpe ratio. This causes the first few months of the Sharpe ratio to be unstable since it is using very few data points to compute the metric. For a true rolling Sharpe ratio, use Pyfolio which we will see in *Chapter 11, Assess Backtest Risk and Performance Metrics with Pyfolio.*

See also

Zipline Reloaded offers robust documentation for using its extensive features. You can find them here:

- Zipline Reloaded documentation:`https://zipline.ml4trading.io`
- An article that describes ingesting the premium US equities data: `https://www.pyquantnews.com/free-python-resources/how-to-set-up-norgate-data-for-zipline-reloaded`

Exploring a mean reversion strategy with Zipline Reloaded

Mean reversion strategies are based on the financial principle that asset prices and returns eventually revert to their long-term mean or average level after periods of divergence or deviation. These strategies operate on the assumption that prices will bounce back to a historical mean or some form of equilibrium after moving away from it, either due to overreaction or other short-term factors. Mean reversion suggests that assets are subject to inherent and stable equilibriums. When prices deviate significantly from these equilibriums, due to factors such as emotional trading, news, or events, they are likely to revert back over time. Traders and algorithms identify assets that have deviated significantly from their historical average price or some other benchmark. This deviation can be measured using various metrics, such as z-scores, Bollinger Bands, or percentage deviations. Before trading a mean reversion strategy, you should empirically test whether the asset actually exhibits mean-reverting behavior. The **Augmented Dickey-Fuller** (**ADF**) test checks for stationarit which is a necessary condition for mean reversion, while the Hurst exponent distinguishes mean-reverting processes (H < 0.5) from trending ones (H > 0.5). The half-life of mean reversion, derived from an Ornstein-Uhlenbeck model, quantifies how quickly deviations decay back to the mean, giving you a practical estimate of holding period. In this recipe, we use the z-score.

In this recipe, we'll use the Zipline Reloaded factor framework to build a portfolio. The strategy buys the top oversold stocks and sells the top overbought stocks.

Getting ready

Most of this recipe will be the same as the recipe demonstrating the momentum factor, with some notable differences:

- We've updated the factor to measure mean reversion and rank our universe based on the top and bottom mean-reverting assets
- We include commission and slippage rules to enhance the realism of the backtest

- We add simple logging to provide feedback during the execution of the algorithm and to demonstrate the available portfolio attributes
- We download benchmark price data and include returns for comparison with our algorithm
- We include a custom function that is executed when the backtest is complete
- We generate an image of the pipeline that shows how the logic filters the stocks in the universe

We assume you have the libraries imported and will skip that step.

How to do it...

We will expand on the previous recipe by adding complexity to our analysis:

1. Set the number of longs and shorts and the lookback periods:

```
N_LONGS = N_SHORTS = 50
MONTH = 21
YEAR = 12 * MONTH
```

2. Create the mean reversion factor:

```
class MeanReversion(CustomFactor):
    inputs = [Returns(window_length=MONTH)]
    window_length = YEAR
    def compute(self, today, assets, out,
        monthly_returns):
            df = pd.DataFrame(monthly_returns)
            out[:] = df.iloc[-1].sub(
                df.mean()).div(df.std())
```

3. Implement the function that returns the pipeline using the factor:

```
def make_pipeline():
    mean_reversion = MeanReversion()
    dollar_volume = AverageDollarVolume(
        window_length=30)
    return Pipeline(
        columns={
            "longs": mean_reversion.bottom(N_LONGS),
            "shorts": mean_reversion.top(N_SHORTS),
            "ranking": mean_reversion.rank( ascending=False),
```

```
        },
        screen=dollar_volume.top(100),
    )
```

4. Implement the function that hooks into the event that fires before trading starts:

```
def before_trading_start(context, data):
    context.factor_data = pipeline_output("factor_pipeline")
```

5. Implement the function that is invoked when the backtest begins. Note the addition of commission and slippage models:

```
def initialize(context):
    attach_pipeline(make_pipeline(), "factor_pipeline")
    schedule_function(
        rebalance,
        date_rules.week_start(),
        time_rules.market_open(),
        calendar=calendars.US_EQUITIES,
    )
    set_commission(
        us_equities=commission.PerShare(
            cost=0.00075, min_trade_cost=0.01
        )
    )
    set_slippage(
        us_equities=slippage.VolumeShareSlippage(
            volume_limit=0.0025, price_impact=0.01
        )
    )
```

6. Add a `print` statement to the same `rebalance` function we created in the last recipe. This `print` statement provides feedback as the algorithm is running:

```
def rebalance(context, data):
    factor_data = context.factor_data
    record(factor_data=factor_data.ranking)
```

7. In the next section of the `rebalance` function, extract the symbols from the `factor_data` DataFrame and record the asset prices:

```
assets = factor_data.index
record(prices=data.current(assets, "price"))
```

8. Now we identify the assets to go long, to go short, and to divest from the portfolio:

```
longs = assets[factor_data.longs]
shorts = assets[factor_data.shorts]
divest = set(
    context.portfolio.positions.keys()) - set(
        longs.union(shorts))
```

9. Finally, we print output to the user and call the `exec_trades` function to execute our desired orders:

```
print(
    f"{get_datetime().date()} | Longs {len(longs)} | Shorts |"
    f"{len(shorts)} | {context.portfolio.portfolio_value}"
)
exec_trades(
    data,
    assets=divest,
    target_percent=0
)
exec_trades(
    data,
    assets=longs,
    target_percent=1 / N_LONGS
)
exec_trades(
    data,
    assets=shorts,
    target_percent=-1 / N_SHORTS
)
```

10. Implement the same exec_trades function as in the previous recipe:

```
def exec_trades(data, assets, target_percent):
    for asset in assets:
        if data.can_trade(
            asset) and not get_open_orders(asset):
            order_target_percent(
                asset, target_percent)
```

11. The analyze function is run after the backtest is complete. We have access to the context object and the output of the backtest in the perf DataFrame. This is useful to run reports or even trigger alerts if certain thresholds are passed. In this example, we simply plot the portfolio value:

```
def analyze(context, perf):
    perf.portfolio_value.plot()
```

12. Use pandas_datareader to compute the daily returns of a benchmark. In this case, we use the S&P 500 index:

```
start = pd.Timestamp("2016")
end = pd.Timestamp("2018")
sp500 = web.DataReader("SP500", "fred", start, end).SP500
benchmark_returns = sp500.pct_change()
```

13. Finally, run the backtest and cache the output:

```
perf = run_algorithm(
    start=start,
    end=end,
    initialize=initialize,
    analyze=analyze,
    benchmark_returns=benchmark_returns,
    before_trading_start=before_trading_start,
    capital_base=100_000,
    bundle="quandl"
)
perf.to_pickle("mean_reversion.pickle")
```

While the backtest is running, you'll see output that resembles the following:

```
2016-01-04 | Longs 0 | Shorts | 1 | 100000.0
2016-01-11 | Longs 0 | Shorts | 1 | 99993.16349999886
2016-01-19 | Longs 2 | Shorts | 1 | 100021.36374999832
2016-01-25 | Longs 2 | Shorts | 2 | 100047.47224999769
2016-02-01 | Longs 3 | Shorts | 3 | 99889.9749999967
2016-02-08 | Longs 2 | Shorts | 2 | 99616.54649999554
2016-02-16 | Longs 2 | Shorts | 0 | 99849.90549999391
2016-02-22 | Longs 1 | Shorts | 0 | 100195.42449999285
2016-02-29 | Longs 1 | Shorts | 0 | 100155.76424999181
2016-03-07 | Longs 2 | Shorts | 1 | 100114.18424999181
2016-03-14 | Longs 0 | Shorts | 0 | 100304.28374999072
2016-03-21 | Longs 1 | Shorts | 2 | 99210.60974998782
2016-03-28 | Longs 1 | Shorts | 0 | 99355.18649998584
2016-04-04 | Longs 1 | Shorts | 0 | 99108.98424998432
2016-04-11 | Longs 2 | Shorts | 1 | 99483.63424998433
2016-04-18 | Longs 2 | Shorts | 0 | 99556.3877499843
2016-04-25 | Longs 2 | Shorts | 0 | 99573.0884999835
2016-05-02 | Longs 4 | Shorts | 0 | 99557.5844999825
2016-05-09 | Longs 3 | Shorts | 1 | 99399.40899998133
2016-05-16 | Longs 3 | Shorts | 2 | 99355.67949998101
2016-05-23 | Longs 3 | Shorts | 2 | 99271.2524999799
2016-05-31 | Longs 1 | Shorts | 2 | 99356.98699997793
2016-06-06 | Longs 4 | Shorts | 3 | 99366.66949997128
2016-06-13 | Longs 3 | Shorts | 1 | 99543.62649996586
2016-06-20 | Longs 2 | Shorts | 1 | 99459.02499996335
2016-06-27 | Longs 4 | Shorts | 1 | 98925.75674996113
2016-07-05 | Longs 0 | Shorts | 3 | 99260.76674996056
2016-07-11 | Longs 3 | Shorts | 2 | 99335.8389999511
2016-07-18 | Longs 1 | Shorts | 1 | 99421.94524994826
2016-07-25 | Longs 0 | Shorts | 2 | 99641.29024993867
2016-08-01 | Longs 0 | Shorts | 2 | 99574.93024993711
```

Figure 9.6: Logs from the algorithm run

14. When the backtest completes, the `analyze` function is invoked and the performance is plotted:

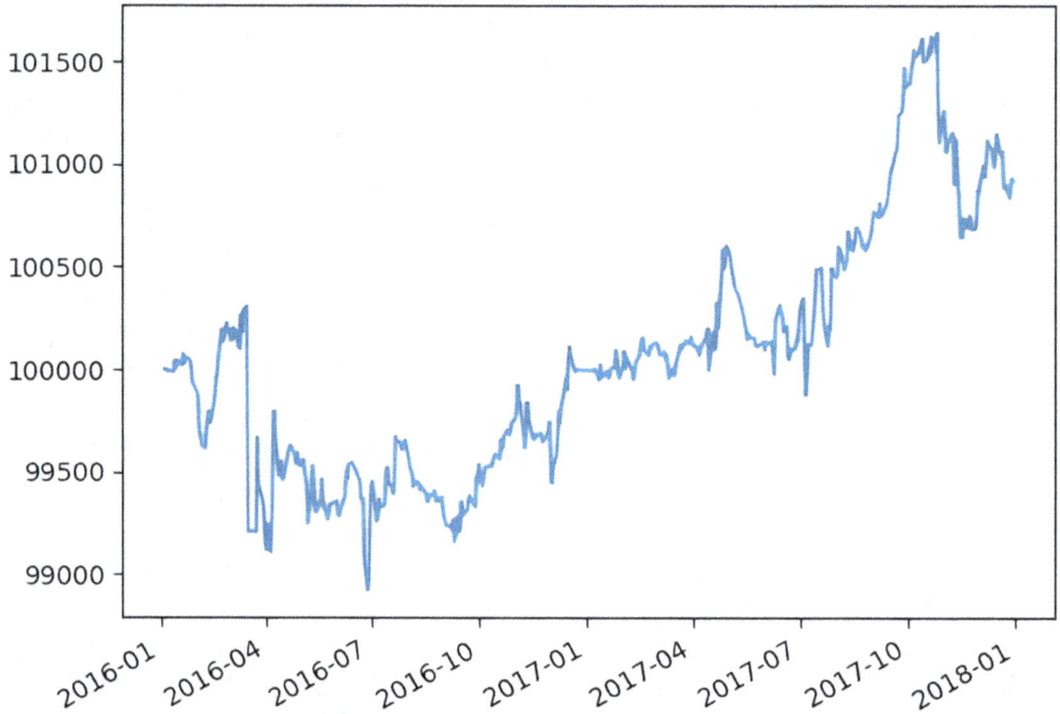

Figure 9.7: Plot automatically generated from the analyze function

> Note
>
> **Important**
>
> The keen eye may spot what looks like a bug: why are we taking long or short positions in only a few stocks when we've set the number of longs and shorts to 50? The answer lies in the sequence in which the `Pipeline` class processes its filters. It's important to note that we've included a screen argument tied to the `dollar_volume` factor. This effectively filters the stocks in the pipeline to only those with a dollar volume exceeding $100,000, and this screening occurs after the long and short selections are made. If you were to remove this screening criterion, the log would display 50 longs and 50 shorts as expected.

How it works...

Our custom factor uses monthly returns as its input, specified by the `Returns` class with a window length set to a constant, `MONTH`, representing a month. The overall window length for the factor is set to a constant, `YEAR`, representing a year. Within the `compute` method, the monthly returns are converted into a DataFrame. The factor's value for each asset is then computed by taking the last month's return, subtracting the mean of all monthly returns, and then dividing by the standard deviation of those returns. This results in a z-score-like metric, indicating how many standard deviations the latest month's return is from the mean, which can be used to gauge mean reversion tendencies for each asset.

The `make_pipeline` function is similar to the one we constructed in the last recipe, except it uses the mean reversion factor. Within the function, an instance of the `MeanReversion` factor is created, which calculates a mean reversion score for each asset. Additionally, the `AverageDollarVolume` class is used to compute the average dollar volume over a 30-day window for liquidity screening. The core of the function is the `Pipeline` object, which is set up to produce three columns:

- `longs`: Identifies the assets with the lowest mean reversion scores (i.e., the most undervalued assets)
- `shorts`: Pinpoints the assets with the highest scores (i.e., the most overvalued assets)
- `ranking`: Provides a rank for each asset based on its mean reversion score in descending order

To ensure the pipeline focuses on liquid assets, a screen is applied that only considers the top 100 assets based on their average dollar volume.

In the `initialize` function, we attach the pipeline and schedule the rebalancing in the same way as the last recipe. However, in this implementation, we include commission and slippage models. The `set_commission` function configures the commission model for US equities to be based on a per-share cost. Specifically, the algorithm will be charged $0.00075 for each share traded, with a minimum trade cost set at $0.01, ensuring that even small trades incur a nominal fee. The `set_commission` function allows for a large range of commission models to match your actual broker's commission schedule. Following this, the `set_slippage` function establishes the slippage model for US equities using the `VolumeShareSlippage` method. This model simulates the impact of an order on the stock price based on the order's size relative to the stock's average volume. The parameters dictate that an order can consume up to 0.25% of the stock's daily volume and that each order will impact the stock price by 1%.

Finally, to compare our algorithm's return to the benchmark, we compute daily returns for the S&P 500 index.

There's more...

Our pipeline is simple: we generate a mean reversion factor, screen the top and bottom stocks for a dollar volume greater than $100,000, and return the results. Zipline Reloaded supports compound factor models where several factors are combined. In those cases, it helps to visualize what's going on. Luckily, we can generate an illustration of how the pipeline is constructed:

```
p = make_pipeline()
p.show_graph()
```

The result is a pictorial depiction of the pipeline:

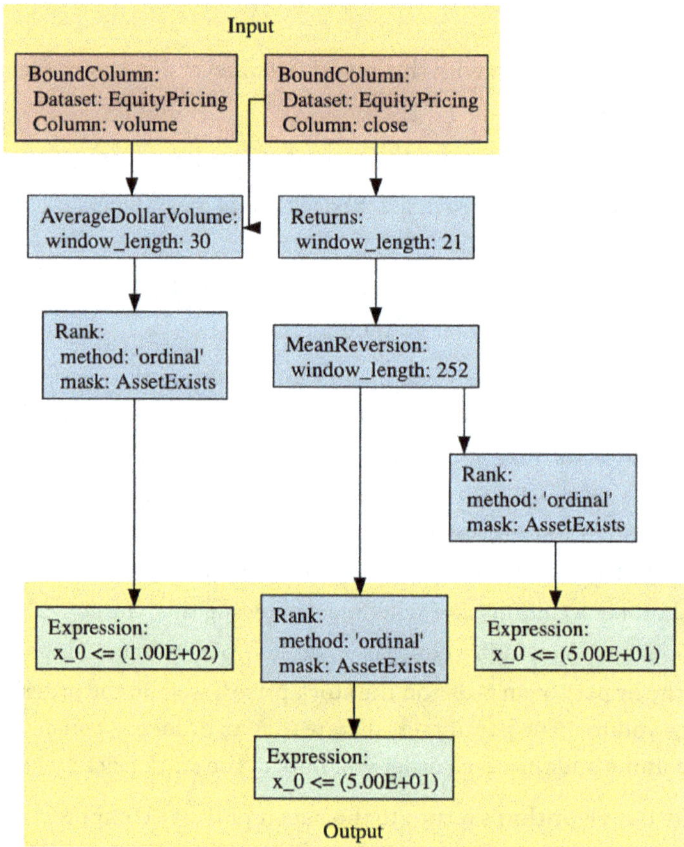

Figure 9.8: Graphical representation of the pipeline

By including returns, Zipline Reloaded computes the rolling alpha and beta of our portfolio against the benchmark. We learned how to hedge the beta and amplify the alpha in the last chapter. Using the output of the backtest, we have these metrics at our disposal.

Plot the rolling beta against the benchmark:

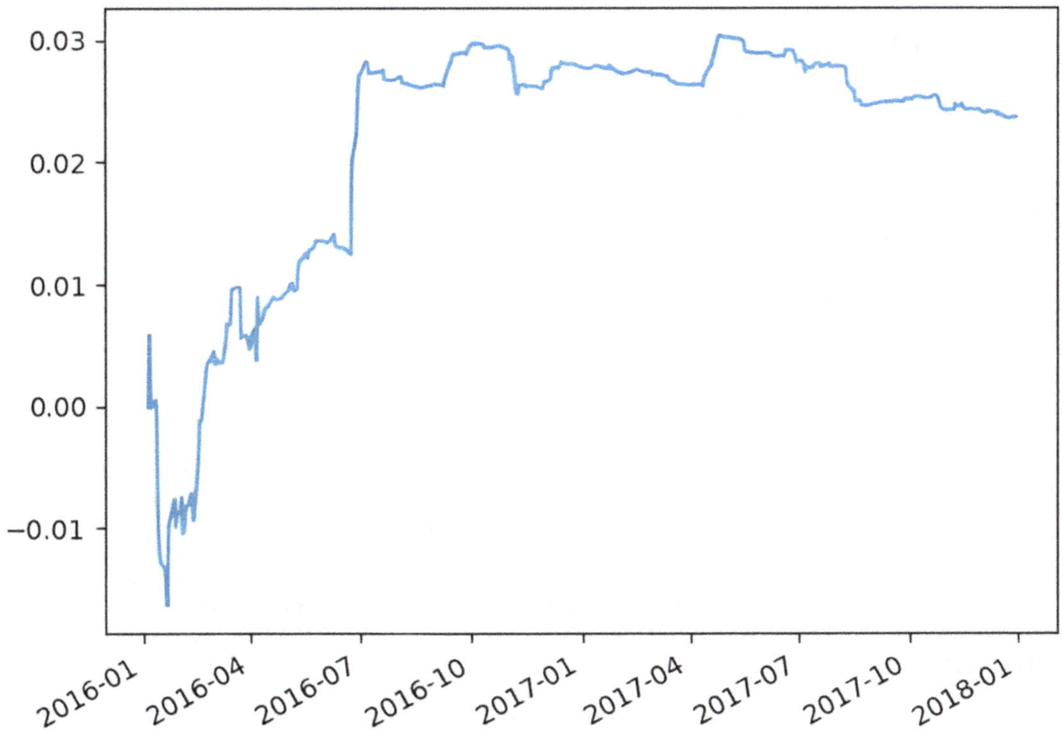

Figure 9.9: Rolling beta of our algorithm's returns against the benchmark

Plot the rolling alpha against the benchmark:

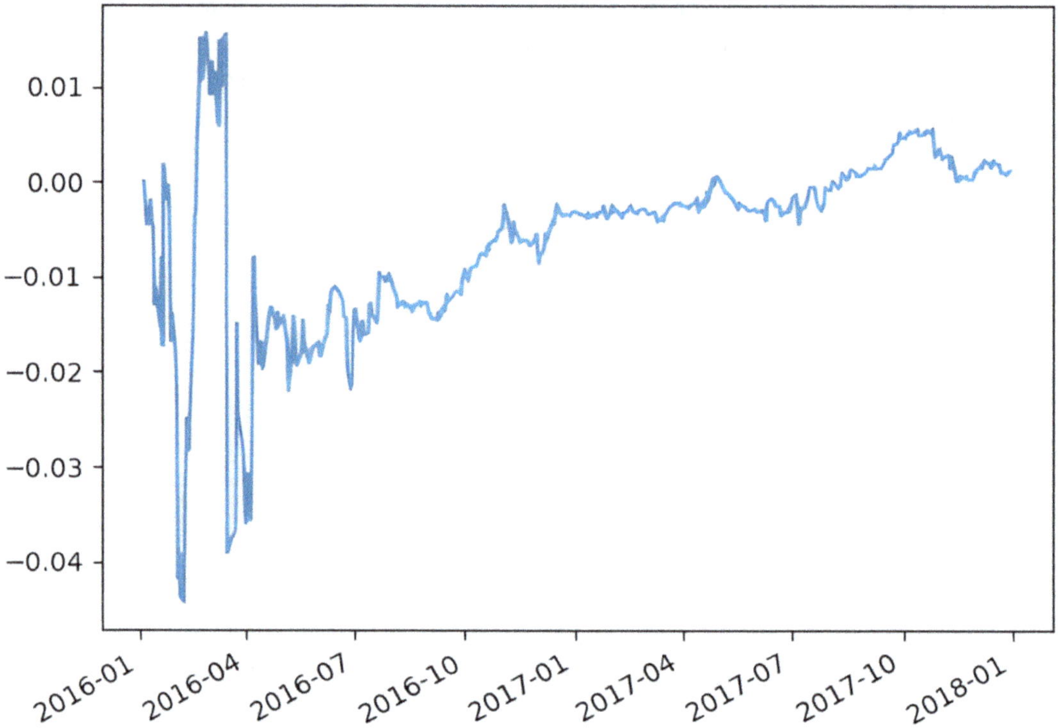

Figure 9.10: Rolling alpha of our algorithm's returns against the benchmark

See also

We went deeper into some more advanced features of Zipline Reloaded. These features aim to create a more realistic simulation of the market dynamics algorithmic traders face every day. To dive deeper, check out the documentation listed here:

- API documentation for the Pipeline API, which describes its available input parameters: `https://zipline.ml4trading.io/api-reference.html#pipeline-api`
- Different built-in slippage models available within Zipline Reloaded: `https://zipline.ml4trading.io/api-reference.html#slippage-models`
- Different built-in commission models available within Zipline Reloaded: `https://zipline.ml4trading.io/api-reference.html#commission-models`

Get this book's PDF version and more

Scan the QR code (or go to `packtpub.com/unlock`). Search for this book by name, confirm the edition, and then follow the steps on the page.

UNLOCK NOW

Note: Keep your invoice handy. Purchases made directly from Packt don't require an invoice.

10

Evaluate Factor Risk and Performance with Alphalens Reloaded

Factor investing is a strategic approach to trading where assets are chosen based on attributes or **factors** that are associated with higher returns. This method differs from traditional investment strategies which focus on asset classes like stocks, bonds, or sectors. Factor investing emphasizes the underlying drivers of risk and return in securities. Much focus is placed by researchers on the statistical analysis of these factors since the edge (measured by predictive power) is often vanishing and results can be misleading. The crux of factor investing lies in the systematic identification and harnessing of these and other factors. By understanding the sources of risk and return, we can aim for returns above traditional benchmarks. It's essential to note, however, that while factor investing can enhance portfolio diversification and potential returns, it does not eliminate risk. Market conditions, economic changes, and other externalities can influence the effectiveness of factor-based strategies at any given time.

In *Chapter 7, Build Alpha Factors for Stock Portfolios*, we explored recipes to construct alpha factors. In this chapter, we explore how to analyze the risk and performance of these alpha factors using Alphalens Reloaded. Alphalens Reloaded is a library designed specifically for performance analysis of predictive alpha factors. It's useful for assessing the quality of signals generated from various factors, which allows us to evaluate how well these signals predict future returns. Alphalens Reloaded integrates with Zipline Reloaded and turns the output of backtests into statistics and visualizations. The library provides various utilities, including tear sheets that consolidate performance metrics and visualizations. These tear sheets can show cumulative returns, turnover analysis, and information coefficients, among other insights.

In this chapter, we present the following recipes:

- Preparing backtest results
- Evaluating the information coefficient
- Examining factor return performance
- Evaluating factor turnover

Preparing backtest results

Zipline Reloaded is a robust backtesting library that has an integrated ecosystem of tools designed to assess trading strategy performance. This ecosystem makes it easier for traders to transition from strategy development to evaluation. An example of an integrated tool is Alphalens Reloaded which is the focus of this chapter.

We learned in *Chapter 9, Event-Based Backtesting Factor Portfolios with Zipline Reloaded* that the output DataFrame of a Zipline backtest provides a detailed analysis of a trading strategy's performance over a specified historical data period. The output includes metrics like cumulative returns, alpha, beta, Sharpe ratio, and maximum drawdown, among many others. We need to manipulate the output DataFrame to extract some of the data so it's suitable for use with Alphalens Reloaded.

This recipe will walk through the process of extracting the relevant information.

Getting ready

To install Alphalens Reloaded in your virtual environment, use `pip`:

```
pip install alphalens-reloaded
```

We assume that a file `mean_reversion.pickle` exists in the same directory as the code for this recipe. The file is the cached output from the Zipline backtest we ran in *Chapter 7, Build Alpha Factors for Stock Portfolios.*

How to do it...

This recipe focuses on manipulating the output of the Zipline backtest using pandas. There's one Alphalens Reloaded method we can use to create a DataFrame used for most analysis in Alphalens Reloaded.

1. Import the libraries we need for the analysis:

```
import pandas as pd
from alphalens.utils import get_clean_factor_and_forward_returns
```

2. Read in the cached backtest output into a DataFrame:

```
mean_reversion = pd.read_pickle("mean_reversion.pickle")
```

3. Construct a DataFrame with symbols in the columns and dates in the rows:

```
prices = pd.concat(
    [df.to_frame(d)
     for d, df in mean_reversion.prices.dropna().items()],
    axis=1
).T
```

Note

Important

A Python list comprehension is a concise way to create lists by iterating over an iterable and applying an expression to each element. It condenses a loop and a list appending operation into a single line of code, making it more readable and elegant. The syntax includes brackets containing an expression followed by a for clause, as we see in *Step 3* above.

4. Convert column names to strings:

```
prices.columns = [col.symbol for col in prices.columns]
```

5. Normalize the timestamps to midnight, preserving time zone information:

```
prices.index = prices.index.normalize()
```

The result is the following DataFrame containing the prices of each asset in the backtest for each day:

	AAL	AAPL	ABBV	AET	AGN	...	ANTM	AMT	PCG	CBS	TMO
2016-01-04 00:00:00+00:00	40.91	105.35	57.61	109.26	307.47	...	NaN	NaN	NaN	NaN	NaN
2016-01-05 00:00:00+00:00	40.91	105.35	57.61	109.26	307.47	...	NaN	NaN	NaN	NaN	NaN
2016-01-06 00:00:00+00:00	40.91	105.35	57.61	109.26	307.47	...	NaN	NaN	NaN	NaN	NaN
2016-01-07 00:00:00+00:00	40.91	105.35	57.61	109.26	307.47	...	NaN	NaN	NaN	NaN	NaN
2016-01-08 00:00:00+00:00	40.91	105.35	57.61	109.26	307.47	...	NaN	NaN	NaN	NaN	NaN
...	...	...	...	...	...	...	...	...	...	...	...
2017-12-22 00:00:00+00:00	NaN	176.42	98.19	177.34	170.91	...	227.02	NaN	NaN	59.00	NaN
2017-12-26 00:00:00+00:00	NaN	170.57	97.75	180.42	164.44	...	225.43	NaN	44.45	60.19	NaN
2017-12-27 00:00:00+00:00	NaN	170.57	97.75	180.42	164.44	...	225.43	NaN	44.45	60.19	NaN
2017-12-28 00:00:00+00:00	NaN	170.57	97.75	180.42	164.44	...	225.43	NaN	44.45	60.19	NaN
2017-12-29 00:00:00+00:00	NaN	170.57	97.75	180.42	164.44	...	225.43	NaN	44.45	60.19	NaN

Figure 10.1: Price data from the backtest output

6. We repeat a similar process for the factor data. Start by constructing a DataFrame with symbols in the columns and factor rank in the rows:

```
factor_data = pd.concat(
    [df.to_frame(d) for d,
        df in mean_reversion.factor_data.dropna().items()],
    axis=1
).T
```

7. Convert column names to strings:

```
factor_data.columns = [
    col.symbol for col in factor_data.columns]
```

8. Normalize the timestamps to midnight, preserving time zone information:

```
factor_data.index = factor_data.index.normalize()
```

9. Create a MultiIndex with `date` in level `0` and `symbol` in level `1`:

```
factor_data = factor_data.stack()
```

10. Rename the MultiIndex:

```
factor_data.index.names = ["date", "asset"]
```

The result is the following: a MultiIndex series with the data and asset in the indexes and the factor ranking in the column:

```
date                       asset
2016-01-04 00:00:00+00:00  AAL      1156.0
                           AAPL     2547.0
                           ABBV      438.0
                           AET       893.0
                           AGN      1371.0
                                     ...
2017-12-29 00:00:00+00:00  ISRG     2449.0
                           DWDP     1277.0
                           ANTM     1510.0
                           PCG      2440.0
                           CBS       292.0
Length: 50275, dtype: float64
```

Figure 10.2: MultiIndex Series containing factor ranks for each day and asset

11. The last step is to create a MultiIndex DataFrame with forward returns, factor values, and factor quantiles:

```
alphalens_data = get_clean_factor_and_forward_returns(
    factor=factor_data, prices=prices, periods=(5, 10, 21, 63)
)
```

The result is the following MultiIndex DataFrame containing the data we need to run all the factor analysis using Alphalens Reloaded:

		5D	10D	21D	63D	factor	factor_quantile
date	asset						
2016-01-04 00:00:00+00:00	AAL	0.004155	-0.050110	-0.037399	0.041066	1156.0	3
	AAPL	-0.064737	-0.082487	-0.084670	0.054770	2547.0	5
	ABBV	-0.064746	-0.045478	-0.055893	0.027773	438.0	1
	AET	-0.036061	-0.040454	-0.053908	-0.064800	893.0	2
	AGN	-0.026344	-0.050997	-0.080561	-0.097310	1371.0	4
...	...	...	...	...	...	...	...
2017-09-29 00:00:00+00:00	ADP	0.004595	0.004595	0.004595	0.004595	1239.0	3
	COL	0.011153	0.024537	0.035920	0.035920	2196.0	4
	BBY	0.059996	0.089902	0.089902	0.089902	2486.0	5
	EFX	0.025883	0.068132	0.037301	0.027976	2501.0	5
	SBAC	0.009967	0.044323	0.044323	0.044323	2390.0	5

Figure 10.3: MultiIndex DataFrame containing clean factor and forward returns for each date and asset

How it works...

After the imports, we need to manipulate the backtest output. First, we construct a DataFrame called `prices` where each column represents a symbol and each row represents a date. We do this by iterating through each row of `prices` using the `items` method which returns an iterator. Each key is the date and each value is a DataFrame representing price data. Each of these DataFrames is converted to a column with the date as the column's name using the `to_frame()` method. The `concat()` function then concatenates these columns horizontally using the `axis=1` argument.

Next, we modify the column names of the `prices` DataFrame to be the symbols since the original column names were Equity objects. Finally, we adjust the row indices of the `prices` DataFrame to normalize the dates to midnight while retaining any time zone information.

To extract the factor data from the backtest output, we follow similar steps. First, we iterate through `factor_data` column, dropping any null values and reshaping the data so that each date corresponds to a unique column. Next, we convert the column names to strings and adjust the dates like before. Finally, the DataFrame is transformed from a two-dimensional table into a one-dimensional series with a hierarchical index. We do this with the `stack` method, resulting in a multi-indexed Series where the primary level of the index is the date and the secondary level is the symbol. For clarity, these levels are named `date` and `asset`.

Now that the DataFrames are prepared, we can call the Alphalens Reloaded `get_clean_factor_and_forward_returns` function. The purpose of this function is to associate factor values with future returns. The output, stored in the variable `alphalens_data`, is a DataFrame that combines the factor data with the subsequent returns based on the provided prices. This merged structure allows us to analyze how specific factor values might have influenced or related to future asset returns. The resulting DataFrame has a MultiIndex with dates and symbols. The columns in the DataFrame represent different forward returns (5D, 10D, 21D, and 63D for 5-day, 10-day, 21-day, and 63-day returns), the factor values and quantile rankings of the factor values. The quantile rankings segment the factor values into groups, with the shown values like "3" or "5" indicating the specific quantile bucket the factor value for an asset falls into on a given date.

This DataFrame will be used for all subsequent analyses.

There's more...

The `get_clean_factor_and_forward_returns` function from Alphalens Reloaded is designed to prepare factor data for subsequent analysis. It aligns factor values with forward returns, ensuring that comparisons between factors and future performance are valid. The function also handles data cleaning tasks such as handling missing values. The result is a structured DataFrame that is optimized for factor analysis. The `get_clean_factor_and_forward_returns` function is flexible in how it aligns the factor data with return data. These are the additional arguments available for controlling this alignment:

- `groupby`: An optional parameter, which, if provided, groups assets based on common characteristics like industry or sector, facilitating sector-neutral analysis.
- `by_group`: A boolean that decides whether to perform computations (like quantile analysis) separately for each group in `groupby` or for the entire dataset.
- `bins`: The number of quantiles to form or specific bin edges. This can be an alternative to the `quantiles` argument.
- `quantiles`: An integer denoting how many quantiles to form. Quantiles segment the factor data, allowing for the examination of returns by factor quantile.
- `periods`: A list of time periods for which forward returns will be computed, e.g., [1, 5, 10] would yield forward returns for 1 day, 5 days, and 10 days.
- `filter_zscore`: Removes outliers based on the z-score. This ensures that extreme factor values, which could be errors or anomalies, do not skew the analysis.
- `groupby_labels`: An optional set of labels for the groups when using the `groupby` argument, useful for more meaningful group naming.

- `max_loss`: The maximum percentage loss that is tolerated in case of missing data. Determines how much missing data is acceptable.
- `zero_aware`: A `boolean` that, if `True`, makes quantile computation treat zeros distinctly, ensuring that they receive their own bin. This is especially useful when zero has a distinct meaning in the factor context.

See also

Factor investing is a broad topic. *Active Portfolio Management: A Quantitative Approach for Producing Superior Returns and Controlling Risk* by Richard C. Grinold and Ronald N. Khan is a staple in the world of quantitative finance and portfolio management. It dives deep into the mathematics and strategies behind managing portfolios actively, including factor-based investing. The book covers various factors, models, and tools, emphasizing the importance of forward returns in the evaluation and prediction of factor performance. For practitioners and students alike, this book provides a comprehensive and rigorous exploration of quantitative techniques in portfolio management. You can buy the book on Amazon here: `https://amzn.to/3RtsovG`

Finally, the Alphalens Reloaded documentation provides examples and details on how to use the code. The documentation can be found here: `https://alphalens.ml4trading.io`

Evaluating the information coefficient

The **Information Coefficient** (**IC**) is a fundamental metric in quantitative portfolio construction. It gauges the predictive power of a forecast relative to future returns. At its core, IC uses the Spearman rank correlation, a non-parametric measure that assesses how well the relationship between two variables can be described using a monotonic function. The IC's value ranges from -1 to 1, with a positive IC indicating a forecast's genuine predictive power, a value near zero indicating an absence of predictive capacity, and a negative value indicating an inverse relationship between the forecast and subsequent returns.

The origins of the IC can be traced back to the 1960s and 1970s. The preliminary idea of the metric was introduced by Jack L. Treynor in the early 1960s as he presented the topic of correlating investment decisions with corresponding outcomes in his writings on performance measurement. By the mid-1970s, Fischer Black, who is also co-credited for the renowned Black-Scholes option pricing model, further honed and expanded upon the concept in academic literature. Today, IC is a cornerstone metric to gauge the predictive power of alpha factors.

Alphalens Reloaded consolidates extensive quantitative research into a single tool tailored for factor evaluation. It simplifies complex methodologies, offering us an easy way to analyze the predictive capabilities of factors.

This recipe will show us how.

Getting ready

For this recipe and subsequent recipes, we assume the imports from the last recipe are available and `alphalens_data` is defined.

How to do it...

Alphalens Reloaded provides tear sheets that provide consolidated summaries of the analyses presented in this recipe. We'll look at each independently to deepen our understanding.

1. Import additional libraries from Alphalens Reloaded to evaluate the IC:

```
from alphalens.performance import (
    factor_information_coefficient,
    mean_information_coefficient,
)
from alphalens.plotting import (
    plot_ic_ts,
    plot_information_table,
)
```

2. Generate the information coefficient for each holding period on each date:

```
ic = factor_information_coefficient(alphalens_data)
```

The result is the following DataFrame with the IC for each day and forward return:

	5D	10D	21D	63D
date				
2016-01-04 00:00:00+00:00	-0.248066	-0.284107	-0.140796	-0.106800
2016-01-05 00:00:00+00:00	-0.248066	-0.284107	-0.140796	-0.106800
2016-01-06 00:00:00+00:00	-0.248066	-0.284107	-0.140796	-0.106800
2016-01-07 00:00:00+00:00	-0.248066	-0.284107	-0.182742	-0.106800
2016-01-08 00:00:00+00:00	-0.248066	-0.263740	-0.182742	-0.085559
...	...	...	...	...
2017-09-25 00:00:00+00:00	-0.009765	0.020817	-0.009796	-0.037130
2017-09-26 00:00:00+00:00	-0.009765	0.020817	-0.009796	-0.094793
2017-09-27 00:00:00+00:00	-0.009765	0.020817	-0.009796	-0.094793
2017-09-28 00:00:00+00:00	-0.009765	0.020817	-0.009796	-0.094793
2017-09-29 00:00:00+00:00	-0.009765	0.020817	0.086333	-0.094793

Figure 10.4: DataFrame containing the IC for each period and forward return

3. Inspect the statistical properties of the IC at each forward return:

```
plot_information_table(ic)
```

The result is the following table containing the mean, standard deviation, and other properties of the IC:

	5D	10D	21D	63D
IC Mean	0.023	0.031	0.018	0.014
IC Std.	0.186	0.165	0.155	0.166
Risk-Adjusted IC	0.124	0.186	0.116	0.084
t-stat(IC)	2.599	3.894	2.426	1.757
p-value(IC)	0.010	0.000	0.016	0.080
IC Skew	0.153	0.104	0.530	0.404
IC Kurtosis	-0.247	-0.554	0.246	-0.221

Figure 10.5: DataFrame containing statistical properties of the IC including mean, standard deviation, risk adjusted IC, t-stat, p-value, skew, and kurtosis

4. Plot the IC over the forward return period to inspect how the alpha decays over longer holding periods as follows:

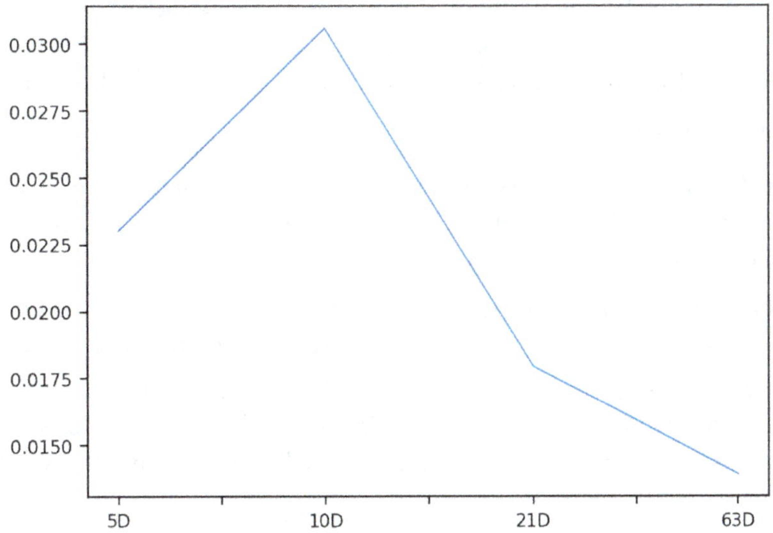

Figure 10.6: Plot demonstrating the decay of the IC as the forward return period lengthens

How it works...

The Spearman rank correlation, often denoted as ρ or Spearman's r, is a non-parametric measure used to assess the strength and direction of the monotonic relationship between two variables. Unlike the Pearson correlation coefficient, which measures linear relationships between continuous variables, Spearman's rank correlation focuses on the relative order of values rather than their absolute magnitudes.

To compute the Spearman rank correlation:

1. Rank each variable separately, assigning ranks from *1* to *N* for a dataset of *N* observations. For tied values, assign the average rank.
2. Calculate the difference between ranks for each observation, denoted as d
3. Square these differences, d^2
4. Use the following formula to compute ρ

$$\rho = 1 - \frac{6\sum d^2}{N(N^2 - 1)}$$

   Where:

   - ρ is the Spearman rank correlation
   - d is the difference between paired ranks
   - N is the number of observations

The resulting ρ will fall between -1 and 1. A value of 1 indicates perfect positive correlation in ranks (i.e., as one variable increases, the other does too), -1 indicates perfect negative correlation in ranks, and a value close to 0 suggests no significant rank correlation.

In the context of the IC using the Spearman rank correlation:

- **Predicted or forward returns**: These are the returns that a factor model anticipates. They are typically derived from the factor scores, which are usually the output of some quantitative model or strategy.
- **Actual returns**: These are the realized returns of assets over a specific period. They serve as the ground truth against which predicted returns are evaluated.

When computing the Spearman rank correlation for the IC, the ranks of both predicted and actual returns are compared. The differences in ranks (*dd*) between these two sets of values are used in the Spearman formula to determine how well the predicted returns' order (or rank) matches the actual returns' order.

Alphalens Reloaded uses the Spearman rank correlation to compare the ranks of the factor values with the ranks of the forward returns. A high correlation would suggest that assets with higher factor scores tend to have higher (or lower, depending on the sign) future returns, affirming the predictive power of the factor.

In *Figure 10.6*, we observe the predictive power of the alpha factor decaying over time. This is referred to as IC decay. In algorithmic trading, it's important to measure how quickly the correlation between predicted and actual returns diminishes. A rapid IC decay indicates that the factor's predictive power is short-lived. Conversely, a slow IC decay suggests that the signal remains relevant for a more extended period, potentially allowing for longer investment horizons. In many trading environments, an IC of 0.05 is considered good while an IC of 0.10 is considered excellent.

There's more...

Alphalens Reloaded ships with plotting functions to visualize how IC evolves through time. To see how the IC using 5-day forward returns evolves through time, use the `plot_ic_ts()` function:

```
plot_ic_ts(ic[["5D"]])
```

The result is a timeseries plot of the IC and its one-month moving average:

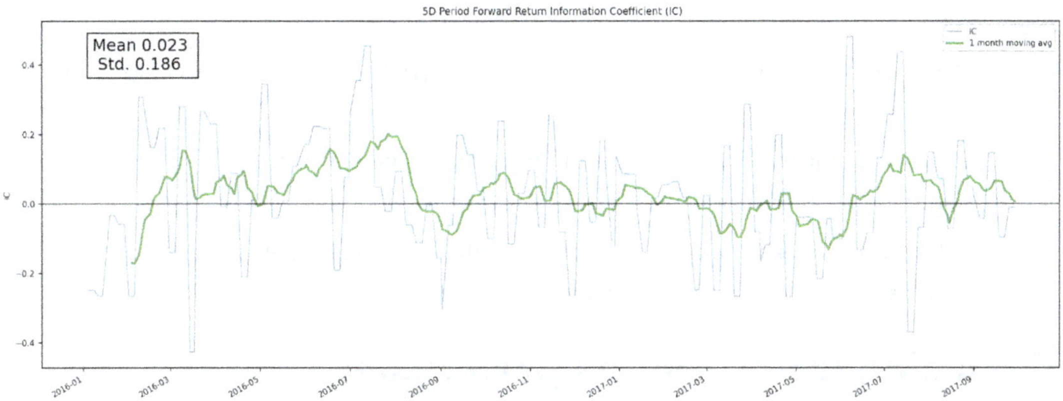

Figure 10.7: Evolution of the IC for 5-day forward returns

Since the return value of the `factor_information_coefficient()` function is a DataFrame, all the methods we learned previously can be used to further analyze the IC. This code resamples the daily IC into the quarterly mean and plots the value for each forward return:

```
ic_by_quarter = ic.resample("Q").mean()
ic_by_quarter.index = ic_by_quarter.index.to_period("Q")
ic_by_quarter.plot.bar(figsize=(14, 6))
```

The result is the following bar chart visualizing the mean IC over each quarter for each forward period:

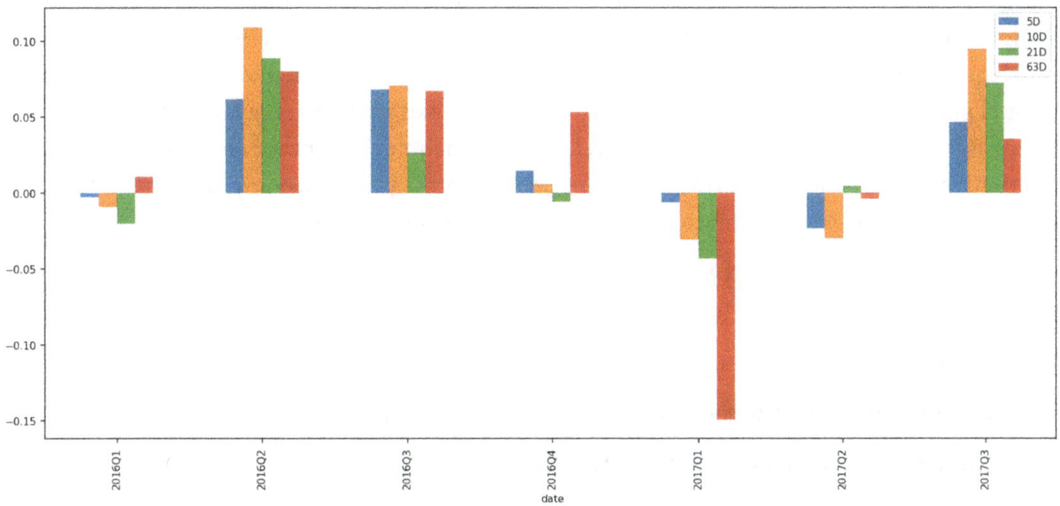

Figure 10.8: Mean IC value per quarter for each forward period

See also

Using the information coefficient is an advanced topic. Here are some resources to get you started:

- Investopedia article describing the information coefficient: `https://www.investopedia.com/terms/i/information-coefficient.asp`
- Details of the Spearman rank correlation coefficient: `https://en.wikipedia.org/wiki/Spearman%27s_rank_correlation_coefficient`

Examining factor returns performance

Factor performance relates to the returns generated by a portfolio constructed explicitly based on specific factor values. These factors can encompass any measurable characteristic or set of characteristics about assets, such as value, momentum, size, or volatility, or in our case, mean reversion. In constructing a factor portfolio, assets with high factor values are held long, while those with low values are held short. This approach seeks to isolate the return attributable solely to the factor under consideration. The primary objective behind computing factor returns is to assess the performance of a factor and determine if it offers a premium over some benchmark return. To ensure that these returns are purely a result of the factor, various adjustments, such as demeaning or group adjustments, are applied.

On the other hand, portfolio returns represent the returns generated by a portfolio based on any chosen investment strategy, which might not necessarily be tied to specific factor values. Such portfolios can be constructed based on criteria like expected returns, risk, fundamental analysis, or technical indicators. The weightings of assets in these portfolios can vary, ranging from equal weighting to market-cap weighting or other schemes. The main aim of evaluating normal portfolio returns is to gauge the efficacy of the investment strategy, which can give us insights into the portfolio's performance relative to benchmarks or other investment alternatives. Unlike factor returns, normal portfolio returns provide a view of the portfolio's performance without the intent to isolate returns due to specific factors.

This recipe will demonstrate the available Alphalens Reloaded functionality to examine factor return performance.

How to do it...

We'll explore how to analyze the return data in the *How it works* section, next.

1. Import additional libraries from Alphalens Reloaded to assess factor performance:

```
from alphalens.performance import (
    factor_returns,
```

```
        factor_cumulative_returns,
        mean_return_by_quantile,
        compute_mean_returns_spread,
        factor_alpha_beta,
    )
```

2. Compute the period-wise, returns for the portfolio weighted by the factor values:

```
returns = factor_returns(alphalens_data)
```

The result is the following DataFrame with the portfolio returns for each forward return period:

date	5D	10D	21D	63D
2016-01-04 00:00:00+00:00	-0.016253	-0.027134	-0.013492	-0.015658
2016-01-05 00:00:00+00:00	-0.016253	-0.027134	-0.013492	-0.015658
2016-01-06 00:00:00+00:00	-0.016253	-0.027134	-0.013492	-0.015658
2016-01-07 00:00:00+00:00	-0.016253	-0.027134	-0.026664	-0.015658
2016-01-08 00:00:00+00:00	-0.016253	-0.026459	-0.026664	-0.011788
...	...	...	...	...
2017-09-25 00:00:00+00:00	-0.003797	-0.001202	0.000069	0.000902
2017-09-26 00:00:00+00:00	-0.003797	-0.001202	0.000069	-0.006470
2017-09-27 00:00:00+00:00	-0.003797	-0.001202	0.000069	-0.006470
2017-09-28 00:00:00+00:00	-0.003797	-0.001202	0.000069	-0.006470
2017-09-29 00:00:00+00:00	-0.003797	-0.001202	0.009394	-0.006470

Figure 10.9: DataFrame with factor-weighted portfolio returns

3. Inspect the returns on a per-asset basis:

```
returns = factor_returns(alphalens_data, by_asset=True)
```

The result is the following MultiIndex DataFrame with each asset return weighted by the associated factor:

		5D	10D	21D	63D
date	**asset**				
2016-01-04 00:00:00+00:00	**AAL**	-0.000006	0.000078	0.000058	-0.000064
	AAPL	-0.001374	-0.001751	-0.001797	0.001162
	ABBV	0.000862	0.000605	0.000744	-0.000370
	AET	0.000211	0.000237	0.000316	0.000380
	AGN	-0.000052	-0.000100	-0.000158	-0.000191
...	...	...	...	...	...
2017-09-29 00:00:00+00:00	**ADP**	-0.000008	-0.000008	-0.000008	-0.000008
	COL	0.000130	0.000285	0.000417	0.000417
	BBY	0.000939	0.001407	0.001407	0.001407
	EFX	0.000411	0.001081	0.000592	0.000444
	SBAC	0.000143	0.000635	0.000635	0.000635

Figure 10.10: MultiIndex DataFrame with per-asset, factor-weighted returns

4. Visualize the factor-weighted, cumulative portfolio returns for the 5-day forward return against the equal-weighted portfolio:

```
pd.concat(
    {
        "factor_weighted": factor_cumulative_returns(
            alphalens_data,
            period="5D"
        ),
        "equal_weighted": factor_cumulative_returns(
            alphalens_data,
            period="5D",
            equal_weight=True
        ),
    },
    axis=1,
).plot()
```

The result is the following plot demonstrating the cumulative return of the portfolios:

Figure 10.11: Plot with the cumulative return of the 5-day forward, factor-weighted portfolio against the 5-day forward, equal-weighted portfolio

5. Compute the mean return for factor quantiles across the forward returns:

```
mean_returns, _ = mean_return_by_quantile(alphalens_data)
mean_returns.plot.bar()
```

The result is the following bar chart visualizing the mean return for each forward return in each quantile:

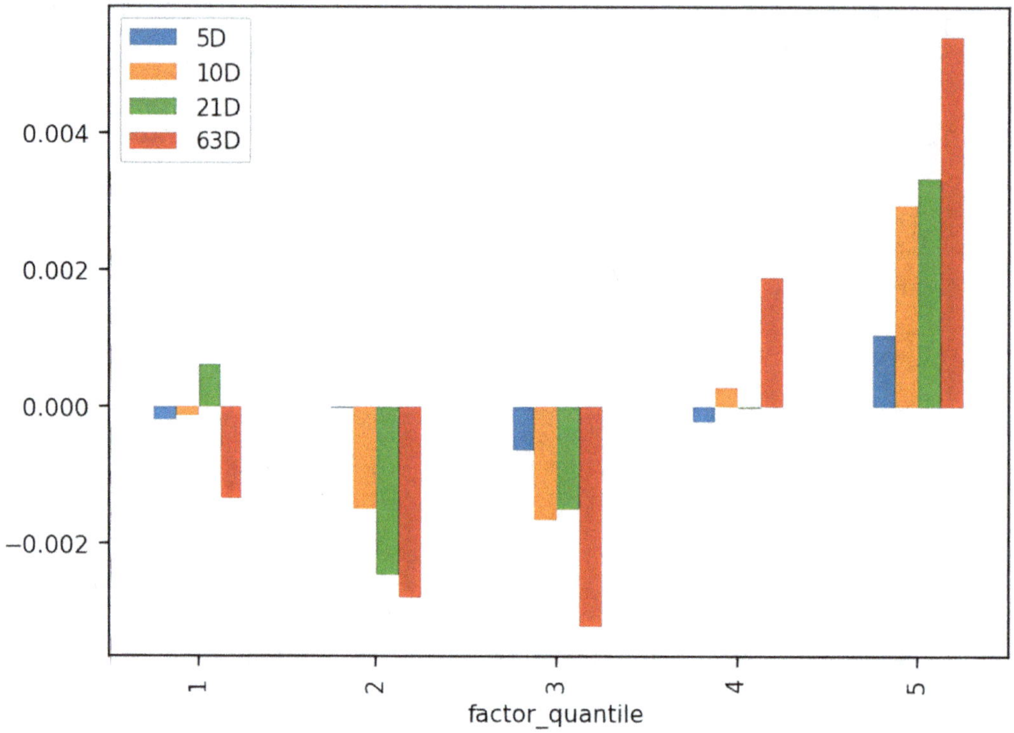

Figure 10.12: Bar chart with the mean factor-weighted portfolio return for each forward return in each quantile

6. Compute the difference in mean returns between the portfolios at the upper and lower quantiles:

```
mean_returns_by_date, _ = mean_return_by_quantile(
    alphalens_data,
    by_date=True
)
mean_return_difference, _ = compute_mean_returns_spread(
    mean_returns=mean_returns_by_date,
    upper_quant=1,
    lower_quant=5,
)
```

7. The result is a DataFrame with the difference between the mean return in the upper and lower quantiles. We can take it a step further and resample the daily values to monthly, take their mean, and plot them:

```
(
    mean_return_difference[["5D"]]
    .resample("M")
    .mean()
    .to_period("M")
    .plot
    .bar()
)
```

8. The result is the following plot of the mean spread per month for the 5-day forward return:

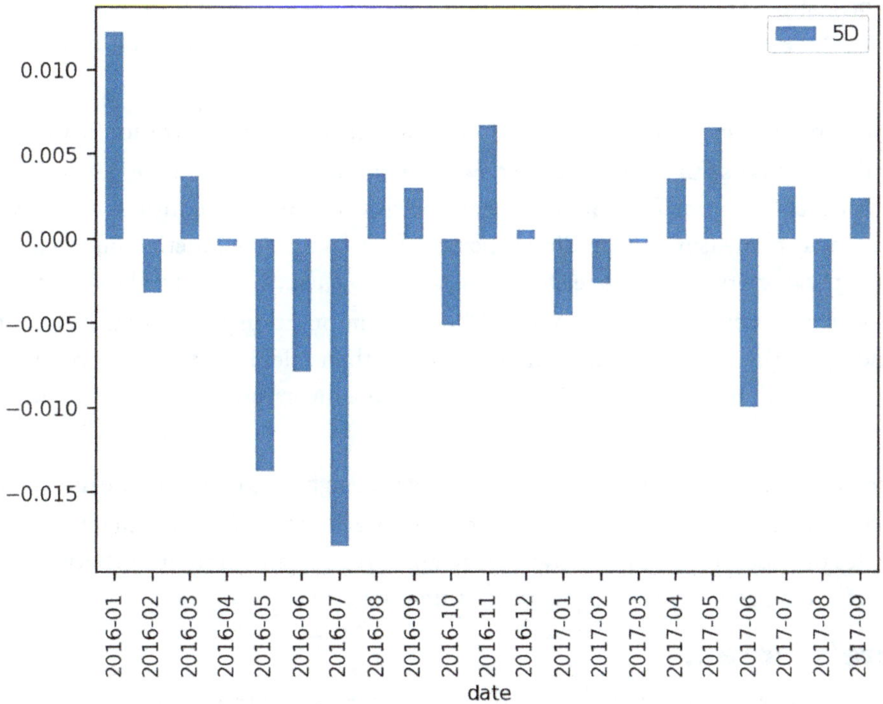

Figure 10.13: Bar chart demonstrating the mean, factor-weighted portfolio returns for the 5-day forward return

How it works...

The `factor_returns()` function is designed to compute the factor-weighted returns. It takes in two primary arguments: `factor_data`, which is a MultiIndex DataFrame that contains factor values, forward returns for each period, and quantiles and `periods`, which is a list of periods for which to compute the returns. For each specified period, it calculates the factor-weighted return by multiplying factor values with forward returns. We can optionally override the factor-weighting and assume an equal-weighted portfolio. This is helpful to compare performance.

The `factor_cumulative_returns()` function is designed to compute the cumulative returns of a factor. The `factor_data` argument is a multi-index DataFrame that contains factor values, forward returns, and group codes. The `period` argument specifies the period for which the cumulative returns are to be calculated, and the `demeaned` argument, when set to `True`, will demean the returns based on the group codes provided in the `alphalens_data` DataFrame. The function computes the mean returns for each date and then determines the cumulative product of these mean returns. The result is a time-series of cumulative returns indexed by date.

The `mean_return_by_quantile()` function computes the mean returns for factors, grouped by quantiles. This is useful to understand how different quantiles of a factor perform over time. In the context of factor portfolio management, the spread between quantiles, which we look at next, is a way to measure the predictive power of the factor. The function offers flexibility through parameters like `by_date`, `demeaned`, `group_adjust`, and `by_group`, which determine how returns are computed and grouped. The core computation groups data by quantiles, and depending on the flags set, by date or group codes, then calculates the mean returns for each group. The result is a MultiIndex DataFrame with the mean returns for each quantile, and optionally, dates and quantiles.

The `compute_mean_returns_spread()` function is designed to compute the mean returns spread for quantiles over a specified period. The spread between the mean return in different quantiles provides insights into how well an alpha factor can differentiate between high and low performing assets over time or across different groups.

There's more...

Using Alphalens Reloaded we can calculate the factor's alpha (representing excess returns) and its beta (indicating market exposure). To do it, we call `factor_alpha_beta`, which performs a regression using the mean return of the factor universe for each period as the independent variable and the average return from a portfolio weighted by factor values for each period as the dependent variable. This is depicted as follows:

```
factor_alpha_beta(alphalens_data)
```

The result is a DataFrame with the annualized alpha and beta across each forward return:

	5D	10D	21D	63D
Ann. alpha	0.006204	0.015760	-0.003038	-0.012823
beta	0.136634	0.123627	0.117090	0.147144

Figure 10.14: DataFrame with the results of a regression on the mean return of the factor universe and average portfolio return

As we learned in *Chapter 7, Build Alpha Factors for Stock Portfolios*, alpha provides a measure of the factor's performance. A positive alpha indicates that the factor has outperformed the benchmark on a risk-adjusted basis, while a negative alpha suggests underperformance. Beta gives insight into the factor's risk relative to the benchmark. A beta greater than 1 indicates that the factor is more volatile than the benchmark, while a beta less than 1 suggests it is less volatile. Over the forward returns of 5 and 10 days, our factor seems to generate positive alpha.

See also

Applied **Quantitative Research** (**AQR**) is a global investment management firm that employs a systematic, research-driven approach to capture investment opportunities across various asset classes. Founded in 1998 by Cliff Asness, David Kabiller, John Liew, and Robert Krail, AQR has become known for its focus on quantitative, data-driven strategies, combining academic research with practical market experience. AQR writes extensively about factor investing. Here's a great paper about measuring factor exposures: `https://www.aqr.com/-/media/AQR/Documents/Insights/Trade-Publications/Measuring-Portfolio-Factor-Exposures-A-Practical-Guide.pdf`

Evaluating factor turnover

In algorithmic trading, factor portfolios form the bedrock of many strategies. As we learned in the last recipe, assets are systematically ranked using the Spearman rank correlation from highest to lowest. Following this ranking, assets in the top quartile are bought and those from the bottom quartile are sold. In this context, turnover quantifies the frequency with which assets are bought or sold to rebalance the designated quartiles.

If a factor exhibits high turnover, it might suggest that the factor's signals are not persistent and could lead to higher trading costs if one were to trade based on this factor. Conversely, a factor with low turnover might indicate more stable signals. By analyzing turnover at the quantile level, we can gain insights into the stability of the factor's rankings across different segments of the asset universe. This can be particularly useful when assessing the viability of a factor for portfolio construction, as it provides a lens into the potential transaction costs and the reliability of the factor's signals.

This recipe will demonstrate the available Alphalens Reloaded functionality to examine turnover.

How to do it...

We'll use Alphalens Reloaded to compute the proportion of assets in a factor quantile that were not in that quantile in the previous period. This is a good way to measure aggregate changes in quartiles across the portfolio:

1. Import additional libraries from Alphalens Reloaded to assess the turnover:

```
from alphalens.performance import (
    quantile_turnover,
    factor_rank_autocorrelation
)
from alphalens.plotting import plot_factor_rank_auto_correlation
```

2. Compute the portfolio turnover for the first quantile:

```
turnover = quantile_turnover(alphalens_data, quantile=1)
```

3. The result is the following Series containing the proportion of assets in the first quantile that were not in that quantile in the previous period:

```
date
2016-01-04 00:00:00+00:00         NaN
2016-01-05 00:00:00+00:00    0.000000
2016-01-06 00:00:00+00:00    0.000000
2016-01-07 00:00:00+00:00    0.000000
2016-01-08 00:00:00+00:00    0.000000
                               ...
2017-09-25 00:00:00+00:00    0.030303
2017-09-26 00:00:00+00:00    0.000000
2017-09-27 00:00:00+00:00    0.000000
2017-09-28 00:00:00+00:00    0.000000
2017-09-29 00:00:00+00:00    0.000000
Freq: C, Name: 1, Length: 440, dtype: float64
```

Figure 10.15: Series containing the proportion of assets in the first quantile that were not in that quantile in the previous period

4. Resample the daily values to monthly and plot the mean turnover for the first quantile:

```
turnover.resample("M").mean().to_period("M").plot.bar()
```

The result is the following bar chart with the mean monthly turnover for the first quantile:

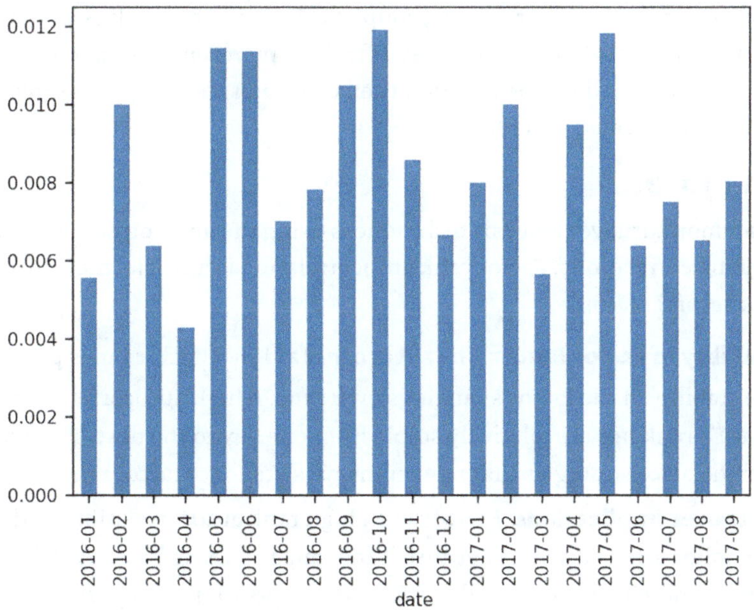

Figure 10.16: Bar chart of the mean monthly turnover for the first quantile

How it works...

The `quantile_turnover()` function calculates turnover for factor quantiles over a specified period. Turnover, in the context of factor portfolio analysis, refers to the rate at which assets within a portfolio are replaced by new assets. High turnover can indicate frequent trading, which might lead to higher transaction costs, while low turnover suggests a more buy-and-hold strategy. By analyzing turnover in the context of factor quantiles, one can assess how stable the factor rankings are over time.

The function takes in the following parameters:

- `alphalens_data`: A multi-index DataFrame that contains factor values, forward returns for each period, the factor quantile/bin that factor value belongs to, and (optionally) the group asset belongs to.
- `quantiles`: An integer or sequence of integers. If an integer, it will select the top and bottom `quantiles` from the factor values. If a sequence, it will define the exact quantiles to compute.
- `period`: The period over which to calculate the turnover. It defaults to '1D', meaning daily turnover.

The function begins by filtering the factor data for the specified quantiles. It then groups the data by date and quantile, and for each group, it calculates the set difference between the current and previous day's assets. This set difference represents the assets that have entered or left the quantile on that day. The function then computes the average turnover for each quantile over the specified period.

There's more...

Another common turnover analysis technique is using the autocorrelation of the factor's daily Spearman rank correlations. Factor rank autocorrelation is a crucial metric in factor portfolio analysis for several reasons:

- **Stability of Factor Ranks**: The `autocorrelationof` factor ranks provides insights into the stability of the factor's rankings over time. A high autocorrelation indicates that the factor's rankings are relatively stable from one day to the next. This stability can be beneficial for strategies that rely on the persistence of factor rankings.
- **Turnover Implications**: Factors with high rank autocorrelation tend to have lower portfolio turnover. This is because if the ranks of assets based on a factor do not change significantly from one period to the next, the positions in a portfolio constructed based on those ranks would also remain relatively stable. Lower turnover can lead to reduced transaction costs, which can enhance the net returns of a strategy.

- **Factor Consistency**: A consistent factor, one that maintains its rank across assets over time, is generally preferred in quantitative strategies. High rank autocorrelation can be an indicator of such consistency. It suggests that the factor is not frequently changing its opinion about the relative attractiveness of different assets.
- **Risk Management**: Understanding the autocorrelation of factor ranks can also aid in risk management. If a factor's ranks are highly volatile (low autocorrelation), it might introduce additional risks in a portfolio strategy. Being aware of this can help in designing appropriate risk controls.

We can measure this with the `factor_rank_autocorrelation()` function. The `factor_rank_autocorrelation()` function computes the autocorrelation of the provided factor's daily ranks. Specifically, it calculates the Spearman rank correlation between the factor values of a particular day and those of the subsequent day. The function takes in the following parameters:

- `alphalens_data`: A multi-index DataFrame that contains factor values, forward returns for each period, and the factor quantile/bin that factor values belong to. The indices are date and asset.
- `period`: The period over which the autocorrelation is computed. It's the lag between the factor values being compared.

```
factor_ac = factor_rank_autocorrelation(alphalens_data)
```

The result is a Series with the daily autocorrelation.

```
date
2016-01-04 00:00:00+00:00         NaN
2016-01-05 00:00:00+00:00    1.000000
2016-01-06 00:00:00+00:00    1.000000
2016-01-07 00:00:00+00:00    1.000000
2016-01-08 00:00:00+00:00    1.000000
                                ...
2017-09-25 00:00:00+00:00    0.787847
2017-09-26 00:00:00+00:00    1.000000
2017-09-27 00:00:00+00:00    1.000000
2017-09-28 00:00:00+00:00    1.000000
2017-09-29 00:00:00+00:00    1.000000
Freq: C, Name: 1, Length: 440, dtype: float64
```

Figure 10.17: Series with the autocorrelation of the factor's Spearman rank

Note

Important

Note in our strategy rebalances on a weekly basis. This means that since there is no opportunity for rebalancing, there will be no turnover except on the weekly rebalance days. We see this reflected in the autocorrelation of 1.

We can use the `plot_factor_rank_auto_correlation()` function to visualize how the autocorrelations change through time.

```
plot_factor_rank_auto_correlation(factor_ac)
```

The result is a time series plot of the autocorrelation:

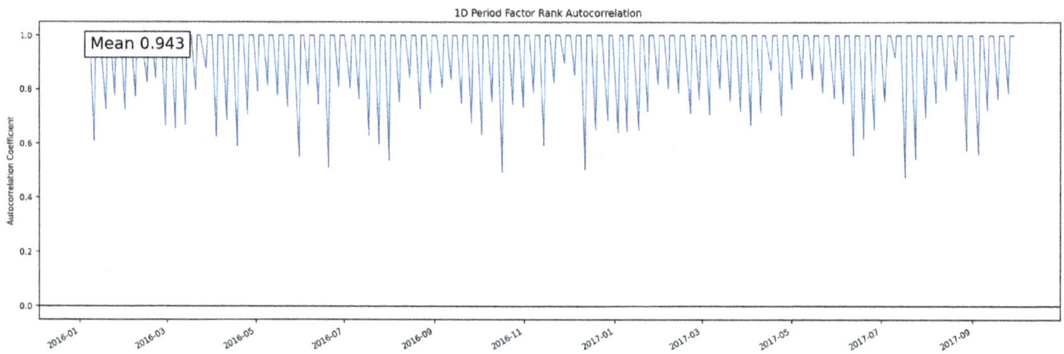

Figure 10.18: Plot visualizing the daily autocorrelation

See also

In case you want to deep dive into the code that computes these metrics, you can do so by visiting the following links:

- Source code for the `quantile_turnover` function: `https://github.com/stefan-jansen/alphalens-reloaded/blob/d4490ba1290f1f135ed398d1b3601569e0e7996b/src/alphalens/performance.py#L575`
- Source code for the `factor_rank_autocorrelation` function: `https://github.com/stefan-jansen/alphalens-reloaded/blob/d4490ba1290f1f135ed398d1b3601569e0e7996b/src/alphalens/performance.py#L620`

Join our community on Discord

Join our community's Discord space for discussions with the authors and other readers:

https://discord.gg/G4YmB6DQvf

11

Assess Backtest Risk and Performance Metrics with Pyfolio

No single risk or performance metric tells the entire story of how a strategy might perform in live trading. Metrics such as the Sharpe ratio, for instance, focus mainly on returns relative to volatility but neglect other risks such as drawdown or tail risk. Similarly, using only maximum drawdown as a measure ignores the risk-adjusted returns and might discard strategies that are robust but temporarily underperforming. The composite view obtained through multiple metrics provides a more nuanced understanding of how the strategy is likely to behave under varying market conditions. Taking it a step further, visualizing risk and performance metrics over time can capture strategy dynamics over time. A strategy might exhibit robust metrics during a bull market but underperform in terms of risk-adjusted returns during a bear or sideways market.

In this chapter, we introduce **Pyfolio Reloaded** (**Pyfolio**), which is a risk and performance analysis library. Pyfolio Reloaded is part of the Zipline Reloaded ecosystem and takes the output of a Zipline Reloaded backtest to build a robust suite of risk and performance metrics. We will walk through the process of using Pyfolio Reloaded to generate risk and performance metrics. Throughout the recipes in this chapter, we'll define the most important metrics to consider when assessing the performance of a backtest.

In this chapter, we present the following recipes:

- Preparing Zipline Reloaded backtest results for Pyfolio Reloaded
- Generating strategy performance and return analytics
- Building a drawdown and rolling risk analysis
- Analyzing strategy holdings, leverage, exposure, and sector allocations
- Breaking down strategy performance to trade level

Preparing Zipline backtest results for Pyfolio Reloaded

In *Chapter 9, Event-Based Backtesting Factor Portfolios with Zipline Reloaded,* we learned how to use Zipline Reloaded to backtest a factor strategy. The output of a Zipline Reloaded backtest includes a DataFrame that details various metrics calculated over the backtest period, such as returns, alpha, beta, the Sharpe ratio, and drawdowns. It also provides transaction logs that capture executed orders, including asset, price, and quantity, giving insights into the trading behavior of the strategy. Additionally, Zipline Reloaded outputs an asset-wise breakdown of the portfolio, detailing the holdings and their respective values, which can be vital for risk assessment and position sizing in the portfolio.

Before we can use the DataFrame, we need to perform some required data preprocessing. Helpfully, Pyfolio Reloaded comes with helper functions that do most of the work for us. In this recipe, we'll read in the DataFrame and prepare it to use with Pyfolio Reloaded. We'll also build a symbol-to-sector mapping and acquire data to represent a benchmark.

Getting ready

We assume you ran the backtest described in *Chapter 9, Event-Based Backtesting Factor Portfolios with Zipline Reloaded,* and have a file called `mean_reversion.pickle` in the current working directory. The pickle file is a serialized version of the DataFrame Zipline Reloaded generated describing the performance results.

How to do it...

We'll use pandas to read the pickle file and the OpenBB Platform to acquire sector data and benchmark prices.

1. Import the libraries:

```
import pandas as pd
from openbb import obb
import pyfolio as pf
obb.user.preferences.output_type = "dataframe"
```

2. Read in the pickle file using the pandas `read_pickle` method:

```
perf = pd.read_pickle("mean_reversion.pickle")
```

The result is the performance DataFrame from the Zipline backtest:

	period open	period close	starting value	ending value	starting cash	...	benchmark period return	benchmark volatility	alpha	beta	sharpe
2016-01-04 21:00:00+00:00	2016-01-04 14:31:00+00:00	2016-01-04 21:00:00+00:00	0.00	0.00	100000.00000	...	0.000000	NaN	NaN	NaN	NaN
2016-01-05 21:00:00+00:00	2016-01-05 14:31:00+00:00	2016-01-05 21:00:00+00:00	0.00	-1977.80	100000.00000	...	0.002012	0.022588	0.000000	-0.000082	-11.224972
2016-01-06 21:00:00+00:00	2016-01-06 14:31:00+00:00	2016-01-06 21:00:00+00:00	-1977.80	-1986.16	101977.78350	...	-0.011130	0.130408	-0.001603	0.005824	-9.192298
2016-01-07 21:00:00+00:00	2016-01-07 14:31:00+00:00	2016-01-07 21:00:00+00:00	-1986.16	-1983.30	101977.78350	...	-0.034566	0.191144	-0.003779	-0.000142	-4.517139
2016-01-08 21:00:00+00:00	2016-01-08 14:31:00+00:00	2016-01-08 21:00:00+00:00	-1983.30	-1986.38	101977.78350	...	-0.045030	0.166229	-0.004494	-0.000074	-6.398478
...	...	...	...	...	...	...	...	...	...	...	...
2017-12-22 21:00:00+00:00	2017-12-22 14:31:00+00:00	2017-12-22 21:00:00+00:00	5747.17	5763.90	95142.41300	...	0.333231	0.103667	0.001123	0.023565	0.306637
2017-12-26 21:00:00+00:00	2017-12-26 14:31:00+00:00	2017-12-26 21:00:00+00:00	5763.90	5696.27	95142.41300	...	0.331820	0.103569	0.000788	0.023615	0.283994
2017-12-27 21:00:00+00:00	2017-12-27 14:31:00+00:00	2017-12-27 21:00:00+00:00	5696.27	64.69	95142.41300	...	0.332873	0.103466	0.001109	0.023621	0.305450
2017-12-28 21:00:00+00:00	2017-12-28 14:31:00+00:00	2017-12-28 21:00:00+00:00	64.69	90.28	100840.72425	...	0.335317	0.103366	0.001211	0.023633	0.313499
2017-12-29 21:00:00+00:00	2017-12-29 14:31:00+00:00	2017-12-29 21:00:00+00:00	90.28	76.95	100840.72425	...	0.328396	0.103344	0.001203	0.023637	0.308825

Figure 11.1: Deserialized DataFrame containing the backtest performance metrics

3. Use the Pyfolio helper function to extract returns, positions, and transactions from the DataFrame:

```
returns, positions, transactions = \
    pf.utils.extract_rets_pos_txn_from_zipline(perf)
```

The result is a pandas Series with strategy returns:

```
2016-01-04 00:00:00+00:00    0.000000e+00
2016-01-05 00:00:00+00:00   -1.650000e-07
2016-01-06 00:00:00+00:00   -8.360001e-05
2016-01-07 00:00:00+00:00    2.860240e-05
2016-01-08 00:00:00+00:00   -3.080170e-05
                                  ...
2017-12-22 00:00:00+00:00    1.658249e-04
2017-12-26 00:00:00+00:00   -6.702257e-04
2017-12-27 00:00:00+00:00    6.617624e-04
2017-12-28 00:00:00+00:00    2.536038e-04
2017-12-29 00:00:00+00:00   -1.320704e-04
Name: returns, Length: 503, dtype: float64
```

Figure 11.2: pandas Series with daily strategy returns

4. The `positions` DataFrames contain the Zipline `Equity` objects as column labels. Replace the object with the string representations:

```
positions.columns = [
    col.symbol for col in positions.columns[:-1]
] + ["cash"]
```

The result is DataFrame with the daily positions, including cash:

	AAL	AAPL	ABBV	ADBE	ADP	...	WDC	WFC	WFM	WMT	cash
index											
2016-01-05 00:00:00+00:00	0.0	0.0	0.0	0.0	0.0	...	0.00	0.00	0.0	0.0	101977.78350
2016-01-06 00:00:00+00:00	0.0	0.0	0.0	0.0	0.0	...	0.00	0.00	0.0	0.0	101977.78350
2016-01-07 00:00:00+00:00	0.0	0.0	0.0	0.0	0.0	...	0.00	0.00	0.0	0.0	101977.78350
2016-01-08 00:00:00+00:00	0.0	0.0	0.0	0.0	0.0	...	0.00	0.00	0.0	0.0	101977.78350
2016-01-11 00:00:00+00:00	0.0	0.0	0.0	0.0	0.0	...	0.00	0.00	0.0	0.0	101977.78350
...	...	...	...	...	...	...	...	...	...	...	...
2017-12-22 00:00:00+00:00	0.0	0.0	0.0	0.0	0.0	...	1936.32	0.00	0.0	0.0	95142.41300
2017-12-26 00:00:00+00:00	0.0	0.0	0.0	0.0	0.0	...	1920.00	0.00	0.0	0.0	95142.41300
2017-12-27 00:00:00+00:00	0.0	0.0	0.0	0.0	0.0	...	0.00	-1950.40	0.0	0.0	100840.72425
2017-12-28 00:00:00+00:00	0.0	0.0	0.0	0.0	0.0	...	0.00	-1961.60	0.0	0.0	100840.72425
2017-12-29 00:00:00+00:00	0.0	0.0	0.0	0.0	0.0	...	0.00	-1941.44	0.0	0.0	100840.72425

Figure 11.3: DataFrame with the position value each day

5. The `symbol` column in the `transactions` DataFrame also contains the Zipline `Equity` objects. Replace the object with the string representations:

```
transactions.symbol = transactions.symbol.apply(lambda s: s.symbol)
```

The result is a DataFrame with the daily transactions:

	sid	symbol	price	order_id	amount	commission	dt	txn_dollars
2016-01-05 21:00:00+00:00	Equity(1228 [GMCR])	GMCR	89.90	6c0bfa6d54d1441baed02c6f0607a864	-22	None	2016-01-05 21:00:00+00:00	1977.80
2016-01-12 21:00:00+00:00	Equity(1228 [GMCR])	GMCR	90.42	17907b8052f64fe3a5bc66e9ed8b09fd	22	None	2016-01-12 21:00:00+00:00	-1989.24
2016-01-12 21:00:00+00:00	Equity(3105 [WMT])	WMT	63.62	23ddc217cfdd4a94b491013377386d8f	-31	None	2016-01-12 21:00:00+00:00	1972.22
2016-01-20 21:00:00+00:00	Equity(3105 [WMT])	WMT	60.84	69aed3b9780e4f5abbd7ecd1ddde5527	31	None	2016-01-20 21:00:00+00:00	-1886.04
2016-01-20 21:00:00+00:00	Equity(994 [ESRX])	ESRX	71.70	6d826744a2df47f5991903b16516fe45	27	None	2016-01-20 21:00:00+00:00	-1935.90
...	...	...	...	...	...	...	...	...
2017-12-27 21:00:00+00:00	Equity(2331 [PYPL])	PYPL	74.59	9d1d861c73eb4a87ad9880c6ec940a82	27	None	2017-12-27 21:00:00+00:00	-2013.93
2017-12-27 21:00:00+00:00	Equity(606 [CMCSA])	CMCSA	40.41	2e36bcbdf6484592bf63b14ad9942aa3	-49	None	2017-12-27 21:00:00+00:00	1980.09
2017-12-27 21:00:00+00:00	Equity(1063 [FDX])	FDX	250.03	ba5adcf1fd4f40db95eebd864b9aead5	-8	None	2017-12-27 21:00:00+00:00	2000.24
2017-12-27 21:00:00+00:00	Equity(2945 [UNP])	UNP	136.32	7a9cda6bb33a4f3b9ec3ed3e718c4a0b	-14	None	2017-12-27 21:00:00+00:00	1908.48
2017-12-27 21:00:00+00:00	Equity(3077 [WFC])	WFC	60.95	2efd159050db4dd4bc144e9891323cdd	-32	None	2017-12-27 21:00:00+00:00	1950.40

Figure 11.4: DataFrame with the transactions each day

6. Extract the symbols from the `positions` DataFrame and use the OpenBB Platform screener to download an overview for each one. The overview includes the sector that we'll use to build the symbol-to-sector mapping:

```
symbols = positions.columns[:-1].tolist()
screener_data = obb.equity.profile(
    symbols, provider="yfinance")
```

The result is a DataFrame with summary information for each symbol:

	symbol	name	stock_exchange	long_description	company_url	...	shares_float	shares_implied_outstanding	shares_short	dividend_yield	beta
0	AAL	American Airlines Group Inc.	NMS	American Airlines Group Inc., through its subs...	https://www.aa.com	...	6.471347e+08	6.661270e+08	53327236.0	NaN	1.580
1	AAPL	Apple Inc.	NMS	Apple Inc. designs, manufactures, and markets ...	https://www.apple.com	...	1.530832e+10	1.566390e+10	99287450.0	0.0052	1.264
2	ABBV	AbbVie Inc.	NYQ	AbbVie Inc. discovers, develops, manufactures,...	https://www.abbvie.com	...	1.762248e+09	1.765870e+09	15927790.0	0.0397	0.593
3	ADBE	Adobe Inc.	NMS	Adobe Inc., together with its subsidiaries, op...	https://www.adobe.com	...	4.467590e+08	4.801530e+08	8007830.0	NaN	1.281
4	ADP	Automatic Data Processing, Inc.	NMS	Automatic Data Processing, Inc. provides cloud...	https://www.adp.com	...	4.083909e+08	4.092910e+08	4142715.0	0.0232	0.785
...	...	...	...	...	...	...	...	...	...	...	...
128	WBA	Walgreens Boots Alliance, Inc.	NMS	Walgreens Boots Alliance, Inc. operates as a h...	https://www.walgreensbootsalliance.com	...	7.131361e+08	8.627130e+08	43268583.0	0.0650	0.793
129	WDC	Western Digital Corporation	NMS	Western Digital Corporation develops, manufact...	https://www.westerndigital.com	...	3.249116e+08	3.265250e+08	21805777.0	NaN	1.521
130	WFC	Wells Fargo & Company	NYQ	Wells Fargo & Company, a financial services co...	https://www.wellsfargo.com	...	3.478506e+09	3.486320e+09	38130739.0	0.0236	1.182
131	WFM	None	YHD	None	None	...	NaN	NaN	NaN	NaN	NaN
132	WMT	Walmart Inc.	NYQ	Walmart Inc. engages in the operation of retai...	https://corporate.walmart.com	...	4.332595e+09	8.063520e+09	43289108.0	0.0128	0.494

Figure 11.5: DataFrame with the screener results for the tickers used in our strategy

7. Build a mapping between each `symbol` and `sector`:

```
sector_map = (
    screener_data[["symbol", "sector"]]
    .set_index("symbol")
    .reindex(symbols)
    .fillna("Unknown")
    .to_dict()["sector"]
)
```

8. The result is a dictionary with symbols as keys and the sector as values. Note for symbols that don't have an associated sector, they're marked as `Unknown`

```
{'AAL': 'Industrials',
 'AAPL': 'Technology',
 'ABBV': 'Healthcare',
 'ADBE': 'Technology',
 'ADP': 'Industrials',
 'AET': 'Unknown',
 'AGN': 'Unknown',
 'AIG': 'Financial',
 'ALXN': 'Unknown',
 'AMAT': 'Technology',
 'AMGN': 'Healthcare',
 'AMZN': 'Consumer Cyclical',
 'ANTM': 'Unknown',
 'ARIA': 'Unknown',
 'ATVI': 'Communication Services',
```

Figure 11.6: Dictionary with a symbol-to-sector mapping for the positions in our backtest

9. Use the OpenBB Platform to download price data for the SPY ETF, which we'll use as the benchmark:

```
spy = obb.equity.price.historical(
    "SPY",
    start_date=returns.index.min(),
    end_date=returns.index.max()
)
spy.index = pd.to_datetime(spy.index)
benchmark_returns = spy.close.pct_change()
benchmark_returns.name = "SPY"
benchmark_returns = benchmark_returns.tz_localize(
    "UTC").filter(returns.index)
```

The result is a pandas Series with daily returns for the SPY ETF:

```
date
2016-01-04 00:00:00+00:00         NaN
2016-01-05 00:00:00+00:00    0.001691
2016-01-06 00:00:00+00:00   -0.012614
2016-01-07 00:00:00+00:00   -0.023992
2016-01-08 00:00:00+00:00   -0.010976
                               ...
2017-12-22 00:00:00+00:00   -0.000262
2017-12-26 00:00:00+00:00   -0.001196
2017-12-27 00:00:00+00:00    0.000486
2017-12-28 00:00:00+00:00    0.002058
2017-12-29 00:00:00+00:00   -0.003770
Name: SPY, Length: 503, dtype: float64
```

Figure 11.7: pandas Series with the daily returns for the SPY ETF

How it works...

The `extract_rets_pos_txn_from_zipline` function takes a DataFrame generated by a Zipline backtest as input and extracts daily returns, net position values, and transaction details. These extracted metrics are returned as a tuple of pandas Series and DataFrames, ready for further analysis or visualization with other Pyfolio functions. The function first normalizes the index of the input DataFrame and sets its time zone to UTC, then extracts the `returns` column for daily strategy returns. It iterates through the `positions` and `transactions` items in the DataFrame to construct daily net position values and transaction details, respectively.

Next, we use a list comprehension to replace each of the column labels in the `positions` DataFrame with strings. We use the pandas `apply` method on the `symbol` column in the `transactions` DataFrame to replace the Zipline Reloaded `Equity` objects with their string representations.

After we extract a list of symbols and download the overview using the OpenBB Platform, we build the symbol-to-sector mapping. We start with the OpenBB Platform output that contains columns `symbol` and `sector`, and sets the index to the `symbol` column. The DataFrame is then reindexed based on the list of `symbols`, fills any missing values with `Unknown`, and finally converts the `sector` column to a dictionary.

Finally, we download and process price data for the SPY ETF which we use as the benchmark in our analysis. The code loads historical data for the dates in our analysis using the `obb.equity.price.historical` method. It then calculates the percentage change of the adjusted closing prices to generate benchmark returns, sets the name of the Series to `SPY`, localizes the time zone to UTC, and filters the Series to match the index of the `returns` DataFrame.

There's more...

You may be wondering why mapping symbols to sectors is important. Incorporating sector information in backtest analysis is crucial for understanding the source of returns and for risk management. Traders often attribute returns to different sectors to identify which segments of the market are driving their portfolio's performance.

This sector-based attribution enables traders to diversify their investments across various sectors, thereby reducing the portfolio's systemic risks associated with any single sector.

Further, by comparing the strategy's returns against a benchmark, like the S&P 500, traders can assess whether the strategy is adding value over and above a passive investment approach. This comparative analysis aids in isolating the strategy's alpha, or risk-adjusted returns, and helps in understanding its behavior relative to the broader market or a specific sector.

See also

Pyfolio offers several helper functions to process Zipline backtest results into a form suitable for further analysis. For more insight into using Pyfolio for risk and performance analysis, see the source code at `https://github.com/stefan-jansen/pyfolio-reloaded/blob/main/src/pyfolio/utils.py`.

To learn more about using Pyfolio Reloaded in practice, check out the cohort-based course, *Getting Started With Python for Quant Finance*, which covers Pyfolio in detail. The URL is `https://www.pyquantnews.com/getting-started-with-python-for-quant-finance`.

Generating strategy performance and return analytics

Traders use strategy performance and return analysis to evaluate the effectiveness of their trading algorithms. Return analysis, often visualized through equity curves, or return distributions, offers insights into the strategy's profitability over time. Temporal analyses, such as monthly or annual return breakdowns, help identify seasonality or long-term trends that may impact future performance.

By comparing these metrics and analyses against a benchmark, traders can isolate the strategy's alpha, or the excess return over a passive investment approach. This review enables traders to make data-driven modifications to their strategies, enhancing profitability and risk management. In this recipe, we explore Pyfolio Reloaded strategy performance and return analytics.

Getting ready

We assume the steps in the *Preparing Zipline Reloaded backtest results for Pyfolio Reloaded* recipe were followed. We'll need `returns`, `positions`, `transactions`, and `benchmark_returns` defined for this recipe.

How to do it...

We'll build a series of using Pyfolio Reloaded that graphically depict strategy performance:

1. Plot the strategy's equity curve against the benchmark. Consider selecting a benchmark that closely represents the strategy you're trading. In this example, we use SPY:

```
pf.plotting.plot_rolling_returns(
    returns, factor_returns=benchmark_returns
)
```

The result is a chart with the strategy's equity curve alongside the cumulative returns of the chosen benchmark.

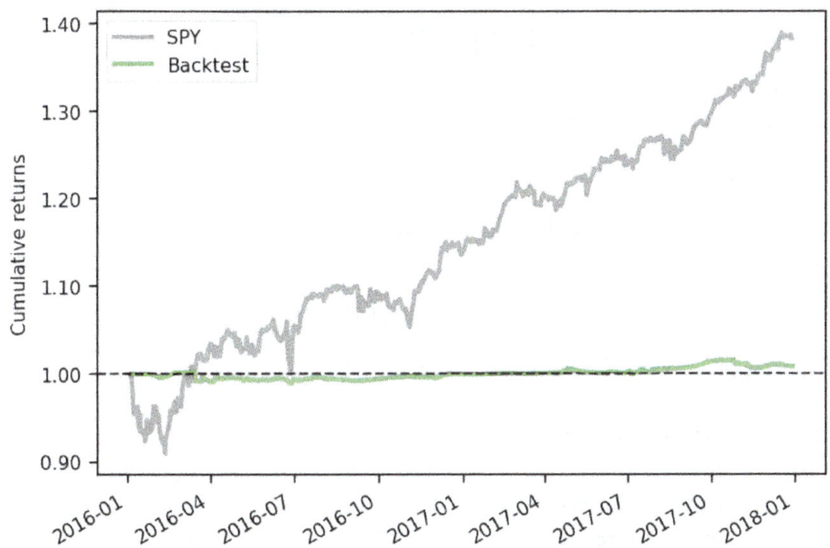

Figure 11.8: Strategy cumulative returns (equity curve) against the benchmark

2. Summarize the distribution of key performance indicators:

```
pf.plotting.plot_perf_stats(
    returns=returns, factor_returns=benchmark_returns,
)
```

The result is a horizontal box plot that depicts the distribution of performance indicators:

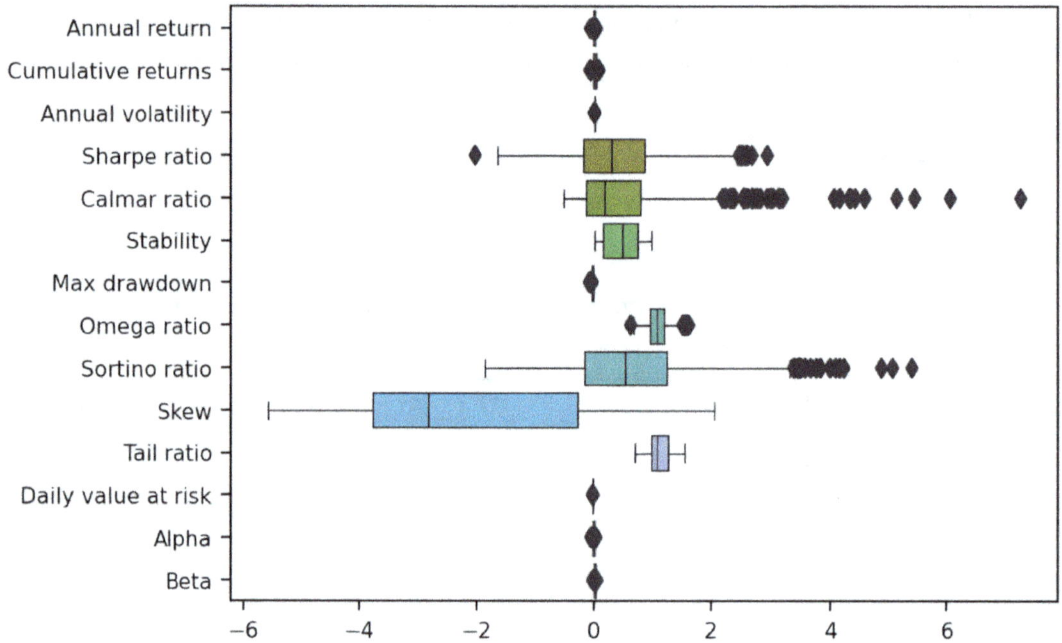

Figure 11.9: Strategy performance metrics

3. Generate a detailed outline of the strategy's performance metrics:

```
pf.plotting.show_perf_stats(
    returns,
    factor_returns=benchmark_returns,
    positions=positions,
    transactions=transactions,
    live_start_date="2017-01-01"
)
```

Note

Important

The `live_start_date` argument in the `show_perf_stats` function separates the backtest and live trading periods. Metrics are calculated separately for the periods before and after this date, which allows for a more nuanced evaluation of the trading strategy's performance. Specifically, the function will display performance statistics for the backtest period up to `live_start_date` and for the live trading period starting from `live_start_date`. Several Pyfolio functions accept this argument.

The result is a pandas DataFrame containing the key performance metrics:

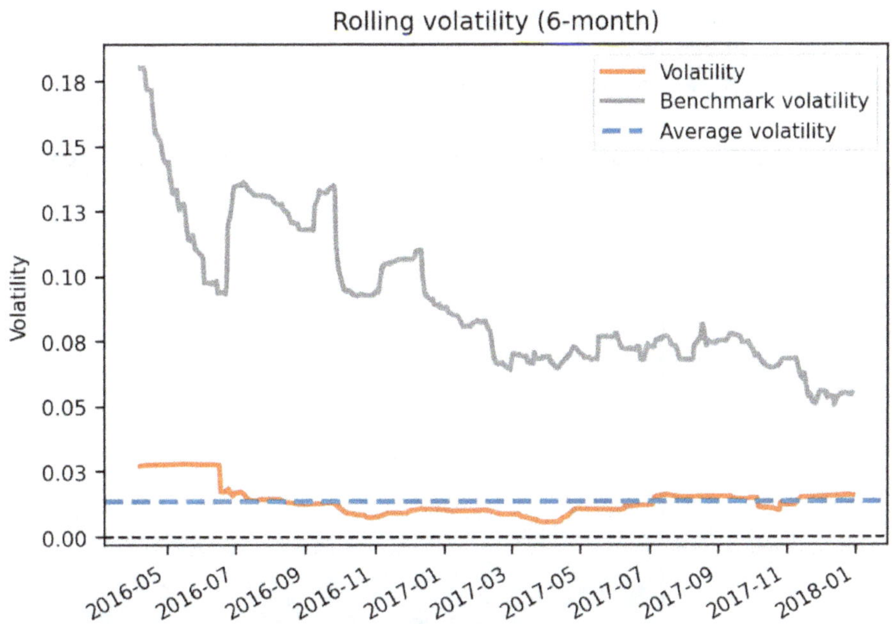

Figure 11.10: Strategy performance metrics

4. Generate a heatmap of the strategy's monthly returns:

```
pf.plotting.plot_monthly_returns_heatmap(returns)
```

The result is a heatmap visualizing the strategy returns during the backtest period:

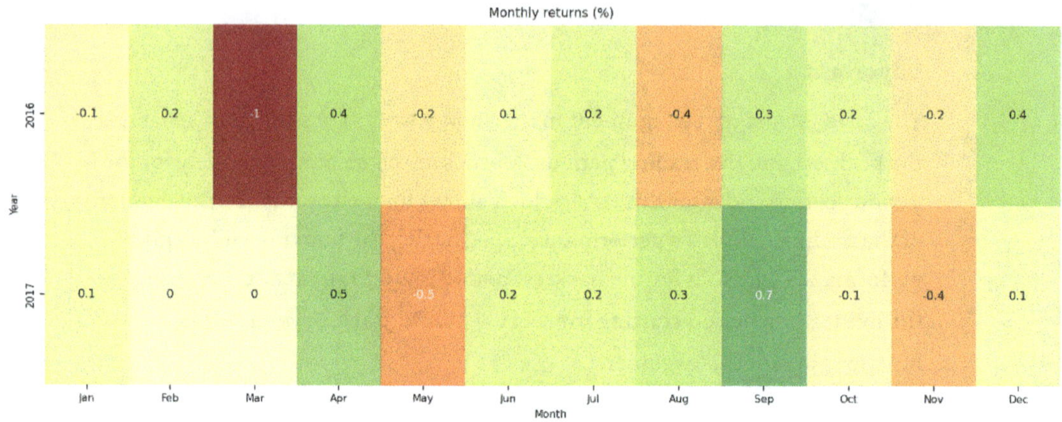

Figure 11.11: Heatmap visualizing the strategy's monthly returns

5. Generate a bar chart of the strategy's annual returns:

```
pf.plotting.plot_annual_returns(returns)
```

The result is a bar chart visualizing the annual returns during the backtest period:

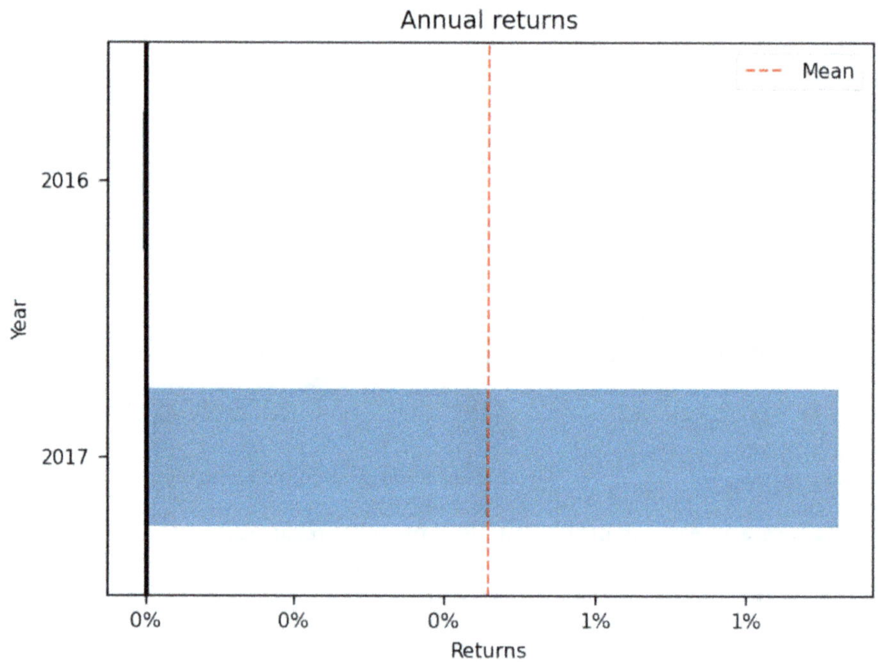

Figure 11.12: Bar chart visualizing the strategy's annual returns

How it works...

Pyfolio does the hard work of parsing the input data and formatting the output charts. Other charts and tables include the following:

- `plot_rolling_returns`: Calculates the rolling returns of a portfolio over a specified window and plots them using Matplotlib.
- `plot_perf_stats`: Iterates through the returns series, extracting each performance metric, and uses Matplotlib's `barh` function to create horizontal bars for each metric.
- `show_perf_stats`: Calculates various performance metrics including annual return, annual volatility, and Sharpe ratio, among others, and then displays these metrics in a formatted table.
- `plot_monthly_returns_heatmap`: Calculates the mean return for each month across years. It then utilizes Matplotlib to generate a heatmap, where the x-axis represents months, the y-axis represents years, and the color intensity indicates the mean return value.
- `plot_annual_returns`: Calculates annual returns by resampling the data to yearly frequency using the mean. It then generates a bar plot of these annual returns using Matplotlib, with the x-axis representing years and the y-axis representing the annual returns.

Now that we covered how the plots are generated, let's review some of the key statistics output by Pyfolio:

- **Calmar ratio**: Calmar ratio is calculated by dividing the **compound annual growth rate** (**CAGR**) of a trading strategy by the maximum drawdown experienced over a specified period
- **Omega ratio**: The omega ratio should be used when return distributions are non-normal or skewed and is calculated by dividing the sum of positive excess returns by the absolute sum of negative excess returns over a given threshold
- **Skew**: Skew is calculated by taking the third standardized moment of the return series, essentially measuring the asymmetry of the return distribution
- **Kurtosis**: Kurtosis is calculated by taking the fourth central moment of the returns series and dividing it by the square of the variance, effectively measuring the "tailedness" of the distribution

- **Value at risk**: Daily **value at risk (VaR)** is calculated by taking the negative of the quantile of the daily returns at a given confidence level, typically 5% or 1% (consider using conditional value at risk, not computed by Pyfolio, which accounts for tail risk)
- **Gross leverage**: Gross leverage is calculated as the sum of the absolute values of long and short positions divided by the portfolio's net asset value at each time point

There's more...

Pyfolio offers more details about a strategy's returns, which can provide more insight into how the strategy performed during the backtest.

1. Create a distribution of monthly returns:

```
pf.plotting.plot_monthly_returns_dist(returns)
```

The output is a histogram with the frequency of monthly returns:

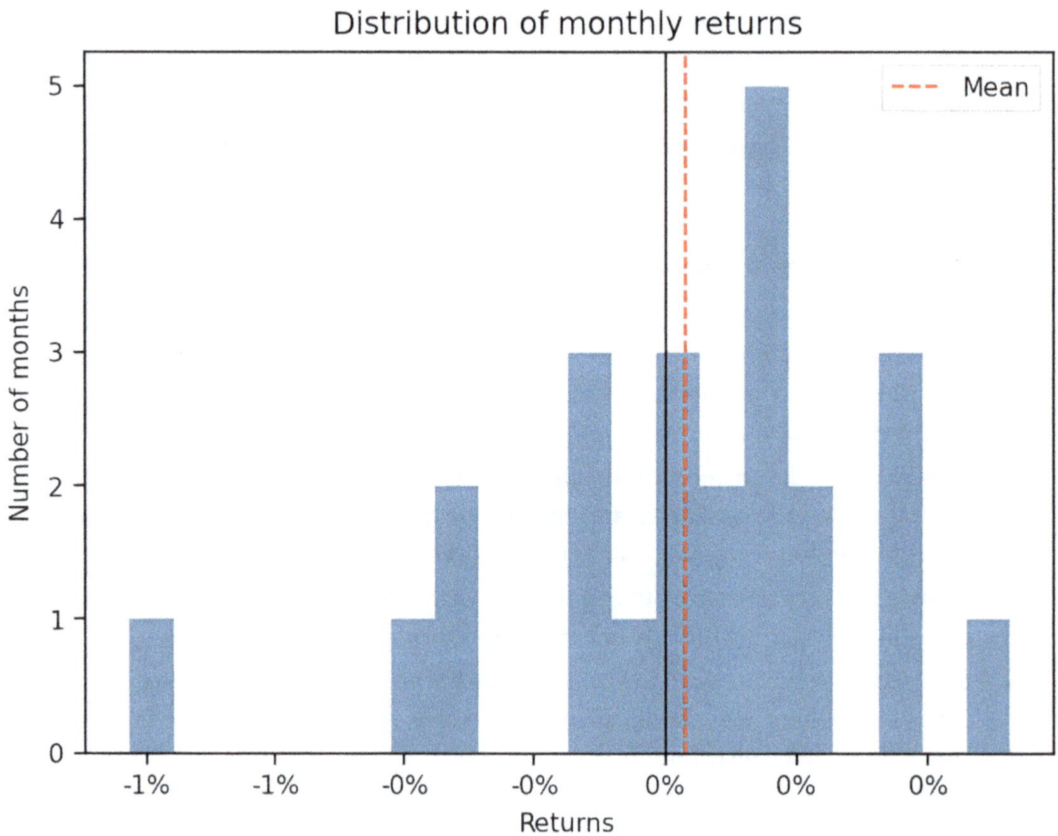

Figure 11.13: Histogram with the frequency of monthly returns

2. Visualize the strategy's daily returns through time:

```
pf.plotting.plot_returns(
    returns,
    live_start_date="2017-01-01"
)
```

The result is a line plot depicting the daily returns:

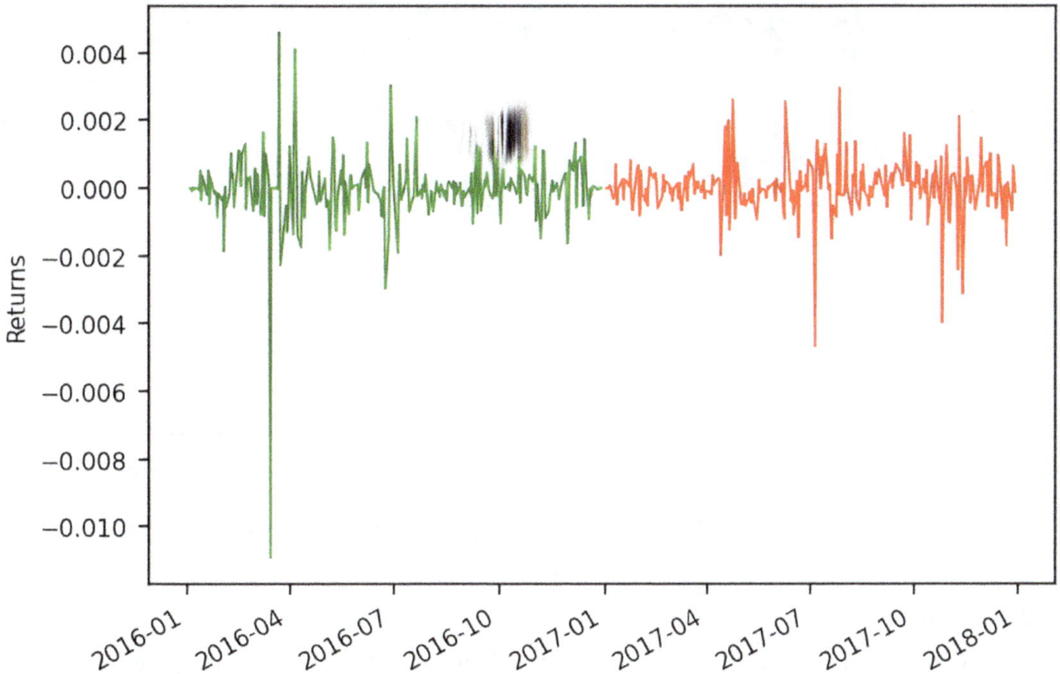

Figure 11.14: Line chart with the daily returns

3. Visualize the return series in quantiles and their cumulative returns for each quantile:

```
pf.plotting.plot_return_quantiles(
    returns,
    live_start_date="2017-01-01"
)
```

The result is a box plot depicting the quantiles of daily, weekly, and monthly returns along with the distribution of cumulative returns:

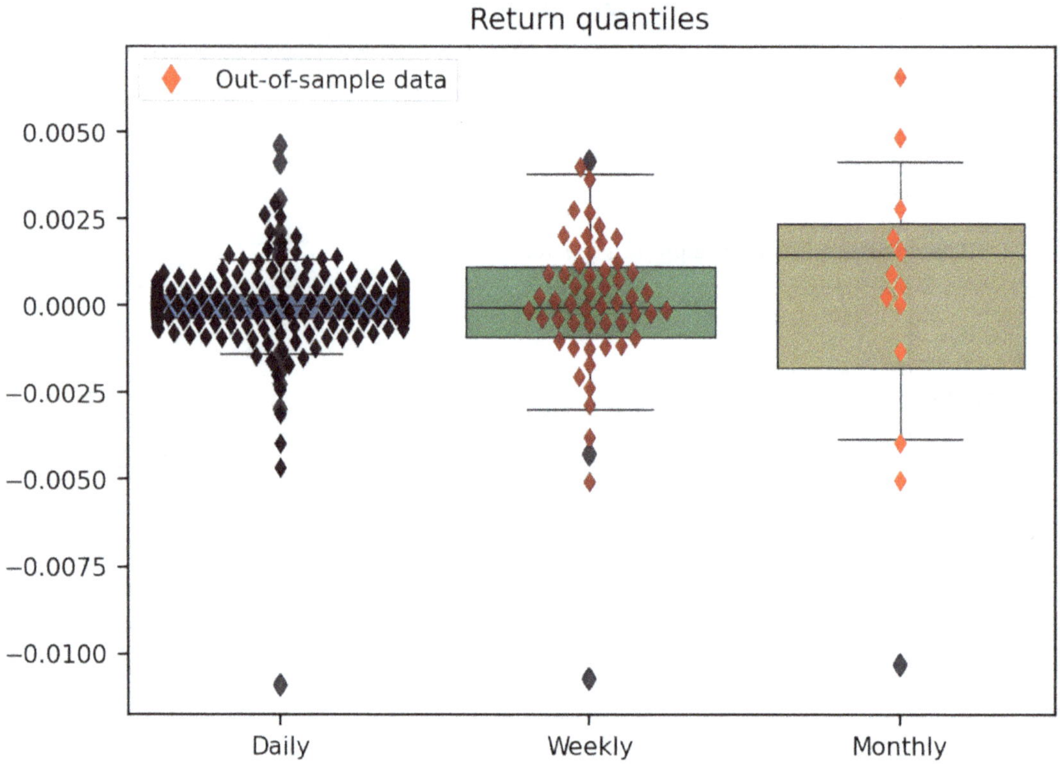

Figure 11.15: Box plot depicting the quantiles of daily, weekly, and monthly returns along with the distribution of cumulative returns

See also

You can dive deeper into Pyfolio's performance and return metrics by reviewing the source code here: `https://github.com/stefan-jansen/pyfolio-reloaded/blob/main/src/pyfolio/plotting.py`

Building a drawdown and rolling risk analysis

A focus only on returns without considering risk is like driving a fast car at high speeds without a seatbelt—it may work for a while, but the consequences can be catastrophic. Risk metrics provide the analytical framework to quantify and manage uncertainty, which lets traders make more informed decisions. These metrics offer insights into the potential volatility, drawdown, and other adverse conditions a strategy might encounter. By incorporating risk analytics into the trading process, traders can better assess the trade-offs between risk and return, optimize their portfolios for maximum risk-adjusted performance, and establish safeguards to mitigate potential losses.

Pyfolio offers several risk metrics to help maintain control of algorithmic trading systems. We'll look at several in this recipe.

Getting ready

We assume the steps in the *Preparing Zipline Reloaded backtest results for Pyfolio Reloaded* recipe were followed in preparation for this recipe. We'll need `returns`, `positions`, `transactions`, and `benchmark_returns` defined for this recipe.

How to do it...

We'll look at Pyfolio Reloaded drawdown analysis and several rolling risk metrics. Rolling risk metrics help traders understand how strategy risk evolves through time.

1. Graphically depict the top 10 drawdowns over the strategy period:

```
pf.plotting.plot_drawdown_periods(returns, top=10)
```

The result is an equity curve depicting the cumulative strategy returns with vertical shading over the periods the strategy was in drawdown:

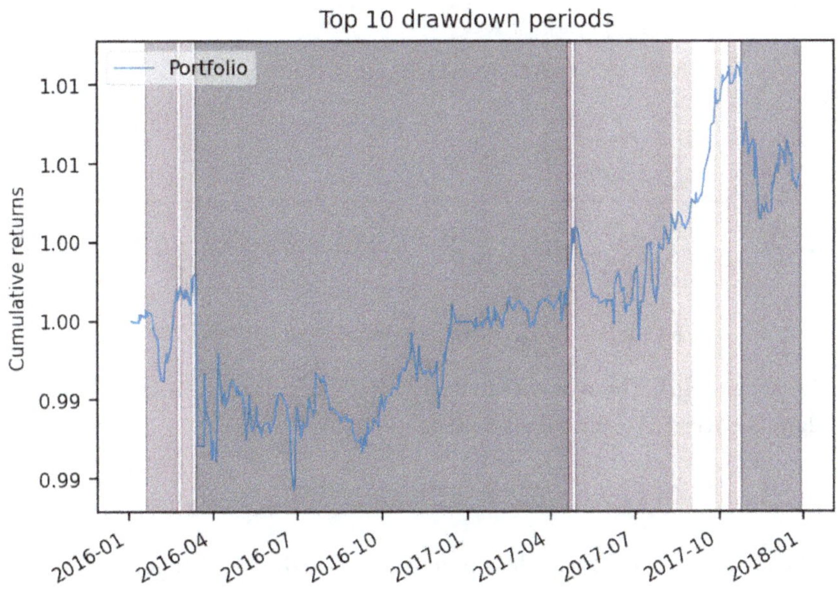

Figure 11.16: Equity curve depicting the cumulative strategy returns with vertical shading over the periods the strategy was in drawdown

2. Visualize the equity drawdown over time:

```
pf.plotting.plot_drawdown_underwater(returns)
```

The result is an **underwater plot** that visualizes the strategy drawdown amounts:

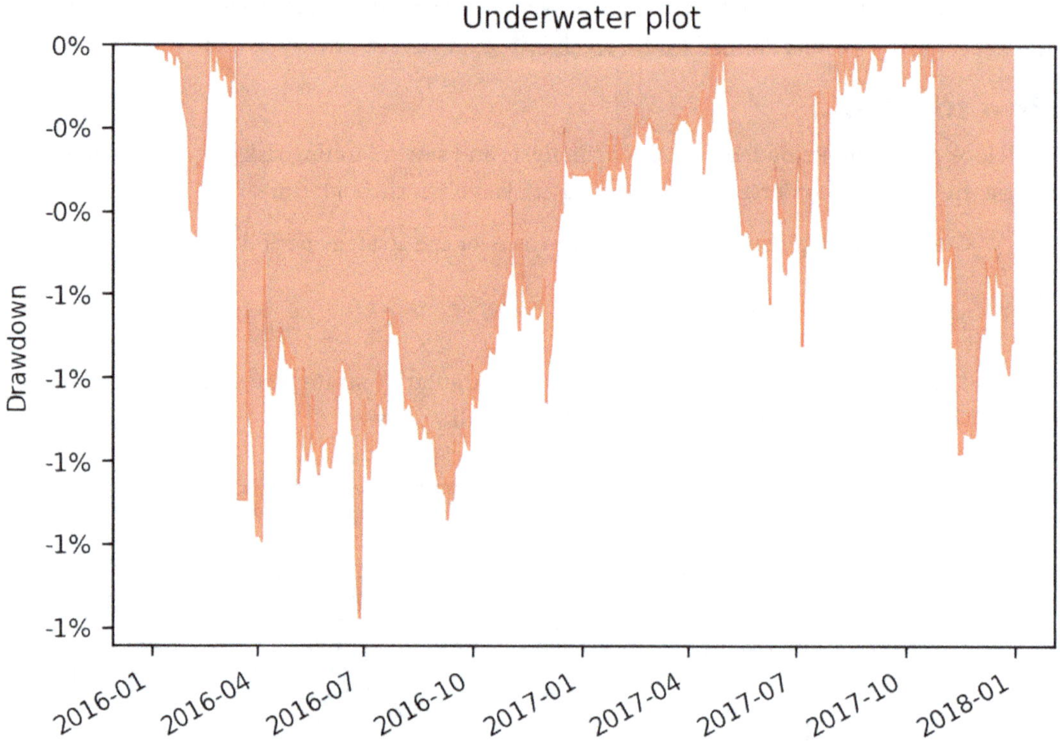

Figure 11.17: Underwater plot visualizing the strategy drawdown amounts

3. Create a table of the worst drawdowns with details of the amount, peak date, valley date, recovery date, and duration:

```
pf.plotting.show_worst_drawdown_periods(returns)
```

The result is a DataFrame detailing the top five drawdown periods:

Worst drawdown periods	Net drawdown in %	Peak date	Valley date	Recovery date	Duration
0	1.37	2016-03-14	2016-06-27	2017-04-20	289
1	0.98	2017-10-25	2017-11-14	NaT	NaN
2	0.72	2017-04-28	2017-07-05	2017-08-10	75
3	0.46	2016-01-20	2016-02-08	2016-02-22	24
4	0.12	2017-04-20	2017-04-21	2017-04-24	3

Figure 11.18: DataFrame detailing the top five drawdown periods

4. Plot the strategy 3-month rolling volatility against the benchmark:

```
pf.plotting.plot_rolling_volatility(
    returns, factor_returns=benchmark_returns, rolling_window=66
)
```

The result is a chart with the rolling 3-month volatility compared to the benchmark:

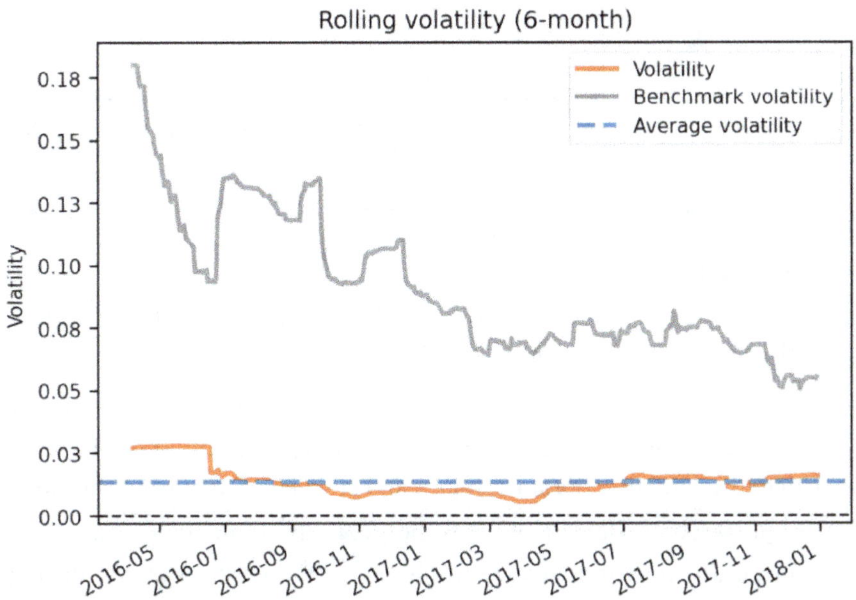

Figure 11.19: Chart with the rolling 3-month volatility compared to the benchmark

5. Plot the strategy 3-month rolling Sharpe ratio, its mean, and the benchmark Sharpe:

```
pf.plotting.plot_rolling_sharpe(
    returns,
```

```
    factor_returns=benchmark_returns,
    rolling_window=66
)
```

The result is a chart with the rolling 3-month Sharpe ratio compared to the benchmark:

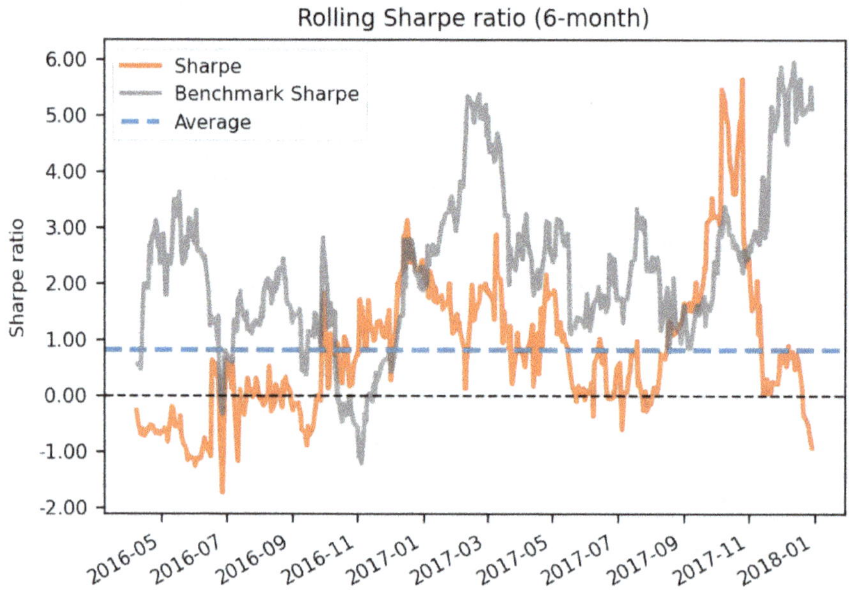

Figure 11.20: Chart with the rolling 3-month Sharpe ratio compared to the benchmark

How it works...

To generate the drawdown and rolling risk metrics, Pyfolio Reloaded uses the same underlying module as the performance and return metrics:

- `plot_drawdown_periods`: Computes the drawdown periods by identifying local maxima and subsequent declines. It then uses Matplotlib to visualize these drawdown periods, highlighting the start, valley, and end of each period on the plot.
- `plot_drawdown_underwater`: Finds the maximum cumulative return up to each point and subtracts the cumulative return from it. It then utilizes Matplotlib to plot the underwater curve, representing the negative drawdowns over time.
- `show_worst_drawdown_periods`: First, this computes the drawdowns, then sorts these drawdown periods and displays the top n worst drawdown periods in a pandas DataFrame.

- `plot_rolling_volatility`: Applies a rolling window and computes the standard deviation of returns within each window. It then uses Matplotlib to plot the computed rolling volatility against time.
- `plot_rolling_sharpe`: Applies a rolling window and computes the Sharpe ratio within each window. It then uses Matplotlib to plot the computed rolling Sharpe ratio against time.

Let's cover some of the key risk metrics we covered:

- **Annual volatility**: The annual volatility is calculated by taking the standard deviation of the daily returns and then annualizing it by multiplying it by the square root of the number of trading days (usually 252).
- **Sharpe ratio**: The Sharpe ratio is calculated as the mean of the excess returns divided by the standard deviation of those excess returns.
- **Max drawdown**: Max drawdown is calculated by identifying the maximum difference between a peak and a subsequent trough in a time series of portfolio values.

There's more...

Pyfolio allows for the overlay of specific event timelines, enabling a comparative analysis of portfolio and benchmark performance during these periods. An example would be assessing performance during the market downturn of what is now considered the New Normal. The following steps show you how:

1. Use `extract_interesting_date_ranges` to extract the strategy returns from pre-defined stress events:

```
times = pf.timeseries.extract_interesting_date_ranges(returns)
```

2. Then join with the benchmark returns, compute the cumulative returns, and plot:

```
(
    times["New Normal"]
    .to_frame("strategy_returns")
    .join(benchmark_returns)
    .add(1)
    .cumprod()
    .sub(1)
    .plot()
)
```

The result is a plot that depicts the strategy returns compared to the benchmark during the stress event:

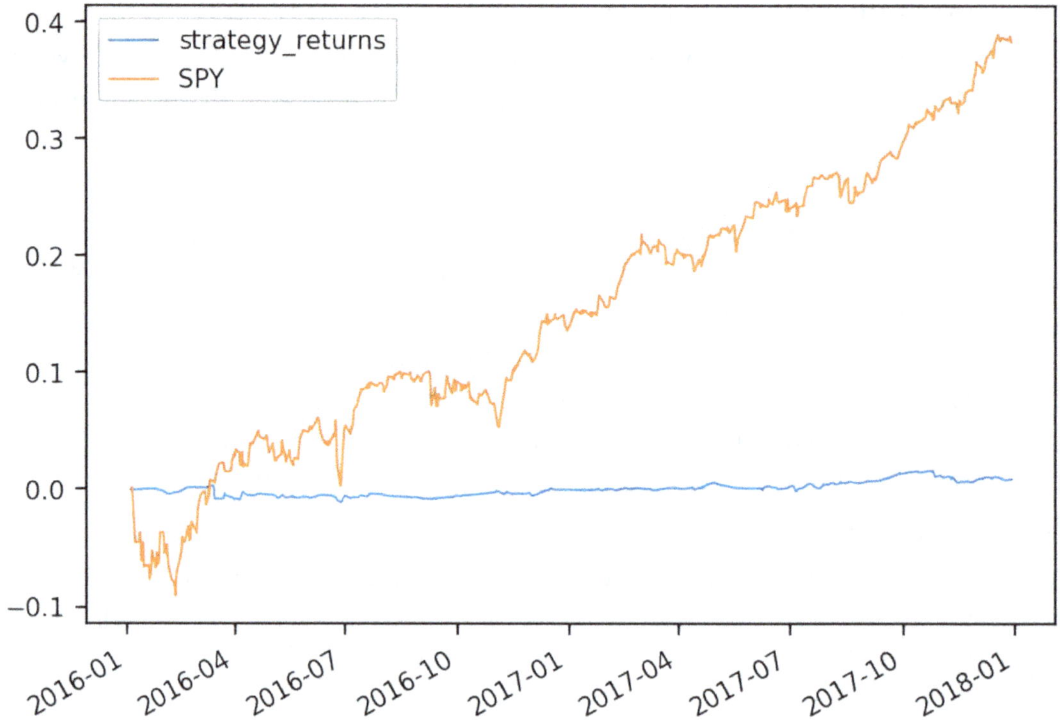

Figure 11.21: Plot that depicts the strategy returns compared to the benchmark during the stress event

See also

To get a list of stress periods and their start and end dates, check into the source code here: `https://github.com/stefan-jansen/pyfolio-reloaded/blob/main/src/pyfolio/interesting_periods.py`

Analyzing strategy holdings, leverage, exposure, and sector allocations

We can extend our strategy analysis with Pyfolio by analyzing holdings, leverage, and sector allocations over time. Analyzing holdings over time helps traders understand the diversification and concentration risks within a portfolio. It helps traders identify overexposure to specific assets, which could be detrimental in adverse market conditions. Leverage analysis is equally important, as excessive borrowing can amplify losses, leading to significant drawdowns or even portfolio liquidation. Monitoring leverage levels over time allows traders to adjust their risk exposure in line with their risk tolerance and market outlook.

Sector allocation analysis provides insights into how diversified the portfolio is across different industries. This is important for risk management, as different sectors respond differently to economic cycles and market events. Understanding sector allocations can help traders optimize their portfolios for various market conditions and potentially enhance returns while mitigating risks. In this recipe, we'll look at how Pyfolio is used for portfolio analysis.

Getting ready

We assume the steps in the *Preparing Zipline Reloaded backtest results for Pyfolio Reloaded* recipe were followed in preparation for this recipe. We'll need `returns`, `positions`, and `sector_map` defined for this recipe.

How to do it...

We'll look at how the strategy holdings, leverage, exposure, and sector allocation evolve throughout the analysis period.

1. Plot the number of daily holdings, average holdings by month, and overall average holdings:

    ```
    pf.plotting.plot_holdings(returns, positions)
    ```

    The result is a plot of the number of daily holdings, average holdings by month, and overall average holdings:

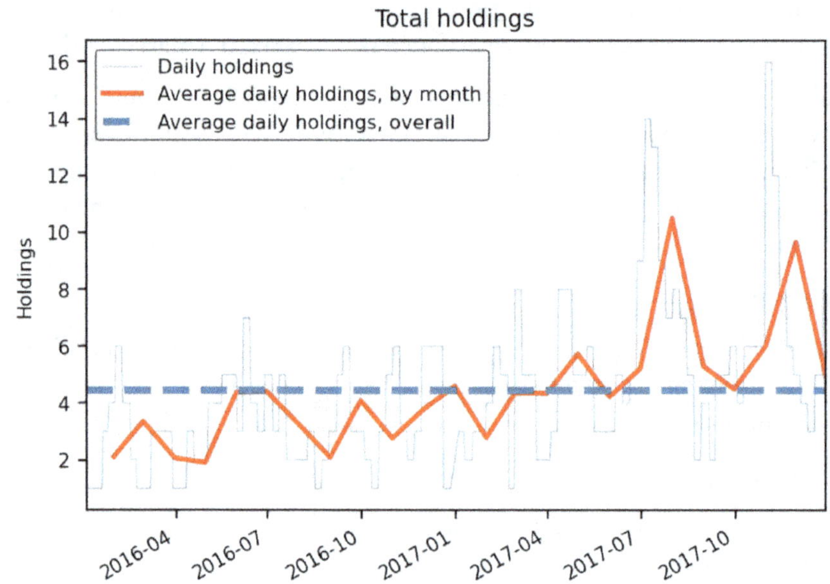

Figure 11.22: Plot of number of daily holdings, average holdings by month, and overall average holdings

2. Plot the number of long and short holdings:

```
pf.plotting.plot_long_short_holdings(returns, positions)
```

The result is a plot of the number of long and short holdings:

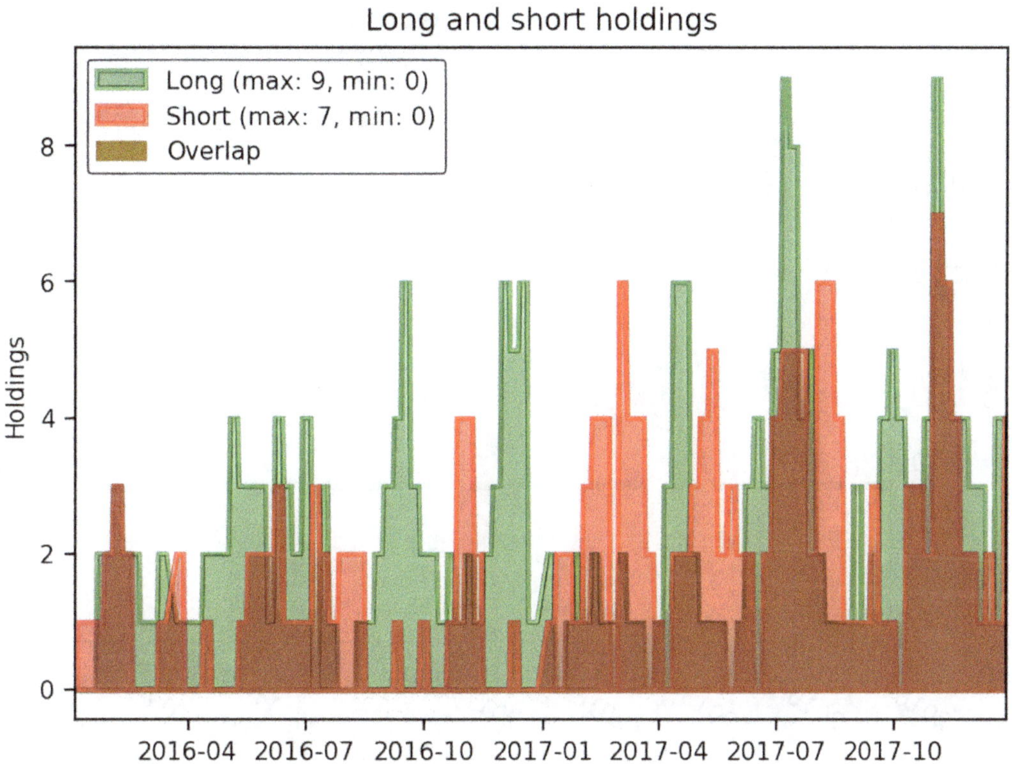

Figure 11.23: Plot of the number of long and short holdings

3. Plot the gross strategy leverage:

```
pf.plotting.plot_gross_leverage(returns, positions)
```

The result is a plot of the gross strategy leverage:

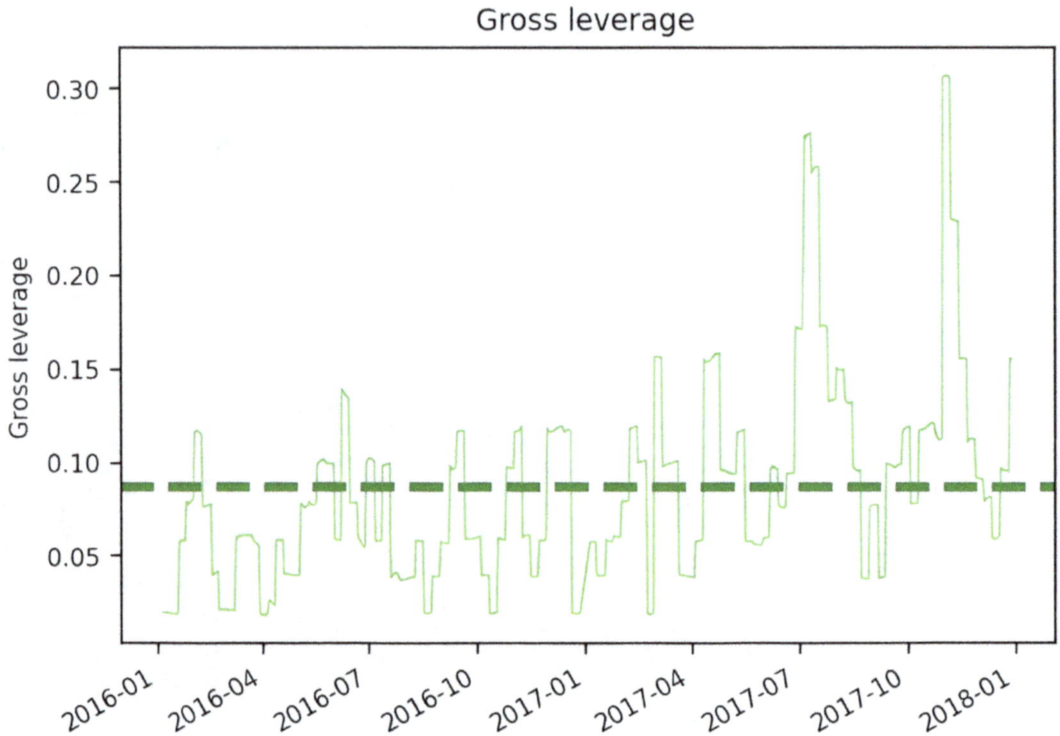

Figure 11.24: Plot of the strategy's gross leverage

4. Plot the long, short, and net exposure:

```
pf.plotting.plot_exposures(returns, positions)
```

The result is a plot of long, short, and net exposure:

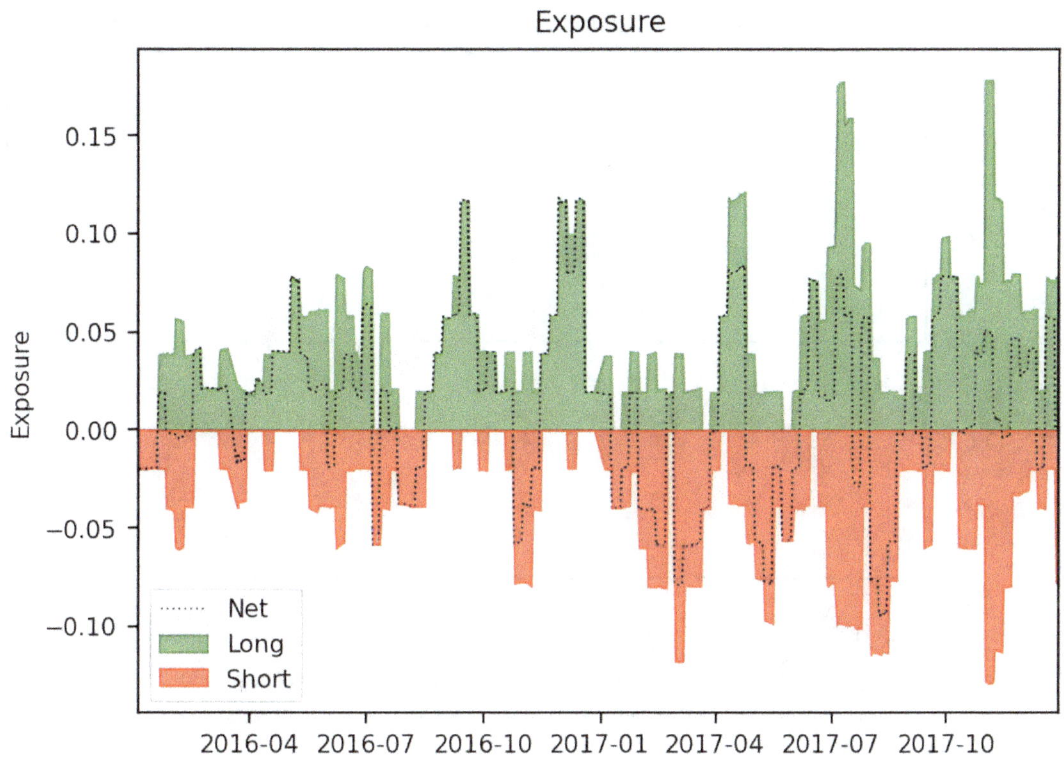

Figure 11.25: Plot of the strategy's long, short, and net exposure

5. Generate a pandas DataFrame with the percentage allocation of each position:

```
positions_alloc = pf.pos.get_percent_alloc(positions)
```

6. Generate a table of the top long, short, and net positions of all time:

```
pf.plotting.show_and_plot_top_positions(
    returns,
    positions_alloc,
    show_and_plot=2
)
```

The result is a pandas DataFrame and chart with the maximum percentage allocation of each of the top 10 strategy holdings:

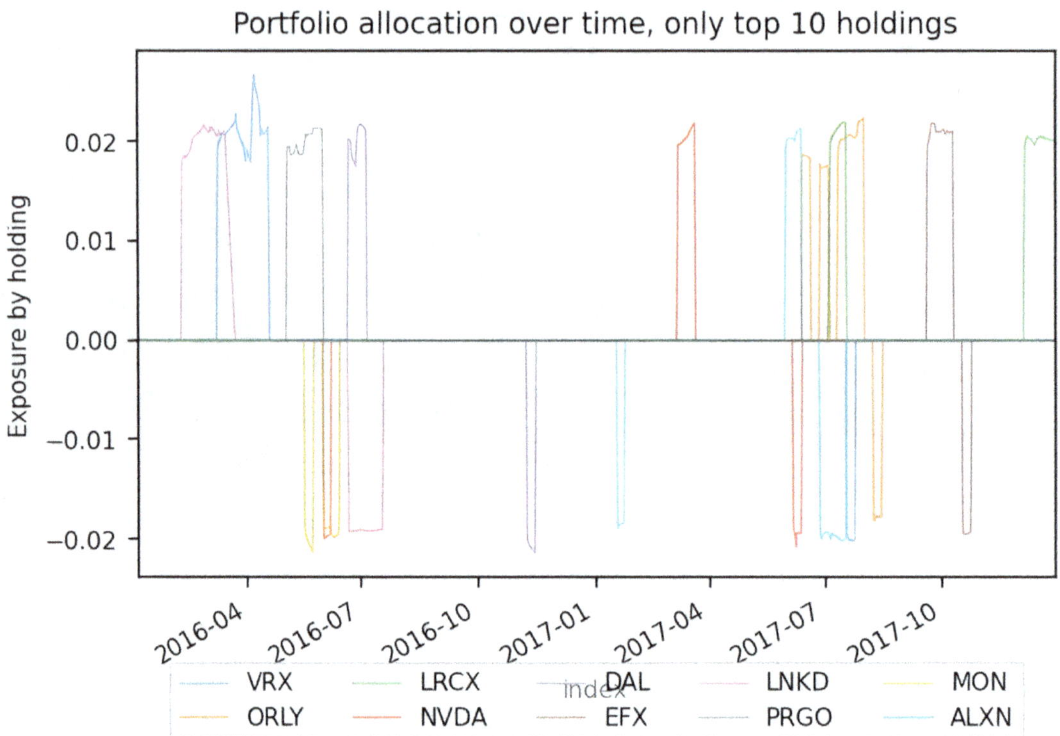

Figure 11.26: pandas DataFrame and chart with the maximum percentage allocation of each of the top 10 strategy holdings

7. Generate the sector allocations based on the positions and sector mapping:

```
sector_alloc = pf.pos.get_sector_exposures(
    positions,
    symbol_sector_map=sector_map
)
```

8. Plot the sector allocation using Pyfolio's `plot_sector_allocations` method:

```
pf.plotting.plot_sector_allocations(
    returns,
    sector_alloc=sector_alloc
)
```

The result is a chart that graphically depicts the strategy's sector allocation, including cash:

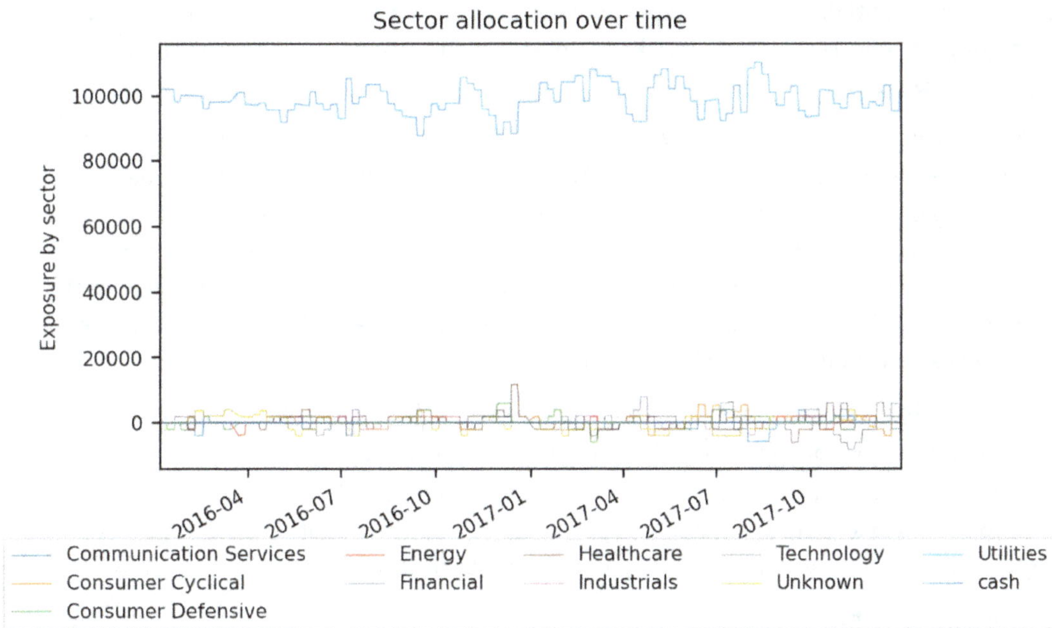

Figure 11.27: Chart of the strategy's sector allocation over time

How it works...

The `plot_holdings` function is designed to visualize the total number of stocks with an active position (either short or long) over time. It takes in a pandas Series of daily returns (`returns`) and a pandas DataFrame of daily net position values (`positions`). The plot gives traders a time-series representation of the strategy's exposure to the market. The daily holdings line gives you an immediate sense of how many positions are held each day, while the monthly and overall averages provide a more smoothed-out perspective, useful for understanding the strategy's typical market exposure.

`plot_long_short_holdings` takes the same arguments as `plot_holdings`. It filters out cash positions and counts the number of long and short positions for each day. Using Matplotlib, it plots these counts as shaded regions over time, with green indicating long positions and red indicating short positions. Conceptually, the plot serves as a visual representation of the strategy's exposure to long and short positions over time.

`plot_gross_leverage` takes `returns` and `positions` and plots the gross leverage over time using Matplotlib. The output provides a time-series view of the strategy's gross leverage which is the ratio of the absolute sum of the long and short positions to the strategy's net asset value. For traders using margin, monitoring gross leverage is critical to quantify the level of risk exposure relative to the portfolio's net asset value. Excessive leverage can amplify both gains and losses, potentially leading to rapid depletion of capital or margin calls. Understanding and managing leverage is essential for risk control and ensuring compliance with trading limits or regulatory requirements.

`plot_exposures` helps visualize the long, short, and net exposure across the strategy. Exposure is calculated by summing the values of either long, short, or all positions on each day and dividing by the sum of all positions on the same day. Long exposure represents the proportion of the portfolio invested in long positions, short exposure indicates the proportion in short positions. The net exposure gives an overall exposure level, which can be interpreted as the strategy's directional bias. A positive net exposure would suggest a bullish stance, while a negative value would indicate a bearish outlook.

`show_and_plot_top_positions` is a snapshot of a strategy's most significant long and short positions. The function takes a pandas DataFrame of positions and a specified number `N` to identify the top N long and short positions by net market value. It then calculates the mean position for each asset over the analysis period. The function outputs a table displaying these top positions and also generates a bar plot to visualize them over time.

Finally, `plot_sector_allocations` calculates the daily sector allocations by aggregating the positions based on the sector mappings for each stock. The plot is a snapshot of the strategy's average exposure to sectors. It is useful for understanding the portfolio's diversification and risk profile across sectors for hedging purposes.

There's more...

If you're trading intraday strategies, transaction costs play an important part in the profitability of a strategy. Transaction costs can be direct, which are the commissions and fees we pay to our broker and exchanges, and indirect, which include market impact and slippage.

Pyfolio has several tools for measuring these costs:

- `plot_turnover`: Plots turnover, which is the number of shares traded for a period as a fraction of total shares. The output displays the daily total, daily average per month, and all-time daily.
- `plot_slippage_sweep`: Plots equity curves at different per-dollar slippage assumptions.
- `plot_slippage_sensitivity`: Plots curve relating per-dollar slippage to average annual returns.
- `plot_capacity_sweep`: Performs a sweep over different starting portfolio values to assess the impact on the Sharpe ratio, considering transaction costs and market slippage, and then plots the resulting Sharpe ratios against the portfolio values.

- `plot_daily_turnover_hist`: Plots a histogram of daily turnover rates.
- `plot_daily_volume`: Plots the trading volume per day.

Active traders that are concerned about their transaction costs can use these additional tools to analyze costs on their strategy performance.

See also

If you're new to asset allocation and why it matters, you can get a good primer at Investopedia here: `https://www.investopedia.com/terms/a/assetallocation.asp`. A concept close to leverage is margin, which is discussed here: `https://www.investopedia.com/terms/m/margin.asp`.

Breaking down strategy performance to trade level

So far in this chapter, we've considered risk and performance metrics at the strategy level. This is an important perspective, but not the only one. In this recipe, we'll use Pyfolio Reloaded to look at the strategy at the trade level. Examining strategy risk and performance at the trade level provides more granular insights into how the returns of the strategy are composed. It lets identify specific trades, or classes of trades, that may be contributing disproportionately to risk or returns. This level of examination helps traders optimize strategy features like trade execution, entry and exit criteria, or even asset class. In this recipe, we'll look at trade-level statistics for our strategy.

Getting ready

We assume the steps in the *Preparing Zipline Reloaded backtest results for Pyfolio Reloaded* recipe were followed in preparation for this recipe. We'll need `transactions` defined for this recipe.

How to do it...

Pyfolio has a utility function to identify a trade from the transaction history. A trade is considered an opening and closing transaction of the same quantity for the same asset.

1. Extract the round trips from the strategy transaction history:

   ```
   round_trips = pf.round_trips.extract_round_trips(
       transactions[["amount", "price", "symbol"]]
   )
   ```

   The result is a pandas DataFrame with the profit or loss, return, and duration of all round trips:

	pnl	open_dt	close_dt	long	rt_returns	symbol	duration
0	-29.89	2016-05-17 20:00:00+00:00	2016-05-24 20:00:00+00:00	True	-0.015012	AAL	7 days 00:00:00
1	78.10	2016-07-19 20:00:00+00:00	2016-08-09 20:00:00+00:00	False	0.039433	AAL	21 days 00:00:00
2	57.12	2016-05-03 20:00:00+00:00	2016-05-24 20:00:00+00:00	True	0.028577	AAPL	21 days 00:00:00
3	-16.51	2017-06-20 20:00:00+00:00	2017-06-27 20:00:00+00:00	True	-0.008758	AAPL	7 days 00:00:00
4	35.88	2017-09-26 20:00:00+00:00	2017-10-10 20:00:00+00:00	True	0.018023	AAPL	14 days 00:00:00
...	...	...	...	...	...	...	...
254	-2.86	2016-01-26 21:00:00+00:00	2016-02-02 21:00:00+00:00	False	-0.044688	WMT	7 days 00:00:00
255	-54.30	2016-01-26 21:00:00+00:00	2016-02-09 21:00:00+00:00	False	-0.028281	WMT	14 days 00:00:00
256	-40.39	2017-01-18 21:00:00+00:00	2017-01-31 21:00:00+00:00	True	-0.019774	WMT	13 days 00:00:00
257	28.62	2017-02-28 21:00:00+00:00	2017-03-07 21:00:00+00:00	False	0.014944	WMT	7 days 00:00:00
258	-86.94	2017-10-31 20:00:00+00:00	2017-11-14 21:00:00+00:00	False	-0.043294	WMT	14 days 01:00:00

Figure 11.28: DataFrame containing the round trips extracted from the transaction history

2. Use the `print_round_trip_stats` function to generate the summary statistics of the strategy trades:

```
pf.round_trips.print_round_trip_stats(
    round_trips.rename(
        columns={"rt_returns": "returns"}
    )
)
```

The result is a series of pandas DataFrames with aggregate and asset-specific statistics:

Summary stats	All trades	Short trades	Long trades
Total number of round_trips	259.00	116.00	143.00
Percent profitable	0.56	0.46	0.64
Winning round_trips	145.00	53.00	92.00
Losing round_trips	114.00	63.00	51.00
Even round_trips	0.00	0.00	0.00

PnL stats	All trades	Short trades	Long trades
Total profit	$861.37	$-599.93	$1461.30
Gross profit	$8204.94	$2347.53	$5857.41
Gross loss	$-7343.57	$-2947.46	$-4396.11
Profit factor	$1.12	$0.80	$1.33
Avg. trade net profit	$3.33	$-5.17	$10.22
Avg. winning trade	$56.59	$44.29	$63.67
Avg. losing trade	$-64.42	$-46.79	$-86.20
Ratio Avg. Win:Avg. Loss	$0.88	$0.95	$0.74
Largest winning trade	$374.66	$167.40	$374.66
Largest losing trade	$-889.20	$-258.42	$-889.20

Duration stats	All trades	Short trades	Long trades
Avg duration	12 days 10:42:51.428571428	12 days 03:47:04.137931034	12 days 16:20:08.391608391
Median duration	8 days 00:00:00	8 days 00:00:00	8 days 00:00:00
Longest duration	35 days 01:00:00	29 days 00:00:00	35 days 01:00:00
Shortest duration	6 days 00:00:00	6 days 00:00:00	6 days 00:00:00

Return stats	All trades	Short trades	Long trades
Avg returns all round_trips	0.26%	-0.46%	0.84%
Avg returns winning	3.18%	2.26%	3.71%
Avg returns losing	-3.46%	-2.74%	-4.35%
Median returns all round_trips	0.31%	-0.21%	0.86%
Median returns winning	2.03%	1.60%	2.50%
Median returns losing	-2.29%	-2.28%	-2.42%
Largest winning trade	19.68%	8.31%	19.68%
Largest losing trade	-46.94%	-15.00%	-46.94%

Figure 11.29: Trade-level summary statistics

3. Plot the duration of each round trip, per asset, over time:

```
pf.plotting.plot_round_trip_lifetimes(round_trips)
```

The result is a plot that visualizes the holding period for each asset traded:

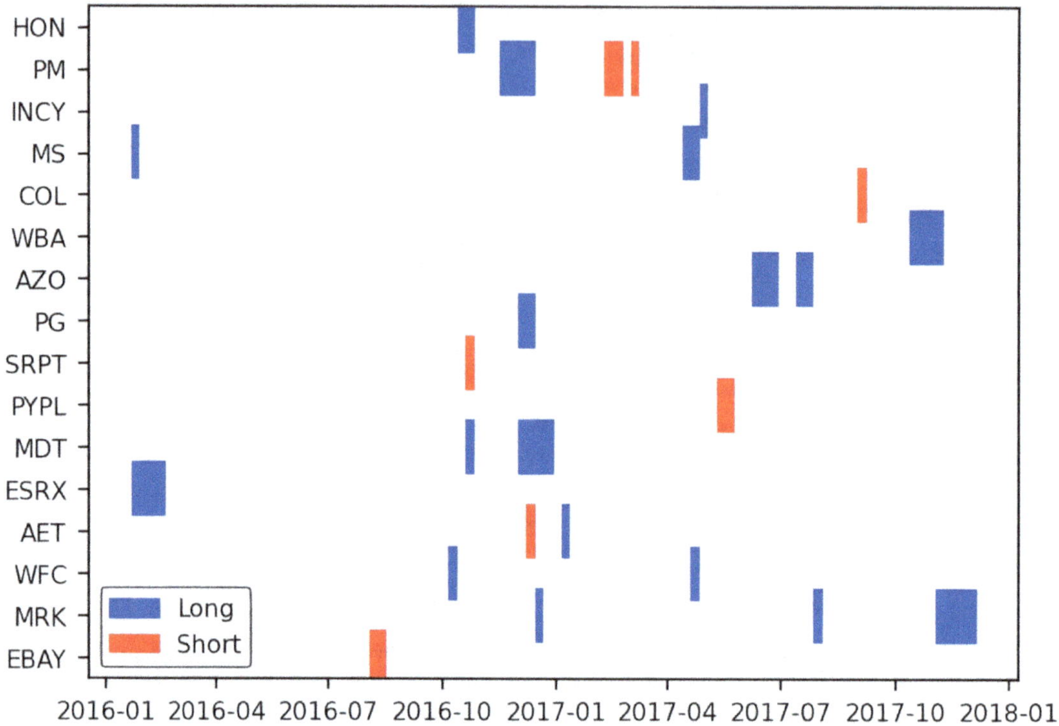

Figure 11.30: Plot visualizing the holding period for each asset traded

How it works...

Round trips are computed by identifying the opening and closing transactions for each asset in a strategy. We start by extracting executed orders from the transactions DataFrame and categorizes them as either "buy" or "sell" based on the sign of the quantity. It then groups these transactions by asset and sorts them by date. For each asset, the algorithm iterates through the sorted transactions to match an opening transaction (buy for long or sell for short) with its corresponding closing transaction (sell for long or buy for short). The time, price, and quantity of both the opening and closing transactions are recorded to compute the round-trip characteristics such as duration, profit and loss, and other relevant metrics.

Conceptually, a round trip is a complete cycle of opening and closing a position in a specific asset, and its analysis is crucial for understanding the effectiveness of our strategy. Metrics derived from round-trip analysis can provide valuable insights into transaction costs, holding periods, and the risk/return profile of individual trades, thereby aiding in strategy optimization and risk management.

Now that we covered how the plots are generated, let's review some of the key statistics output by Pyfolio:

- **Percent profitable**: Calculated by dividing the number of profitable round trips by the total number of round trips
- **Winning round_trips**: Calculated by counting the number of round-trip trades that resulted in a positive profit and loss
- **Losing round_trips**: Calculated by counting the number of round-trip trades that resulted in a negative profit and loss
- **Profit factor**: Calculated by dividing the sum of all profitable trades by the absolute sum of all losing trades
- **Avg. winning trade**: Computed by taking the mean of all profitable trades

There's more...

Depending on our strategy, it's sometimes useful to aggregate the round trip performance statistics by section, instead of by asset. By passing in the `sector_map` dictionary we built in the *Preparing Zipline Reloaded backtest results for Pyfolio Reloaded* recipe, we can aggregate by sector as follows:

1. Apply the sector mapping to the extracted round trips:

```
round_trips_by_sector =
pf.round_trips.apply_sector_mappings_to_round_trips(
    round_trips,
    sector_map
)
```

The result is a pandas DataFrame similar to *Figure 11.28* except aggregated by sector, instead of asset symbol:

	pnl	open_dt	close_dt	long	rt_returns	symbol	duration
0	-29.89	2016-05-17 20:00:00+00:00	2016-05-24 20:00:00+00:00	True	-0.015012	Industrials	7 days 00:00:00
1	78.10	2016-07-19 20:00:00+00:00	2016-08-09 20:00:00+00:00	False	0.039433	Industrials	21 days 00:00:00
2	57.12	2016-05-03 20:00:00+00:00	2016-05-24 20:00:00+00:00	True	0.028577	Technology	21 days 00:00:00
3	-16.51	2017-06-20 20:00:00+00:00	2017-06-27 20:00:00+00:00	True	-0.008758	Technology	7 days 00:00:00
4	35.88	2017-09-26 20:00:00+00:00	2017-10-10 20:00:00+00:00	True	0.018023	Technology	14 days 00:00:00
...	...	...	...	...	...	...	...
254	-2.86	2016-01-26 21:00:00+00:00	2016-02-02 21:00:00+00:00	False	-0.044688	Consumer Defensive	7 days 00:00:00
255	-54.30	2016-01-26 21:00:00+00:00	2016-02-09 21:00:00+00:00	False	-0.028281	Consumer Defensive	14 days 00:00:00
256	-40.39	2017-01-18 21:00:00+00:00	2017-01-31 21:00:00+00:00	True	-0.019774	Consumer Defensive	13 days 00:00:00
257	28.62	2017-02-28 21:00:00+00:00	2017-03-07 21:00:00+00:00	False	0.014944	Consumer Defensive	7 days 00:00:00
258	-86.94	2017-10-31 20:00:00+00:00	2017-11-14 21:00:00+00:00	False	-0.043294	Consumer Defensive	14 days 01:00:00

Figure 11.31: DataFrame with round trips mapped to sector

2. Plot the duration of each round trip, per sector, over time:

```
pf.plotting.plot_round_trip_lifetimes(round_trips_by_sector)
```

The result is a plot that visualizes the holding period for each sector traded:

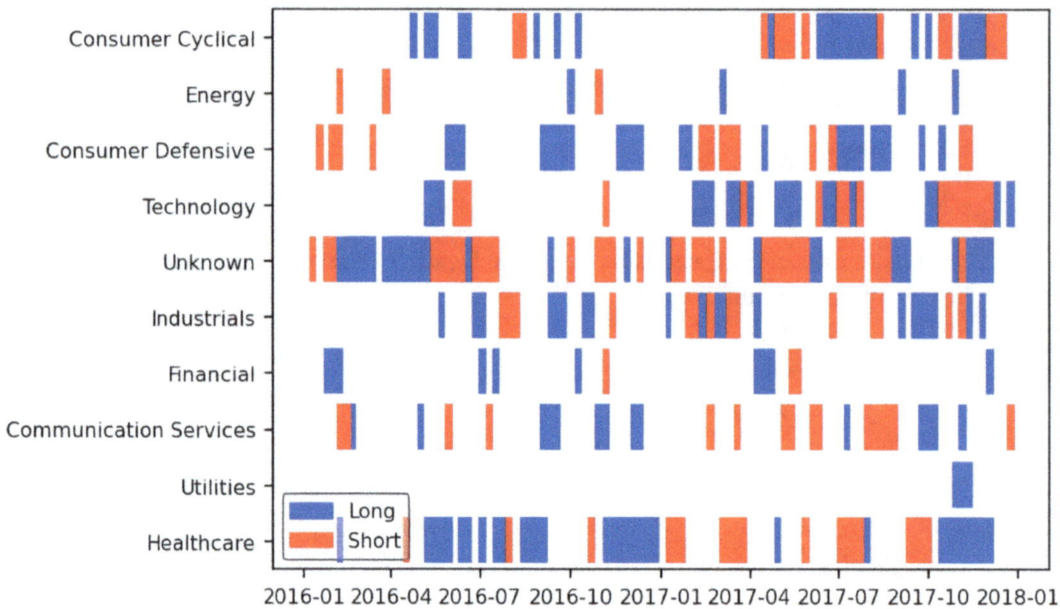

Figure 11.32: Plot visualizing the holding period for each sector traded

See also

As we've said, no single risk or performance metric is enough for a complete picture of your strategy. Pyfolio provides many important risk and performance statistics, but there are more. For a good walkthrough of other important risk and performance metrics, you can refer to blogs online.

Get this book's PDF version and more

Scan the QR code (or go to `packtpub.com/unlock`). Search for this book by name, confirm the edition, and then follow the steps on the page.

UNLOCK NOW

Note: Keep your invoice handy. Purchases made directly from Packt don't require an invoice.

12

Set Up the Interactive Brokers Python API

In *Chapters 1* through *11*, we learned the foundational tools and techniques of algorithmic trading. Now, we'll put this into practice using Python with the **Interactive Brokers** (**IB**) API and **Trader Workstation** (**TWS**). TWS is an advanced trading platform that is used by a wide range of traders, both professional and retail. You may consider alternatives to IB that offer API access. Some other brokers include Alpaca, Think Or Swim, Tasty Trade, and Tradier. When opening an account, make sure to consider market access, account type, commissions, and other factors when selecting a broker. Different brokers and account types may have different costs and restrictions.

TWS is known for its suite of trading tools and features that really enhance the trading experience. TWS is equipped with robust risk management tools so traders can effectively manage and mitigate potential trading risks. IB has unparalleled global market access with the ability to trade across a vast array of financial instruments in 135 markets spanning 33 countries. This feature is useful for traders who want to diversify their portfolios on a global scale.

Further, the paper trading functionality of TWS is an invaluable tool for both novice and experienced traders. It provides a risk-free environment for testing and refining trading strategies using real-time market conditions. This feature is instrumental in helping algorithmic traders develop and hone their algorithms without putting their money at risk. Finally, TWS's API integration is a significant advantage since it exposes all the features of TWS through an API that is accessible with Python. The IB API is especially useful for algorithmic traders since it lets them automate their trading strategies. We will take advantage of the paper trading account and IB API in the next three chapters.

In this chapter, we present the following recipes:

- Building an algorithmic trading app
- Creating a Contract object with the IB API
- Creating an Order object with the IB API
- Fetching historical market data
- Getting a market data snapshot
- Streaming live tick data
- Storing live tick data in a local SQL database

Building an algorithmic trading app

When using the IB API, there's a lot of code that can be reused across different trading apps. Connecting to TWS, generating orders, and downloading data are done the same way despite the trading strategy. That's why it's a best practice to get the reusable code out of the way first. But before we can start building our algorithmic trading app, we need to install TWS and the IB API.

We'll begin with three important topics when using the IB API:

1. The first is the architecture of the IB API, which operates on an asynchronous model. In this model, operations are not executed in a linear, blocking manner. Instead, actions are initiated by requests, and responses to these requests are handled via callbacks.
2. The second concept is inheritance, which is common across all computer programming languages. Inheritance is where a new child class acquires the properties and methods of another, parent, class. Our trading app will inherit functionality from two parent classes provided by the IB API (`EClient` and `EWrapper`).
3. The third concept is overriding where a child class provides the specific implementation for a method that is defined in a parent class.

We'll learn more about how these three concepts function in the *How it works...* section of this recipe.

As we learned in the introduction of this chapter, TWS is IB's trading platform. While running, TWS acts as a server and exposes ports to which the IB API connects. It's through this connection that the IB API operates. In this chapter, we'll install TWS, the IB API, and start building the reusable parts of our algorithmic trading app.

Getting ready

Before we install the IB API, we need TWS installed on our local computer. You can download TWS for your computer from the IB website (`https://www.interactivebrokers.com/en/trading/tws.php#tws-software`). It's available for Windows, Mac, and Linux.

Once it is installed, you can start TWS.

If you have an account, log in. If not, then you can use the Demo account option on the login screen.

We need to change some settings to allow our Python app to connect to TWS. Navigate to **Trader Workstation Configuration** under **Edit** | **Global Configuration** | **API** | **Settings**. You should a screen that looks like this:

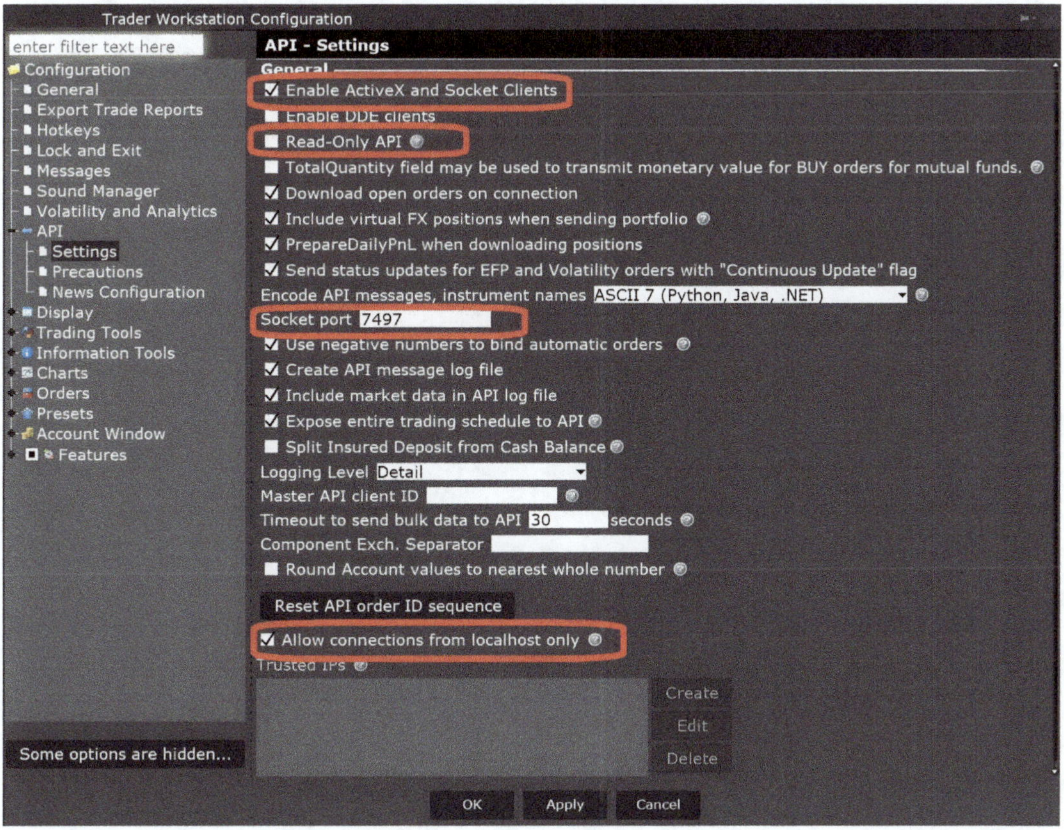

Figure 12.1: Global configuration settings

Make sure to check **Enable ActiveX and Socket Clients**. Check **Read-Only API** if you want extra protection against sending orders to IB. Lastly, check **Allow connections from localhost only** for security.

Make note of the **Socket port**, which you'll need to connect through Python. Depending on whether you logged in with a live or paper trading account, it's either 7497 or 7496.

Note

Important

To work with the IB API live, you need an IBKR Pro account (not IBRK Lite). If you don't want (or can't) set up an IB account, you can use the free demo account. In the free demo account, you will be unable to download or stream market data.

Next, near the top-right corner of TWS, you should see a green button that says **DATA**. By clicking on it, you will see the data farms you're connected to. Note the empty section near the bottom titled **API Connections (listening on *:7497)**. Having this section means you've correctly enabled API connections:

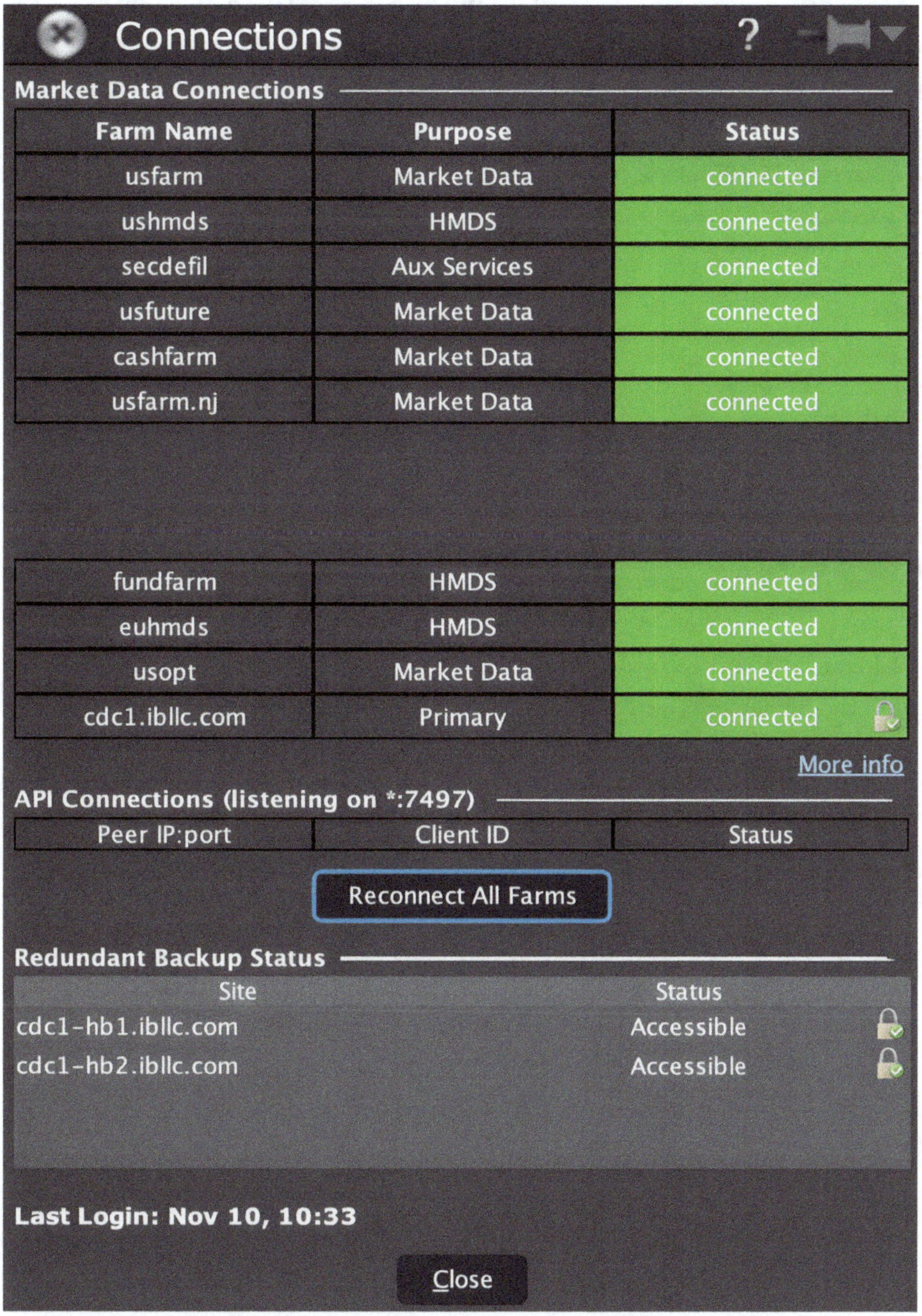

Figure 12.2: Data connections screen showing empty API connections

Once we have TWS set up, you can install the IB API. Download the Python API from the Interactive Brokers GitHub page here: `http://interactivebrokers.github.io/`. Follow the instructions on the download page to download and install the latest stable version of the API for your operating system.

Once you have the IB API set up, create a new directory called `trading-app`. Inside, create the following Python script files:

```
__init__.py
app.py
client.py
wrapper.py
contract.py
order.py
utils.py
```

How to do it...

We'll start by setting up the code we need to connect to TWS through the IB API:

1. Add the following code to the `client.py` file, which imports a base class from the IB API and implements a custom class we'll use to build our trading app:

    ```
    from ibapi.client import EClient
    class IBClient(EClient):
        def __init__(self, wrapper):
            EClient.__init__(self, wrapper)
    ```

2. Add the following code to the `wrapper.py` file, which imports a base class from the IB API and implements a custom class we'll use to build our trading app:

    ```
    from ibapi.wrapper import EWrapper
    class IBWrapper(EWrapper):
        def __init__(self):
            EWrapper.__init__(self)
    ```

3. Add the following code to the `app.py` file, which implements a custom class that we'll develop into our trading app:

    ```
    import threading
    import time
    ```

```
from wrapper import IBWrapper
from client import IBClient
class IBApp(IBWrapper, IBClient):
    def __init__(self, ip, port, client_id):
        IBWrapper.__init__(self)
        IBClient.__init__(self, wrapper=self)
        self.connect(ip, port, client_id)
        thread = threading.Thread(target=self.run, daemon=True)
        thread.start()
        time.sleep(2)

if __name__ == "__main__":
    app = IBApp("127.0.0.1", 7497, client_id=10)
    time.sleep(30)
    app.disconnect()
```

How it works...

The architecture of the IB API operates on an asynchronous model, which is fundamental to understanding its interaction and data flow mechanisms. In this model, operations are not executed in a linear, blocking manner. Instead, actions are initiated by requests, and responses to these requests are handled via callbacks, making the system highly efficient and responsive.

Request-callback pattern

When we interact with the IB API, we typically start by sending a request for an action, such as retrieving market data or placing an order. This request is made through an instance of `EClient`, a component of the API responsible for initiating communication with the IB servers. The `EClient` sends the request and then continues with other tasks, rather than waiting for a response. This non-blocking pattern gets around the **Global Interpreter Lock** (**GIL**) of Python and exemplifies the asynchronous nature of the architecture.

The responses to these requests are not received directly by the `EClient`. Instead, they are handled by another component called `EWrapper`. `EWrapper` is essentially a set of callback functions that are triggered when responses or data from the IB server are received. For instance, when market data is requested, `EWrapper` will have a specific method that gets called when that market data arrives. The user implements these methods in `EWrapper` to define how the data or responses should be processed.

This separation of concerns, where `EClient` handles sending requests and `EWrapper` handles receiving responses, allows for a more organized and manageable code structure. It also enables the handling of multiple simultaneous data streams and requests efficiently. The asynchronous model ensures that the application remains responsive and can process incoming data or events as they occur, which is crucial for real-time trading applications where timely response to market changes is critical.

Inheritance and overriding

`EWrapper` is an interface class that defines a set of callback methods, which are intended to be overridden by our custom class that inherits from `EWrapper`. This inheritance allows us to define specific behaviors for each callback method, tailoring the response to various events, such as receiving market data or order updates. Similarly, `EClient` can be extended, or its methods overridden to customize the way requests to the IB server are made, providing flexibility and control over the interaction with the trading system.

Our trading app class

Our main trading app is a custom class that inherits our custom `IBWrapper` and `IBClient` classes (which in turn inherits the IB API's `EWrapper` and `EClient` classes). This class is designed to initialize and manage our connection to the IB API.

In the `__init__` method of `IBApp`, we initialize `IBWrapper` and `IBClient`, using `IBWrapper.__init__(self)` and `IBClient.__init__(self, wrapper=self)`. This sets up the environment and properties inherited from these parent classes. The `IBClient` initialization specifically requires a reference to an `IBWrapper` instance, which is provided by passing `self`.

Next, we call the `connect` method with the parameters `ip`, `port`, and `client_id`. This method is inherited from `IBClient` and is used to establish a connection to TWS. After we connect, a new thread is created and started using Python's `threading` module. This thread runs the `run` method in a daemon mode, which means it runs in the background and will automatically terminate when the main program exits. The `run` method is responsible for processing incoming messages and events from the IB API. Running this in a separate thread allows the `IBApp` to handle API messages asynchronously without blocking the main execution flow of the application.

There's more...

Now that we have the base code established, we can test our connection.

Using your terminal, run the `app.py` script:

```
python app.py
```

You will see a series of error messages printed on the screen. Don't worry, these are not actually errors. They are just messages indicating you've successfully connected to the IB data farms.

```
ERROR -1 2104 Market data farm connection is OK:usfarm.nj
ERROR -1 2104 Market data farm connection is OK:usfuture
ERROR -1 2104 Market data farm connection is OK:cashfarm
ERROR -1 2104 Market data farm connection is OK:usopt
ERROR -1 2104 Market data farm connection is OK:usfarm
ERROR -1 2106 HMDS data farm connection is OK:euhmds
ERROR -1 2106 HMDS data farm connection is OK:fundfarm
ERROR -1 2106 HMDS data farm connection is OK:ushmds
ERROR -1 2158 Sec-def data farm connection is OK:secdefil
```

Figure 12.3: Output from the IB API showing we successfully connected

> Note
>
> **Important**
>
> Error code `-1` is not actually an error. These are messages indicating successful connections to the IB data farms.

Also note in the TWS data connection screen, we now have a peer IP connected to TWS. That's the Python trading app we built!

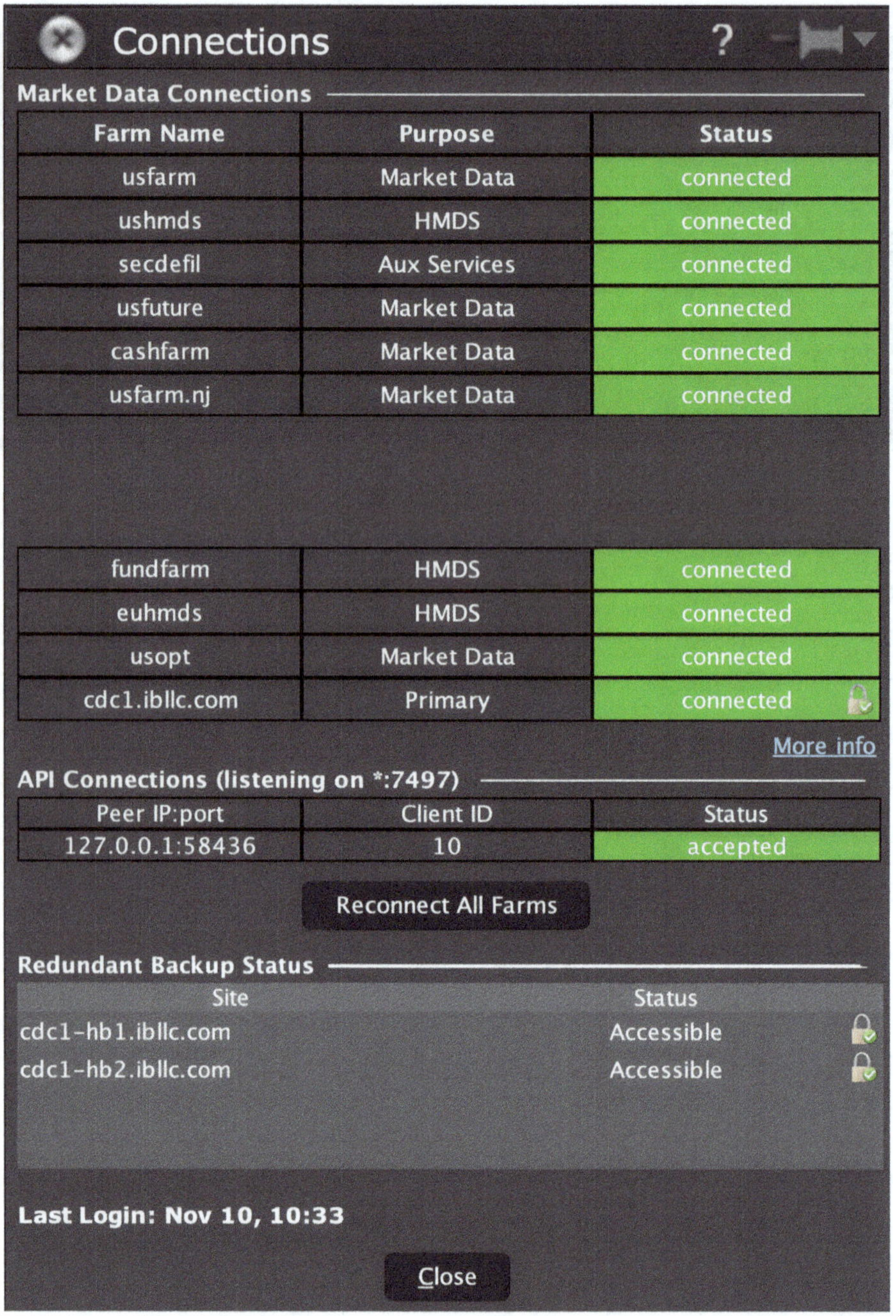

Figure 12.4: TWS data connection screen showing our Python trading app connected to TWS

See also

The IB API has extensive documentation:

- Documentation for the initial setup: `https://interactivebrokers.github.io/tws-api/initial_setup.html`
- Documentation about the `EClient` and `EWrapper` classes: `https://interactivebrokers.github.io/tws-api/client_wrapper.html`
- Documentation about connectivity: `https://interactivebrokers.github.io/tws-api/connection.html`

Creating a Contract object with the IB API

When requesting market data or generating orders, we do it using the IB `Contract` object. An IB `Contract` contains all the information required for IB to correctly identify the instrument in question. Using one class, we can represent a broad spectrum of financial instruments, including stocks, options, futures, and more. In this recipe, we'll create an IB `Contract`.

The `Contract` class is used to define the specifications of a financial instrument that we might want to trade or query. The class has all the necessary details that uniquely identify a financial instrument across various asset classes, such as stocks, options, futures, forex, bonds, and more.

A key attribute of the `Contract` class is `conId` (contract ID), which is a unique identifier assigned by IB to each financial instrument. However, in many cases, we do not need to specify this ID directly. Instead, we typically provide other descriptive attributes that the IB system uses to uniquely identify the contract. These attributes typically include the following:

- `symbol`: The ticker symbol of the asset
- `secType`: Specifying the security type (e.g., `STK` for stock, `OPT` for option, or `FUT` for future)
- `expiry`: The expiration date for derivative instruments
- `strike`: The strike price for options
- `right`: Indicating the option type (call or put)
- `multiplier`: Defining the leverage or contract size
- `exchange`: The primary exchange where the asset is traded

For more complex instruments, additional attributes may be specified, such as `currency` for assets that trade in multiple currencies or on international markets. The `lastTradeDateOrContractMonth` attribute is used for futures and options to specify the contract month. For options and futures, `includeExpired` can be set to indicate whether expired contracts should be considered. The `localSymbol` and `primaryExchange` attributes can provide more specific contract details, especially for instruments where the standard symbol may not be unique.

In this recipe, we'll create custom functions for a future, stock, and option contract.

> Note
>
> **Important**
>
> All financial instruments are called contracts by IB. This might come as a surprise for futures, options, and FX traders when considering stocks being called contracts.

Getting ready

We assume you've created the `contract.py` file in the `trading-app` directory. If not, do it now.

How to do it...

We'll create custom functions that create instances of different types of contracts, set the properties as relevant to the type of financial instrument, and return it.

Add the following code to the `contract.py` file:

```
from ibapi.contract import Contract


def future(symbol, exchange, contract_month):
    contract = Contract()
    contract.symbol = symbol
    contract.exchange = exchange
    contract.lastTradeDateOrContractMonth = contract_month
    contract.secType = "FUT"
    return contract

def stock(symbol, exchange, currency):
    contract = Contract()
    contract.symbol = symbol
    contract.exchange = exchange
    contract.currency = currency
    contract.secType = "STK"
```

```
    return contract

def option(symbol,exchange,contract_month,strike,right):
    contract = Contract()
    contract.symbol = symbol
    contract.exchange = exchange
    contract.lastTradeDateOrContractMonth = contract_month
    contract.strike = strike
    contract.right = right
    contract.secType = "OPT"
    return contract
```

How it works...

The functions are designed to encapsulate the common patterns when creating contracts. The `future` function creates a `Contract` object representing a futures contract. The function takes three parameters: `symbol`, `exchange`, and `contract_month`, which are required to set up the contract. When called, the function creates an instance of the `Contract` class, which is a core component of the IB API for defining financial instruments. This instance, stored in the variable `contract`, is then configured with specific properties: the `symbol` of the futures contract, the `exchange` where it is traded, and the `lastTradeDateOrContractMonth`, which defines the expiration date. Additionally, the security type is set to `FUT`, explicitly marking the contract as a futures contract. The `stock` and `option` functions follow the same pattern.

There's more...

Now that we've defined our contract functions, let's use them. Open `app.py` and add a new import directly under the contract import:

```
from contract import stock, future, option
```

Then right under the instantiation of the app, add the following:

```
aapl = stock("AAPL", "SMART", "USD")
gbl = future("GBL", "EUREX", "202603")
pltr = option("PLTR", "BOX", "20260315", 20, "C")
```

> Note
>
> **Important**
>
> When creating futures and options contracts using code from this book, you may bet an error from IB saying the contract cannot be found. It's likely because it's expired. Make sure to update the expiration date of expirable financial instruments.

The result of the changes is the following code in the `app.py` file:

```
import threading
import time
from wrapper import IBWrapper
from client import IBClient
from contract import stock, future, option
class IBApp(IBWrapper, IBClient):
    def __init__(self, ip, port, client_id):
        IBWrapper.__init__(self)
        IBClient.__init__(self, wrapper=self)
        self.connect(ip, port, client_id)
        thread = threading.Thread(target=self.run,
            daemon=True)
        thread.start()
        time.sleep(2)

if __name__ == "__main__":
    app = IBApp("127.0.0.1", 7497, client_id=10)
    aapl = stock("AAPL", "SMART", "USD")
    gbl = future("GBL", "EUREX", "202403")
    pltr = option("PLTR", "BOX", "20240315", 20, "C")
    time.sleep(30)
    app.disconnect()
```

Running this code will create a stock, future, and option contract, wait for 30 seconds, and then disconnect.

See also

All financial instruments are considered contracts by the IB API. This includes stocks, ETFs, bonds, options, and futures. To read more about the Contract objects, see this URL: `https://interactivebrokers.github.io/tws-api/contracts.html`

Creating an Order object with the IB API

Similar to how a `Contract` object encapsulates the information IB needs for financial instruments, `Order` objects contain all the information required for IB to correctly place orders in the market. IB is famous for having dozens of order types, from simple market orders to advanced algorithms that slowly execute trades based on time or volume conditions. Key attributes of the `Order` class include the following:

- `orderId`: A unique identifier for the order, typically assigned by the client
- `action`: Specifies the action type of the order, such as `BUY` or `SELL`
- `totalQuantity`: The amount of the asset to be bought or sold
- `orderType`: Defines the type of order, such as `LMT` for limit orders or `MKT` for market orders
- `lmtPrice`: The limit price for limit orders
- `auxPrice`: Used for stop or stop-limit orders to specify the stop price
- `tif`: *Time in force*, determining how long the order remains active
- `outsideRTH`: A boolean indicating whether the order can be executed outside regular trading hours
- `account`: Specifies the account the order should be executed from

Additional attributes can be set to further customize the order. These include attributes for advanced order types and conditions, such as `stopPrice` for stop orders, `trailStopPrice` for trailing stop orders, and various attributes for conditional orders. The `Order` class also supports attributes for specifying commission, margin, and other trade-related parameters.

Getting ready

We assume you've created the `order.py` file in the `trading-app` directory. If not, do it now.

How to do it...

We'll create custom functions that create instances of different types of contracts, set the properties relevant to the type of financial instrument, and return it.

Add the following code to the `order.py` file, which implements custom functions to create and return `Order` objects using the IB API:

```
from ibapi.order import Order
BUY = "BUY"
```

```
SELL = "SELL"
def market(action, quantity):
    order = Order()
    order.action = action
    order.orderType = "MKT"
    order.totalQuantity = quantity
    return order
def limit(action, quantity, limit_price):
    order = Order()
    order.action = action
    order.orderType = "LMT"
    order.totalQuantity = quantity
    order.lmtPrice = limit_price
    return order
def stop(action, quantity, stop_price):
    order = Order()
    order.action = action
    order.orderType = "STP"
    order.auxPrice = stop_price
    order.totalQuantity = quantity
    return order
```

How it works...

A market order is executed immediately at the current market price, which should be used with caution in now liquidity instruments since spreads are wide. It prioritizes speed of execution over price, meaning it will be filled quickly but not necessarily at a specific price point. Market orders are commonly used in situations where the certainty of execution is more important than the exact price of the trade. We can define a market order object using the IB API by first instantiating an `Order` object, then assigning either `BUY` or `SELL` to the `action` property, the quantity desired to the `totalQuantity` property, and `MKT` to the `orderType` property.

In similar fashion, we can create a limit order by specifying `LMT` as the `orderType` and a limit price as the `lmtPrice`. A limit order allows traders to specify the maximum price they are willing to pay when buying or the minimum price they are willing to accept when selling. Unlike market orders, limit orders provide price control but do not guarantee execution, as they will only be filled if the market price meets or is better than the limit price.

A stop loss order limits the loss on a position by automatically executing an order when the price reaches a specified stop price. We create a stop loss order by setting `orderType` to `STP` and setting `auxPrice` to the desired stop price.

There's more...

Now that we've defined our order functions, let's use them. Open app.py and add a new import directly under the contract import:

```
from order import limit, BUY
```

Then right under the creation of our contracts, add the following:

```
limit_order = limit(BUY, 100, 190.00)
```

The result of the changes is the following code in the app.py file:

```
import threading
import time
from wrapper import IBWrapper
from client import IBClient
from contract import stock, future, option
from order import limit, BUY
class IBApp(IBWrapper, IBClient):
    def __init__(self, ip, port, client_id):
        IBWrapper.__init__(self)
        IBClient.__init__(self, wrapper=self)
        self.connect(ip, port, client_id)
        thread = threading.Thread(target=self.run, daemon=True)
        thread.start()
        setattr(self, "thread", thread)
if __name__ == "__main__":
    app = IBApp("127.0.0.1", 7497, client_id=10)
    aapl = stock("AAPL", "SMART", "USD")
    gbl = future("GBL", "EUREX", "202403")
    pltr = option("PLTR", "BOX", "20240315", 20, "C")
    limit_order = limit(BUY, 100, 190.00)
    time.sleep(30)
    app.disconnect()
```

Running this code will create a limit order object, wait for 30 seconds, and then disconnect. We'll look at how to submit orders in *Chapter 13, Manage Orders, Positions, and Portfolios with the IB API.*

See also

To read more about the `Order` object and the available order types, check the documentation here: `https://interactivebrokers.github.io/tws-api/available_orders.html`

Fetching historical market data

Requesting historical market data using the IB API is an asynchronous process, emphasizing non-blocking, event-driven data retrieval. To kick off the process, we send a request for historical data by invoking the `reqHistoricalData` method, specifying parameters such as the financial instrument's identifier, the duration for which data is needed, the bar size, and the type of data required. Once the request is made, the IB API processes it and begins sending back the data. However, instead of waiting for all data to be received before continuing with other tasks, the API employs a callback mechanism, specifically the `historicalData` method. This method is called asynchronously for each piece of data received from IB. Each invocation of `historicalData` provides a snapshot of market data for a specific time interval, which we can then process or store. In this recipe, we'll set up the code to request and receive historical market data.

Getting ready

We assume you've created the `app.py`, `client.py`, and `wrapper.py` files in the `trading-app` directory. If not, do it now.

How to do it...

We'll update `app.py`, `client.py`, and `wrapper.py` to request historic market data.

1. Open `client.py` and add the following imports to the top of the file:

```
import time
import pandas as pd
```

2. Create a `list` as a constant after the imports. The strings in this list represent the columns of the DataFrame that we will populate with historical market data:

```
TRADE_BAR_PROPERTIES = [
    "time", "open", "high", "low", "close", "volume"
]
```

3. Inside the `IBClient` class in the `client.py` file, add the following method:

```
def get_historical_data(self, request_id, contract, duration, bar_size):
    self.reqHistoricalData(
        reqId=request_id,
        contract=contract,
        endDateTime="",
        durationStr=duration,
        barSizeSetting=bar_size,
        whatToShow="MIDPOINT",
        useRTH=1,
        formatDate=1,
        keepUpToDate=False,
        chartOptions=[],
    )
    time.sleep(5)
    bar_sizes = ["day", "D", "week", "W", "month"]
    if any(x in bar_size for x in bar_sizes):
        fmt = "%Y%m%d"
    else:
        fmt = "%Y%m%d %H:%M:%S %Z"
    data = self.historical_data[request_id]
    df = pd.DataFrame(data, columns=TRADE_BAR_PROPERTIES)
    df.set_index(pd.to_datetime(df.time, format=fmt), inplace=True)
    df.drop("time", axis=1, inplace=True)
    df["symbol"] = contract.symbol
    df.request_id = request_id
    return df
```

4. Create a method that allows users to request data for more than one contract:

```
def get_historical_data_for_many(self, request_id,
    contracts, duration, bar_size,
    col_to_use="close"):
        dfs = []
        for contract in contracts:
            data = self.get_historical_data(
                request_id, contract, duration, bar_size)
            dfs.append(data)
            request_id += 1
        return (
```

```
            pd.concat(dfs)
            .reset_index()
            .pivot(
                index="time",
                 columns="symbol",
                 values=col_to_use
            )
        )
```

The result of the changes is the following code in `client.py`:

```
import time
import pandas as pd
from ibapi.client import EClient

TRADE_BAR_PROPERTIES = [
    "time", "open", "high", "low", "close", "volume"
]

class IBClient(EClient):
    def __init__(self, wrapper):
        EClient.__init__(self, wrapper)
    def get_historical_data(self, request_id,
        contract, duration, bar_size):
            self.reqHistoricalData(
                reqId=request_id,
                contract=contract,
                endDateTime="",
                durationStr=duration,
                barSizeSetting=bar_size,
                whatToShow="MIDPOINT",
                useRTH=1,
                formatDate=1,
                keepUpToDate=False,
                chartOptions=[],
            )
            time.sleep(5)
            bar_sizes = ["day", "D", "week", "W", "month"]
            if any(x in bar_size for x in bar_sizes):
                fmt = "%Y%m%d"
            else:
```

```
            fmt = "%Y%m%d %H:%M:%S %Z"
        data = self.historical_data[request_id]
        df = pd.DataFrame(data,
            columns=TRADE_BAR_PROPERTIES)
        df.set_index(pd.to_datetime(
            df.time, format=fmt), inplace=True)
        df.drop("time", axis=1, inplace=True)
        df["symbol"] = contract.symbol
        df.request_id = request_id
        return df
    def get_historical_data_for_many(self,
        request_id, contracts, duration, bar_size,
        col_to_use="close"):
            dfs = []
            for contract in contracts:
            data = self.get_historical_data(
                request_id, contract, duration, bar_size)
            dfs.append(data)
            request_id += 1
            return (pd.concat(dfs)
        .reset_index()
        .pivot(
            index="time",
            columns="symbol",
            values=col_to_use
        )
    )
```

5. Next, open the `wrapper.py` file and add the following line of code to the `__init__` method in the `IBWrapper` class:

```
self.historical_data = {}
```

6. Then add the following method to the `IBWrapper` class:

```
def historicalData(self, request_id, bar):
    bar_data = (
        bar.date,
        bar.open,
        bar.high,
```

```
            bar.low,
            bar.close,
            bar.volume,
        )
        if request_id not in self.historical_data.keys():
            self.historical_data[request_id] = []
        self.historical_data[request_id].append(bar_data)
```

The result of the changes is the following code in `wrapper.py`:

```
from ibapi.wrapper import EWrapper
class IBWrapper(EWrapper):
    def __init__(self):
        EWrapper.__init__(self)
        self.historical_data = {}
    def historicalData(self, request_id, bar):
        bar_data = (
            bar.date,
            bar.open,
            bar.high,
            bar.low,
            bar.close,
            bar.volume,
        )
        if request_id not in self.historical_data.keys():
            self.historical_data[request_id] = []
        self.historical_data[request_id].append(bar_data)
```

How it works...

Getting historical data through the IB API clearly demonstrates the request-callback architecture. We get historical data by first requesting it, then processing it through a callback.

Requesting historic data

The `get_historical_data` method accepts four parameters: `request_id`, `contract`, `duration`, and `bar_size`. `request_id` is an arbitrary, but unique identifier for the data request, `contract` specifies the financial instrument for which historical data is being requested, `duration` indicates the time span for the historical data, and `bar_size` defines the granularity of the data.

The valid duration strings are as follows:

Unit	Description
S	Seconds
D	Day
W	Week
M	Month
Y	Year

Figure 12.5: Valid duration strings for requesting historical data

The valid bar size strings are as follows:

Size							
1 secs	5 secs	10 secs	15 secs	30 secs			
1 min	2 mins	3 mins	5 mins	10 mins	15 mins	20 mins	30 mins
1 hour	2 hours	3 hours	4 hours	8 hours			
1 day							
1 week							
1 month							

Figure 12.6: Valid bar sizes for requesting historical data

The method begins by calling `reqHistoricalData`, which is a method provided by the IB API to request historical data. The parameters passed to this function include `request_id`, the `contract` object, an empty string for `endDateTime` (indicating the request is for the most recent data up to the current date), the `duration` of historical data, `bar_size`, and other settings such as `whatToShow` (indicating the type of data required), `useRTH` (data within regular trading hours), `formatDate` (the format of the returned date), and `keepUpToDate` (indicating no need for live updates). These are hardcoded in our implementation, but you can modify them to allow the user to pass their own options.

The available kinds of historic data type strings (`whatToShow`) are as follows:

Type	Open	High	Low	Close	Volume
TRADES	First traded price	Highest traded price	Lowest traded price	Last traded price	Total traded volume
MIDPOINT	Starting midpoint price	Highest midpoint price	Lowest midpoint price	Last midpoint price	N/A
BID	Starting bid price	Highest bid price	Lowest bid price	Last bid price	N/A
ASK	Starting ask price	Highest ask price	Lowest ask price	Last ask price	N/A
BID_ASK	Time average bid	Max Ask	Min Bid	Time average ask	N/A
ADJUSTED_LAST	Dividend-adjusted first traded price	Dividend-adjusted high trade	Dividend-adjusted low trade	Dividend-adjusted last trade	Total traded volume
HISTORICAL_VOLATILITY	Starting volatility	Highest volatility	Lowest volatility	Last volatility	N/A
OPTION_IMPLIED_VOLATILITY	Starting implied volatility	Highest implied volatility	Lowest implied volatility	Last implied volatility	N/A
FEE_RATE	Starting fee rate	Highest fee rate	Lowest fee rate	Last fee rate	N/A
YIELD_BID	Starting bid yield	Highest bid yield	Lowest bid yield	Last bid yield	N/A
YIELD_ASK	Starting ask yield	Highest ask yield	Lowest ask yield	Last ask yield	N/A
YIELD_BID_ASK	Time average bid yield	Highest ask yield	Lowest bid yield	Time average ask yield	N/A
YIELD_LAST	Starting last yield	Highest last yield	Lowest last yield	Last last yield	N/A
SCHEDULE	N/A	N/A	N/A	N/A	N/A
AGGTRADES	First traded price	Highest traded price	Lowest traded price	Last traded price	Total traded volume

Figure 12.7: Valid data types to return for historical data

After sending the request, the method pauses execution for five seconds to allow time for the data to be retrieved and stored in the `historical_data` dictionary, keyed by `request_id`.

> Note
>
> **Important**
>
> The five-second delay is arbitrary and does not guarantee that all data has been received. You can extend this delay or implement more sophisticated methods to check whether data exists in the `historicData` method in the `IBWrapper` class.

The method then determines how to parse the incoming time string depending on whether the requested data is intraday.

Next, the method retrieves the historical data and creates a pandas DataFrame from it. The DataFrame is structured with columns defined by `TRADE_BAR_PROPERTIES`. The index of the DataFrame is set to the time column, which is formatted, and the original time column is dropped. Additionally, a new `symbol` column is added to the DataFrame, containing the symbol of the contract, and `request_id` is stored as an attribute of the DataFrame.

Receiving historic data

The `historicalData` method is a callback and is automatically invoked for each bar of data received from IB following a call to `reqHistoricalData`. When `reqHistoricalData` is called to request historical market data, the IB API responds by sending back this data in individual bar units, with each bar triggering the `historicalData` method. This method then processes and stores each piece of data.

historicalData receives two parameters: request_id and bar. The request_id parameter is the unique identifier associated with the specific request for historical data, which allows the method to differentiate between data from different requests. The bar parameter is an object that contains the historical bar data for the instrument. Within the method, the bar data is structured into a tuple that contains the date (bar.date), the opening price (bar.open), the highest price (bar.high), the lowest price (bar.low), the closing price (bar.close), and the trading volume (bar.volume) for that specific time period.

The method then checks whether the request_id already exists as a key in the historical_data dictionary. If it does not exist the method initializes an empty list under this key. This step ensures that there is a structure in place to store the historical data for each unique request.

Finally, the method appends the bar_data tuple to the list associated with the request_id in the historical_data dictionary. This action effectively stores the historical bar data, allowing the method to accumulate the historical data points for each request over time.

The get_historical_data_for_many method loops through each provided contract, requests the historical data, and concatenates their resulting DataFrames together. The method returns a pivoted DataFrame, which moves the data in col_to_use into the rows and each requested contract into the columns.

There's more...

We now have the code built to request and receive historical market data. Open the app.py file and add the following code block under the definitions of the contracts:

```
data = app.get_historical_data(
    request_id=99,
    contract=aapl,
    duration='2 D',
    bar_size='30 secs'
)
```

The result of the changes is the following code in app.py:

```
import threading
import time
from wrapper import IBWrapper
from client import IBClient
from contract import stock, future, option
```

```
class IBApp(IBWrapper, IBClient):
    def __init__(self, ip, port, client_id):
        IBWrapper.__init__(self)
        IBClient.__init__(self, wrapper=self)
        self.connect(ip, port, client_id)
        thread = threading.Thread(target=self.run, daemon=True)
        thread.start()
        time.sleep(2)
if __name__ == "__main__":
    app = IBApp("127.0.0.1", 7497, client_id=10)
    aapl = stock("AAPL", "SMART", "USD")
    gbl = future("GBL", "EUREX", "202403")
    pltr = option("PLTR", "BOX", "20240315", 20, "C")
    data = app.get_historical_data(
        request_id=99,
        contract=aapl,
        duration='2 D',
        bar_size='30 secs'
    )
    time.sleep(30)
    app.disconnect()
```

After running this code, `data` will contain a pandas DataFrame with the requested historic market data:

```
                            open    high     low   close     volume symbol
time
2023-11-14 09:30:00-05:00  187.69  187.73  187.16  187.47  1168171.0   AAPL
2023-11-14 09:30:30-05:00  187.45  187.51  187.28  187.29   210746.0   AAPL
2023-11-14 09:31:00-05:00  187.28  187.48  187.21  187.23   229337.0   AAPL
2023-11-14 09:31:30-05:00  187.24  187.24  186.73  186.73   197331.0   AAPL
2023-11-14 09:32:00-05:00  186.74  186.90  186.69  186.83   163242.0   AAPL
...                           ...     ...     ...     ...        ...    ...
2023-11-15 15:03:30-05:00  188.41  188.44  188.39  188.40    29656.0   AAPL
2023-11-15 15:04:00-05:00  188.40  188.42  188.34  188.34    15333.0   AAPL
2023-11-15 15:04:30-05:00  188.36  188.36  188.30  188.30    16014.0   AAPL
2023-11-15 15:05:00-05:00  188.31  188.34  188.28  188.34    35756.0   AAPL
2023-11-15 15:05:30-05:00  188.33  188.36  188.32  188.32    15280.0   AAPL

[1452 rows x 6 columns]
```

Figure 12.8: A pandas DataFrame containing requested historic market data

> **Tip**
>
> If you're using an **Interactive Development Environment** (**IDE**) such as **PyCharm** or **VSCode**, you can execute the code in debug mode during development. Debug mode lets you pause the execution of the code to inspect the variables.

See also

To learn more about historical market data, see the documentation at this URL: `https://interactivebrokers.github.io/tws-api/historical_data.html`. For specifics on the following topics, see the associated documentation:

- Requesting historical market data: `https://interactivebrokers.github.io/tws-api/historical_bars.html#hd_request`
- Receiving historical market data: `https://interactivebrokers.github.io/tws-api/historical_bars.html#hd_receive`
- Duration, bar sizes, historical data types available, and available data per instrument: `https://interactivebrokers.github.io/tws-api/historical_bars.html#hd_duration`

Getting a market data snapshot

In the previous recipe, we learned how to get historical data. In some situations, we may need the current market price. In *Chapter 14, Deploy Strategies to a Live Environment*, we'll use the current market price to create methods to target specific values or percentage allocations in our portfolio.

The API uses tick types, each representing a specific category of market data, such as last trade price, volume, or bid and ask. These tick types let us access real-time pricing information, which is important for making informed trading decisions. This recipe will show you how to get real-time market data.

Getting ready

We assume you've created the `app.py`, `client.py`, and `wrapper.py` files in the `trading-app` directory. If not, do it now.

How to do it...

We'll update `app.py`, `client.py`, and `wrapper.py` to request the last price for a contract.

1. Open `client.py` and include the following method in the `IBClient` class after the `get_historical_data_for_many` method:

```
def get_market_data(self, request_id, contract, tick_type=4):
    self.reqMktData(
        reqId=request_id,
        contract=contract,
        genericTickList="",
        snapshot=True,
        regulatorySnapshot=False,
        mktDataOptions=[]
    )
    time.sleep(5)
    self.cancelMktData(reqId=request_id)
    return self.market_data[request_id].get(tick_type)
```

2. Open `wrapper.py` and include the following method in the `IBWrapper` class after the `historicalData` method:

```
def tickPrice(self, request_id, tick_type, price, attrib):
    if request_id not in self.market_data.keys():
```

```
            self.market_data[request_id] = {}
        self.market_data[request_id][tick_type] =
        float(price)
```

3. Add an instance variable in the `__init__` method under `self.historical_data = {}`:

```
self.market_data = {}
```

How it works...

The `get_market_data` method fetches a specific tick type from the IB API. It initiates a market data request for a given financial contract, which we identify by `request_id`, and requests all available ticks by using an empty string for the `genericTickList` argument. The function opts for a single data snapshot, rather than a continuous stream and pauses for five seconds to allow data reception and processing. After the pause, it cancels the data request to free up the request ID. Finally, the function retrieves and returns the specific market data from a dictionary using the request ID and tick type as keys. We default to tick type 4, which is the last traded price.

In the `tickPrice` callback, it first checks whether the `request_id` exists in the `market_data` dictionary and if not, it initializes an empty dictionary for that ID. It then updates the dictionary, setting the `tick_type` key to the received `price`, converted to a float.

The `tickPrice` method will typically retrieve seven different tick types:

Code	Tick Name	Description
1	Bid Price	Highest priced bid for the contract.
2	Ask Price	Lowest price offer on the contract.
4	Last Price	Last price at which the contract traded.
6	High	High price for the day.
7	Low	Low price for the day.
9	Close Price	The last available closing price for the *previous* day.
14	Open Tick	Current session's opening price .

Figure 12.9: Different tick types returned by the IB API

There's more...

To get the last closing price for AAPL, add the following code to `app.py` after we define our AAPL contract:

```
data = app.get_market_data(
    request_id=99,
    contract=aapl
)
```

The `data` variable contains a float representing the last traded price of AAPL.

See also

To learn more about how to request and receive market data using the IB API, see the following resources:

- A list of different tick types: `https://interactivebrokers.github.io/tws-api/tick_types.html`
- Requesting market data: `https://interactivebrokers.github.io/tws-api/md_request.html`
- Receiving market data: `https://interactivebrokers.github.io/tws-api/md_receive.html`

Streaming live market data

Requesting tick-by-tick data involves a real-time, granular approach to market data acquisition. This process begins by invoking the `reqTickByTickData` method, where we specify the unique request identifier, the financial instrument's contract details, and the type of tick data we are interested in (such as `BidAsk`). Upon this request, the IB API starts transmitting data for each individual market **tick**, which is a single change or update in market data.

Unlike bulk historical data retrieval, this method provides data almost instantaneously as market events occur, which lets us build near real-time algorithmic trading applications. The received data is handled through a callback function that is triggered for each tick, capturing detailed information such as price, size, and the time of the tick. By the end of this recipe, you'll be able to stream near-real-time market data from the IB API.

Getting ready

We assume you've created the `app.py`, `client.py`, and `wrapper.py` files in the `trading-app` directory. If not, do it now.

How to do it...

We'll update `app.py`, `client.py`, and `wrapper.py` to request historic market data.

1. Open `client.py` and include the following import at the top of the file:

```
from dataclasses import dataclass, field
```

2. Then add a `dataclass` to represent each price tick below the `TRADE_BAR_PROPERTIES` constant:

```
@dataclass
class Tick:
    time: int
    bid_price: float
    ask_price: float
    bid_size: float
    ask_size: float
    timestamp_: pd.Timestamp = field(init=False)
    def __post_init__(self):
        self.timestamp_ = pd.to_datetime(self.time, unit="s")
        self.bid_price = float(self.bid_price)
        self.ask_price = float(self.ask_price)
        self.bid_size = int(self.bid_size)
        self.ask_size = int(self.ask_size)
```

3. Inside the `IBClient` class in the `client.py` file, add the functions that will start and stop the streaming data:

```
def get_streaming_data(self, request_id, contract):
    self.reqTickByTickData(
        reqId=request_id,
        contract=contract,
        tickType="BidAsk",
        numberOfTicks=0,
        ignoreSize=True
    )
    time.sleep(10)
    while True:
        if self.stream_event.is_set():
            yield Tick(*self.streaming_data[request_id])
```

```
            self.stream_event.clear()
def stop_streaming_data(self, request_id):
    self.cancelTickByTickData(reqId=request_id)
```

The result of the changes is the following code in `client.py`:

```
import time
import pandas as pd
from dataclasses import dataclass, field
from ibapi.client import EClient

TRADE_BAR_PROPERTIES = [
    "time", "open", "high", "low", "close", "volume"
]

@dataclass
class Tick:
    time: int
    bid_price: float
    ask_price: float
    bid_size: float
    ask_size: float
    timestamp_: pd.Timestamp = field(init=False)
    def __post_init__(self):
        self.timestamp_ = pd.to_datetime(self.time,
            unit="s")
        self.bid_price = float(self.bid_price)
        self.ask_price = float(self.ask_price)
        self.bid_size = int(self.bid_size)
        self.ask_size = int(self.ask_size)
class IBClient(EClient):
    def __init__(self, wrapper):
        EClient.__init__(self, wrapper)
    <snip>
    def get_streaming_data(self, request_id, contract):
        self.reqTickByTickData(
            reqId=request_id,
            contract=contract,
            tickType="BidAsk",
            numberOfTicks=0,
            ignoreSize=True
```

```
        )
        time.sleep(10)
        while True:
            if self.stream_event.is_set():
                yield Tick(
                    *self.streaming_data[request_id])
                self.stream_event.clear()
    def stop_streaming_data(self, request_id):
        self.cancelTickByTickData(reqId=request_id)
```

4. Open `wrapper.py` and include the following import at the top of the file:

```
import threading
```

5. Add the following lines of code to the `__init__` method in the `IBWrapper` class:

```
self.streaming_data = {}
self.stream_event = threading.Event()
```

6. Next, add the following method to the `IBWrapper` class:

```
def tickByTickBidAsk(
        self,
        request_id,
        time,
        bid_price,
        ask_price,
        bid_size,
        ask_size,
        tick_atrrib_last
):
    tick_data = (
        time,
        bid_price,
        ask_price,
        bid_size,
        ask_size,
    )
    self.streaming_data[request_id] = tick_data
    self.stream_event.set()
```

The result of the changes is the following code in `wrapper.py`:

```
import threading
from ibapi.wrapper import EWrapper
class IBWrapper(EWrapper):
    def __init__(self):
        EWrapper.__init__(self)
        self.nextValidOrderId = None
        self.historical_data = {}
        self.streaming_data = {}
        self.stream_event = threading.Event()
    <snip>
    def tickByTickBidAsk(
            self,
            request_id,
            time,
            bid_price,
            ask_price,
            bid_size,
            ask_size,
            tick_atrrib_last
    ):
        tick_data = (
            time,
            bid_price,
            ask_price,
            bid_size,
            ask_size,
        )
        self.streaming_data[request_id] = tick_data
        self.stream_event.set()
```

How it works...

Getting streaming data through the IB API requires two steps: first we request it, then we process it through a callback. The tick-by-tick data we stream is the data that corresponds to the data shown in the TWS Time and Sales window.

Note

Important

Time and Sales refers to a real-time data feed that provides detailed information about executed trades for a specific financial instrument. This feed includes the exact time of each trade, the price at which it was executed, and the size of the trade. Time and Sales data is useful for traders who want to analyze order book dynamics in real time.

Requesting streaming data

We start by defining a Python **dataclass** called `Tick`. A Python **dataclass** is a decorator that automatically generates special methods such as `__init__`, `__repr__`, and `__eq__` for classes, primarily used for storing data, simplifying, and reducing boilerplate code.

The `Tick` **dataclass** represents market data ticks with attributes for time, bid and ask prices, and sizes. An additional attribute, `timestamp_`, is defined as a pandas `Timestamp` and excluded from automatic `__init__` method generation using `field(init=False)`. The `__post_init__` method of the **dataclass** converts the `time` attribute from a Unix timestamp to a more readable pandas `Timestamp` format, using `to_datetime`.

The `get_streaming_data` method requires a request ID and a contract to start streaming data. The method requests and yields real-time bid and ask tick data for a specified financial instrument, represented by the `contract` parameter.

The method begins by calling `reqTickByTickData`, a function of the IB API that requests real-time tick-by-tick data. The parameters passed to this function include the following:

- `reqId`: A unique identifier for the data request.
- `contract`: Specifies the financial instrument for which data is being requested.
- `tickType`: Specifies the type of data to stream. Available options are `Last`, `AllLast`, `BidAsk`, and `MidPoint`.
- `numberOfTicks`: A flag to request a specific set of historic ticks or to stream until canceled.
- `ignoreSize`: Whether updates to bid and ask sizes are required.

Following the data request, we delay execution for 10 seconds to ensure that some data is received and buffered before the method starts yielding data.

The method then enters an infinite loop, continuously checking if the thread event `stream_event` is set and when it is, the method yields the `Tick` object with the latest data for the given `request_id`, and then clears the event, readying it for the next batch of data.

Note

Important

A Python generator is a special type of function that returns an iterator, allowing for the generation of items on the fly rather than storing them all in memory at once. When a generator function is called, it doesn't execute its code immediately. Instead, it returns a generator object that can be iterated over. Each iteration over a generator object resumes the function's execution from where it last yielded a value, using the `yield` statement, until it either encounters another `yield` or reaches the end of the function, at which point it raises a `StopIteration` exception.

Receiving streaming data

Depending on the `tickType` requested in the `reqTickByTickData`, IB will use a different callback function. They are as follows:

tickType	Callback
Last	tickByTickAllLast
AllLast	tickByTickAllLast
BidAsk	tickByTickBidAsk
MidPoint	tickByTickMidPoint

Figure 12.10: Callbacks used for each tick type requested

Note

Important

We only implement `tickByTickBidAsk` to respond to the `BidAsk` tick type. You can read more about the type of data that is returned in each of the callbacks at this URL: `https://interactivebrokers.github.io/tws-api/tick_data.html`

We override the `tickByTickBidAsk` provided by the IB API. This callback method is invoked for every tick. Upon invocation, the method first constructs a tuple, `tick_data`, comprising the time, bid price, ask price, bid size, and ask size.

After receiving a tick, the method constructs a `tick_data` tuple with the bid and ask prices and respective volumes. The method then updates a dictionary `streaming_data`, keyed by `request_id`, with this tick data and sets a `stream_event` threading event, signaling that new data has been received and is ready for processing in the `get_streaming_data` method.

There's more...

We now have the code built to request and receive streaming tick data. Open the `app.py` file and add the following code block under the definitions of the contracts:

```
eur = future("EUR", "CME", "202312")
for tick in app.get_streaming_data(99, es):
    print(tick)
```

The result of the changes is the following code in `app.py`:

```
import threading
import time
from wrapper import IBWrapper
from client import IBClient
from contract import future
class IBApp(IBWrapper, IBClient):
    def __init__(self, ip, port, client_id):
        IBWrapper.__init__(self)
        IBClient.__init__(self, wrapper=self)
        self.connect(ip, port, client_id)
        thread = threading.Thread(target=self.run, daemon=True)
        thread.start()
        time.sleep(2)

if __name__ == "__main__":
    app = IBApp("127.0.0.1", 7497, client_id=10)
    eur = future("EUR", "CME", "202312")
    for tick in app.get_streaming_data(99, eur):
        print(tick)
    time.sleep(30)
    app.disconnect()
```

After running this code, you'll see a list of `Tick` objects printed to the console with the details of each tick:

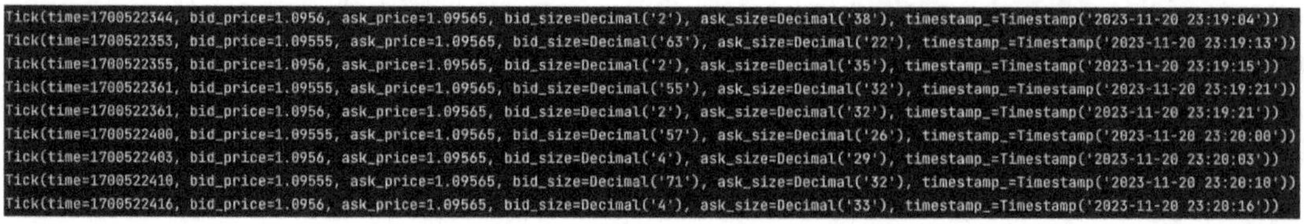

Figure 12.11: Streaming tick data as Tick objects

See also

To learn more about the available types of streaming data, check the following URL: `https://interactivebrokers.github.io/tws-api/market_data.html`. For specifics, check the following URLs:

- Level 1 (top of book) streaming and snapshot data. This is another option for streaming real-time data that was not covered in this recipe: `https://interactivebrokers.github.io/tws-api/md_request.html`.
- Streaming tick data covered in this recipe: `https://interactivebrokers.github.io/tws-api/tick_data.html`

Storing live tick data in a local SQL database

We discussed storing financial market data in *Chapter 3, Accelerate Financial Market Data Analysis with Polars and DuckDB*. In this chapter, we learned several ways of downloading different types of market data for free and storing it in a variety of formats. In *Chapter 5, Build a Quantamental Research Database with Hedge Fund Tools*, we looked at how to use the cutting-edge ArcticDB library to store petabytes of market data. In this recipe, we'll use another storage solution, SQLite, to store streaming tick data in a local relational database.

Getting ready

We assume you've created the `app.py`, `client.py`, `wrapper.py` , and `utils.py` files in the `trading-app` directory. If not, do it now.

We'll also move some of the code currently in `client.py`, to the `utils.py` file. Copy the following code from `client.py` and paste it into `utils.py`:

```
import pandas as pd
from dataclasses import dataclass, field

TRADE_BAR_PROPERTIES = ["time", "open", "high", "low", "close", "volume"]
```

```
@dataclass
class Tick:
    time: int
    bid_price: float
    ask_price: float
    bid_size: float
    ask_size: float
    timestamp_: pd.Timestamp = field(init=False)
    def __post_init__(self):
        self.timestamp_ = pd.to_datetime(self.time, unit="s")
        self.bid_price = float(self.bid_price)
        self.ask_price = float(self.ask_price)
        self.bid_size = int(self.bid_size)
        self.ask_size = int(self.ask_size)
```

Now, remove the code from the `client.py` file and import it from `utils.py`. The result of the changes is the following code in `client.py`:

```
import time
import pandas as pd
from utils import Tick, TRADE_BAR_PROPERTIES
from ibapi.client import EClient
class IBClient(EClient):
    <snip>
```

How to do it...

We'll add methods to our `IBApp` class that will create the SQLite database, generate a connection to our database, and insert tick data into the table.

1. Add the `connection` method to the `IBApp` class in `app.py` and decorate it with the `property` decorator:

```
@property
def connection(self):
    return sqlite3.connect("tick_data.sqlite",
        isolation_level=None)
```

2. Add the `create_table` method to the `IBApp` class:

```
def create_table(self):
    cursor = self.connection.cursor()
    cursor.execute(
        """
        CREATE TABLE IF NOT EXISTS bid_ask_data (
            timestamp datetime, symbol string,
            bid_price real, ask_price real,
            bid_size integer, ask_size integer)
        """
    )
```

3. Add the `stream_to_sqlite` method to the `IBApp` class. Don't worry, we'll go through it in detail next:

```
def stream_to_sqlite(self, request_id, contract,
    run_for_in_seconds=23400):
        cursor = self.connection.cursor()
        end_time = time.time() + run_for_in_seconds + 10
        for tick in app.get_streaming_data(request_id, contract):
            query = """INSERT INTO bid_ask_data (
                timestamp, symbol, bid_price,
                ask_price, bid_size, ask_size)
                VALUES (?, ?, ?, ?, ?, ?)"""
            values = (
                tick.timestamp_.strftime("%Y-%m-%d %H:%M:%S"),
                contract.symbol,
                tick.bid_price,
                tick.ask_price,
                tick.bid_size,
                tick.ask_size
            )
            cursor.execute(query, values)
            if time.time() >= end_time:
```

```
            break
        self.stop_streaming_data(request_id)
```

4. In the `__init__` method of the `IBApp` class, add the following line under the calls to `IBWrapper` and `IBClient`:

```
self.create_table()
```

The result of the changes is the following code in `IBApp`:

```
class IBApp(IBWrapper, IBClient):
    def __init__(self, ip, port, client_id):
        IBWrapper.__init__(self)
        IBClient.__init__(self, wrapper=self)
        self.create_table()
        self.connect(ip, port, client_id)
        thread = threading.Thread(target=self.run, daemon=True)
        thread.start()
        time.sleep(2)
    @property
    def connection(self):
        return sqlite3.connect("tick_data.sqlite",
            isolation_level=None)
    def create_table(self):
        cursor = self.connection.cursor()
        cursor.execute("""
            CREATE TABLE IF NOT EXISTS bid_ask_data (
                timestamp datetime, symbol string,
                bid_price real, ask_price real,
                bid_size integer, ask_size integer)""")
    def stream_to_sqlite(self, request_id, contract,
        run_for_in_seconds=23400):
            cursor = self.connection.cursor()
            end_time = time.time() + run_for_in_seconds + 10
        for tick in self.get_streaming_data(request_id, contract):
            query = """INSERT INTO bid_ask_data (
                timestamp, symbol, bid_price,
                ask_price, bid_size, ask_size) VALUES (
                    ?, ?, ?, ?, ?, ?)"""
            values = (
```

```
                tick.timestamp_.strftime("%Y-%m-%d %H:%M:%S"),
                contract.symbol,
                tick.bid_price, tick.ask_price,
                tick.bid_size, tick.ask_size
            )
            cursor.execute(query, values)
            if time.time() >= end_time:
                break
            self.stop_streaming_data(request_id)
```

How it works...

We first create a class property called `connection`, which establishes and returns a connection to our SQLite database. The `@property` decorator is used to create a property, allowing the `connection` method to be accessed like an attribute without the need to call it as a method.

When the `connection` property is accessed, it creates a connection to an SQLite database file named `tick_data.sqlite`. The `isolation_level=None` parameter sets the transaction isolation level to `None`, which means that the **autocommit** mode is enabled. In **autocommit** mode, changes to the database are committed immediately after each statement, without needing to explicitly call `commit` after each database operation.

The `create_table` method creates a database table named `bid_ask_data`. When this method is called, it first establishes a database cursor, which is an intermediary for executing database commands. The code then executes a `create` SQL command using the `execute` method, which creates the table if it does not exist. When `IBApp` is initialized, we call `self.create_table`, which creates the table if it does not exist.

The `stream_to_sqlite` method stores the tick data in our SQLite database for a specified duration. It starts by creating a database cursor from the established SQLite connection. The method calculates an `end_time` value by adding the specified `run_for_in_seconds` duration (defaulting to 23,400 seconds, or 6.5 hours) to the current time, plus an additional 10 second buffer which makes up for the time we wait for the tick stream to start. It then enters a loop, retrieving streaming data from the `get_streaming_data` method, which yields `Tick` objects containing market data for the given `request_id` and `contract`. For each tick received, the method constructs a SQL insert query to add the tick data into the `bid_ask_data` table, formatting the timestamp and including relevant data such as the contract's symbol, bid price, ask price, bid size, and ask size. The loop continues until the current time exceeds the calculated `end_time`, at which point it breaks, limiting the data streaming to the specified duration.

There's more...

We now have the code built to store streaming tick data. Add the following code block under the definitions of the contracts:

```
es = future("ES", "CME", "202312")
app.stream_to_sqlite(99, es, run_for_in_seconds=30)
```

The result of the changes is the following code in `app.py`:

```
<snip>
if __name__ == "__main__":
    app = IBApp("127.0.0.1", 7497, client_id=10)
    es = future("ES", "CME", "202312")
    app.stream_to_sqlite(99, es, run_for_in_seconds=30)
    app.disconnect()
```

We can inspect the data stored in our SQLite database with DB Browser for SQLite. It's a free tool that gives us a graphical interface to inspect data in SQLite databases. You can download it here: https://sqlitebrowser.org/. Once installed, open up the `tick_data.sqlite` file and navigate to the **Browse Data** tab and you'll see the tick data.

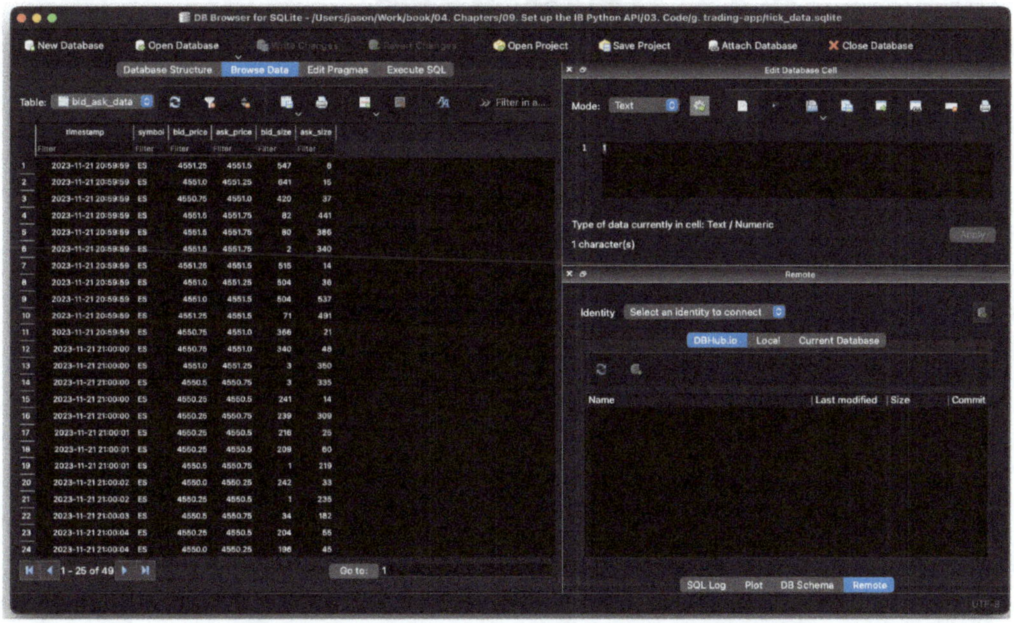

Figure 12.12: Browsing bid ask tick data in our SQLite database

See also

SQLite is a powerful, highly effective solution for local data storage. If you're interested in more details about the `Connection` and `Cursor` objects, you can check the following URLs:

- Documentation for the SQLite `connect` method: `https://docs.python.org/3/library/sqlite3.html#sqlite3.connect`
- Documentation for the SQLite `Cursor` object: `https://docs.python.org/3/library/sqlite3.html#cursor-objects`

Join our community on Discord

Join our community's Discord space for discussions with the authors and other readers:
`https://discord.gg/G4YmB6DQvf`

13

Manage Orders, Positions, and Portfolios with the IB API

In algorithmic trading, efficient management of orders, positions, and portfolio data is critical. Luckily for us, we can do it all using Python. Managing orders encompasses a range of activities, including executing new trades, canceling existing orders, and updating orders to adapt to changing market conditions or shifts in trading strategies. Managing positions involves monitoring and analyzing live position data to track **profit and loss** (**PnL**) in real time. This immediate insight into the performance of individual trades enables traders to make informed decisions on whether to hold, sell, or adjust positions. Further, real-time (or near real-time) portfolio data can generate real-time (or near real-time) risk statistics to improve overall risk management. Portfolio data management involves a comprehensive analysis of the portfolio to assess its performance, understand risk exposure, and make strategic adjustments for optimizing returns. This is especially true when trading stocks on margin or futures, where there is a financial cost and opportunity cost in holding losing positions.

As we've seen, the IB API uses a consistent request-callback pattern that can be used in several aspects of our trading app, including order management, position management, and accessing portfolio details. This pattern allows for the initiation of a request, such as placing or modifying an order, retrieving current position data, or gathering portfolio information, followed by a callback function that handles the response. We'll use this pattern throughout the chapter.

By the end of this chapter, we'll be able to submit and modify orders to IB through Python, obtain key portfolio details including information on liquidity, margin requirements, and open positions, and compute our portfolio's profit or loss.

In this chapter, we present the following recipes:

- Executing orders with the IB API
- Managing orders once they're placed
- Getting details about your portfolio
- Inspecting positions and position details
- Computing portfolio profit and loss

Executing orders with the IB API

In *Chapter 12, Set Up the Interactive Brokers Python API*, we created `contract` and `order` objects. Using these, we can use the IB API to execute trades. But before we can execute trades, we have to understand the concept of the next order ID.

The next order ID (`nextValidOrderId`) is a unique identifier for each order. Since up to 32 instances of a trading app can run in parallel, this identifier makes sure individual orders are traceable within the trading system. `nextValidOrderId` is used to preserve order integrity and prevent overlap between multiple orders submitted simultaneously or in rapid succession. When our trading app connects to the IB API, it receives an integer variable called `nextValidOrderId` from the server that is unique to each client connection to TWS. This ID must be used for the first order submission. Subsequently, we are responsible for incrementing this identifier for each new order.

Getting ready

We assume you've created the `client.py` and `wrapper.py` files in the `trading-app` directory. If not, do it now.

How to do it...

First, we'll add the code to deal with the integer `nextValidOrderId` in the `wrapper.py` file and print out the details of the order's execution:

1. Add an instance variable, `nextValidOrderId`, in the `__init__` method of our `IBWrapper` class:

```
self.nextValidOrderId = None
```

2. Add an implementation of the `nextValidId` method, overriding the method from the inherited `EWrapper` class in our `IBWrapper` class:

```
def nextValidId(self, order_id):
    super().nextValidId(order_id)
    self.nextValidOrderId = order_id
```

3. Add an implementation of the `orderStatus` method, overriding the method from the inherited `EWrapper` class:

```
def orderStatus(
    self,
    order_id,
    status,
    filled,
    remaining,
    avg_fill_price,
    perm_id,
    parent_id,
    last_fill_price,
    client_id,
    why_held,
    mkt_cap_price,
):
    print(
        "orderStatus - orderid:",
        order_id,
        "status:",
        status,
        "filled",
        filled,
        "remaining",
        remaining,
        "lastFillPrice",
        last_fill_price,
    )
```

4. Add an implementation of the openOrder method, overriding the method from the inherited EWrapper class:

```
def openOrder(self, order_id, contract, order,
    order_state):
        print(
            "openOrder id:",
            order_id,
            contract.symbol,
            contract.secType,
            "@",
            contract.exchange,
            ":",
            order.action,
            order.orderType,
            order.totalQuantity,
            order_state.status,
        )
```

5. Add an implementation of the exectDetails method, overriding the method from the inherited EWrapper class:

```
def execDetails(self, request_id, contract,execution):
    print(
        "Order Executed: ",
        request_id,
        contract.symbol,
        contract.secType,
        contract.currency,
        execution.execId,
        execution.orderId,
        execution.shares,
        execution.lastLiquidity,
    )
```

6. Now, open the `client.py` file. Here, we'll add a custom method, `send_order`, under the `__init__` method that accepts a `contract` object and `order` object, increments the `nextValidOrderId` variable, and sends the order to the exchange:

```
def send_order(self, contract, order):
    order_id = self.wrapper.nextValidOrderId
    self.placeOrder(orderId=order_id,
        contract=contract, order=order)
    self.reqIds(-1)
    return order_id
```

The result of the changes is the following code in the `client.py` file:

```
import time
import pandas as pd
from utils import Tick, TRADE_BAR_PROPERTIES
from ibapi.client import EClient
class IBClient(EClient):
    def __init__(self, wrapper):
        EClient.__init__(self, wrapper)
    def send_order(self, contract, order):
        order_id = self.wrapper.nextValidOrderId
        self.placeOrder(orderId=order_id,
            contract=contract, order=order)
        self.reqIds(-1)
        return order_id
    <snip>
```

How it works...

First, we'll cover the overridden methods in the `IBWrapper` class.

When orders are submitted through the `placeOrder` method from the `IBClient` class, `orderStatus`, `openOrder`, `execDetails` from the `IBWrapper` class are invoked depending on the life cycle of the order. They accomplish the following:

- `orderStatus` receives updates about the status of submitted orders
- `openOrder` provides information about orders that have been submitted but not fully executed
- `execDetails` provides detailed information about the execution of an order

Each of these callbacks accepts parameters that are passed from the IB API. In this recipe, we just print out the information. In more sophisticated applications, we can use the events to trigger risk analysis, portfolio updates, or alerts.

When `send_order` is called, it takes a `contract` object and an `order` object. The `contract` object represents the financial instrument to be ordered, while the `order` object contains the details of the order. The first line within the method, `order_id = self.wrapper.nextValidOrderId`, retrieves the next valid order ID from the `IBWrapper` object. The next line, `self.placeOrder(orderId=order_id, contract=contract, order=order)`, is a call to the `placeOrder` method of the IB API. This method is responsible for placing the order with the given `order_id`, `contract`, and `order` details on the IB server. The subsequent call, `reqIds(-1)`, is a request to the server to increment the internal counter for the next valid order ID.

There's more...

We now have everything in place to send orders to IB through the API using Python. To send an order for execution, import our `order` type and the `BUY` constant at the top of the `app.py` file:

```
from order import limit, BUY
```

Then, add the following code after the line that defines the trading app:

```
limit_order = limit(BUY, 100, 190.00)
app.send_order(aapl, limit_order)
```

This uses the `contract` object we set up in *Creating a Contract object with the IB API* and the `order` object we set up in *Creating an Order object with the IB API* recipes from *Chapter 12*.

The result of the changes is the following code in the `app.py` file:

```
import threading
import time
import sqlite3
from wrapper import IBWrapper
from client import IBClient
from contract import stock, future, option
from order import limit, BUY
class IBApp(IBWrapper, IBClient):
    def __init__(self, ip, port, client_id):
        IBWrapper.__init__(self)
```

```
        IBClient.__init__(self, wrapper=self)
        self.create_table()
        self.connect(ip, port, client_id)
        thread = threading.Thread(target=self.run, daemon=True)
        thread.start()
        time.sleep(2)
    <snip>
if __name__ == "__main__":
    app = IBApp("127.0.0.1", 7497, client_id=11)
    aapl = stock("AAPL", "SMART", "USD")
    gbl = future("GBL", "EUREX", "202403")
    pltr = option("PLTR", "BOX", "20240315", 20, "C")
    limit_order = limit(BUY, 100, 190.00)
    app.send_order(aapl, limit_order)
    time.sleep(30)
    app.disconnect()
```

After running this code, you will see a series of messages in the terminal. These messages are a result of the `orderStatus`, `openOrder`, and `execDetails` callbacks being called after the `placeOrder` method was invoked:

```
openOrder id: 9 AAPL STK @ SMART : BUY LMT 100 PreSubmitted
orderStatus - orderid: 9 status: PreSubmitted filled 0 remaining 100 lastFillPrice 0.0
Order Executed:  -1 AAPL STK USD 0000e0d5.6554a46e.01.01 9 100 2
openOrder id: 9 AAPL STK @ SMART : BUY LMT 100 Filled
orderStatus - orderid: 9 status: Filled filled 100 remaining 0 lastFillPrice 188.66
openOrder id: 9 AAPL STK @ SMART : BUY LMT 100 Filled
orderStatus - orderid: 9 status: Filled filled 100 remaining 0 lastFillPrice 188.66
```

Figure 13.1: Message indicating the limit order was executed

Note

Important

In this example, we enter a buy limit order at a price above the current ask, which, at the time of writing, was $188.66. This means that even though the order is a limit order, it will be executed immediately. This is done only for demonstration and testing purposes. In most scenarios, we'd enter a limit order below the best bid to wait for our desired price.

See also

Read more about modifying orders here: `https://interactivebrokers.github.io/tws-api/modifying_orders.html`.

Getting details about your portfolio

The IB API offers a comprehensive snapshot of portfolio data, returning 157 different portfolio values through a single API call. This data provides a detailed view of our portfolios, encompassing a wide range of metrics and data points. Account values delivered via `updateAccountValue` can be classified in the following way:

- **Commodities**: Suffixed by `-C`
- **Securities**: Suffixed by `-S`
- **Totals**: No suffix

In this recipe, we'll build the code to get those data points.

Getting ready

We assume you've created the `client.py`, `wrapper.py`, and `app.py` files in the `trading-app` directory. If not, do it now.

How to do it...

The first step is to incorporate the account number into our `IBApp` class. While an account number is optional for requesting account-level data in a single account structure, it's best practice to specify it in the case of multiple accounts. Then, we'll add the callback to the `IBWrapper` class and add the request method to the `IBClient` class:

1. Modify the `__init__` method of our `IBApp` class by adding `account` as an argument:

```
def __init__(self, ip, port, client_id, account):
```

2. Add the following dictionary to the `__ini__` method in the `IBWrapper` class to store our account details:

```
self.account_values = {}
```

3. Then, add the callback function that responds to the TWS messages:

```
def updateAccountValue(self, key, val, currency, account):
    try:
```

```
            val_ = float(val)
        except:
            val_ = val
        self.account_values[key] = (val_, currency)
```

The result of the changes is the following code in the `wrapper.py` file:

```
import threading
from ibapi.wrapper import EWrapper
class IBWrapper(EWrapper):
    def __init__(self):
        EWrapper.__init__(self)
        self.nextValidOrderId = None
        self.historical_data = {}
        self.market_data = {}
        self.streaming_data = {}
        self.stream_event = threading.Event()
        self.account_values = {}
    <snip>
    def updateAccountValue(self, key, val, currency, account):
        try:
            val_ = float(val)
        except:
            val_ = val
        self.account_values[key] = (val_, currency)
```

4. At the end of the `IBClient` class, add the following method:

```
def get_account_values(self, key=None):
    self.reqAccountUpdates(True, self.account)
    time.sleep(2)
    if key:
        return self.account_values[key]
    return self.account_values
```

How it works...

By now, we're settling into a common pattern: request something to happen in the `IBClient` class and add the results of the call to a dictionary in the `IBWrapper` class. The `updateAccountValue` method is a callback that accepts a key (representing a specific account attribute), a value, a currency, and an account identifier, then stores the value and currency as a tuple in the `account_values` dictionary, keyed by the provided attribute key.

The `get_account_values` method requests account updates, `reqAccountUpdates`, then pauses execution for two seconds to allow time for the account data to be updated. If a specific key is provided, the method returns the value associated with that key from the `account_values` dictionary. If no key is specified, it returns the entire `account_values` dictionary, providing a snapshot of all account-related values.

The IB API returns 157 different account values. Some of the more common ones are as follows:

- `AvailableFunds`
- `BuyingPower`
- `CashBalance`
- `Currency`
- `EquityWithLoanValue`
- `FullAvailableFunds`
- `NetLiquidation`
- `RealizedPnL`
- `TotalCashBalance`
- `UnrealizedPnL`

There's more...

Let's get the net liquidation value of the account. In the `app.py` file, replace the code after the `IBApp` class with the following:

```
if __name__ == "__main__":
    app = IBApp("127.0.0.1", 7497, client_id=10,
    account="DU7129120")
    account_values = app.get_account_values()
    net_liquidation = app.get_account_values("NetLiquidation")
    app.disconnect()
```

The result is the `account_values` dictionary, which contains all 157 account values. Here's a sample:

```
{
    'AccountReady': ('true', ''),
    'AccountType': ('INDIVIDUAL', ''),
    'AccruedCash': (0.0, 'BASE'),
    'AccruedCash-C': (0.0, 'USD'),
    'AccruedCash-P': (0.0, 'USD'),
    'AccruedCash-S': (0.0, 'USD'),
    'AccruedDividend': (0.0, 'USD'),
    'AccruedDividend-C': (0.0, 'USD'),
    'AccruedDividend-P': (0.0, 'USD'),
    'AccruedDividend-S': (0.0, 'USD'),
    'AvailableFunds': (3195.34, 'USD'),
    'AvailableFunds-C': (0.0, 'USD'),
    'AvailableFunds-P': (0.0, 'USD'),
    'AvailableFunds-S': (3195.34, 'USD'),
    ...
    'SMA': (2312528.09, 'USD'),
    'SMA-S': (2312528.09, 'USD'),
    'SegmentTitle-C': ('US Commodities', ''),
    'SegmentTitle-P': ('Crypto at Paxos', ''),
    'SegmentTitle-S': ('US Securities', ''),
    'StockMarketValue': (-769.01, 'BASE'),
    'TBillValue': (0.0, 'BASE'),
    'TBondValue': (0.0, 'BASE'),
    'TotalCashBalance': (5175.9625, 'BASE'),
    'TotalCashValue': (5175.96, 'USD'),
    'TotalCashValue-C': (0.0, 'USD'),
    'TotalCashValue-P': (0.0, 'USD'),
    'TotalCashValue-S': (5175.96, 'USD'),
    'TotalDebitCardPendingCharges': (0.0, 'USD'),
    'TotalDebitCardPendingCharges-C': (0.0, 'USD'),
    'TotalDebitCardPendingCharges-P': (0.0, 'USD'),
    'TotalDebitCardPendingCharges-S': (0.0, 'USD'),
    'TradingType-S': ('STKNOPT', ''),
    'UnrealizedPnL': (-12.9, 'BASE'),
    'WarrantValue': (0.0, 'BASE'),
    'WhatIfPMEnabled': ('true', '')
}
```

Figure 13.2: A sample of the data provided by get_account_values

The result is the `net_liquidation` tuple, which contains the account's net liquidation value and the currency the value is denominated in. Here's what it looks like:

```
net_liquidation
(4408.76, 'USD')
```

Figure 13.3: Net liquidation value of the account

See also

For a complete list of account values and their descriptions, see the following URL: `https://interactivebrokers.github.io/tws-api/interfaceIBApi_1_1EWrapper.html#ae15a34084d9f26f279abd0bdeab1b9b5`

Inspecting positions and position details

To get position-level details from the IB API, including data such as position size, market price, value, average cost, and PnL, we can utilize specific API calls. These calls request detailed information for each position held in an account, with the API responding with the requested data for each position. This enables us to have a comprehensive view of our holdings. In this recipe, we introduce how to get the position data. In the next chapter, we'll make use of it to build a trading strategy.

Getting ready

We assume you've created the `client.py`, `wrapper.py`, and `app.py` files in the `trading-app` directory. If not, do it now.

How to do it...

In the previous recipe, *Getting details about your portfolio*, we used the `reqAccountUpdates` request method in the `IBClient` class to request account details. Calling `reqAccountUpdates` triggers two callbacks. The first is `updateAccountValue`, which we overrode in the `IBWrapper` method. This method returns details about the account. `reqAccountUpdates` also triggers the `updatePortfolio` callback, which returns details about the positions in the account. We'll use the `updatePortfolio` method to get account details using the same `reqAccountUpdates` method:

1. Add a dictionary to the end of the `__init__` method in the `IBWrapper` class to store position details:

```
self.positions = {}
```

2. Add the following method to the end of the `IBWrapper` class:

```
def updatePortfolio(
    self,
    contract,
    position,
    market_price,
```

```
        market_value,
        average_cost,
        unrealized_pnl,
        realized_pnl,
        account_name
    ):
        portfolio_data = {
            "contract": contract,
            "symbol": contract.symbol,
            "position": position,
            "market_price": market_price,
            "market_value": market_value,
            "average_cost": average_cost,
            "unrealized_pnl": unrealized_pnl,
            "realized_pnl": realized_pnl,
        }

        self.positions[contract.symbol] = portfolio_data
```

The result of the changes is the following code in the `wrapper.py` file:

```
<snip>
class IBWrapper(EWrapper):
    def __init__(self):
        EWrapper.__init__(self)
        self.nextValidOrderId = None
        self.historical_data = {}
        self.streaming_data = {}
        self.stream_event = threading.Event()
        self.account_values = {}
        self.positions = {}
    <snip>
    def updatePortfolio(
        self,
        contract,
        position,
        market_price,
        market_value,
        average_cost,
        unrealized_pnl,
        realized_pnl,
```

```
            account_name
        ):
            portfolio_data = {
                "contract": contract,
                "symbol": contract.symbol,
                "position": position,
                "market_price": market_price,
                "market_value": market_value,
                "average_cost": average_cost,
                "unrealized_pnl": unrealized_pnl,
                "realized_pnl": realized_pnl,
            }
            self.positions[contract.symbol] = portfolio_data
```

3. Now, add the following method to the end of the `IBClient` class:

```
def get_positions(self):
    self.reqAccountUpdates(True, self.account)
    time.sleep(2)
    return self.positions
```

How it works...

When `reqAccountUpdates` is called, the `updatePortfolio` callback is triggered for every position in the account. TWS passes details about the position to the method, which are captured in the `positions` dictionary and keyed by the contract's symbol.

The `get_positions` method triggers the callback through the `reqAccountsUpdates` method, waits two seconds, and returns the dictionary containing the positions.

There's more...

To get the current positions in the account, add the following code to the end of the `app.py` file:

```
positions = app.get_positions()
```

The result is a dictionary with position details:

```
{'AAPL': {'contract': 4966399376: 265598,AAPL,STK,,0,0,,,NASDAQ,USD,AAPL,NMS,False,,,,combo:,
  'symbol': 'AAPL',
  'position': Decimal('10'),
  'market_price': 191.30000305,
  'market_value': 1913.0,
  'average_cost': 191.66,
  'unrealized_pnl': -3.6,
  'realized_pnl': 0.0},
 'NVDA': {'contract': 4966396112: 4815747,NVDA,STK,,0,0,,,NASDAQ,USD,NVDA,NMS,False,,,,combo:,
  'symbol': 'NVDA',
  'position': Decimal('-10'),
  'market_price': 487.3200073,
  'market_value': -4873.2,
  'average_cost': 487.27595595,
  'unrealized_pnl': -0.44,
  'realized_pnl': 0.0}}
```

Figure 13.4: Position details of the account

Computing portfolio profit and loss

To get portfolio PnL details from the IB API, we can utilize specific API calls. These calls request the aggregate daily profit or loss, total unrealized profit or loss, and total realized PnL, with the API responding with the requested data. GettingPnL allows us to compute periodic portfolio returns, which, in turn, unlock a suite of risk metrics based on portfolio returns. We'll make use of the dollar profit or loss to compute periodic portfolio returns in the next chapter. In this recipe, we focus on requesting and receiving the portfolio profit or loss.

Getting ready

We assume you've created the `client.py`, `wrapper.py`, and `app.py` files in the `trading-app` directory. If not, do it now.

How to do it...

We'll follow the same pattern in this recipe as in the last few:

1. Add a dictionary to the end of the `__init__` method in the `IBWrapper` class to store position details:

```
self.account_pnl = {}
```

2. Add the following method to the end of the `IBWrapper` class:

```
def pnl(self, request_id, daily_pnl, unrealized_pnl,
    realized_pnL):
        pnl_data = {
            "daily_pnl": daily_pnl,
            "unrealized_pnl": unrealized_pnl,
            "realized_pnl": realized_pnl
        }
    self.account_pnl[request_id] = pnl_data
```

The result of the changes is the following code in the `wrapper.py` file:

```
<snip>
class IBWrapper(EWrapper):
    def __init__(self):
        EWrapper.__init__(self)
        self.nextValidOrderId = None
        self.historical_data = {}
        self.streaming_data = {}
        self.stream_event = threading.Event()
        self.account_values = {}
        self.positions = {}
        self.account_pnl = {}
    def pnl(self, request_id, daily_pnl,
        unrealized_pnl, realized_pnl):
            pnl_data = {
                "daily_pnl": daily_pnl,
                "unrealized_pnl": unrealized_pnl,
                "realized_pnl": realized_pnl
            }
            self.account_pnl[request_id] = pnl_data
    <snip>
```

3. Now, add the following method to the end of the `IBClient` class:

```
def get_pnl(self, request_id):
    self.reqPnL(request_id, self.account, "")
    time.sleep(2)
    return self.account_pnl
```

How it works...

The `pnl` method is a callback function to handle PnL data. When called, it receives an integer `request_id` along with three types of PnL data: `daily_pnl`, `unrealized_pnl`, and `realized_pnl`. The method then constructs a `pnl_data` dictionary with these values and stores it in the `account_pnl` dictionary, keyed by `request_id`, effectively updating the account's PnL information associated with that specific request.

The `get_pnl` method requests PnL data for a specific account. It calls `reqPnL` to send a request to the IB API for PnL information associated with the given `request_id` and account, then pauses for two seconds to allow time for the data to be received and processed before returning the updated PnL data stored in `account_pnl`. Unrealized profit or loss is the potential financial gain or loss on an investment that has not yet been sold for cash. Realized profit or loss is the gain or loss on the asset once it's been sold.

There's more...

At the bottom of the `app.py` file, add the following code to get the account's PnL:

```
pnl = app.get_pnl(request_id=99)
```

The result is a dictionary with the daily, unrealized, and realized PnL:

```
{99: {'daily_pnl': 5.859764794922285,
  'unrealized_pnl': 5.859724294922216,
  'realized_pnL': 0.0}}
```

Figure 13.5: The result of calling get_pnl is a dictionary with the account PnL

See also

The IB API can retrieve PnL data from two different sources: the TWS Account window and the TWS Portfolio window. These sources have different update times, which may result in differing portfolio PnL values. The method described in this recipe requests PnL data from the TWS Portfolio window with a reset schedule specified in the global configuration.

For more details on how portfolio PnL is calculated, see the following URL: `https://interactivebrokers.github.io/tws-api/pnl.html`

Get this book's PDF version and more

Scan the QR code (or go to `packtpub.com/unlock`). Search for this book by name, confirm the edition, and then follow the steps on the page.

UNLOCK NOW

Note: Keep your invoice handy. Purchases made directly from Packt don't require an invoice.

14

Deploy Strategies to a Live Environment

In *Chapter 12, Set Up the Interactive Brokers Python API*, and *Chapter 13, Manage Orders, Positions, and Portfolios with the IB API*, we set the stage to begin deploying low frequency algorithmic trading strategies into a live (or paper trading) environment. High frequency strategies typically focus on streaming tick data, depth of book data, and latency considerations, which are out of the scope of this book. Before we get there, we need two more critical pieces of the algorithmic trading puzzle: risk and performance metrics and more sophisticated order strategies that allow us to build and rebalance asset portfolios. For risk and performance metrics, we will introduce the **Empyrical Reloaded** library, which generates statistics based on portfolio returns. `empyrical-reloaded` is the library that provides the performance and risk analytics behind **Pyfolio Reloaded**, which we learned about in *Chapter 11, Assess Backtest Risk and Performance Metrics with Pyfolio*. In this chapter, we'll use `empyrical-reloaded` to calculate key performance indicators such as the Sharpe ratio, Sortino ratio, and the maximum drawdown, among others, using real-time portfolio return data. To allow us to compute real-time return data while executing trades or other code in our trading app, we'll learn how to run code asynchronously on a thread.

In addition to calculating risk and performance metrics, we will finalize our position management code by introducing methods to submit orders based on a target number of contracts, monetary value, or percentage allocation. This extended functionality unlocks portfolio-based strategies as opposed to only single-asset strategies. Finally, we will introduce three algorithmic trading strategies that you can deploy right away: a monthly factor-based strategy using the `zipline-reloaded` pipeline API that we learned about in *Chapter 9, Event-Based Backtesting Factor Portfolios with Zipline Reloaded*, an options combo strategy, and an intraday multi-asset mean-reversion strategy. These strategies take advantage of the code we've built throughout this book.

This chapter contains the following recipes:

- Calculating real-time key performance and risk indicators
- Sending orders based on portfolio targets
- Deploying a monthly factor portfolio strategy
- Deploying an options combo strategy
- Deploying an intraday multi-asset mean reversion strategy

Calculating real-time key performance and risk indicators

Real-time performance and risk metrics are important for maintaining robust trading strategies. They allow us to compare real-life performance to the performance of our backtests. They provide immediate feedback on the effectiveness of our trading algorithms and let us make adjustments in response to market volatility or unexpected events. By continuously monitoring risk metrics such as drawdowns, volatility, and value at risk, we can effectively manage exposure and mitigate potential losses. Most professional algorithmic traders spend their time analyzing and explaining deviations from the performance that they expect in their backtests to the performance that they observe during live trading. This recipe will introduce the tools we need to do the same.

Getting ready

We'll use `empyrical-reloaded` to compute performance and risk statistics. To install it, use `pip`:

```
pip install empyrical-reloaded
```

At the top of `app.py`, import `Empyrical Reloaded`:

```
import empyrical as ep
```

To calculate real-time performance and risk indicators, we need periodic portfolio returns. Unfortunately, the IB API does not provide a way to retrieve portfolio returns, so we'll need to build our own method. We'll do this by periodically requesting account **profit and loss** (**PnL**) and then using it to compute returns. To allow the rest of our trading app to run independently of the PnL calculations, we'll run the method on its own thread.

Add a new instance variable to `wrapper.py`, which we'll use to capture account PnL. At the end of the `__init__` method in the `IBWrapper` class, add the following:

```
self.portfolio_returns = None
```

Add a method to `client.py` that continuously requests account PnL from the `get_pnl` method we built in *Chapter 11*:

```
def get_streaming_pnl(
    self, request_id, interval=60,  pnl_type="unrealized_pnl"
):
    interval = max(interval, 5) - 2
    while True:
        pnl = self.get_pnl(request_id=request_id)
        yield {"date": pd.Timestamp.now(),
                "pnl": pnl[request_id].get(pnl_type)}
        time.sleep(interval)
```

The method first ensures that the interval between data retrievals is at least three seconds. This accounts for the three-second update time from IB and the two-second wait time in `get_pnl`. In an infinite loop, it retrieves the PnL data and then yields a dictionary containing the current timestamp and the specified type of PnL before pausing for the defined interval duration.

Add a method to stream portfolio PnL and compute the associated returns:

```
def get_streaming_returns(self, request_id, interval, pnl_type):
    returns = pd.Series(dtype=float)
    for snapshot in self.get_streaming_pnl(
        request_id=request_id,
        interval=interval,
        pnl_type=pnl_type
    ):
        returns.loc[snapshot["date"]] = snapshot["pnl"]
        if len(returns) > 1:
            self.portfolio_returns = (
                returns
                .pct_change()
                .dropna()
            )
```

The get_streaming_returns method calculates the periodic PnL. It initializes a pandas Series to store PnL values, then iterates over PnL data snapshots obtained from get_streaming_pnl, adding each PnL value to the returns Series indexed by the snapshot's timestamp. If the Series has more than one entry, it calculates the percentage change in PnL, updating the portfolio_returns attribute with these calculated returns after dropping the NaN values.

In wrapper.py, add the following instance variable at the end of the __init__ method:

```
self.portfolio_returns = None
```

In app.py, update the __init__ method so it resembles the following:

```
def __init__(
    self, ip, port, client_id, account, interval=5):
    IBWrapper.__init__(self)
    IBClient.__init__(self, wrapper=self)
    self.account = account
    self.create_table()
    self.connect(ip, port, client_id)
    threading.Thread(
        target=self.run, daemon=True).start()
    time.sleep(2)
    threading.Thread(
        target=self.get_streaming_returns,
        args=(99, interval, "unrealized_pnl"),
        daemon=True
    ).start()
```

Upon instantiation of our IBApp class, we start two separate threads: one to continuously run the main event loop of the API client and another to stream unrealized PnL returns every five seconds, both beginning their execution after a two-second pause to ensure that the connection is established. This allows us to continue to access the periodic portfolio returns while executing other code.

How to do it...

We'll implement six methods (decorated as properties) to compute performance and risk metrics in our IBApp class using empyrical-reloaded. You should add these methods after the `stream_to_sql` method we added in *Chapter 13, Manage Orders, Positions, and Portfolios with the IB API*.

1. Add a method to compute cumulative returns:

```
@property
def cumulative_returns(self):
    return ep.cum_returns(self.portfolio_returns, 1)
```

2. Add a method to compute the maximum drawdown:

```
@property
def max_drawdown(self):
    return ep.max_drawdown(self.portfolio_returns)
```

3. Add a method to compute the volatility of returns:

```
@property
def volatility(self):
    return self.portfolio_returns.std(ddof=1) * np.sqrt(252)
```

4. Add a method to compute the Omega ratio:

```
@property
def omega_ratio(self):
    return ep.omega_ratio(self.portfolio_returns, annualization=1)
```

5. Add a method to compute the Sharpe ratio:

```
@property
def sharpe_ratio(self): excess_returns = (self.portfolio_returns -
self.risk_free_rate) / 252 return excess_returns.mean() /
excess_returns.std(ddof=1) * np.sqrt(252) /
self.portfolio_returns.std(ddof=1)
```

6. Add a method to compute the percentage and dollar conditional value at risk:

```
@property
def cvar(self):
    net_liquidation = self.get_account_values("NetLiquidation")[0]
```

```
        cvar_ = ep.conditional_value_at_risk(self.portfolio_returns)
        return (cvar_, cvar_ * net_liquidation)
```

How it works...

We'll cover the details of each method in the following sub-sections.

Cumulative returns

To get the cumulative returns of our portfolio, we add the following in the `app.py` file after defining our trading app:

```
app.cumulative_returns
```

The `cumulative_returns` method computes the cumulative returns of our portfolio returns. The first argument, `returns`, is a pandas Series representing the periodic returns of our portfolio. The second argument, 1, specifies the starting value for the cumulative returns calculation. This function effectively calculates the compounded return at each point in time, assuming that the initial investment value is 1. We can use this method to generate the following intraday equity curve by plotting the data from the resulting Series.

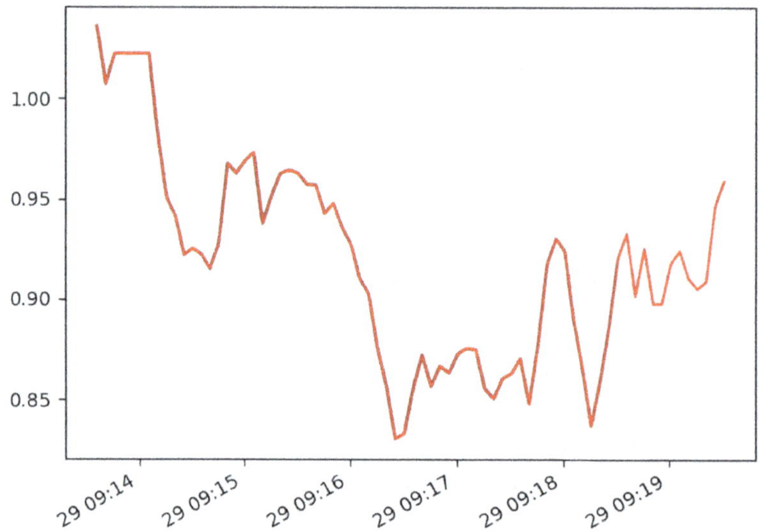

Figure 14.1: An intraday equity curve computed every five seconds based on cumulative returns

Max drawdown

To get the max drawdown of our portfolio, we add the following in the `app.py` file after defining our trading app:

```
app.max_drawdown
```

The `max_drawdown` method computes the maximum drawdown of our portfolio. The maximum drawdown is calculated by determining the largest decrease in value from a portfolio's peak to its lowest point before it reaches a new peak. It's typically expressed as a negative percentage. This metric is crucial in risk management and performance evaluation in algorithmic trading, as it provides insight into the potential downside risk of an investment strategy.

Volatility

To get the volatility of our portfolio, we add the following in the `app.py` file after defining our trading app:

```
app.volatility
```

The `volatility` method calculates the sample standard deviation of portfolio returns. This measure provides insight into the volatility or risk associated with the portfolio over the time period covered by the data. By setting `ddof` to `1`, the calculation adjusts for bias in the standard deviation estimate, making it more accurate for a sample (such as a subset of returns over a specific period) rather than the entire population of returns.

> Note
>
> **Important**
>
> We don't use the `empyrical-reloaded` method in this example because it assumes daily returns. When we compute volatility using `empyrical-reloaded`, it annualizes the volatility metric, which is not appropriate for intraday values.

Omega ratio

To get the Omega ratio of our portfolio, we add the following in the `app.py` file after defining our trading app:

```
app.omega_ratio
```

The `omega_ratio` method calculates the Omega ratio for our portfolio returns. The Omega ratio is a risk-adjusted return measure of an investment asset, portfolio, or strategy, comparing the probability of achieving a threshold return level to the probability of falling below it. It's calculated by dividing the sum of excess returns above a threshold (0 in our case) by the absolute value of the sum of returns below that threshold, where excess returns are annualized if an `annualization` factor is provided (which it is not in our case). In trading, this ratio is particularly useful as it provides a more comprehensive view of the risk-reward tradeoff than traditional measures such as the Sharpe ratio, especially in portfolios with non-normal return distributions.

Sharpe ratio

To get the Sharpe ratio of our portfolio, we add the following in the `app.py` file after defining our trading app:

```
app.sharpe_ratio
```

The `sharpe_ratio` method computes the Sharpe ratio for our portfolio returns. Typically, the `sharpe_ratio` method is computed by first calculating the difference between the returns of the portfolio and the risk-free rate. This excess return is then annualized by multiplying it by the square root of the `annualization` parameter. The annualized excess return is then divided by the standard deviation of the portfolio's returns, which is a measure of the portfolio's risk. Since we are using intraday returns, we won't use `empyrical-reloaded` because it assumes daily returns.

Conditional value at risk

To get the conditional value at risk of our portfolio, we add the following in the `app.py` file after defining our trading app:

```
app.cvar
```

The **Conditional Value at Risk** (**CVaR**), also known as the **Expected Shortfall** (**ES**), is a risk assessment metric that estimates the expected loss in our portfolio under extreme market conditions, focusing on the tail end of the distribution of potential losses. The method first retrieves the `NetLiquidation` value of the account, which represents the total value of the portfolio if all positions were liquidated at current market prices. It then calculates the CVaR of the account's returns using `empyrical-reloaded`'s `conditional_value_at_risk` function, which computes CVaR as the average of the worst-performing returns (those in the tail of the distribution) below a 5% percentile. The method returns two values: the CVaR as a percentage and the CVaR in terms of the actual monetary value, calculated by multiplying the CVaR percentage by the portfolio's net liquidation value.

There's more...

There are more than 40 risk and performance metrics available in `Empyrcal Reloaded`, including rolling metrics and those that compare portfolio returns to a benchmark. Here are a few more you can explore:

- `calmar_ratio`: Ratio of annualized return over maximum drawdown, assessing returns relative to downside risks
- `downside_risk`: Calculates the risk of negative returns, aiding in understanding a strategy's downside volatility
- `sortino_ratio`: Similar to Sharpe, but this focuses only on downside risk and is useful for strategies with asymmetric risk
- `stability_of_timeseries`: Measures consistency of returns; important for assessing strategy reliability over time
- `tail_ratio`: Compares the right (positive) versus left (negative) tail of a distribution, indicating extreme outcome frequency
- `value_at_risk`: Estimates the maximum potential loss over a specified time frame and is crucial for risk assessment
- `excess_sharpe`: Calculates the difference in Sharpe ratio relative to a benchmark; useful for strategy comparison

See also

To learn more about `empyrical-reloaded`, check out the documentation here: `https://empyrical.ml4trading.io/`

Sending orders based on portfolio targets

We now have the components of our trading app built to add flexibility to the way we submit orders. By combining real-time position data and portfolio net liquidation value, we can build more sophisticated order techniques. For example, now that we can access current positions, we're able to dynamically adjust our positions to align with quantity or value targets. Similarly, with live net liquidation value, we can calculate order sizes as a percentage of the portfolio. Building orders based on portfolio percentage targets unlocks advanced portfolio and risk management capabilities. This integration results in a more responsive trading system that is capable of adapting to market changes swiftly and executing orders that are consistently in tune with our overall risk management and investment objectives. In this recipe, we'll implement methods to submit orders based on target values, quantities, and percentage allocations.

Getting ready

We will assume that you've created the `client.py` and `app.py` files in the `trading-app` directory. If you have not, do it now.

We'll start by adding a default market data request ID to the `utils.py` file. Since we cancel market data requests immediately after requesting the data, we can use the same ID.

Open `utils.py` and add the following code after the `TABLE_BAR_PROPERTIES` list:

```
DEFAULT_MARKET_DATA_ID = 55
```

How to do it...

We'll create five separate order methods and three associated helper methods. The order methods will generate the number of contracts to order so that we can achieve the desired portfolio allocation. The helper methods will do the work of calculating the quantities. Add all of the following code under the `send_order` method in the `IBClient` class in the `client.py` file.

1. Add the method that computes the quantity and places an order for a fixed amount of money:

```
def order_value(self, contract, order_type, value, **kwargs):
    quantity = self._calculate_order_value_quantity(
        contract, value)
    order = order_type(quantity=quantity, **kwargs)
    return self.send_order(contract, order)
```

2. Add the method to place an order to adjust a position to the target number of contracts:

```
def order_target_quantity(
    self, contract, order_type, target, **kwargs
):
    quantity=self._calculate_order_target_quantity(
        contract, target)
    order = order_type(
        action=SELL if quantity < 0 else BUY,
        quantity=abs(quantity),
        **kwargs
```

```
    )
        return self.send_order(contract, order)
```

3. Add the helper method that loops through the positions and computes the target number of contracts to order:

```
def _calculate_order_target_quantity(
    self, contract, target
):
    positions = self.get_positions()
    if contract.symbol in positions.keys():
        current_position = positions[
            contract.symbol]["position"]
        target -= current_position
    return int(target)
```

4. Add the method to order the specified asset according to the percentage of the current portfolio value:

```
def order_percent(s
    elf, contract, order_type, percent, **kwargs
):
    quantity = self._calculate_order_percent_quantity(
        contract, percent)
    order = order_type(
        quantity=quantity,
        **kwargs)
    return self.send_order(contract, order)
```

5. Add the associated helper function that computes the percentage of the portfolio based on the net liquidation value and the number of contracts to order:

```
def _calculate_order_percent_quantity(self, contract, percent):
    net_liquidation_value = self.get_account_values(
        key="NetLiquidation")[0]
    value = net_liquidation_value * percent
    return self._calculate_order_value_quantity(contract, value)
```

6. Add the method to adjust a position to a target dollar value. If the position doesn't already exist, the code sends a new order. If the position exists, the code sends an order for the difference between the target value and the current position value:

```
def order_target_value(
    self, contract, order_type, target, **kwargs
):
    target_quantity = self._calculate_order_value_quantity(
        contract, target)
    quantity = self._calculate_order_target_quantity(
        contract, target_quantity)
    order = order_type(
        action=SELL if quantity < 0 else BUY,
        quantity=abs(quantity),
        **kwargs
    )
    return self.send_order(contract, order)
```

7. Add the associated helper method:

```
def _calculate_order_value_quantity(
    self, contract, value
):
    last_price = self.get_market_data(
        request_id=DEFAULT_MARKET_DATA_ID,
        contract=contract, tick_type=4)
    multiplier = contract.multiplier if contract.multiplier
        != "" else 1
    return int(value / (last_price * multiplier))
```

8. Add the method to send an order to update a position to a percent of the portfolio value. If the position doesn't already exist, the code sends a new order. If the position exists, the code sends an order for the difference between the target percent and the current portfolio percent:

```
def order_target_percent(
    self, contract, order_type, target, **kwargs
):
    quantity = self._calculate_order_target_percent_quantity(
        contract, target)
```

```
    order = order_type(
        action=SELL if quantity < 0 else BUY,
        quantity=abs(quantity),
        **kwargs
    )
    return self.send_order(contract, order)
```

9. Add the associated helper method:

```
def _calculate_order_target_percent_quantity(
    self, contract, target
):
    target_quantity = self._calculate_order_percent_quantity(
        contract, target)
    return self._calculate_order_target_quantity(
        contract, target_quantity)
```

How it works...

Our order methods take two required arguments and various keyword arguments based on the order type that's passed. The two required arguments are the contract to trade and the order type to use. The keyword arguments are additional arguments to be passed to the order. The following are the different methods we have to manage orders with our trading app.

Ordering for a fixed amount of money with order_value

The `order_value` method places an order for a specific monetary value rather than a specified quantity of contracts. It calculates the quantity of the asset to be ordered by calling the `_calculate_order_value_quantity` method, which determines the quantity based on the current market price of the asset and its multiplier. This calculation divides the specified dollar value by the product of the asset's last market price and its multiplier (defaulting to 1 if none is specified).

The method then creates an order of the given `order_type` object with the calculated quantity, along with any additional parameters passed via `**kwargs`. Finally, it places the order by invoking `send_order` with the contract and the order.

Ordering to adjust a position to the target number of shares with order_target_quantity

The `order_target_quantity` method adjusts a position to a specified target quantity of contracts. It calculates the quantity by determining the difference between the target quantity and the current position size using the `_calculate_order_target_quantity` method. If the contract already has an existing position, this method adjusts the position to the target by calculating the difference. If no position exists, it treats the target as the total quantity for a new order.

The method then creates an order of the specified `order_type` object, setting the action to `BUY` or `SELL` based on whether the calculated quantity is positive or negative. It uses the absolute value of this quantity. Finally, it places the order by calling `send_order` with the contract and the order.

Ordering to a given percent of current portfolio value with order_percent

The `order_percent` method uses the `_calculate_order_percent_quantity` helper method, which multiplies the portfolio's net liquidation value by the specified percentage, then converts this value into the appropriate quantity of the asset using `_calculate_order_value_quantity`.

The method then creates an order of the specified `order_type` object with this calculated quantity (and any additional parameters passed via `**kwargs`). Finally, it places the order by calling `send_order` with the contract and the newly created order.

Ordering to adjust a position to a target value with order_target_value

The `order_target_value` method adjusts a position to a specified target monetary value for a contract. It first calculates the target quantity of contracts needed to reach the target value using the `_calculate_order_value_quantity` method, which determines the quantity based on the current market price and the contract's multiplier. Then, it calculates the actual quantity to order, taking into account the current position, by using the `_calculate_order_target_quantity` method. This method computes the difference between the target quantity and the current position, treating it as a new order if no position exists or as an adjustment if a position already exists.

The method then creates an order of the specified `order_type` object, setting the action to `BUY` or `SELL` based on whether the calculated quantity is positive or negative, and uses the absolute value of this quantity. Finally, the method places the order by calling `send_order` with the contract and the order.

Ordering to adjust a position to a target value with order_target_value

The `order_target_value` method adjusts a position to a specified target monetary value for a contract. It first calculates the target quantity of contracts needed to reach the target value using the `_calculate_order_value_quantity` method, which determines the quantity based on the current market price and the contract's multiplier. Then, it calculates the actual quantity to order, taking into account the current position, by using the `_calculate_order_target_quantity` method. This method computes the difference between the target quantity and the current position, treating it as a new order if no position exists or as an adjustment if a position already exists.

The method then creates an order of the specified `order_type` object, setting the action to `BUY` or `SELL` based on whether the calculated quantity is positive or negative, and uses the absolute value of this quantity. Finally, the method places the order by calling `send_order` with the contract and the order.

Ordering to adjust a position to a target percent of the current portfolio value with order_target_percent

The `order_target_percent` method adjusts a position so that it represents a specific target percentage of the current portfolio value. This method first calculates the target quantity of the asset needed to achieve the desired portfolio percentage using the `_calculate_order_target_percent_quantity` method. This calculation takes the current value of the portfolio and the target percentage into account, adjusting the position size accordingly. If the position in the specified contract already exists, the method calculates the difference between the current and target percentages and adjusts the position size to match the target.

The method then creates an order of the specified `order_type` object, determining whether to buy or sell based on whether the calculated quantity is positive or negative, and sets the quantity to the absolute value of the calculated amount. Finally, the method places the order by calling `send_order` with the contract and the order.

There's more...

The following examples show how to use the new order methods.

1. In `app.py`, add the following imports at the top of the file:

```
from order import market, limit, BUY, SELL
```

2. In the main section of the file under the instantiation of the trading app, define an AAPL contract:

```
aapl = stock("AAPL", "SMART", "USD")
```

3. Submit a `market` order to buy $1,000 worth of AAPL:

```
app.order_value(aapl, market, 1000, action=BUY)
```

4. Submit a `market` order to adjust the portfolio to be short five shares of AAPL:

```
app.order_target_quantity(aapl, market, -5)
```

5. Submit a `limit` order for AAPL for an equivalent of 10% of the net liquidation value of the portfolio:

```
app.order_percent(
    aapl, limit, 0.1, action=BUY,
    limit_price=185.0
)
```

6. Submit a `stop loss` order to adjust the portfolio to $3,000 worth of AAPL:

```
app.order_target_value(
    aapl, stop, 3000,
    stop_price=180.0
)
```

7. Submit a `market` order to adjust the portfolio so that 50% of the net liquidation value is allocated to AAPL:

```
app.order_target_percent(aapl, market, 0.5)
```

See also

The logic to compute the target values and percentages is based on the `zipline-reloaded` implementation for backtesting. You can review the API reference for details at `https://zipline.ml4trading.io/api-reference.html`.

Deploying a monthly factor portfolio strategy

We'll now integrate the momentum factor we built in *Chapter 7, Build Alpha Factors for Stock Portfolios*, into our trading app. The app is designed to download and process premium U.S. equities data encompassing a comprehensive universe of approximately 20,000 stocks. The advantage of using the premium data is that it lets us build factor portfolios that include the entire universe of U.S.-traded equities.

The trading app is designed to be run on a periodic rebalancing schedule after market hours, typically monthly. Each time it runs, it acquires the latest price data for the entire stock universe. It then computes the momentum factor for these stocks. Based on this computation, the app identifies the top stocks exhibiting the strongest momentum and the bottom stocks showing the weakest momentum. The trading strategy involves going long on the top stocks and short on the bottom stocks.

Our trading app can execute orders that align with a specific target percentage allocation for each stock in the portfolio. This feature simplifies the process of maintaining the desired portfolio balance, requiring only a single line of code to buy or sell shares as needed. This approach lets us rebalance the portfolio so it consistently reflects the target portfolio adjusted for the computed momentum factor.

Getting ready

In *Chapter 9, Event-Based Backtesting Factor Portfolios with Zipline Reloaded*, we explained how to set up Norgate Data for backtesting. For this recipe, we'll rely on that data. If you decide against the paid subscription, you can use the free data described in *Chapter 7, Build Alpha Factors for Stock Portfolios*. Norgate is a premium data provider that offers survivorship-bias–free historical data for equities, ETFs, and futures with high data quality and comprehensive corporate action adjustments. Its Zipline Reloaded integration delivers clean, point-in-time datasets optimized for professional backtesting. The service includes delisted securities, accurate index membership histories, and consistent symbol management, which are critical for realistic simulations. It is designed for researchers who need reliable, production-grade data rather than free or prototype-level alternatives. You can find the page to get the data set up at .

How to do it...

We'll integrate the code we built in *Chapter 7, Build Alpha Factors for Stock Portfolios* into our trading app.

1. In `app.py`, add the following imports to the top of the file and reorder them to adhere to PEP8 specifications:

```
import os
import sqlite3
import threading
import time
import empyrical as ep
import exchange_calendars as xcals
import numpy as np
import pandas as pd
from dotenv import load_dotenv
from zipline.data import bundles
from zipline.data.bundles.core import load
from zipline.pipeline import Pipeline
from zipline.pipeline.data import USEquityPricing
from zipline.pipeline.engine import SimplePipelineEngine
from zipline.pipeline.factors import CustomFactor, Returns
from zipline.pipeline.loaders import USEquityPricingLoader
from zipline.utils.run_algo import load_extensions
from client import IBClient
from contract import stock
from order import market
from wrapper import IBWrapper
load_dotenv()
```

2. Below our `IBApp` class, add the custom momentum factor that `zipline-reloaded` uses to compute the factor value for each asset in our universe:

```
class MomentumFactor(CustomFactor):
    inputs = [USEquityPricing.close, Returns(window_length=126)]
    window_length = 252
    def compute(
        self, today, assets, out, prices, returns
    ):
        out[:] = (
```

```
            (prices[-21] - prices[-252]) / prices[-252]
          - (prices[-1] - prices[-21]) / prices[-21]
        ) / np.nanstd(returns, axis=0)
```

3. Now add a function that creates and returns a `zipline-reloaded` pipeline. The pipeline is responsible for creating a DataFrame with the data that we'll use to select which assets to trade:

```
def make_pipeline():
    momentum = MomentumFactor()
    return Pipeline(
        columns={
            "factor": momentum,
            "longs": momentum.top(top_n),
            "shorts": momentum.bottom(top_n),
            "rank": momentum.rank(ascending=False),
        },
    )
```

4. Now, we'll add the code to generate the weights required to rebalance our portfolio. You'll need to add all of the following code in the main section of the app under the `app = IBApp("127.0.0.1", 7497, client_id=11, account="DU*******")` line. Start with creating a session calendar based on the **New York Stock Exchange** to set the lookback time for computing the momentum. The `top_n` variable determines how many long and short positions we want in our portfolio:

```
top_n = 10
xnys = xcals.get_calendar("XNYS")
today = pd.Timestamp.today().strftime("%Y-%m-%d")
start_date = xnys.session_offset(
    today, count=-252
).strftime("%Y-%m-%d")
```

5. Add the code to load the extension file that we created in the *Getting ready* section of this recipe. After the extension file has been loaded, we can invoke the code to ingest

our data bundle using the premium data subscription. Finally, we will load the data bundle into memory so it's ready to use:

```
load_extensions(True, [], False, os.environ)
bundles.ingest("norgatedata-us-equity-universe")
bundle_data = load("norgatedata-us-equity-universe", os.environ, None)
```

The ingestion can take around 30 minutes once run, so be patient. You should see output resembling the following once the bundling process begins:

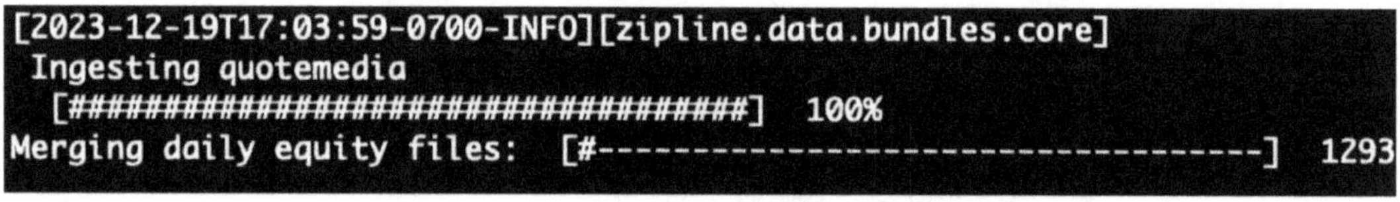

Figure 14.2: The data ingestion process output to the console

6. Add the code that creates the U.S. equity pricing loader, which aligns the price data to U.S. exchange calendars:

```
pipeline_loader = USEquityPricingLoader(
    bundle_data.equity_daily_bar_reader,
    bundle_data.adjustment_reader,
    fx_reader=None
)
```

7. Create the engine that brings the pipeline loader and the bundled data together:

```
engine = SimplePipelineEngine(
    get_loader=lambda col: pipeline_loader,
    asset_finder=bundle_data.asset_finder
)
```

8. Add the code that runs the pipeline and generates the output:

```
results = engine.run_pipeline(
    make_pipeline(),
    start_date,
    today
)
```

9. Clean up the resulting DataFrame by removing records with no factor data, adding names to the MultiIndexes, and sorting the values first by date, then by factor value:

```
results.dropna(subset="factor", inplace=True)
results.index.names = ["date", "symbol"]
results.sort_values(by=["date", "factor"], inplace=True)
```

10. The result is a MultiIndex DataFrame including the raw factor value, boolean values indicating a short or long position, and details on how the stock's factor value is ranked among the universe. The last date in the DataFrame should reflect the last trading day which will allow us to use the results to rebalance our portfolio:

		factor	longs	shorts	rank
date	**symbol**				
2022-12-14	**Equity(20942 [XBIOW])**	-109.975559	False	True	10339.0
	Equity(16489 [ROCGW])	-65.102756	False	True	10338.0
	Equity(3014 [BWACW])	-55.947030	False	True	10337.0
	Equity(18846 [TGVCW])	-40.394871	False	True	10336.0
	Equity(20099 [VIIAW])	-38.196519	False	True	10335.0
...	**...**	...	...	...	...
2023-12-15	**Equity(1113 [APCA])**	15.747811	True	False	5.0
	Equity(11471 [LBBB])	16.065618	True	False	4.0
	Equity(15639 [PUCK])	20.079347	True	False	3.0
	Equity(10485 [IVCB])	20.102028	True	False	2.0
	Equity(14991 [PHYT])	22.416517	True	False	1.0

Figure 14.3: A MultiIndex DataFrame with factor information and trading indicators

11. Use the query method on the results MultiIndex DataFrame to select the long and short positions that will make up our portfolio:

```
longs = results.xs(today, level=0).query(
    "longs == True")
shorts = results.xs(today, level=0).query(
    "shorts == True")
```

12. Create a simple equal-weight to determine how to allocate the assets in our portfolio:

```
weight = 1 / top_n / 2
```

13. Add the code to loop through each of the longs and shorts DataFrames and order a target percent of each asset based on the weight:

```
for row in pd.concat([longs, shorts]).itertuples():
    side = 1 if row.longs else -1
    symbol = row.Index.symbol
    contract = stock(symbol, "SMART", "USD")
    app.order_target_percent(contract, market, side * weight)
```

How it works...

The mechanics of the zipline-reloaded pipeline API are covered extensively in *Chapter 7, Build Alpha Factors for Stock Portfolios*. The contribution of this chapter is to isolate the stocks that we want to go long and short, generate a simple weighting scheme, and send the orders for the target percentage.

The longs and shorts variables are derived from a results DataFrame. For a specific date, the xs method extracts a subset of the DataFrame at a date level, and the query method filters this subset to include only rows where longs or shorts are True, respectively.

The weight variable is calculated as the inverse of twice the number of top stocks (top_n) to be traded, creating an equally distributed allocation among all the stocks.

The for loop iterates over each row of the concatenated longs and shorts DataFrames. For each row, it determines the side of the trade: 1 for long positions and -1 for short positions. The symbol of the stock is extracted from the row's index.

For each stock symbol, a contract object is created using the stock function, which specifies the stock symbol, the exchange, and the currency. Finally, the order_target_percent method is called for each stock, setting the target percentage of the portfolio to be allocated to this stock. The percentage is calculated by multiplying the integer `side` by the `weight` float, effectively scaling the allocation based on whether the position is long or short.

There's more...

You may want to include a screen while building the universe for which to compute momentum and rank. One way to do that is to filter stocks based on their daily average dollar volume, which helps us focus on more liquid and potentially less volatile assets. We can use the `AverageDollarVolume` class, which includes only those stocks that exceed a specified threshold in daily average dollar volume.

To do it, import the class:

```
from zipline.pipeline.factors import AverageDollarVolume
```

Then update the `make_pipeline` function to resemble the following:

```
def make_pipeline():
    momentum = MomentumFactor()
    dollar_volume = AverageDollarVolume(window_length=21)
    return Pipeline(
        columns={
            "factor": momentum,
            "longs": momentum.top(top_n),
            "shorts": momentum.bottom(top_n),
            "rank": momentum.rank(ascending=False),
        },
        screen=dollar_volume.top(100)
    )
```

The screen will apply the filter after it computes the momentum value and ranks the stocks. That means that even though we asked for the `top_n` number of assets to include in the pipeline, we may end up with fewer than `top_n` if they are screened out after ranking.

See also

Learn how to use the Pipeline API in a `zipline-reloaded` backtest at `https://www.pyquantnews.com/the-pyquant-newsletter/backtest-a-custom-momentum-strategy-with-zipline`.

Deploying an options combo strategy

Options can provide algorithmic traders with the ability to express market views that go beyond the linear profit and loss potential of stock trading. Unlike stocks, whose profit or loss is directly tied to the movement of the price on a dollar-for-dollar basis, options are non-linear instruments whose value is affected by multiple dimensions such as the price of the underlying asset, time to expiration, volatility, and interest rates. This multidimensionality allows for strategies that can profit from a range of outcomes.

A straddle strategy includes buying a call and a put option with the same strike prices and expiration dates. This lets traders speculate on the asset's volatility instead of predicting the market's directional movement. This approach makes money for the trader when the underlying asset experiences substantial movement in any direction.

Premium collection strategies such as a short iron condor involve selling both a call and a put spread with the goal of earning the premium from the options sold. This is predicated on the belief that the underlying asset's price will remain within a specific range, leading to the options expiring worthless and the trader keeping the premium collected.

In this recipe, you'll learn how to model options trades in **Trader Workstation** (**TWS**) and submit the orders using Python through the IB API.

Getting ready

We need to add two functions to our `contract.py` file. Open it and add the following code at the end of the file:

```
def combo_leg(contract_details, ratio, action):
    leg = ComboLeg()
    leg.conId = contract_details.contract.conId
    leg.ratio = ratio
    leg.action = action
    leg.exchange = contract_details.contract.exchange
    return leg

def spread(legs):
    contract = Contract()
    contract.symbol = "USD"
    contract.secType = "BAG"
    contract.currency = "USD"
    contract.exchange = "SMART"
```

```
    contract.comboLegs = legs
    return contract
```

These two functions allow us to create the legs of a combo order and use those legs to construct a single tradable instrument.

Note that in the `combo_leg` method, we need to pass in a contract's `conId` string. The `conId` string is a unique identifier maintained by IB. To get the `conId` string, we have to send a request to IB to get the details of that contract maintained by IB. To do that, we use an IB method called `reqContractDetails`. In the `client.py` file, add the following method directly under the `__init__` method in the `IBClient` class:

```
def resolve_contract(self, contract,
    request_id=DEFAULT_CONTRACT_ID):
        self.reqContractDetails(reqId=request_id, contract=contract)
        time.sleep(2)
        self.contractDetailsEnd(reqId=request_id)
        return self.resolved_contract
```

This method takes a contract object, requests the details from IB, and returns its details.

Let's see how it works.

How to do it...

We'll construct an options position called a **strangle**, which will let us bet on an increase in the volatility of the underlying. The following code should be added under the creation of the app under the `if __name__ == "__main__":` line in `app.py`.

1. Add the code to create a long call option contract on TSLA expiring in March 2024 with a strike price of $260:

```
long_call_contract = option("TSLA", "SMART", "202403", 260, "CALL")
long_call = app.resolve_contract(long_call_contract)
```

2. Add the code to create a long put option contract on TSLA expiring on the same date with the same strike price:

```
long_put_contract = option("TSLA", "SMART", "202403", 260, "PUT")
long_put = app.resolve_contract(long_put_contract)
```

3. Convert each resolved contract into a leg of our spread contract:

```
leg_1 = combo_leg(long_call, 1, BUY)
leg_2 = combo_leg(long_put, 1, BUY)
```

4. Pass a list of the legs to the spread function to put the legs together into a single tradable instrument:

```
long_strangle = spread([leg_1, leg_2])
```

5. Create a market order object and send the order to the IB API. In practice, consider using limit orders for options traders:

```
order = market(BUY, 1)
app.send_order(long_strangle, order)
```

How it works...

The `combo_leg` function takes three parameters: `contract_details`, `ratio`, and `action`. It creates an instance of `ComboLeg` and sets `conId`, `ratio`, `action`, and `exchange`. The fully defined `ComboLeg` object is then returned. The `spread` function takes a list of `ComboLeg` objects created by the `combo_leg` function. The function creates an instance of `Contract`, sets its `symbol` to `USD`, `type` to `BAG` (which stands for a **bag** or combination of contracts), `currency` to `USD`, and `exchange` to `SMART`. It then assigns the `legs` parameter to the `comboLegs` attribute of the contract. The complete `Contract` object is then returned.

In this example, we constructed a long straddle. A long options straddle is a market-neutral strategy whereby we purchase both a call option and a put option on the same underlying asset with the same strike price and expiration date. Straddles allow us to bet on volatility rather than the direction of the price movement. The position profits if the underlying asset moves up or down, allowing the trader to exercise one of the options for a profit that exceeds the total cost of both premiums.

We can model options trades in TWS. To get started, click the plus sign to the right of the tabs at the bottom of TWS. Click **Browse** on the right side of the popup to browse predefined layouts. Click **Options** on the left side, then select **Add Layout** on the **Options Trading** card in the top left. Once this has been added, load your favorite underlying. In the **Options Chains** window, toggle **Strategy Builder**.

For example, using the Strategy Builder, we can construct our straddle.

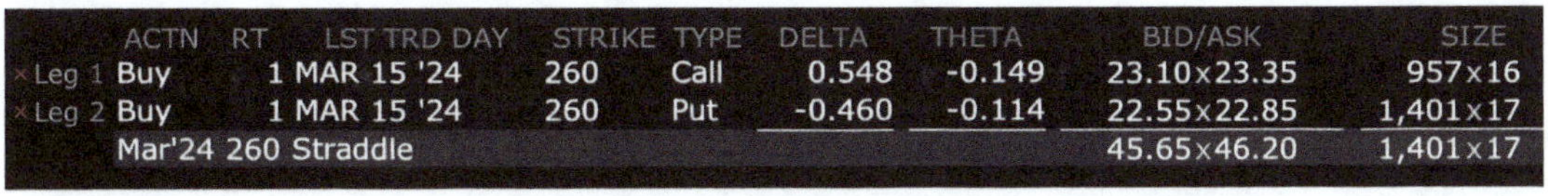

Figure 14.4: A long straddle modeled using the Strategy Builder in TWS

By clicking the **Profile** button just under the **Strategy Builder** window, we can get more details about the strategy, including the payoff charts as shown in the following screenshot:

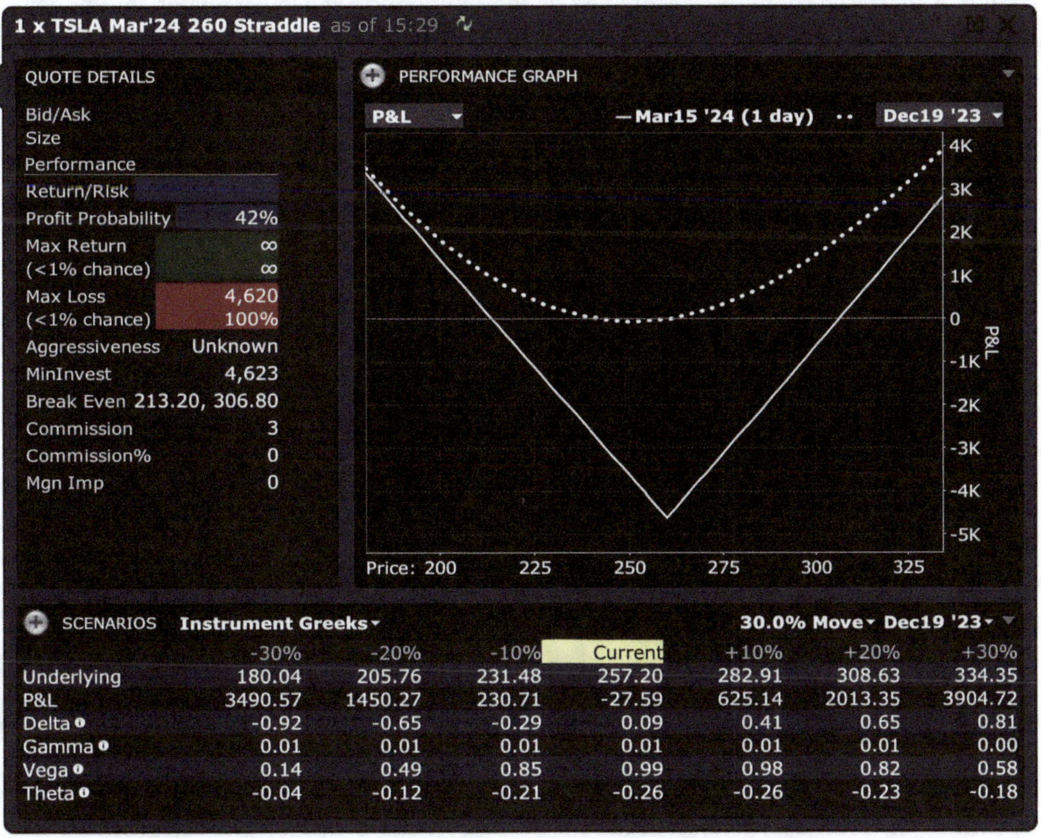

Figure 14.5: A long straddle profile in TWS

After running our app, the legs of the trade will be grouped together in the orders pane as follows:

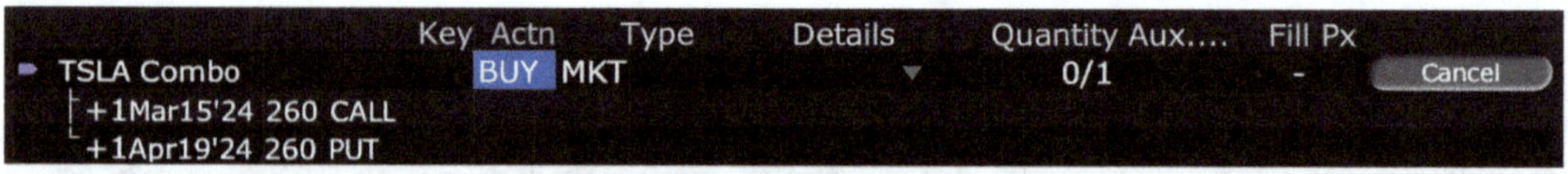

	Key	Actn	Type	Details	Quantity	Aux....	Fill Px	
TSLA Combo		BUY	MKT		0/1		-	Cancel
+1Mar15'24 260 CALL								
+1Apr19'24 260 PUT								

Figure 14.6: Long straddle legs grouped together in the orders pane in TWS

There's more...

Let's model another, more complex strategy called an iron condor. We'll describe a short iron condor. A short iron condor is executed by selling a put option at a lower out-of-the-money strike, purchasing another put with an even lower strike, selling a call option at a higher out-of-the-money strike, and then buying another call with an even higher strike. Typically, all options have the same expiration date. The position is constructed in such a way that we collect the premium from the options sold. The bet is that the underlying asset's price will remain between the inner strikes of the options sold and the options expire worthless. This strategy allows traders to bet on low volatility in the underlying asset's price, aiming to profit from a range-bound market within the span of the options' expiration period.

This strategy is beneficial in a low-volatility environment, where large movements are not expected. It's a limited-risk strategy, as the long options of the spreads act as insurance against substantial adverse moves in the asset's price. The profitability is capped to the premiums received, while losses are limited to the difference between the strikes less the net premium collected.

We can model options trades in TWS. For example, using the Strategy Builder, we can construct our straddle as shown here:

	ACTN	RT	LST TRD DAY	STRIKE	TYPE	DELTA	THETA	BID/ASK	SIZE	
Leg 1	Sell	1	MAR 15 '24	295	Call	0.326	-0.130	10.80x10.95	198x218	Closed
Leg 2	Buy	1	MAR 15 '24	305	Call	0.274	-0.119	8.60x8.75	203x206	Closed
Leg 3	Sell	1	MAR 15 '24	240	Put	-0.322	-0.108	13.75x13.85	2x89	Closed
Leg 4	Buy	1	MAR 15 '24	233....	Put	-0.280	-0.104	11.40x11.55	63x171	Closed
	Total							-4.80x-4.25	203x206	

Figure 14.7: A short iron condor modeled using the Strategy Builder in TWS

By clicking the **Profile** button just under the **Strategy Builder** window, we can get more details about the strategy, including the payoff charts:

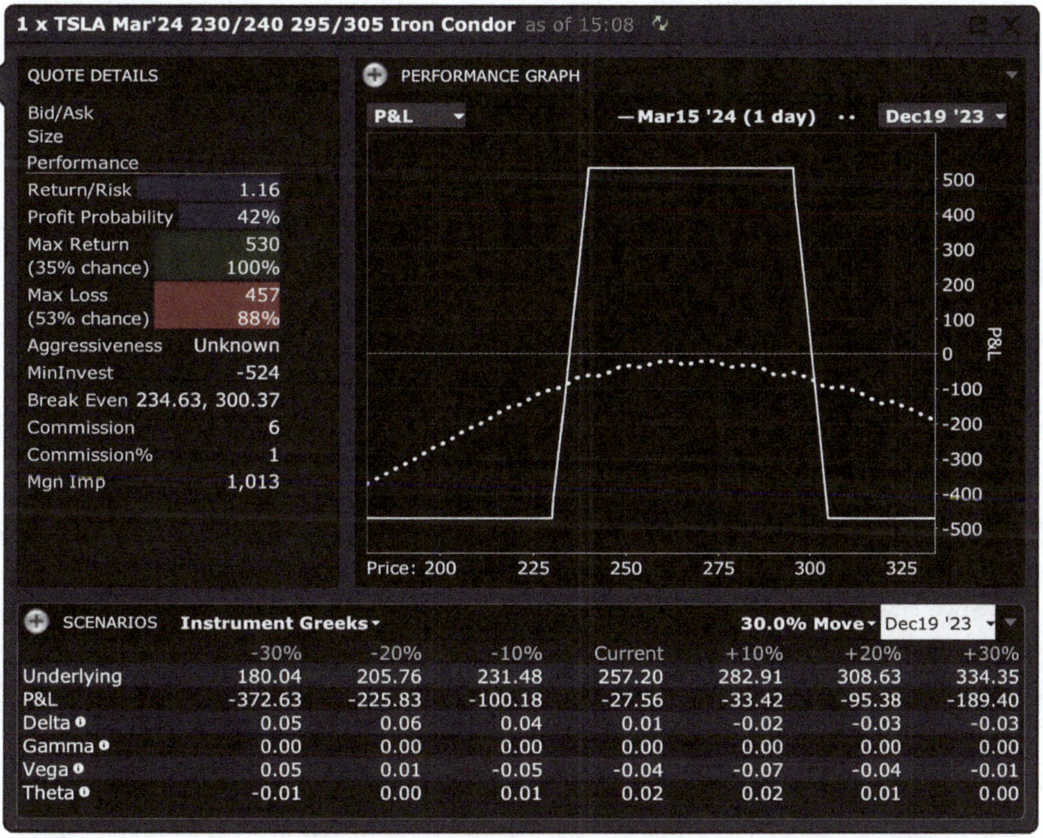

Figure 14.8: A short icon condor profile in TWS

After running our app, the legs of the trade will be grouped together in the **Orders** pane.

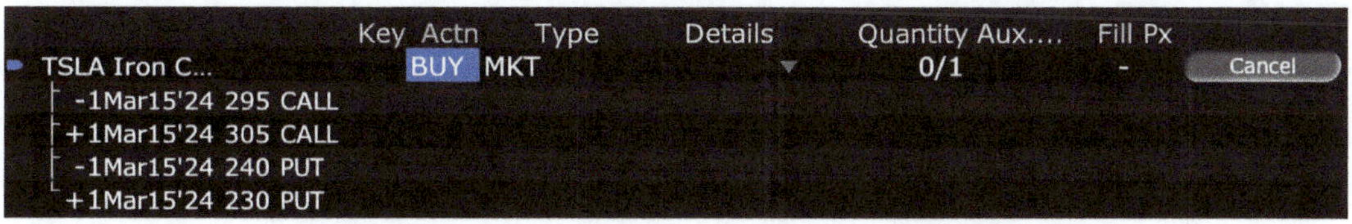

Figure 14.9: Short iron condor legs grouped together in the orders pane in TWS

See also

To learn more about options trading, you can check out the Options Industry Council's website at`https://www.optionseducation.org/`. A great desk reference is one of the most comprehensive guides to options trading on the market: *Options as a Strategic Investment*, which can be found on Amazon: `https://amzn.to/3GQRspX`.

For more information on options spread orders using the IB API, see the documentation: `https://interactivebrokers.github.io/tws-api/spread_contracts.html#bag_opt`

Deploying an intraday multi-asset mean-reversion strategy

In this recipe, we introduce a relative value strategy that uses the crack spread to identify opportunities to buy relatively cheap refiner stocks. The crack spread is a trading strategy in the energy sector that captures the price differential between crude oil and its refined products, most commonly gasoline, and heating oil. Our strategy will use a 1:2:3 combination of one contract of **Heating Oil** (**HO**) futures, two contracts of **NYMEX RBOB Gasoline Index** (**RB**) futures, and short three **Light Sweet Crude Oil** (**CL**) futures.

When trading the crack spread against a refiner stock, we are comparing the profitability of refining operations to the market's valuation of a specific refining company. Refiner stocks should theoretically benefit from a widening crack spread, as their margins improve when the price difference between crude and its products increases. The economic rationale behind our strategy is straightforward: refiners purchase crude oil and sell its refined products. When the spread between the two widens, the refiner's profit margin expands. Consequently, refiner stocks should move in tandem with crack spreads. Other factors such as operational efficiency, regulatory changes, and broader market sentiment can cause the relationship to break down, which we can take advantage of.

In this recipe, we'll build a strategy that identifies times when the crack spread widens substantially but a refiner's stock hasn't reacted proportionally. We'll use the opportunity to go long **Philips 66** (**PSX**), expecting the stock to catch up to the increased profitability suggested by the crack spread.

Getting ready

We assume that you've created the `app.py` files in the `trading-app` directory. If you have not, please do so now.

How to do it...

We'll add the code required to connect to TWS, define the contracts for our strategy, check for trading signals every 60 seconds, and execute trades accordingly. Start by opening `app.py` and replacing any code under the `if __name__ == "__main__":` line with the following.

1. Create the connection to our trading app, replacing `DU*******` with your account number:

```
app = IBApp("127.0.0.1", 7497, client_id=11, account="DU*******")
```

2. Define the refiner stock that we'll trade (in this case, PSX) and the futures contracts that make up the crack spread:

```
psx = stock("PSX", "SMART", "USD")
ho = future("HO", "NYMEX", "202403")
rb = future("RB", "NYMEX", "202403")
cl = future("CL", "NYMEX", "202403")
```

3. Set up a window of time to compute a rolling z-score that we'll use as our trading signal along with the number of standard deviations that trigger a trade:

```
window = 60
thresh = 2
```

4. We'll now set up an infinite loop that will continuously run throughout the trading day. The rest of the code should be under a `while` statement:

```
while True:
```

5. Download the historical data for the four contracts that we just defined. In our example, we'll get one-minute bars over the last week. This will give us flexibility in case we want to extend our lookback window:

```
data = app.get_historical_data_for_many(
    request_id=99,
    contracts=[psx, ho, rb, cl],
    duration="1 W",
    bar_size="1 min",
).dropna()
```

6. Compute the 1:2:3 crack spread and add the data to a new column in our DataFrame that contains the price data:

```
data["crack_spread"] = data.HO + 2 * data.RB - 3 * data.CL
```

7. To normalize the value of the crack spread and the refiner, compute the rolling 60-period rank of the last value as a percentage of the preceding values:

```
data["crack_spread_rank"] = data.crack_spread.rolling(
    window).rank(pct=True)
data["refiner_rank"] = data.PSX.rolling(window).rank(pct=True)
```

8. Compute the difference between the crack spread's 60-period rank and the refiner's 60-period rank:

```
data["rank_spread"] = data.refiner_rank - data.crack_spread_rank
```

9. Compute the rolling 60-period z-score of the difference between the crack spread's rank and the refiner's rank and take the last value as the trading signal:

```
roll = data.rank_spread.rolling(window)
zscore = ((
    data.rank_spread - roll.mean()) / roll.std())
signal = zscore[-1]
```

10. Enter a market order to buy 10 shares of PSX if the current signal is less than the threshold and we do not currently hold a position in PSX. Set the target percent of PSX to 0% if our signal exceeds 0 and we do not currently hold a position in PSX:

```
holding = psx.symbol in app.positions.keys()
if signal <= -thresh and not holding:
    order = market(BUY, 10)
    app.send_order(psx, order)
elif signal >= 0 and holding:
    app.order_target_percent(psx, market, 0)
```

11. Enter a market order to sell 10 shares of PSX if the current signal is greater than the threshold and we do not currently hold a position in PSX. Set the target percent of PSX to 0% if our signal goes below 0 and we do not currently hold a position in PSX:

```
if signal >= thresh and not holding:
    order = market(SELL, 10)
    app.send_order(psx, order)
elif signal <= 0 and holding:
    app.order_target_percent(psx, market, 0)
```

12. Finally, wait for 60 seconds before running the process again:

```
time.sleep(60)
```

The final result should resemble the following in `app.py`:

```
if __name__ == "__main__":
    app = IBApp("127.0.0.1", 7497, client_id=11, account="DU7129120")

    psx = stock("PSX", "SMART", "USD")
    ho = future("HO", "NYMEX", "202403")
    rb = future("RB", "NYMEX", "202403")
    cl = future("CL", "NYMEX", "202403")

    window = 60
    thresh = 2

    while True:
        data = app.get_historical_data_for_many(
            request_id=99,
            contracts=[psx, ho, rb, cl],
            duration="1 W",
            bar_size="1 min",
        ).dropna()

        data["crack_spread"] = data.HO + 2 * data.RB - 3 * data.CL
        data["crack_spread_rank"] = data.crack_spread.rolling(
            window).rank(pct=True)
        data["refiner_rank"] = data.PSX.rolling(
            window).rank(pct=True)
        data["rank_spread"] = data.refiner_rank - data.crack_
```

```
            spread_rank

        roll = data.rank_spread.rolling(window)
        zscore = ((data.rank_spread - roll.mean()) / roll.std())
        signal = zscore[-1]
        holding = psx.symbol in app.positions.keys()

        if signal <= -thresh and not holding:
            order = market(BUY, 10)
            app.send_order(psx, order)
        elif signal >= 0 and holding:
            app.order_target_percent(psx, market, 0)

        if signal >= thresh and not holding:
            order = market(SELL, 10)
            app.send_order(psx, order)
        elif signal <= 0 and holding:
            app.order_target_percent(psx, market, 0)

        time.sleep(60)
    app.disconnect()
```

How it works...

We covered connecting to TWS, defining contract objects, downloading historical data, manipulating data in pandas DataFrames, and submitting orders in previous chapters. Here, we'll focus on how the trading strategy works conceptually.

To run this strategy, we would need to start it at the beginning of the trading day. The algorithm operates in a continuous loop, fetching historical data for the contracts with a one-week duration and a one-minute bar size. For each loop, we calculate the crack spread, which is then ranked over a rolling window along with the rank of PSX stock's performance. The difference between these ranks is used to generate a trading signal. This signal is a z-score, calculated over a rolling window, indicating how many standard deviations the current rank spread is from its rolling mean.

We use the `get_historical_data_for_many` method that we created in *Chapter 12, Set Up the Interactive Brokers Python API*. This method returns a DataFrame with the open, high, low, and closing prices for the PSX equity contract and HO, RB, and CL futures contracts.

> Note
>
> **Important**
>
> As of the time of writing this, the March 2024 contract was the most active contract. You may need to adjust the expiration of the contracts used during your own implementation of this strategy.

The result of acquiring the data is the following pandas DataFrame:

```
symbol                        CL      HO     PSX      RB
time
2023-12-13 09:30:00-05:00  69.36  2.4674  124.78  2.0143
2023-12-13 09:31:00-05:00  69.32  2.4649  124.75  2.0133
2023-12-13 09:32:00-05:00  69.39  2.4677  124.77  2.0155
2023-12-13 09:33:00-05:00  69.47  2.4703  124.94  2.0170
2023-12-13 09:34:00-05:00  69.47  2.4700  124.79  2.0166
...                          ...     ...     ...     ...
2023-12-13 15:55:00-05:00  70.29  2.4908  127.03  2.0638
2023-12-13 15:56:00-05:00  70.29  2.4910  127.09  2.0642
2023-12-13 15:57:00-05:00  70.31  2.4920  127.09  2.0641
2023-12-13 15:58:00-05:00  70.33  2.4919  127.10  2.0646
2023-12-13 15:59:00-05:00  70.36  2.4930  127.16  2.0654
```

Figure 14.10: A pandas DataFrame with historical market data

Now that we have the price data, we're able to compute the crack spread using the same data manipulation techniques that we learned in *Chapter 2, Analyze and Transform Financial Market Data with pandas*. The result of computing the crack spread is a time series that resembles the following chart:

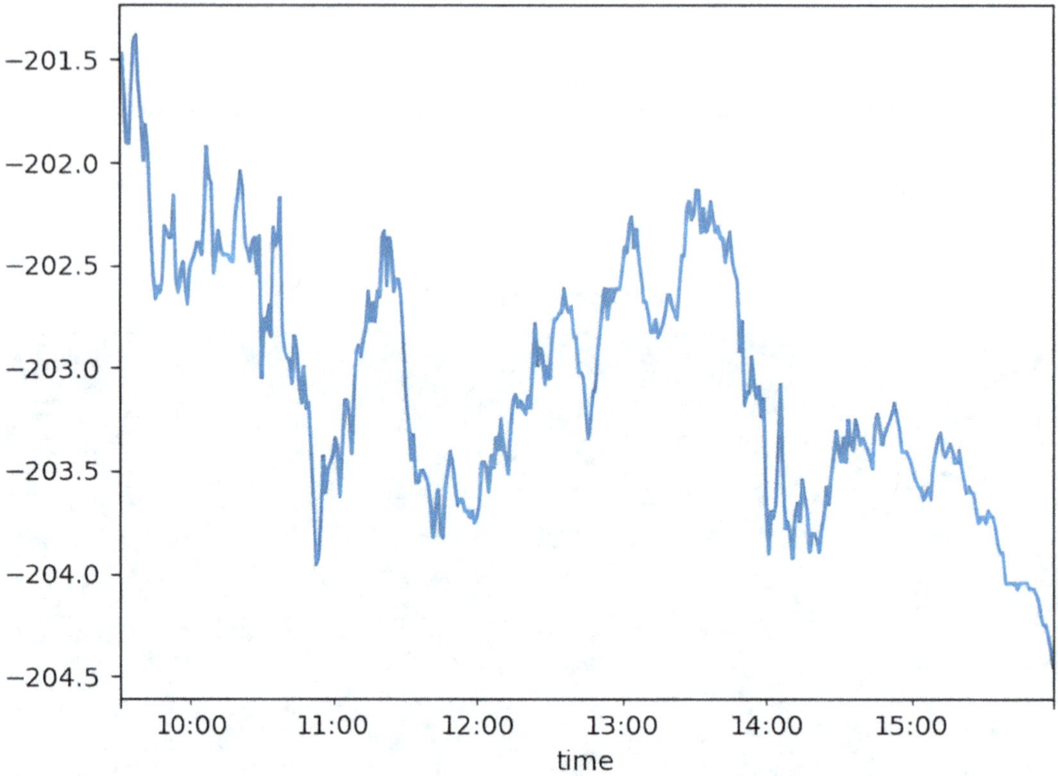

Figure 14.11: A 1:2:3 crack spread plotted over a single trading day

The prices of equities do not go negative, so we need a way to compare the relative value of the crack spread to the refiner that we're trading against. One way to do this is to determine the percent rank of the current price relative to the preceding prices. We use that technique for both the crack spread and the refiner stock. The result of these rolling percentile ranks is two time series that resemble the following chart:

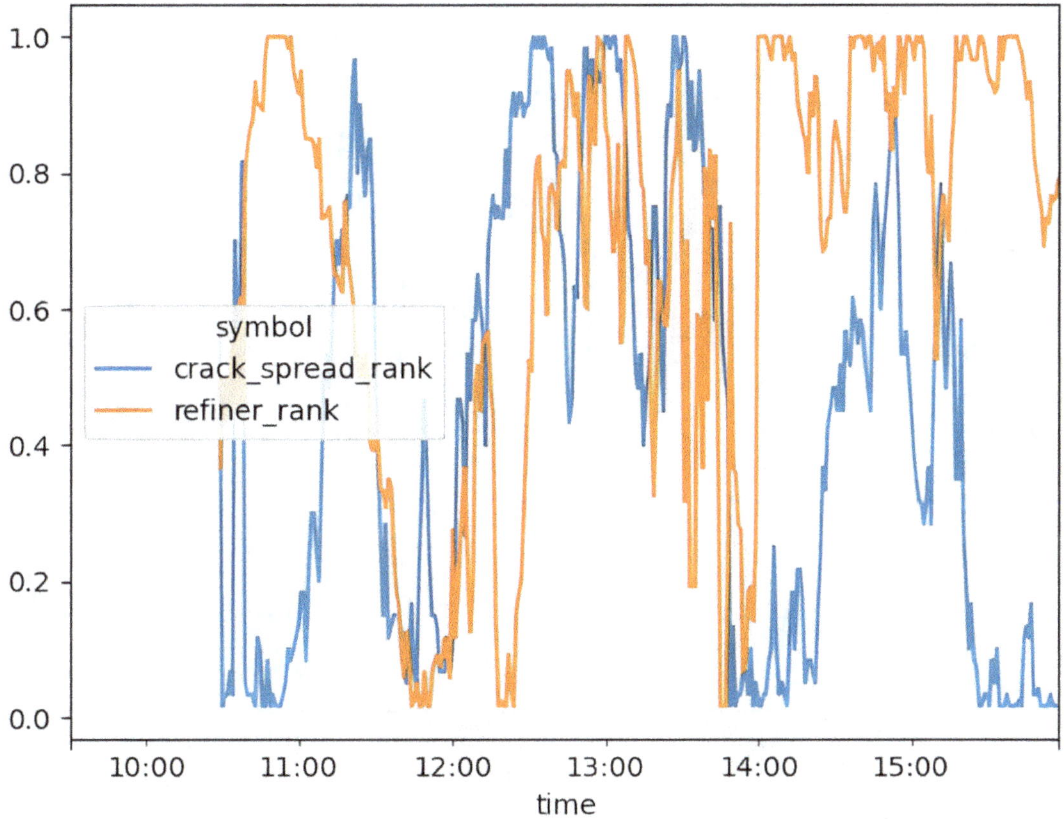

Figure 14.12: The evolution of the price rank of PSX and the crack spread relative to their 60-period windows

Now that the refiner and crack spread prices have been normalized, we can compare them by taking the difference between the two. The result of this difference is a time series that resembles the following chart:

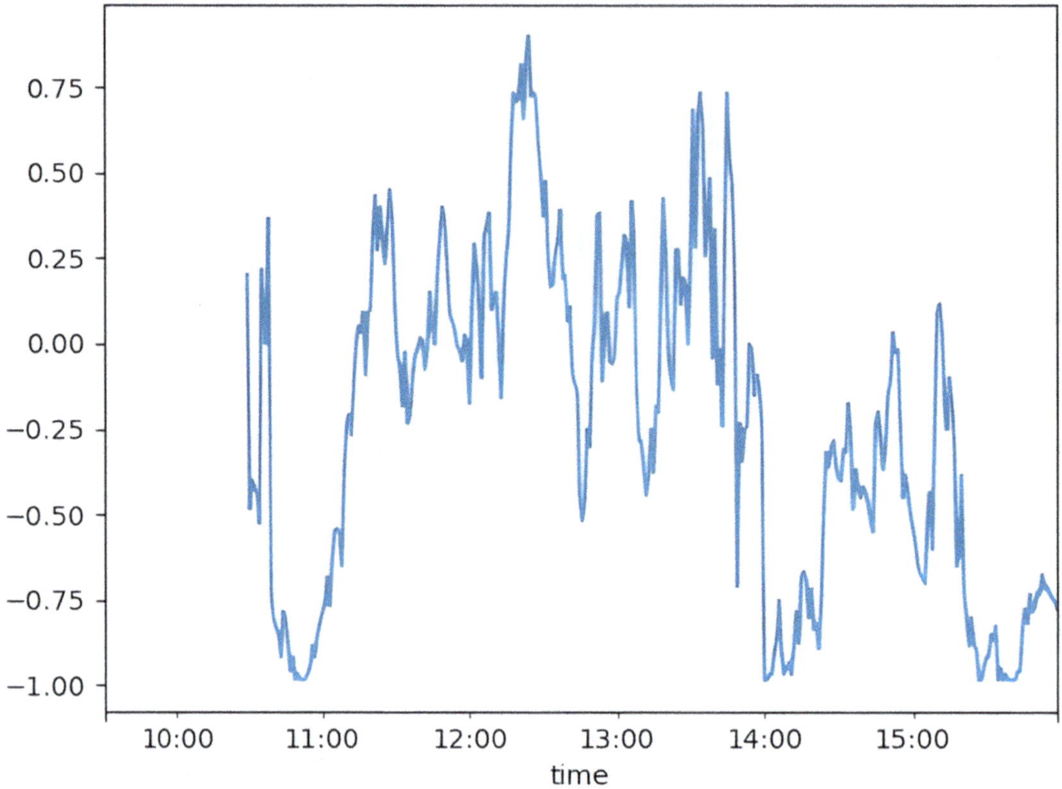

Figure 14.13: The difference between the crack spread's rank and the refiner's rank

We can see some mean reverting behavior, which we can more concisely capture through a z-score. Computing the z-score creates a time series that resembles the following chart:

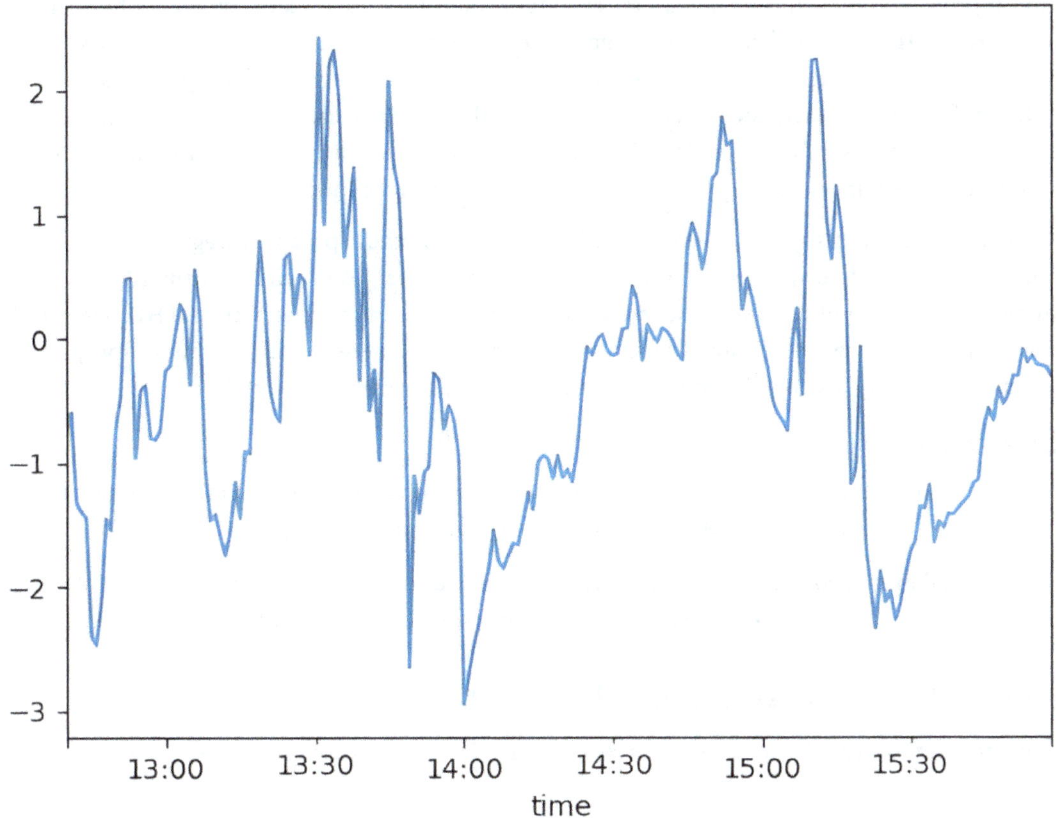

Figure 14.14: A rolling z-score of the differences between the crack spread's rank and the refiner's rank

Trading decisions are made based on this z-score. If the signal is below a negative threshold and PSX is not already held, we enter a buy order. If the signal is non-negative and PSX is held, the position is liquidated to 0. Conversely, if the signal exceeds a positive threshold and PSX is not held, we enter a `sell` order. If the signal is negative and PSX is held, the position is again liquidated. The script pauses for 60 seconds at the end of each loop iteration. This process repeats until we stop execution.

There's more...

In this strategy, we use the crack spread as a relative value indicator. We assume that the relative value of the refiner and the crack spread will oscillate around a mean, which we can exploit. We can also create a spread order and trade the crack spread itself. The crack spread is a type of intercommodity spread by IB.

Intercommodity spreads for futures contracts are constructed using combo legs and combo orders, which allows us to simultaneously trade multiple futures contracts as a single entity.

This approach is particularly relevant for strategies such as crack spreads, whereby the profit is derived from the price differences between related commodities such as crude oil and its refined products. When building these spreads, each leg of the combo order represents a different futures contract, and it's crucial to specify the **local symbol** accurately for each contract. The local symbol is a unique identifier for futures contracts that includes information about the underlying asset, expiration date, and other contract specifics.

IB currently does not support intercommodity spreads for crack spread strategies, which prevents us from directly implementing this particular strategy on their platform. IB does support intercommodity spreads between CL and RB, as well as between RB and HO. We could technically construct a crack spread using a combination of these two intercommodity spreads but the complexity involved makes it easier to just trade the refiner stock.

See also

To learn more about the intuition behind our trade, you can read about the crack spread at `https://www.investopedia.com/terms/c/crackspread.asp`.

You can read more about building combo legs and futures spread contracts using the IB API at `https://interactivebrokers.github.io/tws-api/spread_contracts.html#bag_fut`.

Join our community on Discord

Join our community's Discord space for discussions with the authors and other readers: `https://discord.gg/G4YmB6DQvf`

15

Advanced Recipes for GPU-Accelerated Trading Research

Quantitative trading research is computationally intensive. Factor research, portfolio optimization, and risk modeling require processing millions of rows of market data, fitting models across large cross-sections of assets, and solving complex optimization problems. These workflows are bottlenecked by CPU-bound operations that dominate most quant research codebases.

Graphics processing units (**GPUs**) solve this by executing thousands of parallel operations simultaneously. Unlike CPUs, which have 8-20 cores optimized for sequential tasks, modern GPUs have thousands of cores designed for data-parallel workloads. This architecture makes GPUs ideal for the vectorized DataFrame operations, matrix computations, and graph traversals common in quantitative finance.

NVIDIA's RAPIDS suite (`https://rapids.ai/`) provides GPU-accelerated drop-in replacements for the most popular PyData libraries: cuDF accelerates pandas, cuML accelerates scikit-learn, and cuGraph accelerates NetworkX. These libraries use familiar APIs and in many cases require zero code changes to existing workflows.

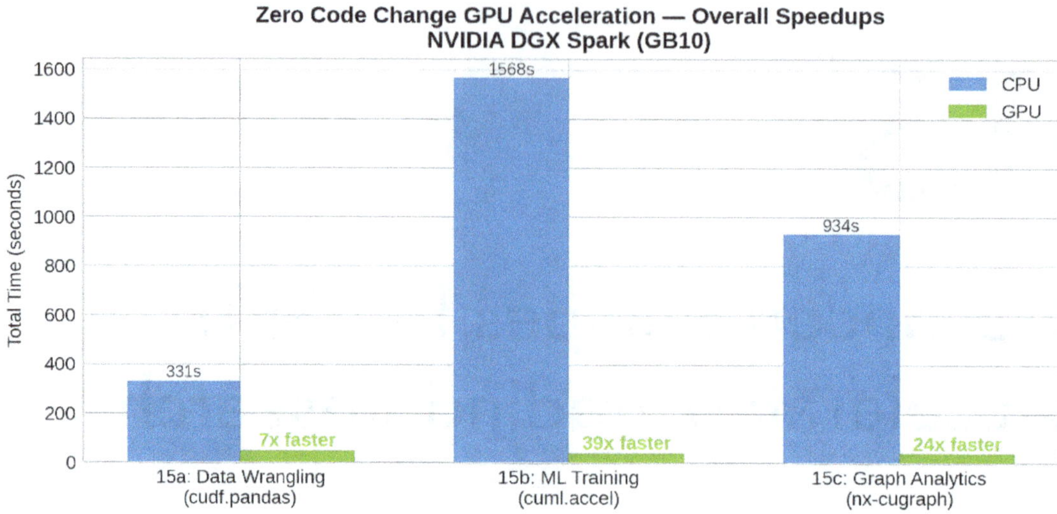

Figure 15.1: Speed ups using the RAPIDS suite of GPU-accelerated libraries

GPU acceleration is not always beneficial. GPUs excel with large datasets, parallelizable operations like groupby-aggregations, matrix math, and graph algorithms. They do not help with small datasets, highly sequential logic, or string-heavy operations that cannot be parallelized.

This chapter sets realistic expectations and benchmarks everything so you know exactly when to reach for GPU acceleration and when to stay on the CPU.

In this chapter, we present the following recipes:

- Accelerating large-scale financial data wrangling with cuDF
- Speeding up factor model training with cuML
- Building GPU-accelerated asset correlation networks with cuGraph
- Running GPU-accelerated portfolio optimization with cuOpt

Technical requirements

All examples in this chapter run on the author's NVIDIA DGX Spark, a desktop-class personal AI supercomputer powered by the GB10 Grace Blackwell Superchip with 128 GB of unified CPU-GPU memory and up to 1 petaFLOP of FP4 AI performance. That said, a DGX Spark is not required. Any computer with an NVIDIA GPU and CUDA compute capability runs every example in this chapter. This includes gaming GPUs (RTX 3060 and above), workstation GPUs (A4000, A6000), data center GPUs (A100, H100), and cloud GPU instances (AWS g5, GCP a2, Google Colab with T4). The RAPIDS libraries detect available GPU hardware automatically. The only practical difference is memory: the DGX Spark's 128 GB unified memory handles the 267-million-row dataset in this chapter without out-of-memory errors, while a 12 GB gaming GPU requires reducing the universe size proportionally.

If your GPU has less than 128 GB of memory, reduce the universe size in each recipe to fit your available memory.

Create the RAPIDS 26.02 environment via conda:

```
conda create -n rapids-26.02 \
    -c rapidsai -c conda-forge \
    rapids=26.02 python=3.12 \
    'cuda-version>=13.0,<=13.1'
conda activate rapids-26.02
```

Alternatively, install via pip using the NVIDIA PyPI index:

```
pip install \
    --extra-index-url=https://pypi.nvidia.com \
    cudf-cu13==26.2.* \
    cuml-cu13==26.2.* \
    cugraph-cu13==26.2.*
```

For the *Running GPU-accelerated portfolio optimization with cuOpt* recipe, install cuOpt and CVXPY:

```
pip install cvxpy
pip install \
    --extra-index-url=https://pypi.nvidia.com \
    cuopt-cu12
```

Accelerating large-scale financial data wrangling with cuDF

Quantitative researchers spend a significant portion of their time on data wrangling: loading historical price data, computing returns, sorting by liquidity, and joining multiple datasets. These operations run sequentially on a single CPU core in pandas, and even with optimized C extensions, processing hundreds of millions of rows takes minutes.

cuDF's pandas accelerator mode provides a zero-code-change path to GPU acceleration. You write standard pandas code and launch your script with `python -m cudf.pandas` instead of `python`. All pandas operations are transparently dispatched to the GPU with automatic CPU fallback. No API changes, no import swaps, no rewriting.

In this recipe, you will process 267 million rows of historical prices for 86,000+ global equities through a quant pipeline: sorting, computing returns, calculating dollar volume, merging sector classifications, and running groupby aggregations. You will run the same script on CPU and GPU to measure the speedup.

Getting ready

This recipe uses the `historical-prices.parquet` file we created in *Chapter 3, Accelerate Financial Market Data Analysis with Polars and DuckDB*.

How to do it...

Follow these steps to build a GPU-accelerated financial data pipeline with cuDF.

1. Import standard data libraries and system utilities for mode detection:

```
import numpy as np
import pandas as pd
import time
import sys
```

2. Detect whether the script is running under the `cudf.pandas` GPU accelerator. When launched with `python -m cudf.pandas`, all pandas operations are transparently dispatched to the GPU with automatic CPU fallback:

```
try:
    is_gpu = "cudf_pandas" in sys.modules or "cudf.pandas" in sys.modules
except Exception:
    is_gpu = False
mode = "GPU (cudf.pandas)" if is_gpu else "CPU (pandas)"
```

3. Load historical price data for 86,000+ global equities from a parquet file. This step is not timed because parquet I/O is disk-bound, not CPU vs GPU:

```
df = pd.read_parquet(
    "historical-prices.parquet",
    columns=["symbol", "date", "close", "volume"],
)
df["date"] = pd.to_datetime(df["date"])
```

4. Build a synthetic sector mapping to simulate a real-world join operation:

```
np.random.seed(42)
symbols = df["symbol"].unique()
sector_map = pd.DataFrame({
    "symbol": symbols,
    "sector": np.random.choice(
        ["Tech", "Health", "Financials", "Energy",
         "Consumer", "Industrials"],
        size=len(symbols),
    ),
})
```

5. Sort the full dataset by symbol and date to prepare for time-series operations:

```
df = df.sort_values(["symbol", "date"]).reset_index(drop=True)
```

6. Compute daily percentage returns for each symbol using grouped `pct_change`:

```
df["return_1d"] = df.groupby("symbol")["close"].pct_change()
```

7. Compute dollar volume (close times volume) and re-sort by date and liquidity:

```
df["dollar_vol"] = df["close"] * df["volume"]
df = df.sort_values(
    ["date", "dollar_vol"], ascending=[True, False]
).reset_index(drop=True)
```

8. Join the sector mapping onto the main DataFrame via a left merge on symbol:

```
df = df.merge(sector_map, on="symbol", how="left")
```

9. Aggregate five daily statistics per sector: mean return, total volume, stock count, and the best and worst single-stock returns:

```
sector_daily = df.groupby(["date", "sector"]).agg(
    mean_return=("return_1d", "mean"),
    total_volume=("volume", "sum"),
    num_stocks=("symbol", "count"),
    max_return=("return_1d", "max"),
```

```
    min_return=("return_1d", "min"),
).reset_index()
```

10. Compute per-symbol summary statistics across their full history:

```
symbol_stats = df.groupby("symbol").agg(
    mean_return=("return_1d", "mean"),
    std_return=("return_1d", "std"),
    mean_volume=("volume", "mean"),
    total_dollar_vol=("dollar_vol", "sum"),
    num_days=("date", "count"),
).reset_index()
```

11. Merge the per-symbol volatility back onto the main DataFrame and flag stocks in the top 10% by historical return volatility:

```
df = df.merge(
    symbol_stats[["symbol", "std_return"]], on="symbol", how="left"
)
vol_threshold = df["std_return"].quantile(0.9)
df["high_vol"] = df["std_return"] > vol_threshold
```

12. Count rows per sector and compute daily market breadth (the number of unique symbols trading each day):

```
sector_counts = df["sector"].value_counts()
daily_breadth = df.groupby("date")["symbol"].nunique()
```

13. Run the script twice using two different launch commands to compare CPU and GPU performance:

```
python 15a_accelerating_large_scale_financial_data_wrangling_with_cudf.py
python -m cudf.pandas
15a_accelerating_large_scale_financial_data_wrangling_with_cudf.py
```

14. The script is identical in both cases. The only difference is the launch command. The result is a 6.8x speedup in execution:

Step	CPU (pandas)	GPU (cudf.pandas)	Speedup
Sort	43.1s	6.4s	6.7x
Returns	16.8s	9.7s	1.7x
Dollar Sort	119.4s	12.4s	9.6x
Merge	28.9s	4.5s	6.4x
Sector Agg	18.7s	1.0s	18.7x
Symbol Stats	13.8s	1.0s	13.8x
Vol Flag	38.4s	6.8s	5.6x
Counts	51.7s	6.9s	7.5x
TOTAL	330.8s	48.7s	6.8x

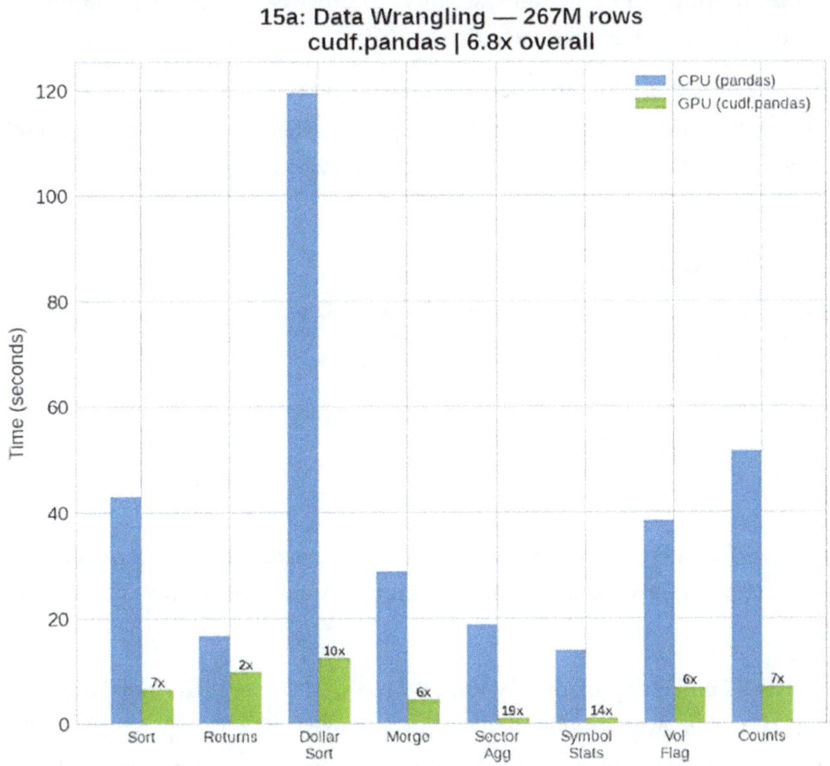

Figure 15.2: Breakdown of where the acceleration happens

How it works...

When you launch a script with `python -m cudf.pandas`, cuDF installs a Python import hook that intercepts the `import pandas` statement. Instead of loading standard pandas, it loads a proxy module. Every DataFrame, Series, and Index object becomes a proxy that wraps either a cuDF GPU object or a pandas CPU object transparently.

When you call an operation like `df.groupby("symbol")["close"].pct_change()`, the proxy dispatches the call to the cuDF GPU implementation first. If the operation succeeds on the GPU, the result remains in GPU memory. If the operation is not supported by cuDF, the proxy automatically transfers the data to CPU memory and falls back to standard pandas. This fallback is transparent to your code.

cuDF stores DataFrames in Apache Arrow columnar format on GPU memory. When you sort 267 million rows, the GPU reads the columns as contiguous memory blocks and applies parallel sorting across thousands of CUDA cores. Groupby aggregations benefit similarly: each group's computation is independent, so the GPU processes all 86,000 symbol groups simultaneously rather than sequentially.

The command-line approach (`python -m cudf.pandas script.py`) is the cleanest way to demonstrate the zero-code-change promise because the script itself is completely standard pandas code. The equivalent Jupyter approach uses `%load_ext cudf.pandas` as the first cell in a fresh kernel.

There's more...

For workflows requiring maximum control over GPU memory and execution, use the explicit cuDF API directly:

```
import cudf
gdf = cudf.from_pandas(df)
gdf["return_1d"] = gdf.groupby("symbol")["close"].pct_change()
```

The explicit API avoids proxy overhead and gives you access to cuDF-specific features. For most quant research workflows, the pandas accelerator mode is sufficient and far more convenient.

> **Note**
>
> For datasets under approximately 100,000 rows, GPU overhead from data transfer and kernel launch latency can make cuDF slower than pandas. The speedup at 267 million rows (6.8x) drops to near parity at 1 million rows and becomes negative below 100K rows. Always benchmark with your actual data sizes.

See also

For more on cuDF, see the documentation:

- Cudf.pandas documentation: `https://docs.rapids.ai/api/cudf/stable/cudf_pandas/`
- NVIDIA blog on cuDF 150x acceleration: `https://developer.nvidia.com/blog/rapids-cudf-accelerates-pandas-nearly-150x-with-zero-code-changes`
- RAPIDS cuDF GitHub repository: `https://github.com/rapidsai/cudf`

Speeding up factor model training with cuML

Cross-sectional factor models are a staple of quantitative equity research. You fit a machine learning model to predict forward returns using features like momentum, volatility, and volume metrics across a universe of stocks. The challenge is iteration speed. When you are testing dozens of feature combinations and hyperparameter settings, each fit-predict-evaluate cycle needs to be fast. Fitting ensemble models like Random Forests on large feature matrices with, for example, 1 million rows and 50 features across a decade of daily equity data takes minutes on a CPU, creating a painful bottleneck in the research process.

cuML's scikit-learn accelerator mode intercepts scikit-learn estimators and executes them on the GPU. This parallelizes the matrix operations behind the estimators and vastly speeds up the operations as we'll see. Like cuDF's pandas accelerator, it uses proxy objects: you launch your script with `python -m cuml.accel`, import scikit-learn as usual, and your code runs on the GPU. Random Forest training sees 40-80x speedups because tree-building and split-finding are embarrassingly parallel.

In this recipe, you will engineer features from the historical price data, sample 2 million observations, and train the popular Random Forest models and KMeans clustering models on both CPU and GPU to measure the speedup.

How to do it...

Follow these steps to GPU-accelerate ML training with cuML:

1. Import standard data and ML libraries using the scikit-learn API:

```
import numpy as np
import pandas as pd
import time
import sys
from sklearn.cluster import KMeans
```

```
from sklearn.ensemble import RandomForestRegressor
from sklearn.ensemble import RandomForestClassifier
```

2. Detect whether the script is running under the `cuml.accel` GPU accelerator:

```
try:
    is_gpu = "cuml.accel" in sys.modules or "cuml" in sys.modules
except Exception:
    is_gpu = False
```

3. Load historical price data and sort by symbol and date:

```
df = pd.read_parquet(
    "historical-prices.parquet",
    columns=["symbol", "date", "close", "volume"],
)
df["date"] = pd.to_datetime(df["date"])
df = df.sort_values(["symbol", "date"]).reset_index(drop=True)
```

4. Compute daily returns and create lagged return features for each symbol. These lags capture short-term momentum and mean-reversion signals:

```
df["return_1d"] = df.groupby("symbol")["close"].pct_change()
for lag in [1, 2, 3, 5, 10]:
    df[f"ret_lag_{lag}"] = df.groupby("symbol")["return_1d"].shift(lag)
```

5. Compute a volume z-score per symbol to normalize trading activity across stocks with different average volume levels:

```
vol_mean = df.groupby("symbol")["volume"].transform("mean")
vol_std = df.groupby("symbol")["volume"].transform("std")
df["vol_zscore"] = ((df["volume"] - vol_mean) / vol_std).fillna(0.0)
```

6. Create the prediction target (next-day return), drop rows with missing values, and clip extreme outliers:

```
df["target"] = df.groupby("symbol")["return_1d"].shift(-1)
df = df.replace(
    [np.inf, -np.inf], np.nan
).dropna().reset_index(drop=True)
```

```
feature_cols = ["return_1d", "ret_lag_1", "ret_lag_2", "ret_lag_3",
                "ret_lag_5", "ret_lag_10", "vol_zscore"]
for col in feature_cols + ["target"]:
    df[col] = df[col].clip(-10.0, 10.0)
```

7. Sample 2 million rows to create a feature matrix large enough for meaningful GPU acceleration:

```
np.random.seed(42)
sample_idx = np.random.choice(
    len(df), size=min(2_000_000, len(df)), replace=False
)
sample_idx.sort()
X = df.loc[sample_idx, feature_cols].values.astype(np.float32)
y = df.loc[sample_idx, "target"].values.astype(np.float32)
```

8. Run a small warmup fit for each estimator to exclude one-time JIT compilation overhead from the benchmark timings:

```
_Xw, _yw = X[:100], y[:100]
KMeans(n_clusters=2, n_init=1, max_iter=1).fit(_Xw)
RandomForestRegressor(n_estimators=5, max_depth=3).fit(_Xw, _yw)
RandomForestClassifier(n_estimators=5, max_depth=3).fit(
    _Xw, (_yw > 0).astype(np.int32)
)
```

9. Train a 100-tree Random Forest regressor to predict next-day returns from lagged return and volume features:

```
rf = RandomForestRegressor(
    n_estimators=100,
    max_depth=12,
    max_features=1.0
)
rf.fit(X, y)
rf_preds = rf.predict(X)
```

10. Cluster 2 million stock-day observations into 20 market regimes using KMeans with 50 random initializations for stability:

```
kmeans = KMeans(n_clusters=20, random_state=42, n_init=50)
kmeans.fit(X)
labels = kmeans.labels_
```

11. Train a 100-tree Random Forest classifier to predict whether next-day returns will be positive or negative:

```
y_dir = (y > 0).astype(np.int32)
rfc = RandomForestClassifier(
    n_estimators=100,
    max_depth=12,
    max_features=1.0
)
rfc.fit(X, y_dir)
rfc_preds = rfc.predict(X)
```

12. Run the script twice to compare CPU and GPU performance:

```
python 15b_speeding_up_factor_model_training_with_cuml.py
python -m cuml.accel 15b_speeding_up_factor_model_training_with_cuml.py
```

The script is identical in both cases. The only difference is the launch command. The result is a 39.2X speedup in execution:

Step	CPU (scikit-learn)	GPU (cuml.accel)	Speedup
Random Forest Regressor (100 trees)	732.2s	17.3s	42.3x
KMeans (k=20, n_init=50)	51.1s	13.0s	3.9x
Random Forest Classifier (100 trees)	784.7s	9.6s	81.7x
TOTAL	1,568.1s	40.0s	39.2x

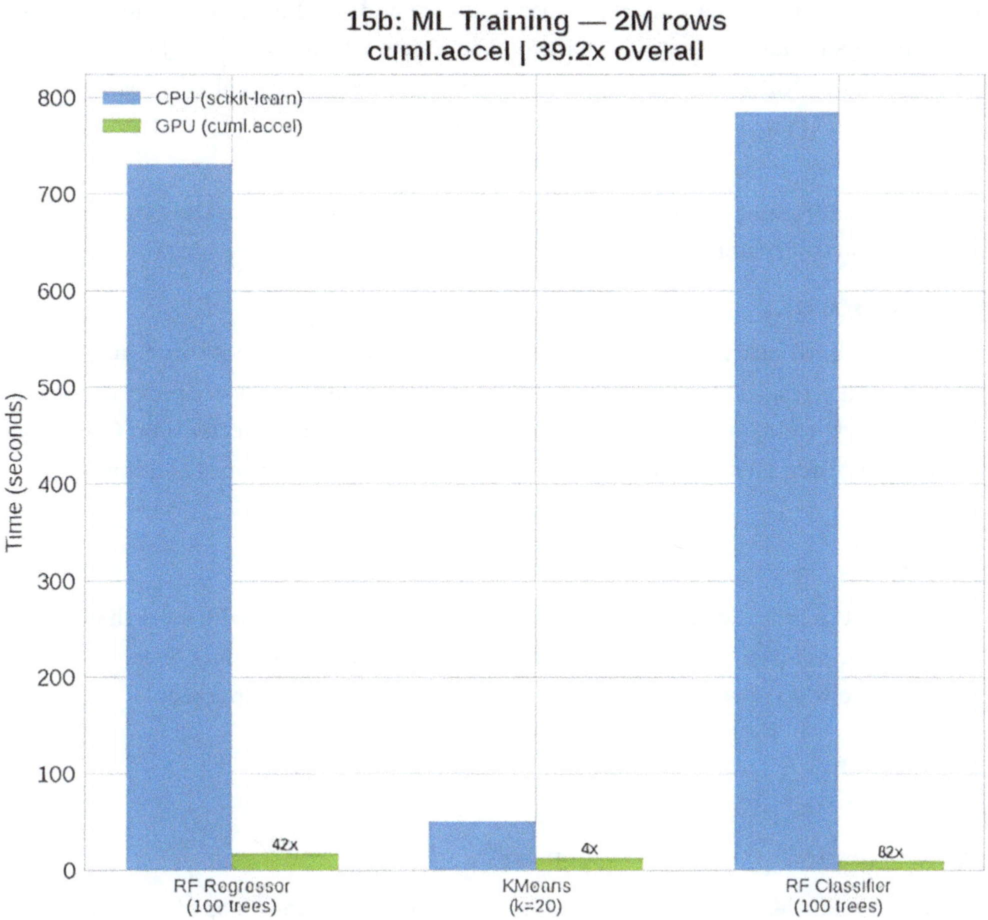

Figure 15.3: Massive acceleration across popular prediction models

How it works...

When you launch a script with `python -m cuml.accel`, cuML installs import hooks that intercept scikit-learn estimator creation. When you instantiate `RandomForestRegressor()`, the result is a proxy estimator that dispatches computation to cuML's GPU kernels. The API is identical to scikit-learn.

Random Forest training is highly parallelizable at two levels. First, each tree in the ensemble is built independently--the 100 trees can be constructed in parallel rather than sequentially. Second, within each tree, the split-point search at each node evaluates all candidate features and thresholds simultaneously. On a CPU, you get limited parallelism via `n_jobs=-1`. On a GPU with thousands of CUDA cores, both levels of parallelism are fully exploited. cuML uses a histogram-based approach to split finding that maps efficiently to GPU memory access patterns.

When an estimator is not yet supported by cuML, the proxy falls back to the CPU scikit-learn implementation transparently.

There's more...

When you load both `cudf.pandas` and `cuml.accel` in the same notebook, the feature matrix loaded via pandas resides on the GPU as a cuDF DataFrame. When cuML's proxy estimator receives this GPU-resident DataFrame for `.fit()`, it reads the data directly from GPU memory without any transfer. This "end-to-end GPU pipeline" provides the fastest configuration.

> Note
>
> **Important**
>
> cuML's GPU acceleration provides the largest speedups on datasets with more than 100,000 rows and models with many estimators (100+ trees). For a quick linear regression on 500 rows, the CPU is faster due to GPU kernel launch overhead.

See also

For more on cuML, see the documentation:

- cuML scikit-learn accelerator documentation: `https://docs.rapids.ai/api/cuml/stable/cuml-accel/`
- NVIDIA blog on cuML zero-code-change: `https://developer.nvidia.com/blog/nvidia-cuml-brings-zero-code-change-acceleration-to-scikit-learn/`

Building GPU-accelerated asset correlation networks with cuGraph

Correlation networks map the pairwise relationships between assets as a graph, where nodes represent stocks and edges connect pairs with high return correlations. Traders use them to spot hidden risk concentrations, build diversified portfolios, and find hedging candidates that sector labels would miss. Unlike a standard correlation matrix, which gives you a flat table of pairwise numbers, a network treats those relationships as connections you can analyze with graph algorithms, surfacing clusters, hubs, and bridges that the matrix alone cannot show. These networks encode market structure: the way stocks group, lead, and depend on one another based on actual return behavior rather than industry classification. Tightly correlated clusters often correspond to sectors, factor exposures, or shared supply-chain linkages.

Community detection algorithms like Louvain find groups of stocks that move together more than they move with the rest of the market, providing a data-driven alternative to traditional sector classifications. Centrality measures like PageRank and betweenness centrality identify the most systemically important assets, the names whose moves ripple outward and whose stress propagates furthest through the network.

NetworkX is the standard Python library for graph analytics, but it runs single-threaded on the CPU. For graphs with thousands of nodes and millions of edges, betweenness centrality alone can take 15 minutes. The nx-cugraph backend for NetworkX provides GPU-accelerated execution with zero code changes. Just set an environment variable and NetworkX dispatches supported algorithms to the GPU automatically.

In this recipe, you will build a correlation network from the 10,000 most-traded stocks in the historical price data, producing a graph with over 7,000 nodes and 1.2 million edges. You will run Louvain community detection, PageRank, and betweenness centrality on both CPU and GPU. With these results, you can build sector-neutral portfolios from data-driven clusters, identify systemically important stocks to monitor for contagion risk, and find hedging pairs whose connections aren't obvious from industry classification alone.

Getting ready

To get ready for this recipe, you need the RAPIDS 26.02 environment with `nx-cugraph` installed. If you installed RAPIDS via conda, `nx-cugraph` is included in the rapids metapackage.

How to do it...

Follow these steps to build a GPU-accelerated asset correlation network.

1. Import NetworkX for graph analytics alongside standard data libraries:

```
import numpy as np
import pandas as pd
import networkx as nx
import time
import os
```

2. Detect whether the `nx-cugraph` GPU backend is active:

```
is_gpu = (
    os.environ.get("NX_CUGRAPH_AUTOCONFIG", "").lower() == "true"
    or "cugraph" in nx.config.backend_priority.algos
)
```

3. Load historical price data, compute daily returns, and pivot to a wide return matrix with dates as rows and symbols as columns. Drop symbols missing more than half their price history:

```
df = pd.read_parquet(
    "historical-prices.parquet",
    columns=["symbol", "date", "close", "volume"],
)
df["date"] = pd.to_datetime(df["date"])
df = df.sort_values(["symbol", "date"]).reset_index(drop=True)
df["return"] = df.groupby("symbol")["close"].pct_change()
returns_wide = df.pivot_table(
    index="date", columns="symbol", values="return"
)
threshold = len(returns_wide) * 0.5
returns_wide = returns_wide.dropna(axis=1, thresh=int(threshold))
returns_wide = returns_wide.replace(
    [np.inf, -np.inf], np.nan
).fillna(0.0)
returns_wide = returns_wide.clip(-1.0, 1.0)
```

4. Select the 10,000 most-traded symbols by total volume to build a graph large enough for meaningful GPU speedups:

```
vol_rank = df.groupby("symbol")["volume"].sum()
vol_rank = vol_rank[vol_rank.index.isin(returns_wide.columns)]
top_symbols = vol_rank.nlargest(10_000).index.tolist()
returns_sub = returns_wide[top_symbols]
```

5. Compute the pairwise correlation matrix across all selected stocks:

```
corr_matrix = returns_sub.corr().values
tickers = returns_sub.columns.tolist()
```

6. Threshold at absolute correlation greater than 0.3 to create edges between correlated pairs. Use absolute correlation as edge weight so all weights are positive:

```
abs_corr = np.abs(corr_matrix)
rows, cols = np.where(np.triu(abs_corr > 0.3, k=1))
edge_df = pd.DataFrame({
    "source": [tickers[r] for r in rows],
    "target": [tickers[c] for c in cols],
    "weight": abs_corr[rows, cols].astype(float),
})
```

7. Build a NetworkX graph from the edge list:

```
G = nx.from_pandas_edgelist(
    edge_df,
    "source",
    "target",
    edge_attr="weight"
)
```

8. Detect communities of correlated stocks using the Louvain algorithm. Stocks within the same community tend to move together:

```
communities = nx.community.louvain_communities(G, seed=42)
```

9. Compute weighted PageRank to identify the most systemically connected stocks in the correlation network:

```
pagerank = nx.pagerank(G, weight="weight")
```

   Compute betweenness centrality to find stocks that serve as bridges between different clusters in the correlation network:

```
betweenness = nx.betweenness_centrality(G)
```

10. Run the script twice to compare CPU and GPU performance. Unlike cuDF and cuML, `nx-cugraph` uses an environment variable rather than `python -m`:

```
python
15c_building_gpu_accelerated_asset_correlation_networks_with_cugraph.py
NX_CUGRAPH_AUTOCONFIG=True python
15c_building_gpu_accelerated_asset_correlation_networks_with_cugraph.py
```

   The script is identical in both cases. The only difference is the launch command. The result is a 23.8X speedup in execution:

Step	CPU (networkx)	GPU (nx-cugraph)	Speedup
Louvain	5.6s	1.1s	5.1x
PageRank	1.3s	0.1s	13.0x
Betweenness Centrality	927.1s	38.0s	24.4x
TOTAL	933.9s	39.2s	23.8x

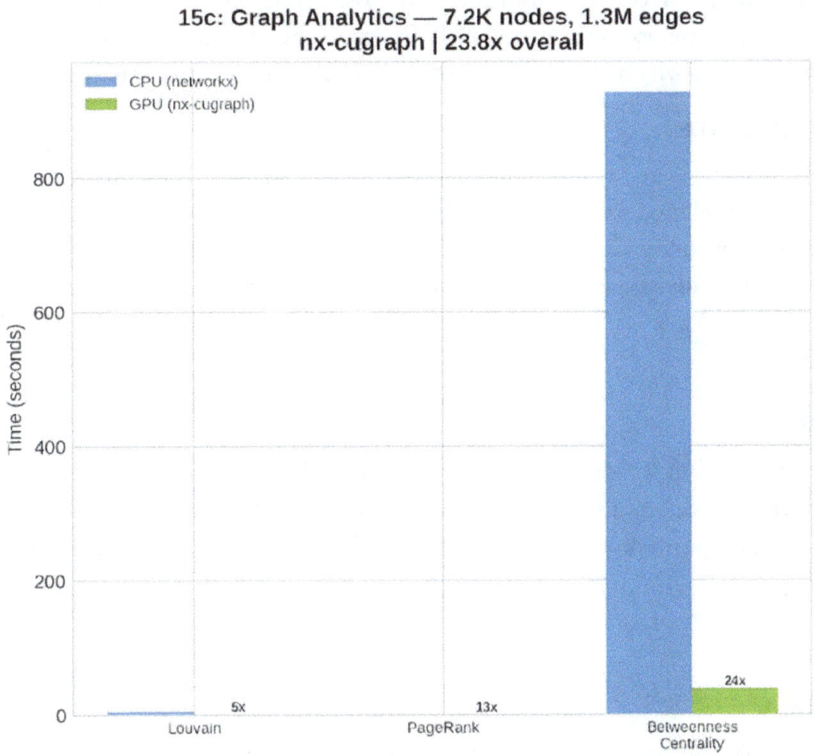

Figure 15.4: Speedups using nx-cugraph across three popular graph calculations

How it works...

Graph algorithms like Louvain, PageRank, and betweenness centrality involve iterative operations across the graph's adjacency structure. Louvain iteratively moves nodes between communities to maximize modularity. PageRank computes the dominant eigenvector of the transition matrix through iterative matrix-vector multiplication. Betweenness centrality requires computing shortest paths from every node to every other node, which is an `O(V * E)` operation. For a graph with 7,209 nodes and 1.27 million edges, that is over 9 billion path computations.

The `nx-cugraph` backend stores the graph in Compressed Sparse Row (CSR) format on GPU memory. When you set `NX_CUGRAPH_AUTOCONFIG=True`, NetworkX's dispatch mechanism checks whether the called algorithm has a cugraph implementation. If it does, NetworkX converts the graph to the cugraph internal format and executes the algorithm on GPU. The result is converted back to standard Python types so all downstream code works unchanged.

For betweenness centrality, the CPU algorithm runs a **breadth-first search** (**BFS**) from each node sequentially. On the GPU, multiple BFS traversals execute simultaneously, and within each BFS, the frontier expansion at each level processes all frontier nodes in parallel. This two-level parallelism is why betweenness centrality sees the most dramatic speedups.

There's more...

The centrality scores and community membership translate directly into quantitative features for cross-sectional models. PageRank identifies the most "systemically connected" stocks. Betweenness centrality identifies stocks that bridge different clusters. Community membership provides a data-driven sector classification that may differ from traditional GICS sectors.

> Note
>
> **Important**
>
> Graph algorithm speedups depend heavily on graph density and algorithm complexity. For very sparse graphs with fewer than 1,000 edges, CPU NetworkX may be faster. Betweenness centrality, with its `O(V * E)` complexity, consistently shows the largest speedups.

See also

For more on `nx-cugraph`, see the documentation:

- Nx-cugraph documentation: `https://rapids.ai/nx-cugraph/`
- Nx-cugraph GitHub repository: `https://github.com/rapidsai/nx-cugraph`
- NetworkX backend dispatch documentation: `https://networkx.org/documentation/stable/reference/backends.html`

Running GPU-accelerated portfolio optimization with cuOpt

Portfolio optimization is where research becomes a tradeable position. You take your return forecasts, risk estimates, and constraints and turn them into actual portfolio weights you can hold. Asset managers, pension funds, and systematic hedge funds run this step constantly, often rebalancing across thousands of assets and stress scenarios to keep portfolios aligned with their mandates. Mean-Variance optimization, introduced by Markowitz in 1952, has well-known limitations: it assumes normally distributed returns and systematically underestimates tail risk. Mean-CVaR (Conditional Value-at-Risk) optimization addresses this by using the expected loss in the worst-case tail scenarios as the risk measure, requiring no distributional assumptions.

The catch is computational cost. CVaR optimization across a large universe with many historical scenarios produces problems with tens of thousands of variables and constraints, and CPU solvers can take minutes per rebalance. That's where the GPU comes in. NVIDIA cuOpt is a GPU-accelerated optimization engine that solves LP, QP, and MILP problems. It integrates with CVXPY as a solver backend, so you formulate your optimization problem using CVXPY's familiar syntax and switch to GPU execution by specifying `solver="CUOPT"`. The CVaR formulation is naturally expressed as a linear program, making it a perfect fit for cuOpt.

This recipe is adapted from NVIDIA's Quantitative Portfolio Optimization Blueprint (`https://github.com/NVIDIA-AI-Blueprints/quantitative-portfolio-optimization`), distilled to the minimum viable workflow that demonstrates GPU-accelerated portfolio optimization using real historical price data. By the end, you'll have a working pipeline that builds tail-risk-aware portfolios in seconds rather than minutes, giving you the headroom to test more scenarios, rebalance more often, and scale to larger universes without rewriting your code.

Getting ready

To get ready for this recipe, you need CVXPY and cuOpt installed:

```
pip install cvxpy
pip install --extra-index-url=https://pypi.nvidia.com cuopt-cu12
```

How to do it...

Follow these steps to implement GPU-accelerated Mean-CVaR portfolio optimization:

1. Import CVXPY for convex optimization alongside standard data libraries. NVIDIA cuOpt is available as a GPU-accelerated solver backend for CVXPY:

```
import warnings
warnings.filterwarnings("ignore")
import numpy as np
import pandas as pd
import cvxpy as cp
import time
```

2. Load historical price data and sort by symbol and date:

```
df = pd.read_parquet(
    "historical-prices.parquet",
    columns=["symbol", "date", "close", "volume"],
)
df["date"] = pd.to_datetime(df["date"])
df = df.sort_values(["symbol", "date"]).reset_index(drop=True)
```

3. Select the top 200 stocks by total trading volume as candidates, then narrow to 50 with sufficient history for reliable estimation:

```
vol_rank = df.groupby("symbol")["volume"].sum().nlargest(200)
candidates = vol_rank.index.tolist()
df = df[df["symbol"].isin(candidates)]
df["return"] = df.groupby("symbol")["close"].pct_change()
```

4. Pivot returns into a wide matrix and clean extreme values. Use the first 50 stocks as the investment universe, where each row represents one historical daily scenario:

```
returns_wide = df.pivot_table(
    index="date", columns="symbol", values="return"
)
returns_wide = returns_wide.dropna(
    axis=1, thresh=int(len(returns_wide) * 0.8)
)
returns_wide = returns_wide.replace(
```

```
    [np.inf, -np.inf], np.nan
).fillna(0.0)
returns_wide = returns_wide.clip(-0.5, 0.5)
tickers = returns_wide.columns.tolist()[:50]
R = returns_wide[tickers].values
n_scenarios, n_assets = R.shape
```

5. Set the CVaR confidence level and risk aversion parameter, then compute expected returns:

```
alpha = 0.95
risk_aversion = 5.0
mu = R.mean(axis=0)
```

6. Define the CVXPY decision variables: portfolio weights, VaR threshold, and auxiliary slack variables for the CVaR linearization:

```
w = cp.Variable(n_assets, name="weights")
gamma = cp.Variable(name="VaR")
s = cp.Variable(n_scenarios, name="slack")
```

7. Compute portfolio return for each historical scenario:

```
portfolio_returns = R @ w
```

8. Define constraints: fully invested, long-only, max 10% per stock, and the CVaR linearization constraints:

```
constraints = [
    cp.sum(w) == 1,
    w >= 0,
    w <= 0.10,
    s >= 0,
    s >= -portfolio_returns - gamma,
]
```

9. Define the objective: maximize expected return minus a risk penalty. The CVaR term penalizes portfolios with large tail losses. This formulation follows Rockafellar and Uryasev (2000):

```
expected_return = mu @ w
cvar = gamma + (1.0 / (n_scenarios * (1 - alpha))) * cp.sum(s)
objective = cp.Maximize(expected_return - risk_aversion * cvar)
```

10. Assemble and solve the optimization problem using NVIDIA cuOpt:

```
problem = cp.Problem(objective, constraints)
problem.solve(solver="CUOPT")
```

11. Extract the optimal weights and display portfolio metrics:

```
weights = w.value
opt_return = expected_return.value
opt_cvar = cvar.value
alloc = pd.Series(weights, index=tickers).sort_values(ascending=False)
top = alloc[alloc > 0.001]
```

On the DGX Spark, cuOpt solves this 50-asset, 7,877-scenario optimization in approximately 0.5 seconds, producing a portfolio with a 15.35% annualized expected return, 1.9% daily CVaR at the 95% confidence level, and 32 active positions.

How it works...

The Mean-CVaR optimization problem is naturally formulated as a linear program when using scenario-based risk. CVaR at confidence level alpha measures the expected loss in the worst (1 - alpha) fraction of scenarios. The Rockafellar-Uryasev (2000) formulation introduces an auxiliary variable gamma (the VaR threshold) and scenario-specific slack variables. The resulting LP has `n_assets + n_scenarios + 1` decision variables and approximately `2 * n_scenarios + n_assets + 2` constraints.

cuOpt solves linear programs on the GPU using the **Primal-Dual Hybrid Gradient for Linear Programming** (**PDLP**) algorithm. PDLP is a first-order method that iteratively updates primal and dual solution vectors using matrix-vector products involving the constraint matrix. These matrix-vector multiplications are the computational bottleneck, and they map directly to GPU parallelism.

CVXPY handles the problem formulation and canonicalization. When you call `problem.solve(solver="CUOPT")`, CVXPY converts the high-level optimization model into the standard LP form that cuOpt accepts, sends it to the GPU solver, and maps the solution back to your named variables.

There's more...

You can add realistic portfolio constraints such as position limits and turnover constraints:

```
constraints_extended = constraints + [
    w <= 0.02,
    cp.norm(w - np.ones(n_assets)/n_assets, 1) <= 0.5,
]
```

The full NVIDIA Quantitative Portfolio Optimization Blueprint at `https://github.com/NVIDIA-AI-Blueprints/quantitative-portfolio-optimization` includes backtesting, rebalancing strategies, and efficient frontier generation. This blueprint provides a robust framework to use NVIDIA's cuOpt technologies for portfolio optimization.

Note

Important

GPU-accelerated optimization provides the largest speedups on large-scale problems with thousands of assets and tens of thousands of scenarios. For 50 assets and 500 scenarios, CPU solvers are fast enough that GPU overhead provides no benefit.

See also

For more on cuOpt and portfolio optimization, see the following resources:

- NVIDIA cuOpt documentation: `https://docs.nvidia.com/cuopt/user-guide/latest/cuopt-python/index.html`.
- NVIDIA Portfolio Optimization Blueprint: `https://github.com/NVIDIA-AI-Blueprints/quantitative-portfolio-optimization`.
- DGX Spark portfolio optimization playbook: `https://build.nvidia.com/spark/portfolio-optimization`.
- CVXPY solver documentation (cuOpt): `https://www.cvxpy.org/tutorial/solvers/index.html`.
- Rockafellar, R. T. and Uryasev, S. (2000), "*Optimization of Conditional Value-at-Risk*," Journal of Risk, Vol. 2, No. 3, pp. 21-41: `https://sites.math.washington.edu/~rtr/papers/rtr179-CVaR1.pdf`.

Get this book's PDF version and more

Scan the QR code (or go to `packtpub.com/unlock`). Search for this book by name, confirm the edition, and then follow the steps on the page.

UNLOCK NOW

Note: Keep your invoice handy. Purchases made directly from Packt don't require an invoice.

16

Unlock Your Exclusive Benefits

Your copy of this book includes the following exclusive benefits:

Follow the guide below to unlock them. The process takes only a few minutes and needs to be completed once.

Unlock this Book's Free Benefits in 3 Easy Steps

Step 1

Keep your purchase invoice ready for *Step 3*. If you have a physical copy, scan it using your phone and save it as a PDF, JPG, or PNG.

For more help on finding your invoice, visit `https://www.packtpub.com/en-us/unlock?step=1`.

> Note
>
> **Note**: If you bought this book directly from Packt, no invoice is required. After *Step 2*, you can access your exclusive content right away.

Step 2

Scan the QR code or go to `packtpub.com/unlock`.

On the page that opens (similar to *Figure 16.1* on desktop), search for this book by name and select the correct edition.

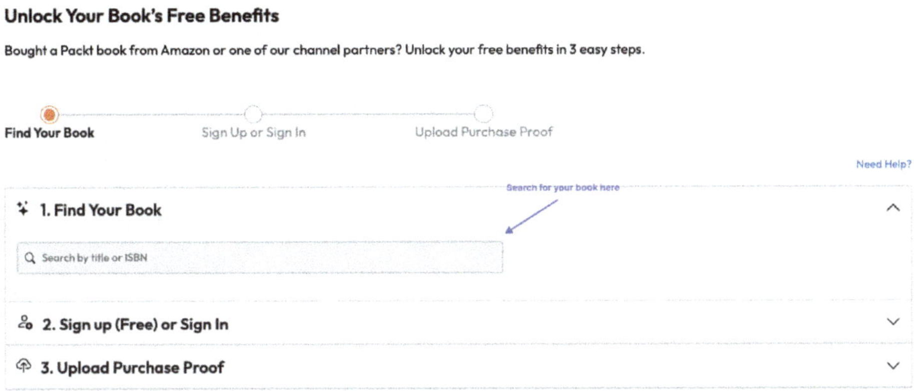

Figure 16.1: Packt unlock landing page on desktop

Step 3

After selecting your book, sign in to your Packt account or create one for free. Then upload your invoice (PDF, PNG, or JPG, up to 10 MB). Follow the on-screen instructions to finish the process.

Need Help

If you get stuck and need help, visit `https://www.packtpub.com/unlock-benefits/help` for a detailed FAQ on how to find your invoices and more. This QR code will take you to the help page.

Note

Note: If you are still facing issues, reach out to `customercare@packt.com`.

packtpub.com

Subscribe to our online digital library for full access to over 7,000 books and videos, as well as industry leading tools to help you plan your personal development and advance your career. For more information, please visit our website.

Why subscribe?

- Spend less time learning and more time coding with practical eBooks and Videos from over 4,000 industry professionals
- Improve your learning with Skill Plans built especially for you
- Get a free eBook or video every month
- Fully searchable for easy access to vital information
- Copy and paste, print, and bookmark content

At www.packtpub.com, you can also read a collection of free technical articles, sign up for a range of free newsletters, and receive exclusive discounts and offers on Packt books and eBooks.

Other Books You May Enjoy

If you enjoyed this book, you may be interested in these other books by Packt:

Machine Learning for Trading, Third Edition

Stefan Jansen

ISBN: 978-1-80324-697-0

- Transform raw data into predictive alpha factors, validated with leak-proof cross-validation
- Master advanced models, from Gradient Boosting Machines to Transformers, Graph Neural Networks, and Reinforcement Learning agents
- Harness Generative AI, Retrieval Augmented Generation, and Causal Inference to make models interpretable, auditable, and compliant with regulatory standards
- Build production-ready trading infrastructure using MLOps, feature stores, and model monitoring to transition research into live capital deployment safely

Python for Finance Cookbook, Second Edition

Eryk Lewinson

ISBN: 978-1-80324-319-1

- Preprocess, analyze, and visualize financial data
- Explore time series modeling with statistical (exponential smoothing, ARIMA) and machine learning models
- Uncover advanced time series forecasting algorithms such as Meta's Prophet
- Use Monte Carlo simulations for derivatives valuation and risk assessment
- Explore volatility modeling using univariate and multivariate GARCH models
- Investigate various approaches to asset allocation
- Learn how to approach ML-projects using an example of default prediction
- Explore modern deep learning models such as Google's TabNet, Amazon's DeepAR and NeuralProphet

Packt is searching for authors like you

If you're interested in becoming an author for Packt, please visit `authors.packt.com` and apply today. We have worked with thousands of developers and tech professionals, just like you, to help them share their insight with the global tech community. You can make a general application, apply for a specific hot topic that we are recruiting an author for, or submit your own idea.

Share your thoughts

Now you've finished *Python for Algorithmic Trading Cookbook, Second Edition*, we'd love to hear your thoughts! Scan the QR code below to go straight to the Amazon review page for this book and share your feedback or leave a review on the site that you purchased it from.

`https://packt.link/r/1806662035`

Your review is important to us and the tech community and will help us make sure we're delivering excellent quality content.

Index

K

L

M

N

O

P

www.ingramcontent.com/pod-product-compliance
Lightning Source LLC
LaVergne TN
LVHW060015210926
848481LV00013B/3711